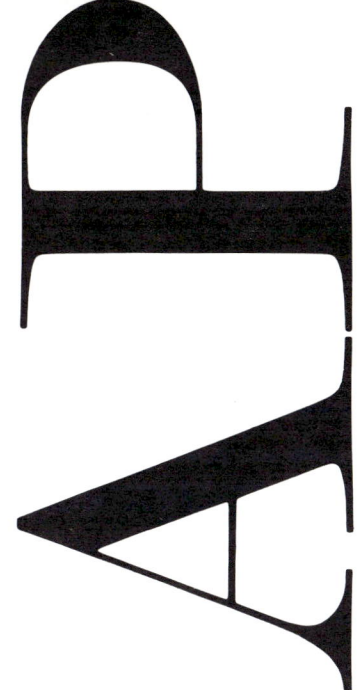

Department of Education and Science
Welsh Office
Department of Education for Northern Ireland

**Assessment of Performance Unit**

# Science
# at Age 13

## A Review of APU Survey Findings 1980-84

Beta Schofield (Editor)
John Bell
Paul Black
Sandra Johnson
Patricia Murphy
Anne Qualter
Terry Russell

London
Her Majesty's Stationery Office

ISBN 0 11 270618 5

# Contents, authorship and analysis       Editor: Beta Schofield

**Analysis**
General survey analysis: Sandra Johnson and John Bell
Pupils' Questionnaires (reported in Chapter 3):
    Anne Qualter and Patricia Murphy
Performance of investigations (reported in Chapter 11):
    1984 survey: Patricia Murphy
    Earlier surveys: Patricia Murphy with Richard Gott
    and Angela Davey

# Tables and figures

# Preface

This report presents a review of the findings of five national surveys on the performance of 13 year old children in science. The surveys were conducted for the Assessment of Performance Unit by research teams at King's College, University of London, and at the University of Leeds. The report gives an overview of the initial series of five annual surveys of this age, carried out between 1980 and 1984. Companion reports are also available for ages 11 and 15, together with a technical report which considers issues of interpretation raised by the monitoring programme ('National assessment: the APU science approach', Johnson, 1989).

This report describes in detail the approach to the surveys and the findings. It is intended primarily for administrators, education advisers and researchers, but it will also be of interest to those teachers who found the previous reports of value. Further copies of this and the other review reports may be purchased from HMSO or through booksellers.

From April 1 1989 enquiries relating to APU publications should be addressed to the School Examinations and Assessment Council (SEAC), Newcombe House, 45 Notting Hill Gate, London W11 3JB.

Details of short reports for science teachers drawing on the findings of the APU surveys are available from the above address.

Reports now available in the series:

| | |
|---|---|
| Number 1 | Science at Age 11 |
| Number 2 | Science Assessment Framework Ages 13 and 15 |
| Number 3 | Science at Age 13 |
| Number 4 | Science Assessment Framework Age 11 |
| Number 5 | Science at Age 15 |
| Number 6 | Practical Testing at Ages 11, 13 and 15 |
| Number 7 | Electricity at Age 15 |
| Number 8 | Planning Scientific Investigations at Age 11 |
| Number 9 | Assessing Investigations at Ages 13 and 15 |
| Number 10 | Metals at Age 15 |
| Number 11 | The Language of Science |

# The research teams

The teams are based at two centres: the Centre for Educational Studies, King's College, University of London*, and the Centre for Studies in Science and Mathematics Education, University of Leeds.

**Team members at King's** (*January 1987*)

| | |
|---|---|
| Director | Paul Black |
| Research and Development (ages 11 and 13) | Patricia Murphy (Deputy Director) Anne Qualter Peter Swatton Robert Taylor |
| Secretary | Julie Jones |

**Team members at Leeds** (*January 1987*)

| | |
|---|---|
| Director | Fred Archenhold |
| Technical Director | Roger Hartley |
| Research and Development (age 15) | Geoff Welford (Project coordinator) James Donnelly |

| | |
|---|---|
| Data Analysis | Sandra Johnson (Deputy Director) John Bell |
| Secretary | Jan Akkermans |

**Past team members**

Dennis Child (Director 1982–83); Angela Davey (1982–84); Brenda Denvir (Jan–Aug 1981); Rosalind Driver (1977–82, Deputy Director 1979–82); Reed Gamble (1982–85); Richard Gott (1980–84, Deputy Director 1982–84); Wynne Harlen (1977–1984, Deputy Director (1978–84); Jenny Head (1981–84); Peter Kelly (Director 1977–78); Nasrin Khaligh (1984–85); David Layton (Director 1977–82); Brian Maher (1979–83); Cynthia Millband (1980–81); Tony Orgee (1982–85); David Palacio (1980–85); Terry Russell (1982–86); Beta Schofield (1977–85, Deputy Director 1985); Karen Spencer (1985–86); Ardrie VanderWaal (1979–80); Iain Watson (1984–85); Christopher Worsley (1978–82); Fiona Wylie (1980–82).

---

* Formerly Centre for Science and Mathematics Education, Chelsea College

# Acknowledgements

The monitoring teams would like to thank the many people who contributed to the various phases of work involved in conducting the surveys and producing this report.

The monitoring framework and test questions used were the result of a number of years of development work cooperatively undertaken by the teams at King's College, University of London, and at the University of Leeds in collaboration with the Science Steering Group.

Many visitors from overseas made valuable contributions, in some cases during the development of the framework and in others in the question writing and trialling phase. Thanks are due in particular to John Theobald and Marjory Martin from Australia and Joyce Glasgow from the West Indies.

Mrs B. A. Bloomfield and her staff at the Monitoring Services Unit were responsible for obtaining the co-operation of the schools drawn in the sample and making all the administrative arrangements with Heads and teachers for both written and practical testing.

Science advisers in the local education authorities helped by nominating teachers as practical testers and then arranging for their release from normal teaching duties. Dr N. B. Evans, HMI, arranged for the translation of test materials into Welsh. In Northern Ireland, Mr I. W. Milligan, HMI, made arrangements for the recruitment of testers.

Philip Harris Ltd supplied the apparatus for the practical testing. The care and ingenuity of members of their staff have been greatly appreciated.

The administration of the practical tests, a demanding part of the exercise, was undertaken by science teachers from England, Wales and Northern Ireland. Thanks are also due to those who marked the written tests.

The conduct of the surveys themselves depended on the goodwill and cooperation of pupils and staff in the survey schools. We are particularly grateful to the teachers who undertook the various time-consuming tasks involved in administering the tests, without whose help this survey would not have been possible.

Special thanks are due to Julie Jones for all her efforts and for using her organisational skills in assembling this review; and to Cliff Wakeling for his highly professional handling of the equally critical stage from final draft to publication.

Lastly, the authors are indebted to Mrs Jackie McDermott for producing the index.

# Introduction

## 1.1 The nature of the review reports

This is one of a set of four complementary volumes, three of which report in turn for the three ages (11, 13 and 15 years) at which the Assessment of Performance Unit science surveys have been conducted, while the fourth concentrates on the more technical aspects of the exercise. Their preparation marks the end of the first phase of the APU Science surveys during which the monitoring teams at Leeds and Chelsea*, in consultation with the Science Steering Group, have developed the assessment framework with its matching bank of questions, conducted a series of five annual surveys and reported the results.

Earlier reports have been concerned primarily with findings of surveys conducted in one particular year; in this review report, however, the intention is to draw on results from all five surveys. Where detailed results from the final survey in June 1984 are needed in order to substantiate summaries of performance, they are usually given in appendices; rather fewer questions than usual are reproduced in the text itself, and readers may be referred to earlier reports for question examples.

The assessment has differed from traditional science examinations of pupils of a specified age in two major ways: it has focused on the performance of a population rather than of individuals, and on the process-related skills of science rather than its content. Some consequences of these two characteristics are outlined in sections 1.2 and 1.3, respectively.

## 1.2 The sampling procedure

Between 1980 and 1984 annual surveys of pupils from all types of school in England, Wales and Northern Ireland were conducted at age 11, 13 and 15, except that Wales and Northern Ireland were not included in the first year at age 13. Although the aim was to describe how the population of 13 year old pupils performed in science, it was only necessary to test a sample of that population. Each year the sample was obtained in a two-stage operation. First a sample of schools was drawn randomly but within constraints designed to ensure that it would reflect the national pattern with respect to region of the country, size of entry and type of school; then about 26 pupils were randomly selected by date of birth from each of the sample schools. At age 13, this has produced samples of up to 15,000 pupils; these were divided into about 26 equivalent sub-samples, each being allocated a different package of paper-and-pencil questions intended to last for about an hour. Some of these pupils also took one of three different types of practical test.

Since the purpose of the assessment was to arrive at a survey description of science performance for the population as a whole, it was possible to protect the anonymity of pupils, of schools, and of the education authorities involved.

## 1.3 The assessment framework

A single statement of scientific performance was considered to be less helpful than a profile report related to the processes of science and not just to the content. After a great deal of consultation and discussion, a number of assessable process-related skills were identified and organised into a framework of six categories, some of which were subsequently subdivided. Not all the resulting subcategories (shown in Table 1.1, p. 2) have been assessed each year. Those shown in bold correspond to those listed in recent publications. Each subcategory was more clearly defined in terms of generalised *question descriptors*; these were evolved during the stage when questions and mark schemes were being scrutinised to check their relationship to the assessment framework. A revised set of these question descriptors appears as Appendix 4. Although the framework is the same for all three ages, the emphasis differs from age to age; this point is taken up again in Chapter 13.

Questions in any of the above subcategories need a content vehicle. It is not possible to set questions in which either process or content is isolated; performance involves the interaction of the two. Thus some way of labelling content was seen to be required. Two dimensions of question-content were used: the context

---

\* The Chelsea Centre for Science and Mathematics Education took part in an intercollegiate merger and is now incorporated in the Centre for Educational Studies, King's College, University of London.

**Table 1.1** *The assessment framework (ages 13 and 15)*

| Category | Subcategories | Mode of testing |
|---|---|---|
| 1 Use of graphical and symbolic representation | **Using graphs, tables and charts** Using scientific symbols and conventions | Written |
| 2 Use of apparatus and measuring instruments | **Using measuring instruments** **Estimating physical quantities** **Following instructions for practical work** | Group practical |
| 3 Observation | **Making and interpreting observations** | Group practical |
| 4 Interpretation and application | i **Interpreting presented information** Judging the applicability of statements to data Distinguishing degrees of inference ii **Applying: biology concepts** **physics concepts** **chemistry concepts** Generating alternative hypotheses | Written |
| 5 Planning of investigations | **Planning parts of investigations** **Planning entire investigations** Identifying or proposing testable statements | Written |
| 6 Performance of investigations | **Performing entire investigations** | Individual practical |

evoked by the question and the concepts needed by the pupil in order to answer it. The *context* dimension was divided into three broad ranges, relating to 'everyday', 'science' (often sub-divided into biology, physics and chemistry), and 'other school subject'. The *concept* dimension was divided first by a demarcation line between 'everyday' concepts or items of knowledge and those likely to have been covered in school science lessons. The establishment of a list encompassing this second group was the result of extensive research into school and examination syllabuses, and of consultation with teachers from over 100 schools. It consists of concept-related statements grouped under a number of headings (see Appendix 5). Thus each question could be labelled not only with the name of the process-related category which it was written to assess, but also by context and concept.

It was necessary to arrange for the assessment to take account of the science performance of pupils of differing ages (11, 13 and 15 years) across the complete ability range at each age. Although there is likely to be some common ground in the period before pupils are offered options, there is still a great variety of science activity within schools. Consequently, in order to allow pupils to demonstrate their ability, questions were written with a very wide range of style, content and mode of testing, subject to financial and logistical constraints associated with nation-wide assessment. Thus some categories were assessed using paper-and-pencil

tests, others by practical work; some questions were open-ended, some had coded answers; some practical tests took the form of a circus of tasks, while in others pupils were observed one at a time, and their actions recorded on checklists. Details of the various modes of testing used are given in Chapters 5 to 11, where each category is discussed in turn, and in the teachers' report, 'Science assessment framework, Ages 13 & 15', Murphy and Gott, 1984.

As the surveys proceeded, and more and more information was gathered, it became clear that the banks of questions set up initially would benefit from some modification. In some cases, questions originally written for one age group were found to be suitable also for another, and became incorporated in the corresponding bank. In others, differences in marking of apparently similar questions at different ages were eradicated. This rationalization of the question banks had more relevance to some subcategories than to others, and is discussed, where appropriate, in later chapters of this report.

## 1.4 Alternative ways of reporting

The two preceding sections have shown that the aim of the assessment programme is to describe the science performance of the population (rather than the individual), and to break down the report by categories related to 'process-skills'. The results are presented in two main ways: at the subcategory level and at the question level. In the first case a mean score for the population is estimated from the performances of individual pupils in the sub-sample taking the given subcategory test. In the second case the mean score of the individual pupils taking a given question is found. The subcategory score is the more useful for consideration of variation of performance with school and pupil variables, since the wide range of questions involved tends to even out uncharacteristic peaks and troughs in performance which might be associated with specific questions. However, results for individual questions often give some insight into pupils' understanding, especially where the frequency of occurrence of particular responses or types of response has been recorded for each of a group of questions sharing a common property, such as a specific concept demand. Reporting at the subcategory level is in any case not always appropriate; sometimes each question in the group within a subcategory appears to present unique demands in that performance is likely to be heavily influenced by factors other than, or additional to, the generalised skill which is under consideration.

Where a subcategory performance level is appropriate, the test is usually constructed by drawing a random selection of about 60 questions from the relevant pool of questions within the bank, the pool ideally containing about three times the number of questions in the test. In the case of Category 3, **Observation**, however, the cost of administering a test of 60 questions is prohibitive, and the number of questions is therefore reduced to 45. In Category 2, **Use of apparatus and measuring instruments,** the number of *radically* different questions that can be written is limited; the cost of apparatus, moreover, is particularly high. For these reasons, a fixed test is used for the assessment of this category rather than one assembled by random selection from a large pool of questions. In Category 6, **Performance of investigations**, since each pupil is individually observed by a trained tester, it would not be financially or logistically possible to include a large enough number of investigations in a survey for the category to be validly represented either by random sampling or by use of a fixed test. In practice, six questions is the maximum number used in any one survey, and each is reported separately.

## 1.5   Supplementary research investigations

The system of producing a test by random selection of questions from a large pool within the bank was chosen so that different but equivalent tests could be made available for use on different occasions. Coupled with the very wide variety of questions needed to cover the ranges of pupil ability, school courses and question types involved, this system provides limited opportunities for systematic investigation of pupil response; for example, of the effect of varying *one* factor in a task while holding others constant. For even if there were suitable sets of questions in the bank, there is no guarantee that all, or indeed any, will be selected. Nor is it likely that the number of questions focusing on one particular aspect of science–a single concept, perhaps– would by chance be sufficient to allow justifiable conclusions to be drawn about pupil understanding. Consequently, specially designed questions were included in some surveys over and above those required for obtaining subcategory scores. Responses to these 'probe' questions have been analysed and the results used to illuminate initial findings from earlier surveys.

Probes fall into three main groups. They may lie within a single category; they may cross two or more categories; or they may lie outside the framework altogether. The first group will be reported in the appropriate category chapter; for example, a probe set up to investigate the possibility of using line drawings or photographs instead of actual measuring instruments in the assessment of pupils' ability to record scale readings, is reported in Chapter 6, **Use of apparatus and measuring instruments.** Discussion of the second group is to be found in Chapter 12, which is concerned with cross-category links in performance. An example of an investigation which lies outside the framework is that

into pupils' out-of-school activities and interests; this is reported in Chapter 3.

## 1.6   Dissemination of information about the science surveys

From the outset of the project, the Science Steering Group and monitoring teams alike have been concerned to involve the science teaching community in their activities and to seek advice as to the details of the framework and corresponding tests to be adopted. This concern led to the distribution in October 1977, more than two years before the first survey, of a Consultative Paper (DES, 1977) offering a preliminary discussion of suitable criteria for assessment, and inviting comment from interested parties. More than 60 responses, many from institutions and groups, were received by the Steering Group; not until they had been sifted and considered were firm decisions on the proposed assessment framework reached. By September 1978 a 'Science Progress Report' (DES, 1978a) had been compiled, and was distributed in the same way as the earlier Consultative Paper. In it, decisions with regard to the assessment framework were described, as well as plans for setting up a bank of questions and for the organisation of the survey. The detailed list of science knowledge and concepts discussed in section 1.3 was provided as an appendix to this report.

While the two documents described above were being prepared, several liaison groups consisting of teachers and others involved in science education were set up. Members of these groups were actively involved in categorising and scrutinising questions in preparation for the monitoring. In July 1979 a meeting was held in which the 30 or so participants, all distinguished in the field of science education, considered the validity of the assessment framework. Members of both groups continued to be involved in a consultative capacity for several years. As results came in and reports of surveys were published, the role of the monitoring team with respect to these and other groups began to shift away from advice-seeking towards information-giving; discussion meetings tended to be replaced by workshops designed to help participants to become familiar with the process-related category system, and the new types of question needed to match it. Later still there was a further shift towards discussion of the possible implications for science teaching of the survey findings.

The report of the first survey at age 13, which took place in 1980, was published by HMSO (DES, 1982a). Because of the relative unfamiliarity of the process-oriented framework, it was necessary to give substance to the definitions of categories and subcategories by publishing nearly 100 question examples in that report. Their inclusion also served to emphasise the very large range of content and question-type thought necessary to establish each subcategory performance level. Because of the high cost of such a production, subsequent research reports were produced in a low-cost format and given a limited free distribution. These reports also include many question examples. Since some of the findings were seen to have direct interest for teachers of science, shorter and more specifically focused reports were written with a teacher audience in mind. These have been distributed free to all schools. The published output of the monitoring teams to date (1989) has included 12 research reports (four at each age), and 11 teachers' reports, as well as a number of occasional papers and contributions to professional journals. The four review reports, of which this is one, are of course, additional to this list.

The change in the nature of the reports is paralleled by a change in the relationship of the APU to the teaching profession. In 1978, in the period following the appointment of the science monitoring teams, the emphasis was on the intention to reflect the curriculum rather than to influence it, and many teachers were indifferent to, if not suspicious of, the exercise. A number of factors have combined to promote interest not only in the results of the surveys, but also in the techniques of assessment which have been developed, including the questions themselves. Among these are the pressures towards the provision of science for all and a balanced science curriculum, and towards emphasising the processes as well as the content of science, which have been expressed in the DES policy statement 'Science 5–16' (DES, 1985c). The increase in interest has been made evident by the more positive response of teachers attending meetings organised to discuss results.

The introduction of the GCSE and the associated National Criteria for the conduct of examinations (JCNC, 1985), with the emphasis on giving all pupils an opportunity to show how much, rather than how little, they can do, is focusing attention on the levels of performance in science which are currently achieved by pupils, particularly those of average and low ability. The graded assessment movement has similarly alerted teachers to the need to be aware of the kind of science activity likely to afford success to pupils of various abilities and ages. The type of data available from the science surveys can inform the debate about grade-related criteria, and some use of the data has already been made during the development phase of the GCSE grade-related criteria.

**2**

# Science resources and provision for 13 year olds in the schools

## 2.1 Introduction

The opportunity has regularly been taken in the annual surveys to gather supplementary information about the resources which the schools have available for science, and also about the ways in which schools organise their provision for science for pupils at this age. The information is gathered by means of a questionnaire which all participating schools are asked to complete (a copy of the questionnaire used in the 1984 survey is reproduced as Appendix 2). The response rate to the questionnaire among participating schools has always been very high–certainly above 95 per cent.

In every survey of 13 year olds to date schools have been asked about their financial resources, about their general laboratory and technician provision, and about the curriculum choice they make available to pupils at this age. Naturally, as the survey programme has developed so also have the school questionnaires evolved so that new or more detailed information might be gathered. In particular, the questions have probed more specifically about the extent to which the science resources in schools have been made available to their pupils *aged 13*.

This chapter considers the findings which have emerged from the various questionnaire enquiries over the period. Where the same or similar questions have been included in a number of the questionnaires, comment will be offered as appropriate about the stability of the response pattern over that period of time. As usual, unless otherwise stated, tables will relate to data from the 1984 survey.

Following previous practice, figures are always given separately for England, Wales and Northern Ireland. They are also provided separately for up to five different types of school within England. These are independent schools, Grammar schools, Secondary Modern schools, and two categories of Comprehensive school, termed 'Junior' Comprehensives and 'Senior' Comprehensives, distinguished by the presence or absence of examination classes. 'Junior' Comprehensives are defined as all Comprehensive schools with a leaving age of 15 or younger, and therefore include Middle

schools. 'Senior' Comprehensives comprise all Comprehensive schools with a leaving age above 15; these will be 11–16 and 11–18 Comprehensives in the main. Independent and Grammar schools are sometimes considered together as a single group where it has been established that their resource levels and organisational patterns are similar.

For the first time figures are given by school type in Northern Ireland: the two types are Grammar and Secondary Intermediate. Since the majority of schools in the samples and in the school population in Wales are 'Senior' Comprehensives, a breakdown by type of school would here be of limited value.

The chapter begins by considering the science courses schools provide for their 13 year old pupils, and moves on to review the findings about the ways schools group these pupils for science work, about the proportion of total learning time given to this area of the curriculum, and about the science qualifications of the teachers of science to this age-group. Finally, the schools' current levels of laboratory accommodation are explored, with comment on the implications for any proposed expansion of science teaching in the schools.

It should be noted that although information has always been gathered in the questionnaires about schools' general levels of funding and about their levels of expenditure on *science*, this aspect of resourcing is not discussed here. There are two reasons for this: firstly, rather detailed information about schools' levels of capitation income is available from other sources (particularly, the publications of the Chartered Institute of Professional Finance and Accountancy–CIPFA). Secondly, it was remarked in earlier science reports that the questions on finance were those most frequently omitted by school respondents. This was presumably because they objected to providing the information, or because producing the figures, particularly for science expenditure, would have been an especially onerous task. Thirdly, there have been comments from schools to the effect that levels of expenditure on specific areas of the curriculum–such as science–actually vary from year to year; this is certainly the case for breakdowns of expenditure *within* a department (on books, consumables, and so on).

## 2.2 Science-course provision and teaching materials used

Every survey questionnaire has included an enquiry about the science courses made available to 13 year olds. In the first survey in the series this enquiry took the form of an invitation to indicate which specific science courses *each* sample pupil was studying. It became immediately clear from the results that this was an unnecessarily detailed method of enquiry, since in the great majority of schools *all* 13 year olds follow the same course or course combination—most commonly a single General Science course (throughout this chapter the term 'General Science' is intended to embrace all the various kinds of integrated course in science, variously known as General Science, Integrated Science, Combined Science, and so on). In subsequent surveys, therefore, schools have simply been asked *whether* they provide a common curriculum in science at this age, and if so what form this takes.

There is no evidence in the annual results of any change in the situation over the period of the surveys, either in terms of an underlying trend or a sharp change between particular years. The data in Table 2.1, together with that gathered in the previous surveys at this age, indicate that at the time of testing between 70 per cent and 80 per cent of the schools in England and Northern Ireland provided a single General Science course which all their 13 year old pupils were constrained to follow; in Wales the corresponding proportion of schools was lower at around 60 per cent. About a fifth of the schools in England and Wales and a lower 15 per cent of those in Northern Ireland provided their pupils in this age-group with separate courses in the three major sciences.

Of the remaining schools a few allowed individual pupils an element of choice. The majority constrain their more able 13 year olds to follow separate courses in the three main sciences, while their average and less able pupils studied General Science or, less frequently, followed two courses in physical and biological science,

respectively. The proportion of schools not providing one of the two main kinds of common science curriculum has always been higher in Wales than in the other two countries (roughly 25 per cent over the survey period, compared with 10–15 per cent in both England and Northern Ireland).

The general pattern varies from one type of school to another, as Table 2.1 shows. For instance, the cumulated survey data suggest that a higher proportion of 'Junior' Comprehensives in England (mainly Middle schools) provide a single General Science course compared with the 'Senior' Comprehensives (85–90 per cent and 75–80 per cent respectively); a lower proportion of Independent and Grammar schools offer their pupils science in this integrated form (about a third of schools), favouring instead separate specialist courses (half the schools). More than a quarter of the few Secondary Modern schools either provide a common curriculum in science which is different from the two major kinds or else allow an element of choice to their pupils.

The picture for the Secondary Intermediate schools in Northern Ireland very much resembles that for the 'Junior' Comprehensives in England. The Grammar schools in Northern Ireland appear to be almost evenly split between those providing a common course in General Science and those providing compulsory courses in the three main sciences.

It must be recognised, of course, that General Science can take many forms. The relative emphasis given to the biological and the physical sciences, and the particular topics studied within these main areas, is very much in the control of the individual school, or even teacher. This flexibility and the consequent anticipated variety in course content has precluded any attempt in these surveys to explore the actual nature of the science experience of different pupils following ostensibly the same science course. As noted later, there is a preponderance of biologists among the teachers of General Science to this age-group. It is possible, therefore, that there might be a greater emphasis on biological science

**Table 2.1** *The science courses provided for 13 year olds*
(Percentage of all schools offering each common course or courses)

|  | No. of schools | General Science | Physics, Chemistry and Biology | Other common | No common curriculum |
|---|---|---|---|---|---|
| England | 320 | 66 | 18 | 13 | 3 |
| Wales | 90 | 58 | 18 | 12 | 12 |
| Northern Ireland | 116 | 74 | 15 | 3 | 8 |
| **England only:** |  |  |  |  |  |
| 'Senior' Comprehensive | 183 | 73 | 13 | 9 | 5 |
| 'Junior' Comprehensive | 51 | 84 | 4 | 12 | 0 |
| Independent/Grammar | 64 | 30 | 51 | 19 | 0 |
| Secondary Modern | 22 | 68 | 5 | 27 | 0 |
| **Northern Ireland** |  |  |  |  |  |
| Grammar | 31 | 52 | 45 | 0 | 3 |
| Secondary Intermediate | 85 | 82 | 4 | 5 | 9 |

than on physical science in the courses. Unfortunately, no survey information is available which directly illuminates this issue.

Information is available about some of the learning resource materials in use with this age-group in science. Indeed, survey evidence is that schools make as much or more use of their own resource materials in the science work of their 13 year olds as they do of the most popular commercially available packages. About a third of the schools from England and Wales which took part in the 1983 survey indicated that they used their own resource materials in the main, another third indicated that they made main use of the Nuffield Combined Science publications. These figures compare with about a fifth and fewer than a tenth, respectively, of the schools from Northern Ireland.

The Scottish Integrated Science materials were more frequently used in the schools of Northern Ireland (30–40 per cent) than in those of England and Wales (about 10 per cent). The Insight to Science materials, on the other hand, were used as a main resource in around a tenth of the schools in each country. Within England, the 'Junior' Comprehensives made more use of the Nuffield materials than did all other types of school. (Full details about this resource enquiry are given in the report of the 1983 survey–DES, 1986a.)

Many schools also take advantage of local field centres in their science work, of course, and occasionally organise industrial and other educational visits for their pupils. The 1980 and 1981 questionnaires included a question on this kind of activity. The results suggest that more than half the Comprehensive schools in England use field centres compared with rather few Independent or Grammar schools (about 15 per cent). Industrial visits, the data suggest, are three times as likely to be organised for 13 year olds in 'Senior' Comprehensive than in 'Junior' Comprehensives (roughly 60 per cent and 20 per cent of schools, respectively). Such visits are organised by about a third of the Independent and Grammar schools.

## 2.3  Organisational patterns in science provision

In the last three annual surveys at this age the schools which took part were asked to indicate which one of four possible pupil grouping strategies best described their science classes at this age. The four possibilities were: mixed-ability grouping, banding, streaming and setting.

Mixed-ability classes were defined as containing the full range of pupil ability within the age-group as a whole 'relative to the national population'. Banding and streaming were both defined as methods by which entire classes of pupils would be ranked in terms of some measure of general ability, pupils in these classes staying together for all their lessons including science. The defined difference between banding and streaming is that the ability range *within* streamed classes is expected to be narrower than that within a banded class (in banding there are usually several classes of roughly similar ability spread within a single broad band). Setting is a strategy whereby pupils are *only* separated or are *further* separated for lessons in particular subjects on the basis of their relative abilities in those subjects (in this case science).

In brief, the findings indicate that about two-fifths of the Comprehensive schools in England teach their 13 year olds in mixed-ability groups, the rest are divided evenly between banding, streaming and setting (ie roughly a fifth of schools indicating each strategy). The pattern for Comprehensive schools in Wales is similar, except that rather fewer adopt a mixed-ability approach at this age (about 30 per cent) and rather more adopt a banding strategy (about two-fifths compared with the one-fifth in England). Such figures, although available, are not readily interpretable for the Northern Ireland schools since this country still retains a selective system.

Among the Comprehensive schools in England the evidence is that very many more of the 'Junior' Comprehensives adopt a banding strategy compared with the 'Senior' Comprehensives (33 per cent and 15 per cent of schools, respectively).

In the later surveys in the series schools have been asked a number of questions about *individual* teaching groups in science. One of these questions related to the spread of pupil ability within each group. Schools were asked to describe each teaching group as 'high ability', 'average ability', 'low ability', 'remedial' or 'mixed ability'. Of course, the schools' responses would inevitably be school-bound to some extent, since classes might be judged relative to other classes in the same schools rather than against some more general notion of 'high' or 'low' ability as it might apply more widely.

Despite this potential comparability problem the findings from this particular enquiry are clear. More than three-quarters of the teaching groups following separate specialist courses contained a relatively narrow ability spread: these groups were almost as often 'low' or 'average' ability as 'high ability'. In contrast, the General Science groups were more often mixed-ability: just about two-fifths were mixed-ability, in fact, the rest of one or other narrow ability spread (none clearly predominated). About 5 per cent of the teaching groups were described as remedial.

Of especial import is the strong relationship between ability spread and size of teaching group. The survey data illustrate unequivocally the known tendency for schools to arrange for pupils of lower ability to be taught in smaller classes.

Table 2.2 provides the group size information for the teaching groups within those Comprehensive schools in England which provided a single General Science course for all their 13 year olds. The picture presented by the Table is very similar also for those teaching groups within Comprehensive schools providing separate courses in the three main sciences. *In general*, about a third of the 'low-ability' groups and all but a handful of remedial classes contain fewer than 21 pupils. In contrast around a third or so of the 'high-ability' groups contain 31 or more pupils. The *majority* of teaching groups other than remedial classes contain between 26 and 30 pupils.

**Table 2.2** *Relationship between size of teaching group and ability of pupils*

(Percentage of groups within each ability level containing indicated numbers of pupils – English Comprehensive schools providing a common General Science course to all their 13 year olds)

| Ability Level | No. of groups | Number of pupils | | | |
|---|---|---|---|---|---|
| | | <21 | 21–25 | 26–30 | 31 + |
| High ability | 207 | 2 | 13 | 57 | 28 |
| Average ability | 165 | 4 | 17 | 66 | 13 |
| Low ability | 229 | 30 | 30 | 35 | 5 |
| Remedial | 71 | 90 | 4 | 6 | 0 |
| Mixed ability | 468 | 4 | 31 | 59 | 6 |

The same striking association between the general ability level of a teaching group and its size has emerged to the same, if not greater, degree among those survey schools from Wales. As mentioned earlier, the Northern Ireland schools are selective, so that any breakdowns by ability of teaching group will be of questionable meaning.

Looking at the data another way, the evidence is that 85–90 per cent of the smallest teaching groups are lower-ability or remedial classes, while 50 per cent or so of the largest teaching groups contain the more-able pupils. This undoubtedly explains the relationship which has consistently emerged in the surveys at this age between performance and size of teaching group: pupils in smaller groups producing *lower* test scores than their peers in larger groups.

**Table 2.3** *Time spent on science by teaching groups following different courses*

(Percentage of groups within each time range in English Comprehensives)

| Common courses | No. of groups | Number of periods per week | | | | |
|---|---|---|---|---|---|---|
| | | 1–2 | 3 | 4 | 5 | 6 |
| General Science | 1249 | 6 | 15 | 43 | 22 | 14 |
| Physics, Chemistry and Biology | 178 | 0 | 20 | 12 | 2 | 66 |

Enquiries have been included in every survey question-naire about the amount of time spent on science by this age-group. The results have clearly indicated that there is a very strong connection between the course curriculum provided to the pupils and the amount of time they spend on science in their schools. The clearest example of this is the difference in time spent on science between those pupils following a single integrated course and those pupils studying separate specialist subjects.

Table 2.3 illustrates this point well. Since there is no evidence in the survey data of any notable difference in the amount of time allocated to science for groups of different ability, Table 2.3 provides the time breakdown for *all* groups within each kind of common curriculum. General Science courses are normally allocated four teaching periods a week at most, while specialist courses are either allocated one or, more frequently, two periods each a week (a period is typically 35 or 40 minutes long). Thus, the differencce in time allocation between pupils studying General Science and those following courses in the three main sciences is generally two periods per week, equivalent to more than an hour of learning time each week.

Survey data have also indicated that the majority of science classes at this age receive all their lessons in a laboratory (about 85 per cent). Most of the other 15 per cent of classes receive at most one or two lessons a week in a classroom. Only a handful of classes receive *all* their science lessons in a classroom.

The question which has not been asked is the *kind* of laboratory in which lessons usually take place. It is not possible, for example, to indicate the extent to which lessons focusing on Physics (whether in a specialist course or in a General Science course) actually took place in a Physics laboratory, or similarly whether the Biology or the Chemistry lessons took place in specialist Biology or Chemistry laboratories.

## 2.4 Qualifications of teachers of science to 13 year olds

Information has been sought in every survey about the science qualifications of teachers teaching science in the schools. The findings are that, *overall*, about 95 per cent of all the science teachers in the survey schools, not just those teaching 13 year olds, have been found to hold an academic qualification in science (defined as either a degree in a science subject or a BEd or teaching certificate with science as the main subject). The majority of these teachers are, in fact, science graduates (about 70 per cent); of these degree holders about two-thirds in England and Wales also hold a Postgraduate Certificate in Education (PGCE) compared with about one-third in Northern Ireland.

The evidence from the surveys is that almost a third of all science teachers are qualified in Biology, almost a quarter in Chemistry and about a fifth in Physics. Fewer than a tenth of these teachers will be qualified in some other specialist science or in integrated science. The 1984 survey data reveal some marked differences between male and female science teachers in terms of the subject of their qualifications. Half the women teachers were qualified in Biology, one in five in Chemistry and just about one in twenty in Physics. In contrast, similar proportions of male teachers were qualified in Physics or Chemistry as were qualified in Biology (about one in four in each case).

Considering now those particular teachers who were teaching science to 13 year olds, Table 2.4 shows that lower proportions of these teachers were qualified in Physics or in Chemistry than in the school as a whole. For instance, roughly one in ten of these teachers held Physics qualifications compared with one in five of *all* science teachers. In the case of Chemistry, the discrepancy appears to be less at roughly one in five compared with one in four.

**Table 2.4**  *Subject qualifications of teachers of General Science to 13 year olds*

(Percentage of classes in English Comprehensive schools taught by teachers with qualifications in indicated subject)

| Subject of qualification | Level of ability of group | | | | |
|---|---|---|---|---|---|
| | High | Average | Low | Remedial | Mixed |
| Biology | 36 | 36 | 36 | 33 | 37 |
| Other biological science | 9 | 10 | 12 | 9 | 8 |
| Chemistry | 21 | 23 | 15 | 16 | 25 |
| Physics | 15 | 12 | 12 | 14 | 11 |
| Other physical science | 5 | 7 | 8 | 7 | 5 |
| General science | 8 | 6 | 8 | 10 | 8 |
| No science qualification | 6 | 6 | 9 | 10 | 6 |
| Number of teaching groups | 189 | 145 | 200 | 69 | 484 |

A point of particular interest in Table 2.4 is the similarity between teaching groups of different abilities in terms of the qualifications of their science teachers. For instance, there seems to be no evidence that the teaching groups containing the more-able pupils are allocated teachers with Biology or with Physics qualifications more often than are those groups of less academically inclined pupils.

This is the case also for teaching groups of different abilities within the 'separate-subject' schools. In other words, there is no indication that more-able groups are preferentially treated with regard to the qualifications of the teachers assigned to them. The numbers of teaching groups available for analysis are small in this case, but the evidence is that the less academically able pupils are as likely as the average or more-able pupils to receive their specialist science teaching from teachers holding formal qualifications in the appropriate sciences.

As Table 2.5 shows, in these 'separate-subject' schools and in the 'narrow ability' classes, Biology courses were more likely to be given by teachers qualified in Biology than were Chemistry or Physics courses to be given by a teacher qualified in the appropriate subject.

The picture for the mixed-ability classes is rather different. Here the subject most likely to be taught by a teacher with the appropriate subject qualification is Chemistry. Of particular interest, perhaps, is the fact that fewer than a third of the Biology classes were taken by teachers qualified in this subject; rather disquieting is the evidence that fully a quarter of these classes learn their Biology with a teacher possessing no formal qualification in *any* science subject (though these classes are admittedly few in number, and in even fewer schools).

The findings together indicate some important differences in the science experience of 13 year olds, depending on whether they are following a single integrated science course or specialist courses in the main sciences. Pupils following General Science courses are typically taught by one or at most two teachers only, and these are more likely to hold qualifications in Biology than in Physics or Chemistry. In contrast, pupils following three separate specialist courses will usually be taught by three different teachers with a good chance that these teachers will between them have qualifications representing the three main sciences.

In view of this it must be possible that 'General Science' pupils might benefit in Biology *at the expense of* Physics and, though to a lesser extent, Chemistry. Indeed, the likelihood of these pupils being taught the Chemistry or the Physics in their integrated courses by

**Table 2.5**  *Subject qualifications of teachers of specialist subject courses to 13 year olds in 1984†*

(Percentage of classes in English Comprehensives taught by a teacher qualified in indicated subject)

| Subject of lesson | Level of ability of group | Science subject qualification of teacher | | | | |
|---|---|---|---|---|---|---|
| | | Biology | Chemistry | Physics | Other | None |
| Biology | Narrow | 66 | 7 | 6 | 20 | 1 |
| | Mixed | 30 | 15 | 0 | 29 | 26 |
| Chemistry | Narrow | 21 | 49 | 3 | 25 | 2 |
| | Mixed | 16 | 60 | 0 | 24 | 0 |
| Physics | Narrow | 16 | 7 | 53 | 23 | 1 |
| | Mixed | 12 | 0 | 38 | 47 | 3 |

† Numbers of groups: 138 'Narrow' (53 'high' ability, 27 'average', 58 'low') and 27 'mixed'.

teachers with qualifications in these subjects is very much lower than that of 'specialist subject' pupils being taught their Chemistry or Physics courses by teachers qualified in these particular subjects. As Table 2.4 has shown, about one in five and one in ten General Science classes are taught, respectively, by teachers with qualifications in Chemistry or Physics. This compares with about 50 per cent of the separate subject classes in each case (see Table 2.5).

Even for Biology there is a clear difference between general and specialist classes. Roughly one in three of the former compared with two in three of the latter learn their Biology from someone with a formal Biology qualification. Mixed ability classes following separate subject courses resemble the General Science classes in this particular respect.

## 2.5 Laboratory provision and technician support

Earlier in this chapter it was noted that an extremely small proportion of teaching groups at this age were taught all their science in a classroom environment. On the contrary, the great majority of 13 year olds receive *all* their science lessons in laboratories. There is little evidence then that 13 year olds suffer unduly in this respect from pressure on laboratory accommodation for examination classes further up the school.

There is evidence (gathered in the surveys of 15 year olds) that limited laboratory availability instead constrains the variety of science courses offered to the older pupils. In other words, most schools provide the laboratory space currently required by examination classes for their specialist subject and, presumably, General Science courses, and use any spare laboratory capacity for science teaching lower down the school rather than for extending the range of science courses provided to their older pupils (see the review report at age 15–DES, 1988b). If schools are already making full use of their available laboratories, the implications for schools of a commitment to an entirely practically based 'science for all' are clear.

In the report of their extensive survey of education in English secondary schools HMI provided a rough but nevertheless useful criterion by which the adequacy of a school's laboratory accommodation in this context might be judged (DES, 1979). Since the criterion depends on knowledge of the number of form-entries and of laboratories in an individual school, this information was gathered in the school questionnaires used in the later APU surveys so that adequacy of laboratory accommodation might be explored.

The HMI criterion is based on the assumption that pupils aged from 11 to 16 will study science for about a sixth of their curriculum time (ie 6 periods in a 35-period week) and that their science work will be practically based. Allowing one period per day for general laboratory maintenance, there will be available in each laboratory about 30 hours teaching time in a 35-period week or 35 hours in a 40-period week. An n-form entry school with y year-groups within the age-range 11–16 would then need $6ny/30$ in $7ny/35$ (ie $ny/5$) laboratories in order to accommodate such a practically based science teaching load.

HMI considered that schools with sixth forms would need one further laboratory over this basic number to meet their extra requirements. For the purposes of these APU surveys schools with ages of intake below 11 were considered to need laboratory accommodation only for the science courses taken by pupils of 11 and over.

Applying this criterion, a 5-form entry 11–16 Comprehensive school would need five laboratories while a 5-form entry 11–18 school would need six laboratories to be considered adequately provided (five plus one extra for the additional sixth-form needs). A 3-form 8–12 middle school would need a single laboratory and a 3-form entry 13–16 school would need at least two laboratories to be considered similarly adequately provided.

Of course, when evaluating the accommodation in their sample schools, HMI had available to them information about the particular circumstances obtaining in each. Consequently, the result of applying this general criterion was often modified for individual schools in the light of this information. It should be noted that similar circumstantial information is *not* available for the present survey schools. Nevertheless, the findings which have emerged from an application of HMI's rough criterion are illuminating.

In the earlier science survey reports comments were offered about the adequacy of the laboratory accommodation in the sample of schools which took part in each *particular* survey. The 1980 and 1981 figures, in fact, were based either on a notional form-entry size (in the surveys of 15 year olds) or on the number of science teaching groups (in the surveys of 13 year olds). In the case of estimated form-entries the total number of pupils in each school between the ages of 11 and 16 was divided by 35–in retrospect this was too high a divisor to apply, since a more typical form size is around 30 pupils. The number of teaching groups has also proved an unsuitable divisor in the HMI criterion index, since there are often more teaching groups in science than there are administrative forms at age 13.

From 1982 onwards the school questionnaires have asked specifically for the number of form entries, so that it has been possible to apply the HMI index more meaningfully to the later data. Table 2.6 presents the results for the sample of secondary schools which were

**Table 2.6** *Proportions of schools with adequate numbers of laboratories to be able to accommodate a practically based science curriculum (comprising 20 per cent of total available school learning time) for all pupils aged 11–16\**

|  | No. of schools | Percentage of schools with adequate numbers of laboratories |
|---|---|---|
| England | 558 | 65 |
| Wales | 130 | 69 |
| Northern Ireland | 145 | 34 |
| **Within England** |  |  |
| Independent | 88 | 83 |
| Grammar | 18 | 100 |
| Comprehensive to 18 | 120 | 74 |
| Comprehensive to 16 | 64 | 56 |
| 'Junior' Comprehensive | 51 | 39 |
| Secondary Modern | 18 | 44 |
| **Within Northern Ireland** |  |  |
| Grammar | 36 | 86 |
| Secondary Intermediate | 108 | 16 |

\* Based on questionnaire responses to the 1984 surveys at ages 13 and 15.

involved in either or both the 1984 surveys at ages 13 or 15. Table 2.6 suggests that, as far as HMI's criterion is concerned, almost all the Independent and Grammar schools in England have enough laboratories to be able to extend their science provision to *all* their pupils. This is the case also for the Grammar schools in Northern Ireland.

For the Comprehensive and Secondary Modern schools in England and Wales the picture is rather different. Around a quarter of the Comprehensive schools with sixth forms and a third or more of other Comprehensives and Secondary Modern schools seem still to have too few laboratories for such a broad provision of practically based science to be a possibility. This is *despite* a slight improvement in laboratory availability in English Comprehensive schools over the period of the surveys.

The Secondary Intermediate schools in Northern Ireland are the least well provided of all school types in terms

of available laboratories. Fewer than a fifth of the Secondary Intermediate schools in Northern Ireland would be considered to have enough laboratories to accommodate entirely practically based science courses for all their pupils amounting to an average of a sixth of total curriculum time. Among these schools the coeducational and the girls' schools would appear to be even less well provided with laboratories than the boys' schools, as will be seen more clearly later.

This differential laboratory provision among the different types of maintained school can be even more clearly illustrated by looking at the ratio of the number of pupils aged 11 to 16 in the schools to the number of laboratories the schools have available. Table 2.7 presents the relevant information for the maintained schools in the three countries which took part in one or other of the 1984 surveys of 13 year olds or of 15 year olds.

Within England Table 2.7 shows a clear gradation in the level of laboratory provision from the rather privileged Grammar schools at one end through the Comprehensives with sixth forms and those without to the particularly poorly supported Secondary Moderns at the other.

The contrast between the laboratory availability in the Grammar and Secondary Modern schools in England and between that in the corresponding Grammar and Secondary Intermediate schools in Northern Ireland is stark. The evidence is that, while 80–90 per cent of the Grammar schools enjoy a ratio of 100 or fewer pupils per laboratory, 50 per cent of the Secondary Modern schools in the England and 16 per cent of the Secondary Intermediate schools in Northern Ireland have high ratios of 175 pupils or more to each laboratory.

These ratios are readily translated into implications for practically based teaching in science. For instance, a ratio of 100 pupils per laboratory would mean that if all the pupils aged 11 to 16 in the school were to spend 100 per cent of their *total* learning time in a science

**Table 2.7** *Laboratory availability in schools of different types*
(Percentage of schools in each range in the 1984 surveys at ages 13 and/or 15)

| Type of school | No. of schools | No. of pupils in school per laboratory | | | | |
|---|---|---|---|---|---|---|
|  |  | <100 | 100–124 | 125–149 | 150–175 | 176+ |
| **England** |  |  |  |  |  |  |
| Grammar | 18 | 89 | 6 | 6 | 0 | 0 |
| Comprehensive to 18 | 120 | 28 | 28 | 28 | 10 | 6 |
| Comprehensive to 16 | 64 | 3 | 12 | 27 | 31 | 27 |
| Junior Comprehensives | 51 | 2 | 2 | 6 | 12 | 78 |
| Secondary Modern | 18 | 0 | 11 | 16 | 22 | 50 |
| **Wales** |  |  |  |  |  |  |
| Comprehensives | 110 | 14 | 31 | 26 | 19 | 10 |
| **Northern Ireland** |  |  |  |  |  |  |
| Grammar | 36 | 81 | 13 | 3 | 0 | 3 |
| Secondary Intermediate | 108 | 17 | 25 | 26 | 16 | 16 |

laboratory, then they would have to be taught in groups of 100 pupils each. If, on the other hand, any pupil within this age-range were to spend 20 per cent of total learning time in practically based science work, then the original ratio of 100 pupils per lab means that groups of 20 pupils at a time could undertake their science activity in a laboratory. Similarly, a ratio of between 100 and 124 would imply science group sizes of between 20 and 25 pupils; a ratio between 125 and 149 implies group sizes of 25 to 30 pupils, and so on. These conversions make sense, of course, only if it would be logistically possible to divide any year-group into equally sized groups for their science activity.

Given this, Table 2.7 suggests that 80 per cent or so of Grammar schools not only have enough laboratories to allow them to provide a practically based science curriculum to all their 11–16 pupils for a sixth their total learning time on average, but they have sufficient laboratories to be able to teach these pupils in group sizes of 25 or fewer pupils. A similar proportion of Secondary Modern/Intermediate schools would only be able to support this level of practically based science provision if their pupils undertook their science activities in groups of 30 pupils or more.

The differential provision of laboratories in the single-sex and mixed schools of Northern Ireland mentioned earlier is also more clearly illustrated with this ratio approach. Table 2.8 presents the figures; this table like the previous one is based on those Grammar and Secondary Intermediate schools which took part either in the 1984 survey of 13 year olds or in that of 15 year olds or both. These together form more than half of the population of such schools in the country as a whole.

The evidence in Table 2.8 is that even among the Grammar schools the girls' schools have far fewer available laboratories than do the boys' schools. Among the Secondary Intermediate schools the difference in current provision is even more striking. The girls' Secondary Intermediate schools are much less well provided with laboratories than are the boys' Secondary Intermediates. The picture for the girls' schools is bleaker than even Table 2.8 suggests, for those 7 schools classified into the 175+ group actually have closer to 300 than 200

pupils per laboratory, ie 60 pupils per teaching group for all pupils to receive practically based science.

This apparent dearth of laboratory accommodation in the girls' schools might well be one of the main reasons why almost a third of the girls in Northern Ireland have been found to be studying no science course at all at age 15–not even the traditional Biology (see the review report at Age 15–DES, 1988b).

As mentioned earlier, it is not possible to comment here on the *kinds* of laboratories the schools do already have available, but it is likely that Physics and Chemistry laboratories will be in shorter supply than Biology laboratories–particularly in the girls' schools. The implications for a move to practically-based science for all pupils to age 16 are clear. Indeed, with their present laboratory space it is difficult to see how an attempt might be made to redress the current imbalance in science-taking between boys and girls, without pupils lower down the school losing some of the time they now enjoy in a laboratory environment.

The HMI secondary survey report also proved useful in providing a criterion for judging the adequacy of a school's technician support: schools with three or fewer laboratories per full time technician being considered by the HMI to be adequately supported (DES, 1979). The 1984 survey data reveal a rather uniform picture, with about a third of schools of most types having enough technician support to meet this criterion satisfactorily. The only figures which differ are those for Secondary Modern schools in England and Secondary Intermediate schools in Northern Ireland–44 per cent (of just 18 schools) and 18 per cent (of 67 schools), respectively.

## 2.6   Summary

The school questionnaires used in the various annual science surveys have together provided a wealth of information about the circumstances in which 13 year olds study science in their schools.

**Table 2.8**   *Laboratory availability in schools of different types in Northern Ireland*
(Percentage of schools in each range in the 1984 surveys at ages 13 and/or 15)

| Type of school | No. schools | No. of pupils in school per laboratory | | | | |
| --- | --- | --- | --- | --- | --- | --- |
| | | <100 | 100–124 | 125–149 | 150–175 | 176+ |
| **Grammar** | | | | | | |
| Boys' | 8 | 100 | 0 | 0 | 0 | 0 |
| Girls' | 12 | 75 | 17 | 8 | 0 | 0 |
| Mixed | 16 | 75 | 18 | 0 | 0 | 1 |
| **Secondary intermediate** | | | | | | |
| Boys' | 18 | 39 | 33 | 22 | 6 | 0 |
| Girls' | 16 | 0 | 13 | 32 | 13 | 43 |
| Mixed | 74 | 15 | 26 | 26 | 20 | 13 |

The data suggest that pupils at this age are far more likely to be following a single General Science course than any other, unless they attend Independent or Grammar schools in which case they would be following separate-subject courses in Biology, Chemistry and Physics.

The time spent on science by 13 year olds in school depends very much on whether they study an integrated science or the three separate sciences. Pupils in the former group are most likely to spend at most four periods a week in science activity, while pupils in the latter group generally enjoy six periods a week of science.

The schools are as likely to be using their own resource materials as any which are commercially available (about a third of surveyed schools claimed to use their own). Of the more popular commercially available materials, Nuffield Combined Science featured most strongly in England and Wales (about a third of schools made main use of these) while the Scottish Integrated Science materials were relatively widely used in Northern Ireland (30–40 per cent of schools compared with about 10 per cent in England and Wales). Insight to Science was used as a main resource in about one in ten of all schools. Some use was also made of field centre and industrial visits in the science work of many 13 year olds.

Banding, streaming and setting were all used to some extent by Comprehensive schools in England and Wales to place 13 year olds into teaching groups for science, although the majority of schools simply created mixed-ability groups (the schools in Northern Ireland are already selective). 'Junior' Comprehensive schools (mainly middle schools) were more likely to use banding than were the 'senior' Comprehensives (11–16 and 11–18 schools in the main).

Survey evidence is that in England and Wales less-able pupils are highly likely to be learning their science in small groups of 20 or fewer pupils. The most-able pupils, on the other hand, are almost as likely to be taught in larger groups of more than 30 pupils. This difference in treatment is more marked for separate-subject courses than it is for General Science.

About two-thirds of the teachers of science to 13 year olds hold a science degree, and about a quarter have a BEd or a teaching certificate with science a main com-ponent. Roughly one in twenty of the teachers teaching science to this age-group have no formal qualification in *any* science subject. Half the female science teachers were qualified in Biology, about one in five in Chemistry and about one in twenty in Physics. For each main science about a quarter of the male science teachers held a formal qualification.

A higher proportion of the teachers of science to this age-group were qualified in Biology (about a third) than were qualified in Chemistry (20–30 per cent), Physics (about 15 per cent) or indeed integrated science in any form (fewer than 10 per cent). A consequence of this is that pupils studying General Science are very much less likely to be taught the Physics or Chemistry in their courses by teachers with matching subject qualifications than are those pupils studying these subjects in specialist courses. The same is actually true, though to a lesser degree, in Biology.

In view of the already existing subject imbalance among the teachers of science to this age-group, it must be of some interest that the schools do not appear to adopt a policy of differential assignment of their subject teachers to groups of different academic ability. The more-able pupils are not apparently in any way pref-erentially treated by receiving all their subject teaching from the available teachers qualified in the appropriate subjects. Neither indeed is there any difference in the amount of time provided to the various teaching groups for science work. Time in laboratories is *also* shared equally where there is insufficient laboratory space to accommodate all classes at this stage. The only observ-able concession to the different needs of pupils of dif-ferent abilities in science is the deliberate manipulation of class size, so that the less-able pupils are taught in more manageable smaller groups.

There is little indication in the survey data that 13 year olds suffered at the time of testing from pressure on laboratory accommodation. The majority of teaching groups received *all* their science lessons in laboratories, and only a tiny handful of groups were taught entirely in classrooms. On the other hand, few of the maintained schools without sixth forms currently have enough laboratories to enable them to accommodate an entirely practically based science curriculum for *all* pupils aged 11 to 16 of the kind currently under consideration. This is especially the case for the Secondary Intermediate schools in Northern Ireland, and among these the situation is most severe for the girls' schools and the mixed schools.

# 3

# Pupils' interests and perceptions relating to science

## 3.1 Introduction

The review of survey findings at age 13 has focussed largely on children's performance in science. The surveys, however, have also been concerned to discover some of the reasons for *variations* in children's performance. To this end a good deal of research has been carried out by the science teams. This research has included the administration of a number of probes: packages of questions targeted to address specific issues.

The chapter describes one aspect of this research work: that aspect concerned with pupils' interests, as they pertain to science, outside and inside school; their perceptions of some of the science tasks used in the surveys; their perceptions of suitable careers for themselves and others; and finally their view of the importance of science for different career choices.

## 3.2 Background

An investigation of the relationship between pupil attributes and achievements was undertaken to facilitate the interpretation of the survey data and to promote the development and refinement of the questions used in the assessment.

Part of this investigation included a review of survey performance by gender carried out across the three ages (see Johnson and Murphy, 1986). In this review the performance of girls and boys in each category of the assessment framework was presented and discussed. The results for pupils of age 11 in 1980 showed that, on four out of five science tests, girls and boys performance was not significantly different. The one test difference in favour of the boys was in the application of physics concepts. A general performance effect noted across all the tests was associated with the content of the questions; that is, with the information, object, event or data presented to the children. The effect of content on performance was observed particularly on questions about electricity where, irrespective of the need to apply conceptual understanding, girls did less well than boys. Girls tended, on the other hand, to score higher on questions where they had to make observations; and on many questions about health and

nutrition, or on those set in a clearly domestic context. At age 13 the results were very similar, except that the test differences in favour of the boys extended to include interpretation of graphical information. At age 15 boys performed at a significantly higher level on *four* out of *seven* tests. These included the application of physics *and* chemistry concepts, the use of symbolic representations and the interpretation of presented information. The findings at test and question level were replicated at the three ages over the five years of surveys up to and including 1984, and are very similar to the findings of other assessment exercises (Hobbs *et al*, 1979, NAEP, 1978).

In the same review it was noted that only about one girl in every five chose to study physics once the subject became optional. This finding was associated in the review with the performance discrepancy observed in the application of the physics concepts at each age. It appeared, however, that the performance disadvantage in physics was never fully overcome, even by able girls studying physics. Attention was also drawn to research carried out in other countries, and replicated in the APU Science results at age 11, about the differences, established early and persisting, in the interests and voluntary pastimes of boys and girls. The review concluded that the early socialisation experiences of boys and girls might have a profound effect on their attitudes to science and on their subsequent performance in, and liking of, the subject.

At ages 13 and 15, no attempt was made, before 1984, to collect affective data; the focus of the research work carried out to increase the interpretability of survey results had been linked more closely to question attributes than to pupil attributes.

In summary, by 1983 there had been some assessment of affective outcomes at age 11 but none at ages 13 and 15. There had been a review of gender differences in performance which took account of other research findings. The effect on the validity, reliability and interpretability of APU measures of external influences was thus recognised. Further to the studies mentioned there had been a number of in-depth studies, informed by survey results, carried out at age 13 (see Chapter 11 for discussion). The intention of these studies was to identify possible influences acting on pupils when responding to questions in the various categories of the framework.

The combination of insights gained into the possible relationships between pupil attributes and achievement led to a set of research questions being raised for consideration in the age 13 survey in 1984. Of course any work in this area is of necessity complex and based on interlinked hypotheses. This was kept in mind during the selection of the research questions to be pursued. Account had also to be taken of the constraints imposed by the demands of a national survey. The decision made at age 13 was to consider a set of hypotheses about performance determinants which were related to, and significant for, the assessment exercise and for classroom practice.

The following issues were selected for consideration:

- pupils' interests in science topics and applications
- pupils' science-related experiences
- pupils' perceptions of science activities
- pupils' views of their own performance on science activities
- pupils' views of different jobs and the relevance of science to them

## 3.3  Questionnaire development

Five questionnaires were produced (see Appendix 3) to address the above issues. The questionnaires were self-administered. Four questionnaires were included at the end of a written test package (one questionnaire per package) and given to separate sub-samples of pupils of the order of 3,000. These questionnaires used a Likert-type five-point attitude scale. A further questionnaire was administered at the end of the circuses of practical questions.

The first questionnaire 'Topics of interest' was concerned with pupils' interest in science topics. The APU Science team had produced a list of science concepts and knowledge (see Appendix 5) to define for question writers the extent of the concept domain at each age. The list was unique in that it was written to be appropriate for 11 year olds in primary schools through to 15 year olds in secondary schools. As mentioned in Chapter 1, the list had a common structure across the three ages and was generated by a process of dialogue between team members and teachers. The list included those concept statements which it was reasonable to expect pupils of 11, 13 and 15 years of age to have met in their science lessons. The age 13 list was a sub-set of the age 15 list and subsumed the list for age 11.

The 'Topics of interest' questionnaire included, where possible, science concept statements from the list paired with a statement of application which was dependent on the same concept. An example of such a pair of statements is 'How sound travels' and 'How balloons can be used to help teach deaf children'. The purpose was to see if the more abstract expression of a concept affected pupils' reactions to it, and to see if pupils who were interested in one of the paired statements would be interested in the other. In addition, it was hoped to find out whether groups of pupils tended to be positive about the applications of science rather than about its abstract formulations. The issue of 'girl-friendly science' was also kept in mind when developing this questionnaire (Smail 1984, GASAT 11, 1983). Is it the case, as believed by many researchers in the field, that girls are interested in topics of social and human relevance, or is it the specific content of science which determines their interest? Clearly the questionnaire could not fully address such complex issues, but it was hoped at least to cast some light on the matter at age 13. (The questionnaire finally produced included 48 topics of interest, listed at random.)

The second questionnaire attempted to identify the different experiences the pupils bring to the learning situation. The questionnaire included a selected list of activities which children might pursue outside school and which might influence their attitudes to, and achievements in, science. In the development of this particular questionnaire there was an attempt to produce an overlap with one developed at age 11; the outcome was an overlap of approximately 50 per cent, although the wording of the statements was not always identical. In the questionnaire at age 13 the pupils were also asked to say whether they had a sister or a brother or both. It was thought that access to some of the activities listed might depend quite heavily on playing with siblings' toys, or sharing their out-of-school interests. The questionnaire asked the pupil to state how often they undertook a particular activity, and whether they would be interested in doing more of it.

The third questionnaire was the most complicated, and due to the time required for analysis the available results are limited in scope. It was developed in order to consider the relationships between the pupils' perception of scientific activities, their liking of them and their view of their *competence* in them. Discussion of the development of this questionnaire is included here to emphasise that the five questionnaires had a linked aim and a common background of development. Some results will also be discussed in section 3.6. The questionnaire was given to the pupils after they had completed a circus of **Observation** tasks or **Using measuring instruments** tasks. The **Observation** tests required children to *use*, rather than *explain*, their knowledge, to model a variety of resources either overtly everyday or scientific in nature. The children had, then, to select the relevant observations and, in many instances, use them to describe a generalisation or to make a prediction. The 'content' is an *integral* part of the observation tasks. The observation tests offered an alternative way of presenting the content of science to children to that used in the 'Topics of interest' questionnaire. The questionnaire asks the pupils their opinion of what the task they had just completed was about. They were then asked to comment on how well they liked it, how it

**Figure 3.1** *Topics of interest in order of popularity*

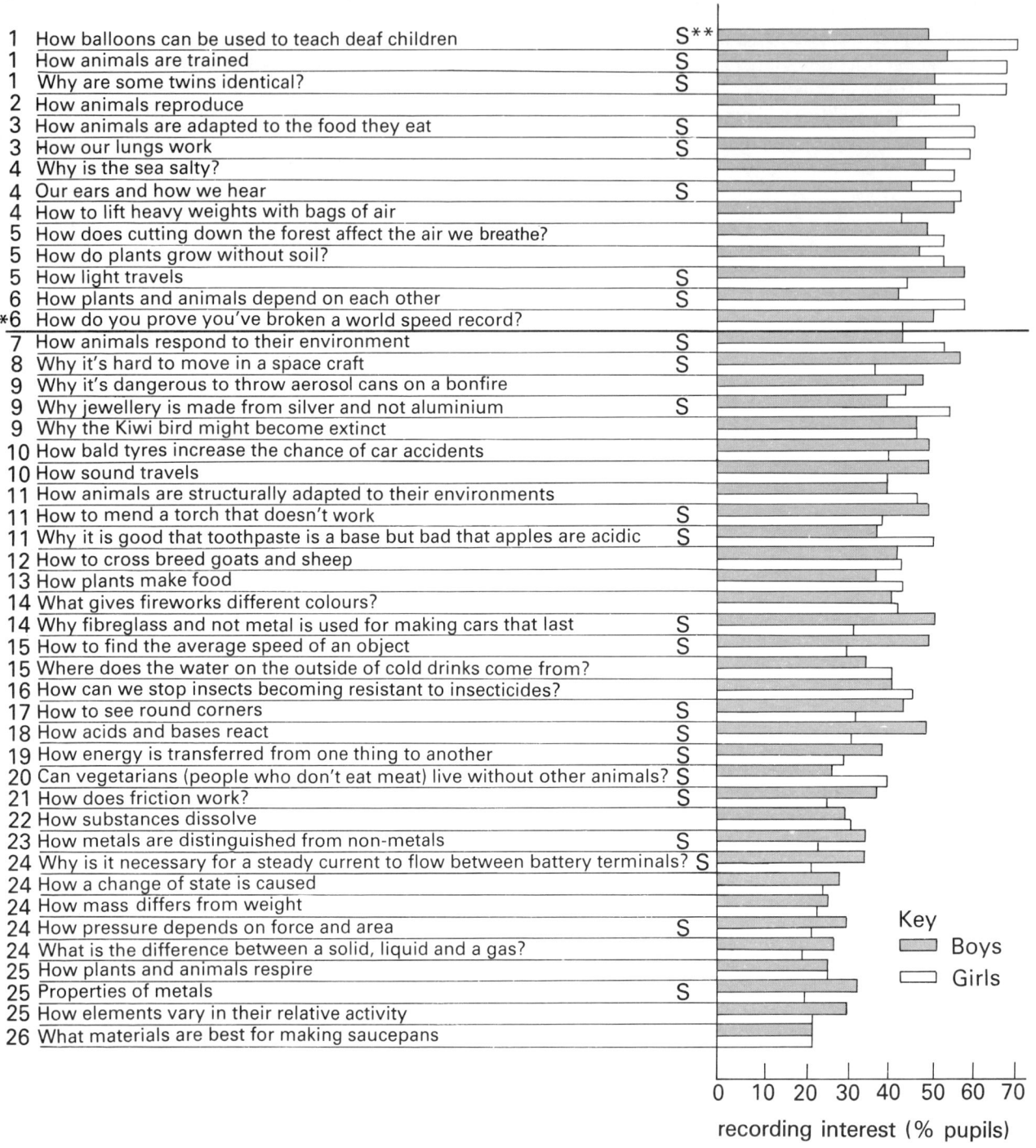

| | | |
|---|---|---|
| 1 | How balloons can be used to teach deaf children | S** |
| 1 | How animals are trained | S |
| 1 | Why are some twins identical? | S |
| 2 | How animals reproduce | |
| 3 | How animals are adapted to the food they eat | S |
| 3 | How our lungs work | S |
| 4 | Why is the sea salty? | |
| 4 | Our ears and how we hear | S |
| 4 | How to lift heavy weights with bags of air | |
| 5 | How does cutting down the forest affect the air we breathe? | |
| 5 | How do plants grow without soil? | |
| 5 | How light travels | S |
| 6 | How plants and animals depend on each other | S |
| *6 | How do you prove you've broken a world speed record? | |
| 7 | How animals respond to their environment | S |
| 8 | Why it's hard to move in a space craft | S |
| 9 | Why it's dangerous to throw aerosol cans on a bonfire | |
| 9 | Why jewellery is made from silver and not aluminium | S |
| 9 | Why the Kiwi bird might become extinct | |
| 10 | How bald tyres increase the chance of car accidents | |
| 10 | How sound travels | |
| 11 | How animals are structurally adapted to their environments | |
| 11 | How to mend a torch that doesn't work | S |
| 11 | Why it is good that toothpaste is a base but bad that apples are acidic | S |
| 12 | How to cross breed goats and sheep | |
| 13 | How plants make food | |
| 14 | What gives fireworks different colours? | |
| 14 | Why fibreglass and not metal is used for making cars that last | S |
| 15 | How to find the average speed of an object | S |
| 15 | Where does the water on the outside of cold drinks come from? | |
| 16 | How can we stop insects becoming resistant to insecticides? | |
| 17 | How to see round corners | S |
| 18 | How acids and bases react | S |
| 19 | How energy is transferred from one thing to another | S |
| 20 | Can vegetarians (people who don't eat meat) live without other animals? | S |
| 21 | How does friction work? | S |
| 22 | How substances dissolve | |
| 23 | How metals are distinguished from non-metals | S |
| 24 | Why is it necessary for a steady current to flow between battery terminals? | S |
| 24 | How a change of state is caused | |
| 24 | How mass differs from weight | |
| 24 | How pressure depends on force and area | S |
| 24 | What is the difference between a solid, liquid and a gas? | |
| 25 | How plants and animals respire | |
| 25 | Properties of metals | S |
| 25 | How elements vary in their relative activity | |
| 26 | What materials are best for making saucepans | |

Key
- Boys
- Girls

0  10  20  30  40  50  60  70

recording interest (% pupils)

\* The line between the activities in rank order 6 and 7 denotes the point above which 50 per cent or more of the pupils indicated that they would like to know more about the topics.

\*\* S indicates that the difference in the percentages of girls and boys recording interest in the topic is significant at the 1 per cent level.

related to their experiences of other science activities, and how well they thought they had done on it. The pupils had to answer these questions for two tasks that they had just completed. They were also asked to say which was their favourite task in the test, and how they felt they had done overall. Finally they were asked about their science lessons in school and whether they intended to continue with science after the third year. Essentially this questionnaire was developed to see how pupils perceived these types of tasks and whether their perception matched that of the team. In addition it was hoped to establish whether attributes of the question, or the pupil, or a combination of both, affected their perception, and/or their performance, of a task.

The fourth questionnaire was concerned to establish pupils' view of the suitability of a variety of jobs for themselves; for girls; and for boys. The fifth questionnaire was linked to the fourth but in this questionnaire pupils' views of the relevance of science, for the same list of jobs, was sought and the effect, if any, this had on their view of the job's suitability for themselves; for girls; and for boys. These questionnaires were included in the investigation to gain another insight into pupils' perceptions of science and the effect that these might have on their approaches and responses to science in schools. The questionnaires were trialled in schools, originally with a more extensive list of jobs, covering as wide a range as possible. This was to inform decisions as to which jobs were recognised and understood by the pupils. Built into the questionnaire were two distinct aspects. These were *job type* and *job status*. Thus 'pairs' of jobs, one from each end of the status spectrum, were included where this was appropriate. An example of such a pair was 'bank manager' and 'bank clerk'. The final questionnaire listed 44 jobs in total, with status spread at random within it.

## 3.4 Topics of interest

In Figure 3.1 (p. 16) the topics are listed in order of overall popularity, as judged by the pupils stating a desire to know more about them. In the same figure, for each topic, interest by gender is indicated. Where there is a significant difference (at the 1 per cent level) in the interest shown by boys and girls, an 'S' has been placed alongside the respective bars in the figure. Note also that the topics which are most popular with *all* pupils, ie >50 per cent, are more often the topics in which girls express a significantly greater interest. The most popular subjects do not spread across the contents of science, nor are they located in any particular one. There is, however, a predominance of biological statements in which all pupils claim to be more interested. There is also noticeable in the data a positive trend towards an interest in the applications of science. It must be said that the general level of interest in all of the topics is not high.

The sample of pupils responding to the questionnaire was split into two groups, girls and boys. Within each group, using the same criteria as above, those topics which 50 per cent or more of the sub-sample expressed a desire to know more about were identified. The results for each group are listed in Tables 3.1 and 3.2.

**Table 3.1** *Topics which 50 per cent or more girls expressed an interest in knowing more about*

| Topic | % of Girls |
|---|---|
| How balloons can be used to help teach deaf children | 71 |
| Why are some twins identical? | 70 |
| How animals are trained | 69 |
| How our lungs work | 59 |
| Our ears and how we hear | 59 |
| How plants and animals depend on each other | 59 |
| How animals reproduce | 58 |
| Why is the sea salty? | 56 |
| Why jewellery is made from silver and not aluminium | 55 |
| How does cutting down forests affect the air we breathe? | 54 |
| How animals respond to their environment | 54 |

**Table 3.2** *Topics which 50 per cent or more boys expressed an interest in knowing more about*

| Topic | % of Boys |
|---|---|
| How light travels | 60 |
| Why it is hard to move in a space-craft | 58 |
| How to lift heavy weights with bags of air | 56 |
| How animals are trained | 54 |
| How does cutting down forests affect the air we breathe? | 51 |
| Why fibreglass and not metal is used for making cars that last | 51 |
| How do you prove you've broken a world speed record? | 51 |
| Why are some twins identical? | 51 |
| Why is the sea salty? | 50 |
| How sound travels | 50 |
| How to mend a torch which doesn't work | 50 |
| How bald tyres increase the chance of car accidents | 50 |

Tables 3.1 and 3.2 show that boys expressed an interest in more topics than girls. The type of topic preferred also shifts when the boys and girls are considered separately. Three out of four of the 'girls'' topics are biological in nature. However two of these topics are of equal interest to both boys and girls. Two thirds of the 'boys'' topics of interest are physics-orientated and are generally to do with the applications of science.

Tables 3.3 and 3.4 list the topics in which girls as a group expressed a significantly greater interest than boys, and vice versa. The lists include *all* topics which were preferred by boys or girls to a significantly greater extent, and therefore include these topics of less intrinsic interest *generally* than the ones highlighted in Tables 3.1 and 3.2.

It would appear that girls, rather than opting for, say, applications of science as a category in preference to the more abstract statements, seem to have responded to the very specific content listed.

**Table 3.3** *Topics in which girls expressed a significantly greater interest (at the 1 per cent level) than boys*

| | Topic | Percentage expressing an interest in knowing more about a topic | |
|---|---|---|---|
| | | Girls % | Boys |
| | How balloons can be used to help teach deaf children | 71 | 48 |
| | Why are some twins identical? | 70 | 51 |
| | How animals are trained | 69 | 54 |
| | How animals are adapted to the food they eat | 61 | 43 |
| (a)* | How plants and animals depend on each other | 59 | 43 |
| | How our lungs work | 59 | 49 |
| | Our ears and how we hear | 59 | 46 |
| | Why jewellery is made from silver and not aluminium | 55 | 40 |
| | How animals respond to their environment | 54 | 44 |
| | How plants make food | 44 | 36 |
| (a) | Can vegetarians (people who don't eat meat) live without other animals? | 40 | 26 |
| | Why it's good that toothpaste is a base but bad that apples are acidic | 49 | 37 |

\* The letters on the left indicate the paired statements as each statement in a pair is denoted by the same letter.

17

**Table 3.4**  *Topics in which boys expressed a significantly greater interest (at the 1 per cent level) than girls*

| Topic | | Percentage expressing an interest in knowing more about a topic | |
|---|---|---|---|
| | | Boys % | Girls |
| (a)* | How light travels | 60 | 44 |
| | Why it's hard to move in a space craft | 58 | 37 |
| (b) | How to lift heavy weights with bags of air | 56 | 44 |
| (c) | Why fibreglass and not metal is used for making cars that last | 51 | 31 |
| (d) | How do you prove you've broken a world speed record? | 51 | 44 |
| | How sound travels | 50 | 40 |
| (e) | How to mend a torch that doesn't work | 50 | 38 |
| (f) | How bald tyres increase the chance of car accidents | 50 | 41 |
| | How acids and bases react | 49 | 31 |
| (g) | Why it's dangerous to throw aerosol cans on a bonfire | 49 | 45 |
| (d) | How to find the average speed of an object | 49 | 29 |
| (a) | How to see round corners | 44 | 32 |
| (h) | How energy is transferred from one thing to another | 39 | 29 |
| (f) | How does friction work? | 37 | 25 |
| (e) | Why it is necessary for a steady current to flow between the terminals of a battery? | 34 | 21 |
| (i) | How metals are distinguished from non-metals | 34 | 23 |
| (c) | Properties of metals | 33 | 20 |
| (h) | Is there such a thing as perpetual motion? | 30 | 23 |
| (i) | How elements vary in their relative activity | 30 | 21 |
| (b) | How pressure depends on force and area | 30 | 21 |
| (g) | What is the difference between a solid, a liquid and a gas? | 27 | 19 |

* The letters on the left indicate the paired statements as each statement in a pair is denoted by the same letter.

In the list of topics in Table 3.4, in which significantly more boys than girls expressed interest, there is a definite trend to *include* the science concept statements. In most cases both statements in a pair are included (see letters next to the topics in the table).

There is a difference in the topics in which boys and girls expressed an interest. Some of the most popular topics were of interest to both girls and boys, notably the biological ones. Girls were more interested in topics related to plants and animals and their care, rather than in applications across contents. The boys' topics of interest were more often physical science ones. If boys expressed an interest in a topic they were generally interested in both the concept statement and the application.

These different interests of boys and girls may well be reflected in their performance on different questions used in the survey. It has been mentioned in the review of gender differences in performance that girls tended to do better than boys at all ages on questions concerning health, nutrition and reproduction and on many questions which are set in a clearly 'domestic' context. Similarly, boys at all ages performed at a higher level on questions concerned with the application of physics concepts. Thus the pattern of difference in interests matches the pattern of difference in performance.

The data presented in this section could be interpreted as indicating the limited scope of girls' interest in science topics. The results suggest that any widening of the topics they see as relevant and of interest to them cannot be achieved by resorting to applications *per se*. Rather, the results indicate that attempts must be made to link the applications of science to the broader context of the world and its living inhabitants.

## 3.5  Out-of-school activities

The second questionnaire was an attempt to probe some of the influences bearing on pupils' science studies and performance. It was considered likely that those pupils who pursue hobbies which embody some science skills and content would bring to school science some knowledge of the subject area and a predisposition towards it. The possibility that the *desire to do more of certain kinds of activity* would link with a *positive attitude to science* was also considered—pupils were therefore also asked if they would be interested in doing more of each activity listed. Furthermore, the possibility of access to certain activities was probed by asking pupils if they had brothers or sisters; this was in the expectation that girls with brothers might be more likely to become involved in boys' hobbies, and vice versa.

Before commencing a discussion of the results on this questionnaire it is important to note the possibility of viewing them from several perspectives. In the discussion in the review report at age 11 (DES, 1988a) the activities listed are referred to as 'science-relevant'. To an extent this relevance is indisputable. There are clear links with science in terms of the content of some of the activities and in the 'hands on' skills deployed in others. However, it is possible that, in regarding certain activities as relevant to science, one is imposing a particular view of science and hence of what is necessarily relevant. It is a matter of some concern, expressed throughout this chapter, that a fresh look at science is made which might result in links between pupils' activities and their relevances for science being forged rather than assumed. The process of assuming relevance from any standpoint means that other activities are automatically considered as irrelevant.

Two-thirds of the activities listed in the questionnaire were more popular with boys than girls; indeed, of the activities prefered more by girls than boys, only one was of interest to more than 28 per cent of the girls questioned. Figure 3.2 (p. 19) clearly illustrates the loading towards boys' interests in the questionnaire.

Box plots (see section 3.7 for a discussion of this form of data representation) have been drawn to display the levels of popularity of the activities listed (see Figure A3.1, p. 191). Again the loading towards the boys' interests is clear from the different levels of the medians

**Figure 3.2** *Differences between the percentages of boys' and girls' stated preference for listed activities*

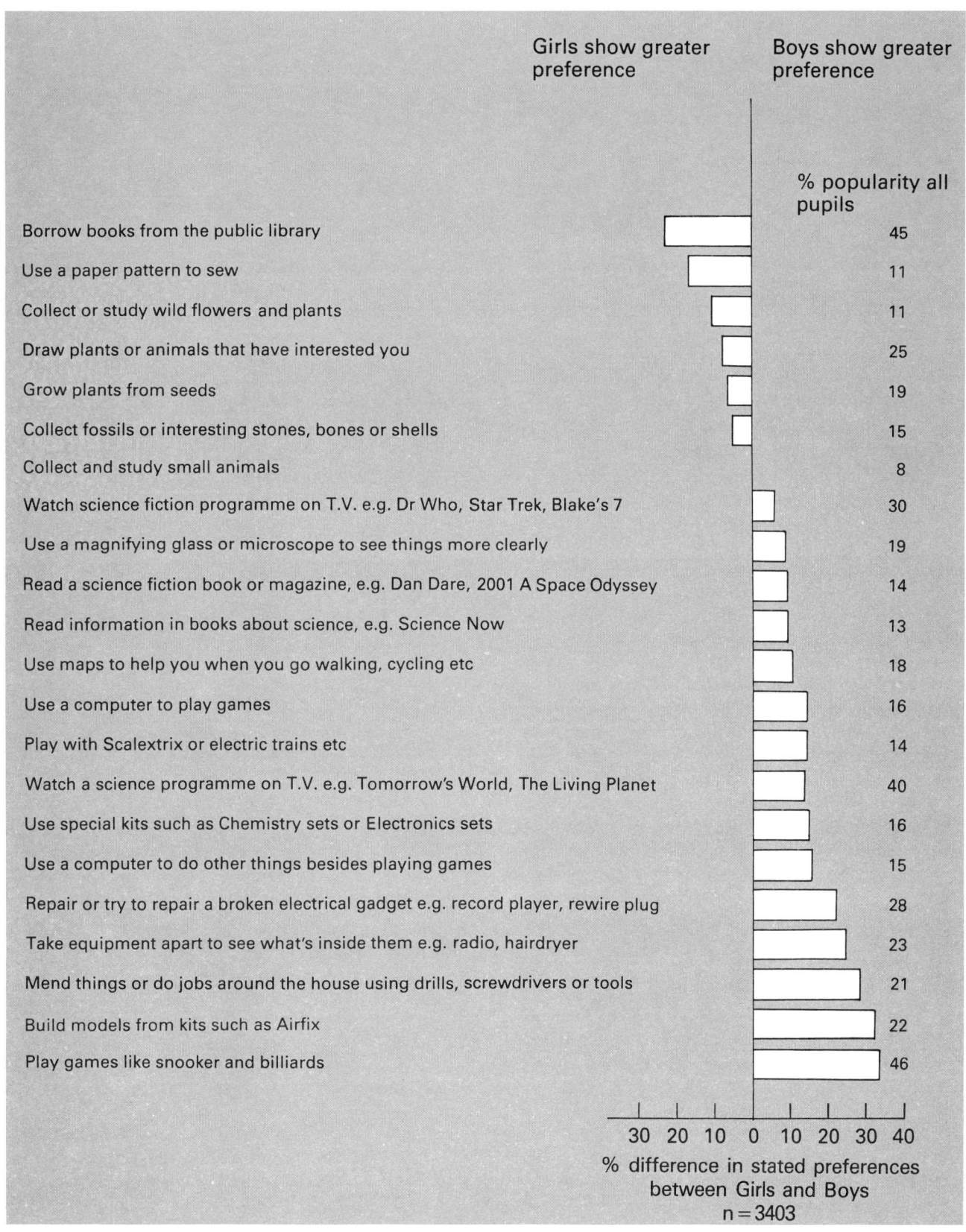

| | Girls show greater preference | Boys show greater preference | % popularity all pupils |
|---|---|---|---|
| Borrow books from the public library | | | 45 |
| Use a paper pattern to sew | | | 11 |
| Collect or study wild flowers and plants | | | 11 |
| Draw plants or animals that have interested you | | | 25 |
| Grow plants from seeds | | | 19 |
| Collect fossils or interesting stones, bones or shells | | | 15 |
| Collect and study small animals | | | 8 |
| Watch science fiction programme on T.V. e.g. Dr Who, Star Trek, Blake's 7 | | | 30 |
| Use a magnifying glass or microscope to see things more clearly | | | 19 |
| Read a science fiction book or magazine, e.g. Dan Dare, 2001 A Space Odyssey | | | 14 |
| Read information in books about science, e.g. Science Now | | | 13 |
| Use maps to help you when you go walking, cycling etc | | | 18 |
| Use a computer to play games | | | 16 |
| Play with Scalextrix or electric trains etc | | | 14 |
| Watch a science programme on T.V. e.g. Tomorrow's World, The Living Planet | | | 40 |
| Use special kits such as Chemistry sets or Electronics sets | | | 16 |
| Use a computer to do other things besides playing games | | | 15 |
| Repair or try to repair a broken electrical gadget e.g. record player, rewire plug | | | 28 |
| Take equipment apart to see what's inside them e.g. radio, hairdryer | | | 23 |
| Mend things or do jobs around the house using drills, screwdrivers or tools | | | 21 |
| Build models from kits such as Airfix | | | 22 |
| Play games like snooker and billiards | | | 46 |

30  20  10  0  10  20  30  40
% difference in stated preferences
between Girls and Boys
n = 3403

for boys and girls. It is also noticeable that those hobbies preferred more by girls than by boys are not actually *very popular* with girls, but rather they are *very unpopular* with the boys. The activity which is by far the most popular with the girls, whilst not being unpopular with the boys, is borrowing books from the public library. This activity is also the only one which was included in the absence of any overt links with science. It was, in fact, included at age 13 because of a concern that interest in particular activities might relate to pupils' backgrounds rather than their scientific interests.

There were only three of the listed activities which showed *no* difference between boys and girls in their desire to pursue them further. These were 'watch science fiction on TV', 'Use a computer to play games', and 'Use a magnifying glass or microscope'. For these three activities there were small differences, in favour of boys, in the proportion of pupils actually pursuing them often. It is therefore possible that given the opportunity these differences might disappear. It is noteworthy that the results at age 11 show a marked difference in favour of the boys in the numbers showing an interest in 'Watching science fiction on TV' and in 'Using a microscope'.

Part of this questionnaire was concerned with the gender of the pupils' siblings, because it was considered likely that this might have an effect on the individuals exposure to certain pastimes. However, very little difference in 'out-of-school' activities has been detected between boys or girls with sisters, brothers, sisters and brothers, or neither (see Figure A3.2, p. 192).

## 3.6 Task perception

The third questionnaire was set to consider pupils' perceptions of the questions used in the tests of **Observation** and **Use of apparatus and measuring instruments**. The purpose of this questionnaire has been described in section 3.3 of this chapter. A primary aim included establishing a description of the pupils' perception of the various tasks and contrasting it with the view as stated in the assessment categories. A secondary aim was to look for relationships between question attributes, pupil attributes and pupils' perception of the questions. A third aim was to describe what pupils considered to be their normal school science experience and to establish their interest in pursuing the subject after the third year.

The amount of data available from this questionnaire is large. The first step in the analysis was to produce a description of the data which dealt with both a theoretical expectation and the actual outcomes which reflect the pupils' alternative views.

The first stage of description of the data collected from the questionnaire for the **Observation** circuses is presented here. There were responses from 2,600 pupils randomly spread across boys and girls and 29 different tasks (an average of 90 responses per task). The tasks cover the contexts of science, 'physics', 'chemistry' and 'biology' (broken down into animal and plant), but in this random sample there were only two 'everyday' tasks. The results for these two tasks are included for completeness but are not referred to in the text. The context label was assigned to the tasks by the assessor and not the pupils.

The first aspect of the data considered was the pupils' responses to the question 'What was the question about?'. The responses were categorised under general headings which were then detailed for each task. Example 3.1 includes a description of the categories for one of the tasks. The general categories included those responses which refer to the nature of the task, ie the relationship and/or variables to be observed—the *outcome*; those which describe what they are to

**Example 3.1** *Category 3 example 'Tracks'*

Question example

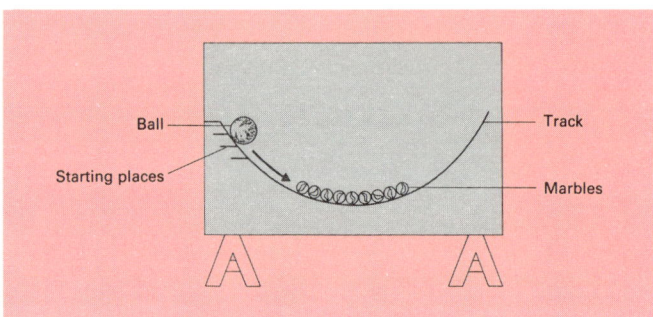

You have been given different kinds of ball in a pot, and a board with a track and nine marbles as shown in the diagram.

a) Roll one of the balls down the track so that it hits the row of marbles.

Do this again with the same ball but starting at different places on the track. Look carefully at what happens. You do not have to write anything.

b) Do the same thing with the rest of the balls in the pot.

Think about what you have noticed and the different balls you used. Each time something happens to the end marble. What does the movement of the marble depend on?

.................................................................................................

.................................................................................................

.................................................................................................

.................................................................................................

Categories of pupils response to 'what was this question about?'

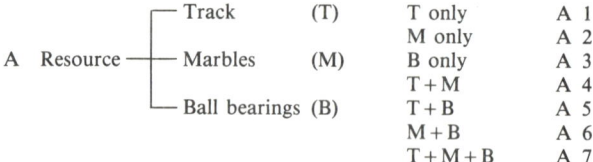

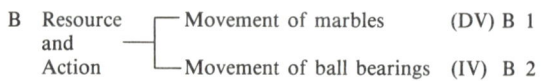

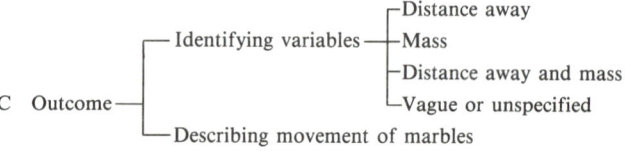

observe—the *action* and those which refer to the objects within the task—the *resource*. The mark schemes for all of the **Observation** tasks focused on the *outcomes*. Overall no credit was given for general descriptions of the action or the resource. In the first analysis the general categories of response rather than the detail were considered.

A contingency Table (3.5) was drawn up of pupil response against task content. The purpose of the table was to see if there was any relationship between the way in which pupils described a task and the content of that task. The cells in the table were inspected to see if the numbers in the cells differed from what might have been expected for a completely random distribution.

**Table 3.5**  *Pupils' response by task content*

| | Task content: percentage responses | | | | |
|---|---|---|---|---|---|
| Pupils' response | Physics | Chemistry | Animal | Plant | Everyday |
| Outcome | 56 | 56 | 68 | 62 | 62 |
| Action | 21 | 28 | 1 | – | 20 |
| Resource | 20 | 15 | 28 | 37 | 16 |
| Other | 4 | 1 | 1 | 1 | 2 |

There are some significant relationships between the task content and the type of pupils' response. More pupils than expected described tasks in a 'physics' and 'chemistry' context by *the action* to be observed. Significantly fewer pupils described the biological tasks in this way. There were, in fact, more physics tasks than biology tasks which required the pupils to observe an event over time, but this was not the case for the chemistry tasks. None of the biological questions was concerned with the observation of events, which reflects both the nature of the subject and the consequence of testing time constraints. Pupils clearly saw these tasks in terms of how to observe—the outcome (65 per cent), or as a resource alone (32 per cent). Because of these findings the next table considered the tasks in terms of whether the task required the pupils to (i) observe a fixed resource, eg comparing two materials, such as polythene and perspex, or classifying a collection of teeth; or (ii) an event over time, for example, the movement of ball bearings on a track, or of ink in sticks of chalk. The first group of tasks have been referred to as *static* (n = 25), and the second as *dynamic* (n = 20).

Table 3.6 shows the way that pupils describe the task and the nature of the observation to be made.

**Table 3.6**  *Pupils' perception of tasks of different resource types*

| | Percentage response | |
|---|---|---|
| Pupils' perception | Static | Dynamic |
| Outcome | 68 | 52 |
| Action | 4 | 29 |
| Resource | 27 | 16 |
| Other | 3 | 3 |

Pupils more often described a 'dynamic' task by the action to be observed, whereas in the 'static' tasks they tended to describe the outcomes. On this type of task more pupils also described the question by the resource alone.

The next relationship in the data to be considered was whether the content of the task affected pupils' expressed liking or dislike of it. Table 3.7 shows this relationship for the sub-groups of boys and girls

For boys and girls there appeared to be little difference between their liking for the physics and chemistry tasks. The chemistry tasks were liked more than the physics ones. There was, however, a tendency for both boys and girls to express more dislike for the questions about animals, the girls showing a stronger tendency to dislike the 'animal' questions. This is interesting in the light of earlier discussions. The 'animal' tasks were all based on static resource and were concerned with comparison and matching. The specific content ranged from animal intestines (photograph) to insects' legs, teeth and crab shells, and from skulls to photographs of moths—a far cry from the 'person orientated' biology described by the pupils' interests.

It is perhaps worth noting that the content of the tasks, ie physics, chemistry, etc, is defined by the assessors, but when pupils were asked about their view of the content most were unable to identify the tasks as specifically physics, chemistry or biology and often described them as outside of their school science experience. It is significant that the pupils tended to perceive this type of task in terms of the observations required rather than their specific content. This perhaps

**Table 3.7**  *Pupils' expression of their liking for tasks with different contents*

| | Percentage response | | | | | | | | | |
|---|---|---|---|---|---|---|---|---|---|---|
| | Physics | | Chemistry | | Animal | | Plant | | Everyday | |
| Liking | Boys | Girls | Boys | Girls | Boys | Girls | Boys | Girls | Boys | Girls |
| Positive | 50 | 49 | 60 | 58 | 40 | 33 | 41 | 40 | 58 | 69 |
| Negative | 23 | 25 | 18 | 19 | 31 | 43 | 29 | 26 | 21 | 9 |
| Neutral | 27 | 26 | 22 | 23 | 29 | 24 | 30 | 34 | 21 | 22 |

**Table 3.8** *Pupils' assessment of their own performance for tasks with different content*

| View of performance | Percentage response | | | | | | | | | |
|---|---|---|---|---|---|---|---|---|---|---|
| | Physics | | Chemistry | | Animal | | Plant | | Everyday | |
| | Boys | Girls | Boys | Girls | Boys | Girls | Boys | Girls | Boys | Girls |
| Good | 51 | 32 | 35 | 30 | 37 | 39 | 52 | 29 | 40 | 46 |
| Average | 33 | 45 | 37 | 36 | 38 | 30 | 35 | 39 | 41 | 32 |
| Bad | 8 | 7 | 13 | 16 | 8 | 17 | – | 6 | 12 | 7 |
| Can't tell | 8 | 16 | 15 | 18 | 17 | 14 | 13 | 26 | 7 | 15 |

accounts for the shift in their stated liking for 'science content' *vis-à-vis* the 'Topics of interest' results—section 3.4, p. 17.

Table 3.8 shows the sub-groups of boys and girls who expressed a liking for the tasks and their stated view of their performance on them. The purpose of displaying the results in this way was to see if there was a relationship between pupils liking a task and their belief in their competence on it.

The results indicated that there was a tendency for girls to rate their performance lower than the boys. There was also a larger proportion of girls who said they could not judge their own performance. Exceptions arose in the case of the animal and everyday tasks. The boys' results indicated that they rated their performance on the physics and plant tasks more positively. For both the sub-groups of boys and girls who expressed a dislike of the tasks there was no apparent relationship between their view of their performance and the content of the task.

The next possible relationship considered was between the pupils' liking for a task and the type of observations, ie static or dynamic, which was demanded (see Table 3.9).

**Table 3.9** *Pupils expressing a liking for tasks of different resource type*

| Liking | Percentage response | | | |
|---|---|---|---|---|
| | Static | | Dynamic | |
| | Boys | Girls | Boys | Girls |
| Positive | 45 | 40 | 57 | 56 |
| Negative | 28 | 33 | 19 | 20 |
| Neutral | 27 | 27 | 24 | 24 |

Many pupils expressed quite definite views about their preferences, and there was a tendency for pupils to favour the dynamic questions.

Pupils were also asked whether they were interested in pursuing science after the third year. This last question was not put to the children in terms of the separate subjects because of the results found during trialling, ie

that few pupils perceive this type of task in terms of a specific subject area. Table 3.10 shows a breakdown of pupils stating a positive or a negative intention or else stating a minimal interest.

**Table 3.10** *Pupils' stated intentions of studying science after the third year*

| Intention | Girls | Boys |
|---|---|---|
| Yes | 41 | 45 |
| A little | 32 | 25 |
| None | 13 | 7 |
| No opinion | 15 | 23 |

More boys than girls stated no opinion on the matter. More girls than boys stated that they wanted either to do a little science only, or to do none at all. A very similar number of boys and girls expressed a positive intention to continue science which, given the actual subject take-up, is very interesting. It could well be that the large proportion of pupils stating a desire to do little science or expressing no opinion eventually choose subjects on the basis of their appropriateness to their proposed careers. In section 3.8 (p. 28) this point is discussed further.

## 3.7 Suitable jobs

In looking at pupils' stated job preferences it was decided to focus on the proportions of pupils recording either a positive or a negative response. This effectively reduced the five-point scale of response to a two-point scale. However, before doing this, pupils' responses on the five point scale were investigated. Cross-tabulations (contingency tables) were established to look at the *extent* of the differences in the job preferences between boys and girls. Where a statistically significant difference (1%) in the overall pattern of response occurred and this coincided with a 10%, or greater, difference in preference when looking only at pupils' positive or negative responses, then this was taken to represent a *marked* difference in pupils' responses and hence to be noteworthy. It is differences of this order of magnitude which are represented in Table 3.11 and Figure 3.3 (p. 25).

Table 3.11 (p. 24) provides an alternative way of showing the information given in Figure 3.3 by assembling the jobs into three groups: those which are preferred more by boys, those which are preferred more by girls and those for which neither boys nor girls can be said to show any greater preference. The jobs are listed in order of the magnitude of the difference in stated preference.

To draw attention to those jobs which girls and boys responded to in markedly different ways a method of data representation has been chosen which suits the data and the form of analysis used (Tukey, 1977, Erikson and Nosanchuk, 1979). This method is used in the remaining sections of the chapter.

The first step in the analysis of the data presented in this section was to look at those jobs which were considered suitable by a large proportion of pupils and those jobs which were not considered by many pupils to be suitable. Other salient features of the data also needed to be depicted, such as the general level of popularity of the majority of jobs, and the range of levels of popularity.

The data is displayed in a box plot. The first step in constructing the plot is to identify the median. This is done by looking at the full range of levels of popularity, ie the percentages considering each job to be suitable, and selecting the middle level which splits the data in half. The median value for the upper half of the data is then obtained (the upper quartile) followed by the median value for the lower half of the data (the lower quartile). Half of the data then falls between the upper and lower quartiles. It also follows that a quarter of the data lies above the upper quartile and a quarter lies below the lower quartile. It is the jobs above the upper quartile and below the lower which we spell out as being of *particular interest* for the purposes of comparing different sub-samples.

The jobs which are amongst the *most* and *least* popular can be arranged in order of popularity above and below the central 'box' of jobs. This highlights those jobs which fall outside the 'centre' of the data. However some data points might be very much more or very much less popular than others; to highlight these instances any data points falling more than 1.5 times (a step) the distance of the inter-quartile range away from the 'box' is plotted as an outlier, a line (whisker) is drawn to indicate the length of the steps. This method is that suggested by Tukey (1977) for dealing with such data.

Figure 3.4 (p. 26) shows the results for the 'Suitable jobs' questionnaire displayed in this way. It includes three representations of the data:

(a) what all pupils select for themselves,
(b) what boys select as suitable for themselves,

(c) what girls select as suitable for themselves.

The picture of the data obtained in b) and c) of Figure 3.4 is very similar to that which was obtained for 'all' pupils when considering those jobs which are suitable for boys and girls. The jobs of 'driver', 'garage mechanic' and 'electrician' are seen as very definitely 'boys'' jobs. In contrast, 'secretary', 'typist', 'hairdresser' and 'shop assistant' are among those jobs considered to be definitely 'girls'' ones. These results give the impression that pupils' preferences closely reflect the reality of the current job market.

In addition, boys and girls *agreed* as to what is a 'boys'' job, what is a 'girls'' job and which jobs are neutral. However, when the fine detail is considered there were some notable exceptions. A number of jobs were seen by *more* girls than boys as being *very* suitable for boys. These were 'plumber', 'engineer', 'steelworker', 'petrol pump attendant', 'farmer', 'porter' and 'caretaker'. In the case of 'steelworker' and 'caretaker' these jobs were generally unattractive to both sexes. The unattractiveness of the job may well influence a pupil into disallowing it as a job associated with them. Thus if a girl positively does not want a particular job then for her it might become a 'boys'' job.

One job was an exception to the trend described above and that was 'driver'. Although more boys that girls saw this as a suitable job for themselves, *more girls* than boys thought that this job would be suitable for girls. In general however, boys and girls shared a very similar view of what 'girls'' jobs were.

Among those jobs with *no* gender difference in choice for self, a number were seen by girls as more suited to boys. These were 'scientist', 'chef', 'police officer', 'professor' and 'doctor'. In each case the difference lay in the proportions of girls who saw the jobs as *very suitable* for boys. This is perhaps because girls saw these as predominantly *mens'* jobs, which they currently are, but did not think this would stop them personally going in for such jobs. Or it may be the case that when some girls were selecting jobs they saw as suitable for 'boys' then any career they do *not* wish to pursue themselves they more positively labelled as a 'boys'' job.

Part of this questionnaire had embedded within it the notion of 'job status'. This was achieved by including, in random positions, pairs of jobs of the same nature but with an hierarchical difference. It was hypothesised that there might well be a gender difference in career orientation as exemplified by pupils opting for high-status jobs such as a 'professor' or a 'doctor' with a long-term career structure implied. Of particular interest was the hypothesis that girls who opt for a high-status job may well have a *less* stereotypically, constrained view.

Three relatively high-status jobs were selected for further study, one from each of the job groups which are below.

**Table 3.11** *'Suitable jobs'—Jobs suitable for self**

| Greater preference shown by boys | | | | Greater preference shown by girls | | | | Greater preference shown by neither sex | | | |
|---|---|---|---|---|---|---|---|---|---|---|---|
| Job | % All | % Boys | % Girls | Job | % All | % Boys | % Girls | Job | % All | % Boys | % Girls |
| Engineer | 34 | 58 | 11 | Hairdresser | 36 | 9 | 63 | Computer programmer | 47 | 52 | 43 |
| Garage mechanic | 31 | 51 | 11 | Typist | 38 | 11 | 64 | Scientist | 37 | 41 | 33 |
| Electrician | 31 | 49 | 11 | Secretary | 41 | 17 | 66 | Factory worker | 29 | 32 | 24 |
| Plumber | 22 | 44 | 6 | Nurse | 34 | 11 | 57 | Lab technician | 24 | 27 | 21 |
| Bricklayer | 26 | 45 | 8 | Librarian | 36 | 19 | 54 | Professor | 11 | 14 | 8 |
| Machinist | 26 | 43 | 10 | Teacher | 32 | 19 | 44 | Police Officer | 34 | 36 | 33 |
| Steel worker | 19 | 35 | 6 | Shop assistant | 50 | 39 | 61 | Solicitor | 29 | 30 | 28 |
| Farmer | 34 | 49 | 20 | Cashier | 44 | 33 | 55 | Member of Parliament | 17 | 19 | 17 |
| Petrol pump att. | 20 | 33 | 9 | Café worker | 34 | 22 | 44 | Clerical worker | 19 | 14 | 23 |
| Driver | 50 | 62 | 38 | Social worker | 25 | 15 | 34 | Office cleaner | 16 | 11 | 20 |
| Farm worker | 31 | 43 | 20 | Post office worker | 35 | 26 | 43 | Chef | 38 | 35 | 41 |
| Factory manager | 30 | 41 | 20 | Shopkeeper | 53 | 44 | 61 | Bank clerk | 37 | 35 | 40 |
| Architect | 27 | 37 | 19 | Journalist | 36 | 30 | 41 | University lecturer | 17 | 14 | 19 |
| Bank manager | 30 | 38 | 22 | | | | | Doctor | 33 | 31 | 34 |
| Member of forces | 37 | 45 | 30 | | | | | | | | |
| Porter | 16 | 22 | 9 | | | | | | | | |
| Caretaker | 17 | 22 | 11 | | | | | | | | |

n=1671

* A difference in the percentages of greater than 10 per cent expressing a preference for a job is taken as a marked difference. The jobs are listed in the order of the magnitude of difference in stated preference between boys and girls.

24

**Figure 3.3** *'Suitable jobs'. Differences between the percentages of girls and of boys stating a job to be suitable for themselves*

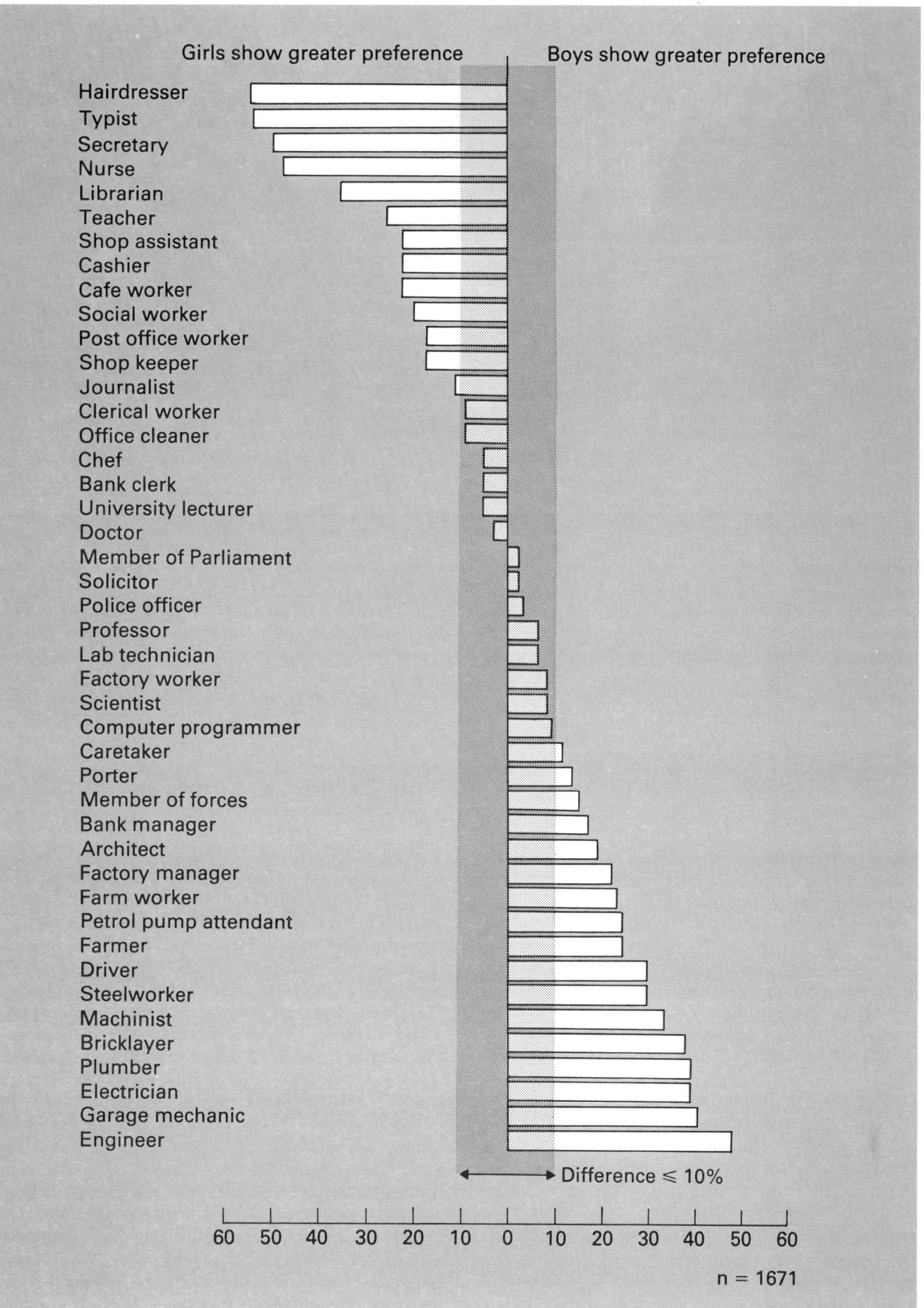

**Figure 3.4** *'Suitable jobs'. Percentage of pupils seeing jobs as suitable for themselves*

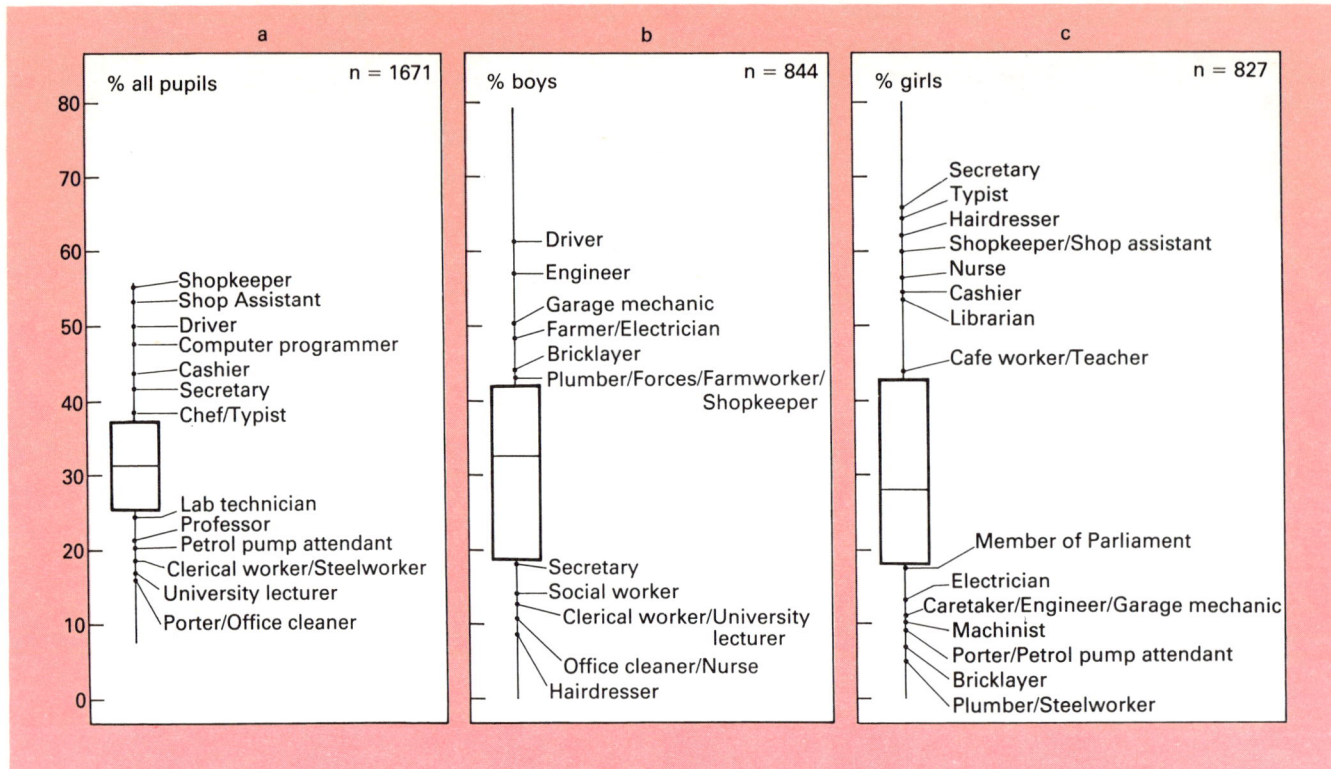

doctor (33 per cent)—a job of equal popularity with both sexes;

**teacher** (32 per cent)—a job more popular with girls than with boys;

**architect** (27 per cent)—a job more popular with boys than girls.

The second stage of analysis looked at the sub-sample of pupils (n = 182) who thought **doctor** was a suitable job for themselves. This sub-sample was then split into boys and girls and considered in terms of how the boys viewed jobs as suitable for boys and how the girls viewed jobs as suitable for girls. Figure 3.5 (p. 27) includes the following data:

– *Jobs seen as suitable for boys:*
  selected by the sub-sample of boys who chose 'doctor' as suitable;
  selected by the boys who saw 'doctor' as unsuitable.

– *Jobs seen as suitable for girls:*
  selected by the sub-sample of girls who chose 'doctor' as suitable;
  selected by the girls who saw 'doctor' as unsuitable.

If the data for the boys are considered it can be seen that there is a very similar spread to that obtained for the boys in Figure 3.4. There is, however, a more generally positive attitude to jobs evidenced by the position of the median and the range of the data indicated by the size of the box. The jobs which the 'doctor' boys regard as more suitable tend to be the more scientific ones and are usually of a higher status than for the boys who do not regard 'doctor' as suitable. Even so, this sample of boys still includes the popular 'boys'' jobs in their preferences. The least popular jobs for these boys are still the 'girls'' jobs, including interestingly 'nurse', which suggests that status had some significance in the boys choice of 'doctor'.

Turning to the girls who consider 'doctor' as suitable one can discern a difference in the overall data to those obtained for those girls not citing 'doctor' as suitable. There is a larger spread resulting from more polarization of job preference. There does not appear to be an increase in 'high-status' job preference nor in the popularity of the more scientifically orientated jobs. What is most noticeable is the very high popularity of 'nurse' for those girls who regard 'doctor' as being a suitable job. This would suggest that it is not status which is influencing the girls' choice but rather the job's content, ie the caring for people.

More of the girls who see 'doctor' as suitable also view more favourably the jobs of 'farmer', 'engineer', 'garage mechanic', electrician' and 'factory manager', although this is not shown on the figure. This suggests that these girls are less bound by stereotypes than others who do not see 'doctor' as suitable. This goes against the general trend in the data in Figure 3.4 which shows the gender-specific nature of jobs.

**Figure 3.5** *'Suitable jobs'. Percentages of boys and girls seeing jobs as suitable for themselves. (Contrasting sub-samples according to the suitability of 'doctor' for self)*

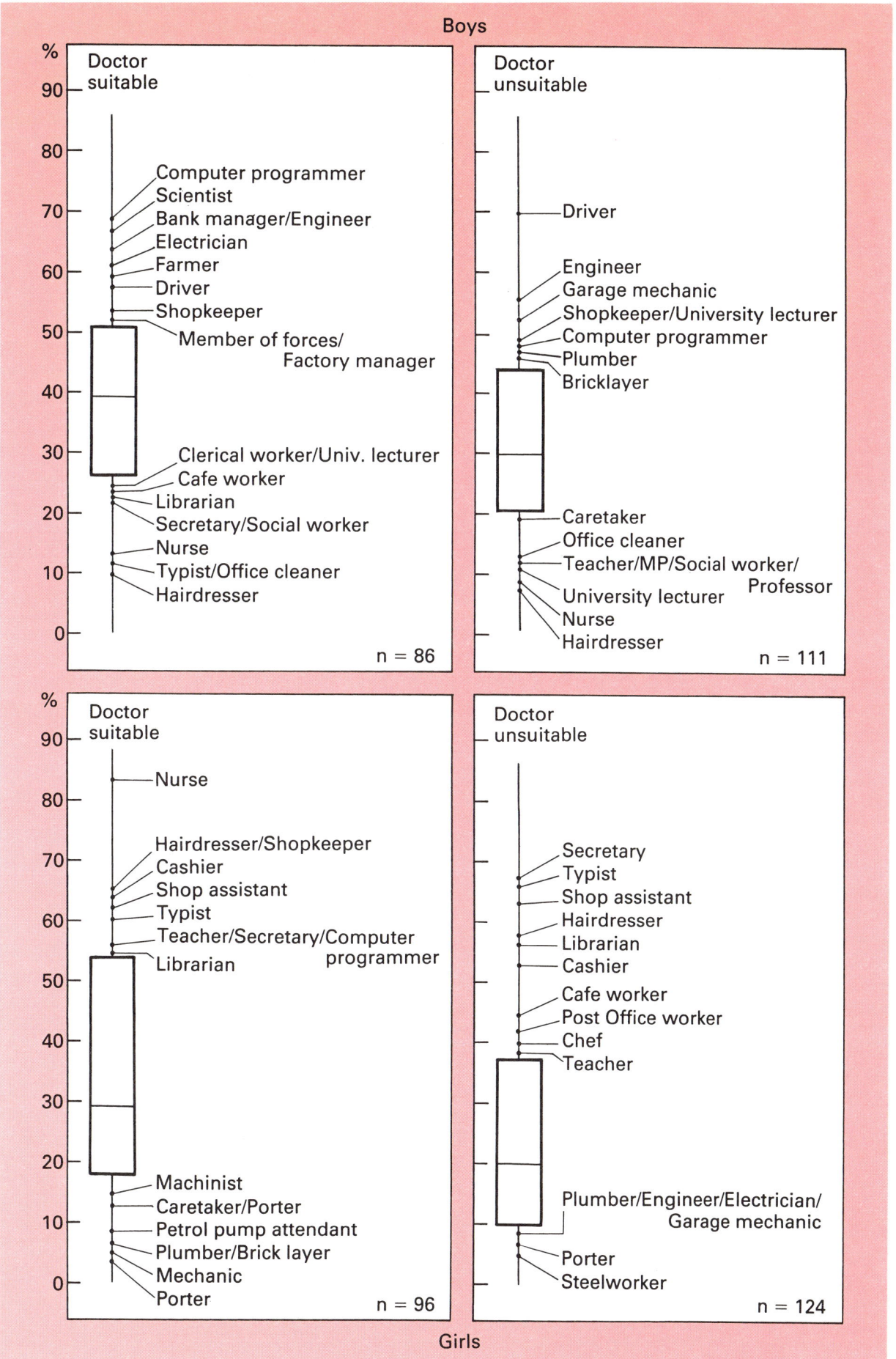

The results for the two other high-status jobs considered, 'teacher' and 'architect', are included in Appendix 3, Figures A3.3 and A3.4 (pp. 194–5).

The results for the three sub-samples of girls (the 'doctor' group, the 'teacher' group and the 'architect' group) show that there is a more positive attitude towards jobs for these sub-samples than for the group of girls as a whole. This is evident from the increase in the median value for the sub-samples and the greater spread of the data indicated by the size of the boxes. However, there is no real change in the distribution patterns of job preference; nor is there a significant shift in orientation towards higher status jobs. On the other hand, a shift for the boys is noticeable in the results for the 'doctor' sub-sample. Boys who selected 'doctor' as suitable for themselves also selected other high-status jobs but did not select 'nurse', which remained very unpopular. Yet 'nurse' is very highly favoured by the girls in the 'doctor' sub-sample.

## 3.8  Jobs and science

The 'Jobs and science' questionnaire complements and extends the information obtained by the 'Suitable jobs' questionnaire. The first part of the questionnaire required a separate sample of pupils to record the suitability of each job for themselves. Pupils were then asked to consider the importance of science for each job. Table 3.12 (p. 29) lists the jobs according to the size of the differences in preference shown by boys and girls. The percentages of pupils stating science to be an important aspect of each job is also given. In addition in Table 3.12 there is an indication of any differences in the way a job was categorised to that found in the 'Suitable jobs' data. Thus, N denotes a previously 'neutral' job, G a 'girls'' and B a 'boys''. Figure 3.6 displays the differences in percentages of boys and girls stating jobs to be suitable for themselves; this was a repeat of the exercise carried out in Figure 3.3.

**Figure 3.6**  *'Jobs and science'. Difference between percentage of girls and boys stating a job to be suitable for themselves*

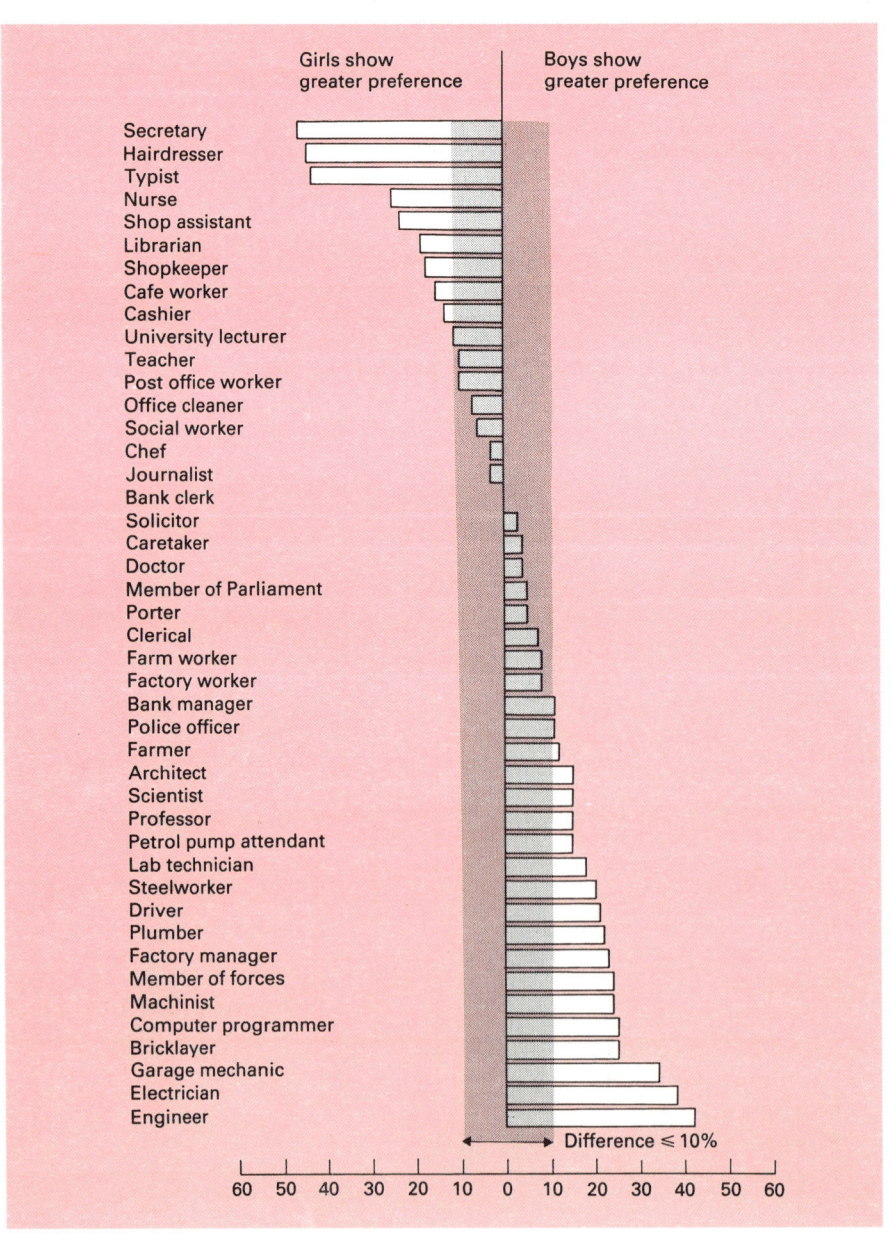

**Table 3.12** 'Jobs and science'–Jobs suitable for self

(Jobs ordered according to size of difference in percentage of boys and girls expressing a preference. A difference greater than 10 per cent is taken to indicate a marked difference as in Table 3.11).*

### Greater preference shown by boys

| Job | % All | % Boys | % Girls | % imp. of Science |
|---|---|---|---|---|
| Engineer | 32 | 53 | 13 | 48+ |
| Electrician | 30 | 49 | 12 | 55+ |
| Garage mechanic | 26 | 42 | 9 | 38+ |
| Bricklayer | 18 | 31 | 7 | 14− |
| Computer programmer N | 45 | 57 | 33 | 58+ |
| Machinist | 27 | 34 | 11 | 58+ |
| Member of forces | 35 | 48 | 25 | 35+ |
| Factory manager | 26 | 38 | 16 | 29+ |
| Plumber | 17 | 28 | 7 | 35+ |
| Driver | 43 | 53 | 33 | 15− |
| Steelworker | 16 | 25 | 6 | 31+ |
| Lab technician N | 25 | 31 | 14 | 68+ |
| Petrol pump attendant | 13 | 20 | 6 | 17− |
| Professor N | 13 | 30 | 16 | 68+ |
| Scientist N | 32 | 39 | 25 | 80+ |
| Architect | 29 | 37 | 23 | 36+ |
| Farmer | 28 | 34 | 23 | 47+ |

### Greater preference shown by girls

| Job | % All | % Boys | % Girls | % imp. of Science |
|---|---|---|---|---|
| Secretary | 35 | 12 | 58 | 15− |
| Hairdresser | 29 | 7 | 51 | 17− |
| Typist | 33 | 11 | 54 | 12− |
| Nurse | 31 | 13 | 48 | 67+ |
| Shop assistant | 38 | 27 | 50 | 9− |
| Librarian | 29 | 20 | 38 | 14− |
| Shop keeper | 43 | 35 | 52 | 12− |
| Café worker | 26 | 18 | 33 | 10− |
| Cashier | 35 | 28 | 41 | 13− |
| University lecturer N | 15 | 20 | 31 | 50+ |

### Greater preference shown by neither sex

| Job | % All | % Boys | % Girls | % imp. of Science |
|---|---|---|---|---|
| Police officer | 36 | 41 | 31 | 29+ |
| Bank manager B | 27 | 32 | 23 | 16− |
| Factory worker | 21 | 24 | 16 | 24− |
| Farm worker B | 27 | 31 | 23 | 22− |
| Clerical worker | 15 | 14 | 7 | 18− |
| Porter B | 11 | 13 | 8 | 6− |
| Member of Parliament | 15 | 18 | 12 | 25+ |
| Doctor | 33 | 35 | 31 | 78+ |
| Caretaker B | 12 | 14 | 10 | 12− |
| Solicitor | 27 | 29 | 26 | 24+ |
| Teacher G | 30 | 25 | 35 | 70+ |
| Post Office worker G | 28 | 23 | 33 | 11− |
| Office cleaner | 12 | 8 | 15 | 8− |
| Social worker G | 18 | 15 | 21 | 17− |
| Chef | 36 | 35 | 37 | 17− |
| Journalist G | 31 | 31 | 32 | 21− |
| Bank clerk | 33 | 33 | 33 | 19− |

n = 3482

* The median value for percentage of pupils seeing science as important for all jobs is 23 per cent. The percentage of pupils seeing each job as important for science is given with a + where science is more important than average and a − where science is less important.

B beside a job title indicates that in Table 3.1 that job showed a markedly greater preference by boys.

G beside a job title indicates a job which in Table 3.1 showed a markedly greater preference by girls.

N beside a job title indicates a job which in Table 3.1 did not show a markedly greater preference by either sex.

The patterns in the data described in Figures 3.3 and 3.6 are much the same except that some of the jobs change categories from Table 3.11 to 3.12. These are 'computer programmer', 'professor', 'scientist' and 'shopkeeper'. The first three move from being neutral in the 'Suitable jobs' to being 'boys'' jobs. All three of these jobs are those for which pupils see science as being important. This suggests that some pupils hold a very particular view of these jobs possibly cued by the images of men in white coats and glasses. The movement of some jobs to being considered neutral is generally the result of fairly small changes in the proportions selecting them as suitable. The job of teacher, which moves from 'girls'' to neutral, is a possible exception. The percentage of girls stating teaching as suitable for themselves and for girls generally drops in the 'Jobs and science' questionnaire, whilst the percentage of boys selecting it rises. Seventy per cent of all pupils see science as being very important for teaching. Could it be that in this context pupils are thinking of the job 'science teacher' rather than 'teacher' in general? Of the seven jobs for which more than 55 per cent of the pupils consider science to be important, four actually swing in the direction of being 'boys'' jobs. These observations will be considered further in the later discussion.

Box plots depicting the distribution of job preferences were drawn up for the data from the 'Jobs and science' questionnaire (Figure 3.7). When the results for the two questionnaires are compared the *similarity* in the patterns of job preference is the most noticeable character-

istic. Notwithstanding, there is a general tendency for the levels of popularity to be depressed in the 'Jobs and science' data; this is highlighted by the lower medians in each case. Although the patterns of job preference are similar, there are some differences in the stated preferences of the boys. In particular 'computer programmer' becomes the most popular job for boys and 'scientist' moves upwards to be in the top 25 per cent of suitable jobs.

In the previous discussion (in which the data from the 'Suitable jobs' questionnaire are compared with those from 'Jobs and science'), three observations have been made:

- More than three quarters of the jobs in which boys showed a greater preference were jobs for which science is seen to be important. This compares with a fifth of the jobs for which girls showed a greater preference (note the plus and minus signs in the 'importance of science' column in Table 3.12);

- There is a general depression in the proportions of pupils seeing jobs as suitable for themselves;

- There is a slight change in the distribution patterns of boys' jobs to raise the comparative suitability of 'computer programmer' and 'scientist', both jobs being considered by pupils to have a large science component.

These three points suggest that there is a *context filter* in operation in the 'Jobs and science' questionnaire.

**Figure 3.7** *'Jobs and science'. Percentage of pupils seeing jobs as suitable for themselves*

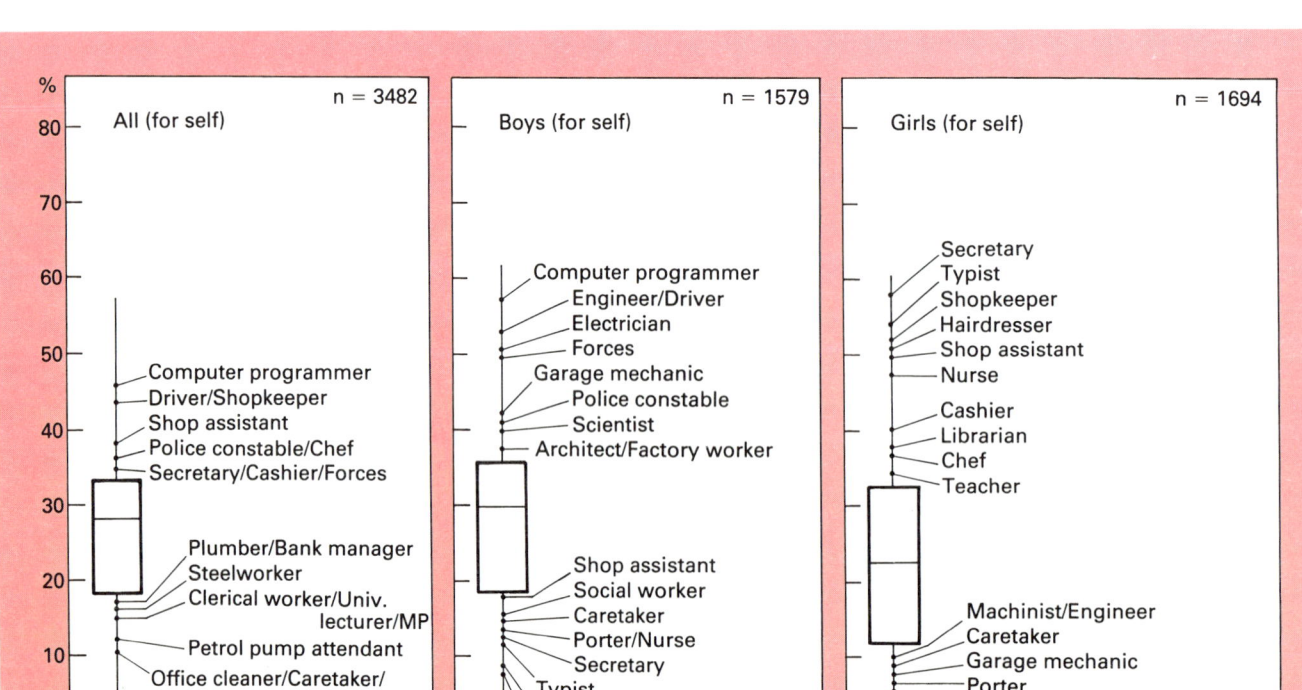

That is to say that the pupils try to construe the questioner's meaning and, in doing so, take the juxtaposition of science relevance with the suitability of jobs as the major cue. The outcome of this is a general depression in the stated suitability of jobs. This may explain why so many pupils see science as important for teaching, because they are here considering the job to be that of science teacher and professor as science professor.

Moreover a context effect may serve to explain why some jobs, seen as having a large science component, swing away from the position they held in the 'Suitable jobs' questionnaire towards being more strongly preferred by boys. It may be that in picking up the science context cue boys more readily state a preference for those jobs for which they see science as playing an important part. The phenomenon of a context filter is a commonly observed feature in pupils' performance within the APU category-based tests, and it is interesting to note its occurrence here.

The section of the 'Jobs and science' questionnaire which asked the pupils to state the importance of science for each job is considered next. There were no significant differences noted in the distribution patterns of the importance of science to jobs for boys and girls. However, there were significant differences in the numbers of boys and girls attaching importance to science in the case of six jobs. Girls saw science as having more importance than did boys for 'hairdresser', 'secretary' and 'nurse'. Boys saw relatively more importance for science for 'professor', 'computer programmer' and 'electrician'. Thus *more* pupils see the relevance of science in certain jobs which they are likely to see as suitable *for themselves*. This could be the first glimmerings of a career-orientation effect. In general, the importance of science ascribed to each job by the 13 year old pupils seems to be directed by an understanding of the *content* of the job itself, rather than the qualification needed to enter the job. It could also be that science is not perceived as a qualification at this age. Rather, pupils who have considered careers in particular jobs may be more aware of the relevance of science to the jobs.

It was considered possible that in the context of the 'Jobs and science' questionnaire, those pupils who tend to select high-status jobs would not only select other jobs of high status' but also, being perhaps more confident about their science abilities than other pupils, be more likely to select high-status jobs with a perceived high science content.

In the first instance it was decided to look at 'teacher' as for this job it does seem that the 'context filter' has had more effect than simply to depress the level of job popularity (see Figure 3.8, p. 32).

For the boys who see 'teaching' as suitable for themselves, there is an increase in the relative popularity of

'scientist', 'doctor', 'professor' and 'lab technician', all of which are seen as having as high science content. For the girls, the distribution patterns are almost identical to those for the 'Suitable job' data. However it is interesting to note that 'computer programmer' becomes less popular with the girls who see teaching as suitable when they make their selection in a science context. Thus it seems that in deciding that 'computer programmer' has a high science content the girls are more likely to reject it as suitable for themselves.

In no case are high science content jobs allotted a higher degree of popularity by the girls in the 'Jobs and science' questionnaire than in the 'Suitable jobs' questionnaire. This suggests that the 'context filter' operates in a different way for boys and girls. For girls the science context simply serves to depress the levels of popularity of all jobs. For boys, although we have noted the general depression in job popularity, it is the case that those boys who favour jobs with a high science content tend also to be more positive about other jobs seen to have a high science content. This is further highlighted in the case of 'teacher' where it seems that boys translate the job 'teacher' in the science context to 'science teacher' and are consequently more positive about this job and other jobs with a high science content.

Among those pupils who select high-status jobs, the sub-groups of boys and girls stating each of the three high-status jobs ('teacher', 'doctor' [A3.6, p. 197] and 'architect' [A3.7, p. 198]) to be suitable for themselves, there is a tendency for them to be more positive about jobs in general. This is evidenced by the increase in the median values and the greater spread of the data above the medians. Pupils selecting one high-status job are more likely to select other high-status jobs. Thus those pupils selecting 'doctor' were more likely to select 'teacher' and 'architect', those selecting 'teacher' to choose 'doctor' and 'architect', and those selecting 'architect' to choose 'doctor' and 'teacher'. In regard to the question of a reduction in the stereotyped view of job suitability, the boys in all these sub-groups are more likely than other boys to select the 'girls'' jobs of 'hairdresser', 'cashier', 'secretary' and 'nurse'. Girls in all three sub-groups are more likely to see the 'boys'' jobs 'bank manager', 'plumber', 'machinist', 'electrician' and 'factory manager' as suitable for themselves. There is a suggestion that pupils choosing high-status jobs have a less gender-stereotyped view than others.

## 3.9 Discussion

In section 3.2 (p. 14) of this chapter a number of issues were raised which had not so far been answered by the data collected. The results discussed in this chapter have illuminated some of these.

**Figure 3.8** *'Jobs and science'. Percentage of boys and girls seeing jobs as suitable for themselves. (Contrasting sub-samples according to the suitability of teaching for themselves)*

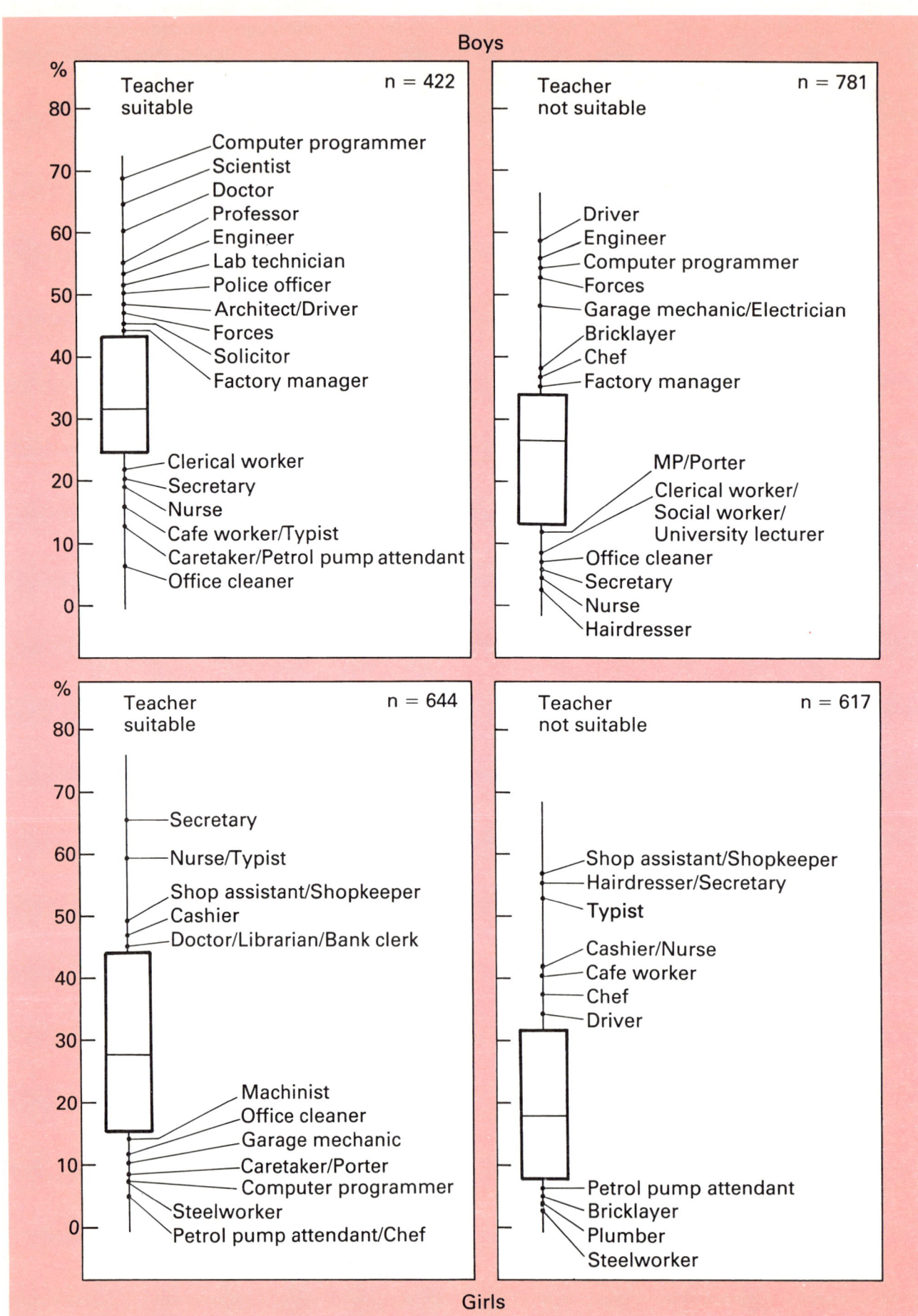

## Interest in science topics

One of the questionnaires looked at pupils' interest in knowing more about certain topics within science. The results showed that girls expressed an interest in topics related to people or other animals, their function and the relationships between them and other living things. The topics which girls expressed significantly *more* interest in than others were also the topics that were rated as most popular by *all* pupils.

The boys showed an interest in *more* topics than did girls, with a *physical science* orientation apparent in the interests expressed. Boys, unlike the girls, were interested in knowing more about both the applications of science *and* the science concepts embedded within the application. Expressing an interest in a topic suggests one has an understanding of what is entailed and its relevance to oneself. It is possible, therefore, that different pupil interests reflect different understandings of relevance. This point is raised because of its significance for several research findings (some mentioned in this chapter), and for the possible routes curriculum developers might take in establishing ameliorating strategies.

In other words: does one accept girls' more constrained set of interests as given and unchangeable, or should one attempt to teach science through broadly social and environmental applications? Or is the issue of relevance the key, so that the question raised is 'what are the processes by which pupils perceive relevance to themselves and therefore interest in particular topics and subjects?' An outcome of the latter question may not be to produce what is termed girl-friendly science, but rather to produce a learning environment within science which enables pupils to construct relevance and to have their assumptions of relevance (or lack of it) questioned and broadened.

## Science-related out-of-school activities

The results for the questionnaire on 'Out-of-school activities' showed that the activities listed which were chosen to be relevant to science in school corresponded largely to those in which boys engaged and girls did not. It was also the case that girls expressed little interest in the activities generally. If it is accepted that scientific activity in schools reflects the values and interests of those most commonly engaged in it, it is quite possible that in identifying 'science relevant' activities one might in fact be imposing a stereotypical view of the subject. To avoid this potential bias it is necessary to consider alternative perspectives of science and the relevance of children's out-of-school activities in broader terms. This is a particularly difficult challenge to meet because science educationists are products of a system themselves and are as affected by societal influences as other people.

One way forward did seem to be implied in the results of the third questionnaire, although this is very tentative

at this stage. Pupils appeared to enjoy a wide range of science content when it was part of tasks with overt procedural demands rather than overt conceptual demands. Tasks with this attribute may provide suitably motivating 'vehicles' for *introducing* pupils to a wide body of content from which their interests may develop.

## Career aspirations

One of the issues concerned the pupils' expectations. The expectation identified as potentially influential was that of career aspiration. The results show that the most popular jobs for boys are that of 'driver' or 'engineer' and for girls 'secretary', 'typist' or 'hairdresser'. Boys and girls share very similar perceptions about the sex appropriateness of particular jobs. These shared views conform for the most part with conventional patterns of employment in society. There does appear to be a shift from age 13 to age 15 (DES, 1988b) but more in terms of the nature of the perceived convention. At age 15 the pattern of job preference which emerges has closer links to the reality of the job market available to school leavers than that given by 13 year olds.

## Importance of science for jobs

When the pupils' view of sex-appropriate jobs was elicited in the questionnaire which asked about the importance of science for jobs, a 'context filter' appeared to operate. The context seemed to cue the pupils to view the jobs in terms of science content. There was therefore a swing towards a greater preference by boys for jobs for which science was seen to be important. The pupils at age 13 appeared to ascribe science relevance on the basis of the content of the job itself rather than seeing it as a necessary qualification for job entry. When pupils had to consider the importance of science for jobs *along* with their view of the jobs suitability this had the effect of orientating a group of boys more towards certain jobs because of the perceived relevance of science for them. Thus, for the boys, perceiving a *high* science content in a job made it *more* popular with them. However, for girls in general it tended to produce another barrier between them and certain careers. In the results for the 'Suitable jobs' questionnaire there were 13 girls' jobs and 17 boys' jobs. In the 'Jobs and science' questionnaire results the number of boys' jobs remained the same but the girls' were reduced by a third.

For the majority of pupils, their common sense predisposition to accept societal sex roles means that at age 13, when pupils in general are less aware of the meaning and significance of subject qualifications in terms of career openings, boys assume school subjects such as science to be relevant to a *wider* set of potential jobs. Girls on the other hand assume a *narrow* range of jobs; and many assume that the need for such subjects as science for a job identifies it as *unsuitable* for them.

It is clear that the assumptions held by pupils concerning jobs will dramatically affect their subsequent choice of relevant subjects at age 14.

### Significance of job status

The results also indicated that pupils selecting one high-status job would be more likely to select others. This effect is more pronounced for boys than for girls. Girls' choice was influenced by job content, which could override status considerations. The sub-groups of pupils who tended to select high-status jobs also tended to hold a less gender-stereotyped view of job suitability. It was also noticeable that girls who opted for high-status jobs were more positively aware of what jobs were suitable and what jobs were not: their preference was more polarized.

## 3.10   Future work and implications

In response to an issue raised at the beginning of this chapter in section 3.2, was it possible to identify the experiential differences of pupils? The 'Out-of-school' questionnaire has been useful, but problematic. It would seem that attempting the *a priori* identification of significant science-related experiences produces a narrow perspective. It is likely that other pupil pastimes could contribute to science performance, but were not included in the list. A redevelopment of this questionnaire would be useful; this might best be informed by some open ended questions put to 13 year olds in interviews or on paper. This could lead to the drawing up of an alternative list of 'Out-of-school activities', which may provide a richer source of data to inform discussion on the influences of pupils' experiences on science performance.

In the secondary analysis of the 'Suitable jobs' and 'Jobs and science' questionnaires, sub-samples of pupils choosing high-status jobs were considered. This analysis could be continued and extended by looking at other sub-groups of pupils, such as those choosing low-status jobs, those selecting clerical jobs, and those selecting jobs which tend to be selected by the opposite sex.

The 'Topics of interest' questionnaire has provided some insights into the way different groups of pupils perceive science topics and their preferences for them. The results showed that the gender differences are not by any means simple reflections of the three science subjects, nor do they fit the dichotomy of application versus the more abstract statements. However, there are quite noticeable links between the kinds of statements selected more by boys and those selected more by girls.

Very little analysis has so far been carried out as to the effects on pupil responses of the context, content and the particular concepts implicit in the statements. The work which has been done in this area suggests that further analysis could yield some rewarding results. With the support of an understanding of the relationships between pupil performance on certain tasks and the effects on pupils of their context, content and concept dependencies, it may be possible to point to some useful implications for teaching from this work.

The results obtained indicate that two tasks need to be done in the future. The first is to use the results to refine the questionnaires. This refinement will involve the rejection of redundant questions and the inclusion of additional ones. It is only when this task has been completed that an efficient and effective study of the links between external factors and pupils' performance on the tests can be carried out. Secondly there is scope in the data already collected for further analysis, which will allow us to paint a broader picture of pupil attributes and will increase our potential to interpret the links between these attributes and performance.

# 4

# Pupils' science performances

## 4.1 Introduction

One of the main purposes of the science survey programme is to monitor pupils' levels of performance in each of a number of different aspects of science activity. As indicated in Chapter 1 the assessment framework consists of a range of categories and sub-categories of activity. These are fully discussed in relation to the assessment of 13 year olds in the chapters which follow.

The general structure of the assessment framework was decided before the monitoring programme began; detail has been added and modifications made as testing experience has been gained. Another early decision concerned the method of question selection for survey administration. The general strategy was to be to select questions as needed from 'dynamic' question pools; it remained only to decide the criteria for this selection. The decision for the science programme was to adopt a domain-sampling approach, and to make random selections of suitable numbers of questions to create each subcategory survey test. The random sample of 13 year olds selected to be tested is assumed to represent the population of pupils of this age in schools in England, Wales and Northern Ireland. In a similar way, each randomly-selected set of questions is assumed to represent the population of questions relating to the particular aspect of science performance under consideration. Full details of the pupil and question selection strategies are given in the associated technical report (DES, 1989).

There are some notable exceptions to this domain-sampling approach in science. Cost constraints, for instance, are occasionally so severe that the administration of large numbers of questions to represent a subcategory is not always feasible. The particular instance of this is the case of **Performance of investigations**. The tasks which have been developed in this category necessarily require one-to-one administration by trained personnel, who carry with them to the schools appropriate sets of equipment and other resources (see Chapter 11 for full information). Each task engages pupils for 20 to 30 minutes at a time, so that in the typical hour-long test session two such tasks is the maximum which can be attempted and each administrator can test only three or four pupils per school visit.

Logistic constraints are also important in dictating alternative question selection strategies. The apparatus demand in the practical category **Use of apparatus and measuring instruments**, for instance, is so complex that it soon proved impossible to organise the administration of truly 'random' selections of questions. Partly as a consequence of this, and partly in recognition of the dubious value of sampling measuring instruments and pieces of apparatus each year, it was decided to focus on *particular* sets of instruments and apparatus, and on a *particular* range of practical tasks. The resulting set of questions therefore now constitutes a 'fixed' test, and this is administered to both 13 and 15 year olds in their respective surveys (see Chapter 6 for details).

For most subcategories in the assessment framework domain-sampling of questions *has* proved a possibility —at least in later years once the question pools had begun to approach an appropriate size (150 + questions). In this particular chapter we consider overall 'test' performances for these subcategories, beginning with the results of the 1984 survey and moving on to consider the picture which has emerged over the initial five-year survey series. It should be noted that whenever reference is made to statistical significance this will be at the 5 per cent level.

## 4.2 Pupils' subcategory performance levels in 1984

Seven subcategories at age 13 were represented in the 1984 survey by collections of questions randomly selected from relevant question pools. These are (with the numbers of questions selected and the ways in which they were packaged shown in brackets):

— Using graphs, tables and charts          $(90-6\times15)$
— Making and interpreting observations      $(45-3\times15)$
— Interpreting presented information         $(90-6\times15)$
— Applying biology concepts                  $(60-4\times15)$
— Applying chemistry concepts                $(60-4\times15)$
— Applying physics concepts                  $(60-4\times15)$
— Planning parts of investigations           $(60-4\times15)$

The testing time usually demanded of individual pupils at ages 13 and 15 is one hour. Early pilot studies indicated that around 15 questions is the most appropriate number to include in a test package occupying this time at age 13. Consequently, the questions used in the surveys are typically distributed among test packages so that each contains around 15 questions.

For instance, the 45 questions relating to the practical subcategory **Making and interpreting observations** were distributed randomly among three different test packages. These were administered in the form of circuses, ie the resources required for particular tasks are set up on tables or work benches, and pupils circulate around these spending equal amounts of time at each table or bench (see Chapter 7).

The 400+ pencil and paper questions selected to represent the other six subcategories named above were divided into 28 test packages, again containing 15 questions each. In this particular survey, any one 'written test' package contained questions from just one subcategory.

Each of the 28 'written test' packages was administered to a different random sub-sample of roughly 500 pupils drawn from almost as many different schools. The practical circuses were each attempted by different sub-samples of around 650 pupils from about 85 schools. *In total* around 2,000 pupils were involved in the practical testing, and between 2,000 and 3,000 pupils were involved in the assessment of each of the non-practical subcategories. See Appendix 1 for further details of sample selection and test administration.

During processing of the pupils' responses, percentage scores are first calculated for each pupil. These are produced simply by averaging the series of individual question scores achieved by the pupil, and expressing this average as a percentage of the maximum possible 'test score'. Estimates of the 'population' performance levels of each of a number of identifiable pupil groups (such as boys and girls) are computed on the basis of these individual scores, weighting appropriately to allow for imbalance in sample representation (see Appendix 1 and associated technical report—DES (1989)—for details). The performance level estimates for 1984 are shown in Table 4.1.

There are three main features in the data of Table 4.1. Firstly, as has become familiar, the performance levels of pupils are higher when **Using graphs, tables and charts** than they are for every other science activity. This has been the case in every survey to date at every age. This is not to say, of course, that the 'skill' of using symbolic representation (if such exists) is necessarily inherently 'easier' or even better practised than that of interpreting data or of planning investigations. Pupils are simply more successful in demonstrating a basic level of competence in this area as it is realised in the kinds of questions developed for the science surveys, and as it is rewarded in the mark schemes used.

Secondly, the differences in the mean scores of boys and girls are large enough to reach statistical significance for the subcategories **Using graphs, tables and charts** (in favour of girls), **Applying physics concepts** (in favour of boys) and **Planning parts of investigations** (in favour of girls). The physics result has been a particularly strong and consistent feature in every survey at every age. The tendency for girls to produce slightly higher mean performance scores than boys in the 'planning' subcategory was also a feature in the performance data of 1983 (the only other year in which this activity was assessed in a comparable form).

Thirdly, the mean scores for pupils in Wales are lower than those of their peers in England and Northern Ireland on all aspects of the assessment framework except the practical subcategory **Making and interpreting observations** (the differences reach statistical significance in all cases except 'planning'). Northern Ireland pupils produced performance levels equal to those of their counterparts in England on most subcategories, the only exceptions again being the practical **Observations** subcategory (on which their mean performance was significantly lower) and the subcategory **Applying physics concepts**. As we will see later, this pattern confirms that found in previous surveys at this age.

Within England, pupils in the South produced slightly higher mean scores than pupils in the North (typically, statistically significant differences were of around 2 to 3 percentage points), with the Midlands either equalling the South or falling somewhere in-between. Greater differences have usually emerged when schools drawing from distinctly different types of catchment area have been considered, and this survey is no exception. As Table 4.2 shows, pupils in comprehensive schools drawing from mainly inner city areas produced lower average scores than all others, and pupils in

**Table 4.1** *Pupils' subcategory performance levels in 1984†*

(Mean per cent scores—weighted population estimates)

| Subcategory | | All | Boys | Girls | Eng | Wales | NI |
|---|---|---|---|---|---|---|---|
| Using graphs, tables | mean | 65.8 | 64.6 | 67.0 | 65.9 | 63.5 | 67.1 |
| and charts | s.e. | 0.6 | 0.8 | 0.7 | 0.6 | 1.0 | 0.9 |
| Making and interpret- | mean | 37.2 | 36.1 | 37.9 | 37.4 | 37.3 | 34.4 |
| ing observations | s.e. | 0.7 | 0.8 | 0.6 | 0.7 | 0.9 | 1.1 |
| Interpreting presented | mean | 42.4 | 43.1 | 41.9 | 42.5 | 39.7 | 42.8 |
| information | s.e. | 0.5 | 0.7 | 0.6 | 0.6 | 0.8 | 0.9 |
| Applying biology | mean | 27.0 | 27.5 | 26.6 | 27.1 | 25.0 | 27.0 |
| concepts | s.e. | 0.4 | 0.6 | 0.5 | 0.5 | 0.8 | 0.6 |
| Applying chemistry | | | | | | | |
| concepts | mean | 27.9 | 27.4 | 28.3 | 28.0 | 25.7 | 28.4 |
| | s.e. | 0.5 | 0.6 | 0.5 | 0.5 | 0.9 | 0.7 |
| Applying physics | | | | | | | |
| concepts | mean | 29.0 | 30.6 | 27.4 | 29.1 | 27.4 | 27.8 |
| | s.e. | 0.4 | 0.5 | 0.5 | 0.5 | 0.7 | 0.6 |
| Planning parts of | | | | | | | |
| investigations | mean | 32.0 | 31.2 | 32.9 | 32.1 | 31.2 | 32.4 |
| | s.e. | 0.5 | 0.6 | 0.6 | 0.5 | 0.8 | 0.7 |

†Sample size details given earlier.

**Table 4.2** *Performance levels in 1984 broken down by catchment area*

(Unweighted mean per cent scores for pupils in English comprehensive schools)

| Subcategory | Rural | Prosp. subur. | Mixed urban | Unpros. subur. | Inner city |
|---|---|---|---|---|---|
| Using graphs, tables and charts | 67 | 68 | 64 | 58 | 57 |
| Making and interpreting observations | 39 | 38 | 38 | 33 | 30 |
| Interpreting presented information | 44 | 46 | 41 | 38 | 33 |
| Applying biology concepts | 29 | 28 | 26 | 23 | 21 |
| Applying chemistry concepts | 29 | 31 | 27 | 24 | 19 |
| Applying physics concepts | 31 | 32 | 28 | 26 | 22 |
| Planning parts of investigations | 32 | 34 | 31 | 28 | 26 |

comprehensive schools drawing mainly from rural or prosperous suburban areas consistently produced the highest mean scores (see Report No 4–DES, 1986a–for an explanation of the way schools were classified on the basis of teachers' estimates of the proportions of their pupils who were drawn from different kinds of catchment area). This same pattern of performance has emerged as strongly in the surveys at ages 11 and 15 in language and mathematics as in science.

As far as connections between pupil performance and other school characteristics are concerned, it must be said that the survey data has revealed very little. Searching for 'school effects' is always a difficult exercise (see DES, 1989). But in this case, with the kind of data available, exploring merely for statistical *associations* between variables was always likely to prove an unfruitful occupation. This is partly because of the sampling scheme and test administration strategy employed here ('light-sampling' of pupils in schools and many different test packages administered in each school), but more particularly because of the highly complex nature of the school system itself (see the Age 11 Review Report–DES 1988a, for comment on the primary sector) and of the organisation of science teaching within it (see Chapter 2 for the picture at age 13).

The only association large enough to be worthy of note in the survey data at age 13 has been the familiar one between performance and size of teaching group: the smaller the group the *lower* the science performance levels of the pupils. When this finding was first presented in survey reports (see DES, 1982a, 1984a) it was suggested that an explanation might lie in the common practice in schools of teaching less-able pupils in smaller groups.

From 1982 onwards the school questionnaires at this age have gathered additional information from the participating schools about *individual* science teaching groups so that this possible explanation could be explored. As Chapter 2 shows, it is indeed the case that the more-

able pupils are generally taught in large groups of typically 26–30 pupils and less-able pupils are taught in smaller groups of fewer than 21 pupils. A similar performance association with a similar likely explanation has been reported also in the review report in mathematics (Foxman *et al*, 1985).

## 4.3 Reviewing performance patterns over time

The 1984 survey was the last in the initial series of five surveys. This is therefore an appropriate time to review the cumulated test data for evidence of consistency in the performance picture produced from year to year, and also for indications of systematic change over the period.

Before engaging in such a review it is essential to draw attention to three major factors which will have affected the reliability of performance estimates, and hence of sub-group comparisons, within and between surveys. This is particularly important to do, since the effect of these factors can sometimes only be guessed at and cannot be allowed for in analysis. The factors essentially concern *question-sampling effects, school participation effects*, and *marking effects*.

The analysis approach which has been adopted in this assessment programme is based on the assumption that the random samples of questions and of pupils (and their schools) involved in any survey represent their populations in known ways. The voluntary participation of schools in the surveys, with the consequent degree of non-participation, causes problems in determining the extent to which the school samples *have* been representative of the school population from year to year. Schools are selected for survey involvement by a random-sampling procedure, and the pupils selected for testing in the surveys are drawn from those invited schools which agree to take part. Table 4.3 shows the numbers of schools which in 1980–84 took part in the surveys of 13 year olds in England, Wales and Northern Ireland, and also in parentheses indicates these as a percentage of those invited.

As Table 4.3 shows, the participation rates have differed from survey to survey in all three countries.

**Table 4.3**

*Numbers of schools which participated in the surveys*
(Bracketed figures indicate these schools as percentages of those invited to participate)

| Year | England | | Wales | | Northern Ireland | |
|---|---|---|---|---|---|---|
| 1980 | 448 | (77) | — | — | — | — |
| 1981 | 345 | (84) | 122 | (87) | 125 | (87) |
| 1982 | 314 | (83) | 87 | (81) | 83 | (78) |
| 1983 | 451 | (87) | 85 | (75) | 85 | (70) |
| 1984 | 326 | (85) | 94 | (68) | 119 | (73) |

After the first survey the rate of participation of schools in England increased slightly, and has since remained fairly steady at around 85 per cent. In Wales and Northern Ireland the participation rates have usually been lower; indeed they steadily decreased over the period (surveys of 13 year olds began in these two countries in 1981), until in 1984 just about 70 per cent of the relatively small numbers of invited schools in each of these countries actually took part in the survey.

Schools which have declined to take part in particular surveys have sometimes done so because they had very recently been involved in one or more previous surveys (most commonly in those of 15 year olds in mathematics, language or science). This has affected secondary schools in Wales and Northern Ireland much more than those in England, simply because the population of schools in these countries is not large and around half of the available schools are actually needed in any one survey. Indeed, the pressure on secondary schools in Wales and Northern Ireland became extremely great once annual surveys were in operation in all three curriculum areas each year. Because of this a single sample of schools was eventually selected for each 'round' of monitoring at age 15, and these schools each accommodated testing in maths, language and science—using different pupil samples for each subject area.

Whatever the reasons for schools declining to take part in surveys, the fluctuating participation rates must be a factor contributing to test score variation over the period—particularly in Wales and Northern Ireland where relatively small numbers of schools are actually involved in each survey. The assessment of the practical subcategory **Making and interpreting observations** will have been particularly vulnerable in this respect, since the pupils who take part in the practical testing are drawn from even fewer schools than are those who undertake written tests.

The degree to which the samples of questions represent their respective question pools from year to year is less uncertain. Of greater uncertainty is the degree to which the pools themselves represent their respective question populations. The main problem here is that these 'populations' of questions do not actually exist in concrete terms. They rather 'potentially' exist. Since they are not in practice real, it is difficult to character-ise them completely. After all, what is this activity labelled **Applying biology concepts**? How can it be measured? What kinds of questions should be used? The general ways in which the Science Team attacked this problem is shown by the questions developed for use in the survey programme. Detailed descriptions, with numerous exemplar questions, have been offered in earlier reports at every age, and further discussion is given in the following chapters of the present report.

However, it is not possible to describe any question

pool in a completely comprehensive way. Cumulated testing experience has suggested numerous question features which appear to influence pupils' performance. These include, for example, mathematics dependence, form of data representation, strength of 'science' context, degree of scientific knowledge required, presence or absence of pictorial cues, and so on. Clearly, it is difficult and not particularly helpful to attempt to draw up a multi-dimensional grid which would adequately serve as a pool and hence test specification. It is feasible only to decide some major features (such as question format, task requirement, and so on), and to describe the compositions of the pools in terms of these.

Question pools of sufficient size (estimated at 150 + questions) for domain-sampling to be an option did not exist prior to the first surveys in the series. The pools have therefore been continually growing over the entire survey period, until they have reached their present sizes. A consequence of this is that the comparability of the survey tests drawn from these growing pools from year to year must be in some doubt—in the earlier years because pool and test sizes were small and in later years because of the rationalisation exercise described in Chapter 1. The developmental histories of the sub-categories at age 13 are detailed later in this chapter.

Finally, a comment on script-marker effect is in order. The scripts from any one written test package are shared between two markers at most (practising science teachers, trained for this purpose). Each marker is thus responsible for marking around 300 scripts. Marker reliability studies carried out during the 1980 survey indicated that there was high agreement between three independent markers on the rank order in which they would place the same pupils (the traditional indication of marker reliability). However, when the pupils' scores were averaged there were in some cases differences of between two and four percentage points in the three figures produced (see DES, 1984a, Appendix 11). In other words, if the same 'test' were marked indepen-dently by two or more different markers and population estimates produced, these estimates of population performance could differ by as much as four percentage points. Much attention has been given to mark schemes since this time in efforts to 'tighten' them, but no further formal reliability studies have been conducted. This has clear implications for a test-score review over the five-year period.

All three of the factors discussed above will undoubtedly have contributed to fluctuations in the performance-level estimates over the five years, creating variation over and above that attributable to pupil, school and question-sampling effects and to 'real' changes in the performance levels of the population of 13 year olds. It will also mean that differences will need to be rather substantial before they can be adjudged to be significant in any sense.

Bearing this in mind we move on to review the cumulated test data. Performance data are reviewed for six of the seven domain-sampled subcategories: these are **Using graphs, tables and charts, Making and interpreting observations, Interpreting presented information, Applying biology concepts, Applying chemistry concepts** and **Applying physics concepts**. The seventh subcategory **Planning parts of investigations** has only been assessed in the same form twice–in 1983 and 1984–and so is not considered here. For ease of communication the mean percentage scores are rounded to the nearest percentage point.

Since the random sampling of questions has ensured that the overall standard deviations of raw scores have remained fairly stable from year to year within any particular subcategory, it has not proved necessary to resort to score standardisation when reviewing differences in the levels of performance of pupil groups such as boys and girls.

Although comments are occasionally made about the statistical significance of particular performance differences, it should be recognised that differences which reach statistical significance are not necessarily of any educational importance. Similarly, a lack of statistical significance does not mean that a performance difference is to be ignored. Small differences which persistently emerge in the same direction over most or all surveys are likely to be worth attention and may well have pedagogical implications, despite the fact that they may be too small to reach statistical significance.

## 4.4  Using graphs, tables and charts

This subcategory–which is fully discussed in Chapter 5–was created by amalgamating two original subcategories: **Reading information from graphs, tables and charts** and **Representing information as graphs, tables and charts**. First survey results confirmed a high correlation between pupil performance on these two related aspects, and it seemed more efficient to assess them in combination (at age 11 the two aspects have been retained for separate assessment and reporting). Table 4.4 provides the developmental history of the subcategory over the survey period.

In common with other similar tables in this report, Table 4.4 shows, for each year in which the sub-

category was assessed: the number of questions available in the question pool; the number of questions randomly selected for administration in the survey for that year; the way in which the questions were distributed among different hour-long test packages; the approximate number of pupils who attempted each package, and the approximate number of schools from which these pupils were drawn; and, finally, the estimated mean percentage scores for all 13 year olds in the three different countries.

Table 4.4 shows very clearly the scale of pool expansion over the period, with the initial pool of 54 questions having been continually supplemented until it reached its present size of 273. Despite this degree of growth the mean performance score estimates fluctuate only slightly between 1980 and 1983–all changes well within sampling limits. However, the effect of the pre' 84 pool rationalisation and expansion referred to earlier is readily seen in the Table. At age 13, 129 questions were 'absorbed' into the pool from the pools at other ages, with 99 of these coming from the existing pool of questions originally developed for administration to 11 year olds. The result of this severe change in both the size and nature of the pool is the jump in mean scores of 10 percentage points between 1983 and 1984.

A noteworthy feature in the data of Table 4.4 which concerns national performance patterns is the failure of the pupils in Wales to match the performance levels of their peers in England and Northern Ireland (the performance differences between Wales and the other countries reach statistical significance in 1981, 1982 and 1984). As indicated earlier this finding is not confined to this particular subcategory, but has emerged for almost every aspect of science performance assessed in written mode (the pattern for the only practical subcategory discussed in this chapter–**Observations**–is inconsistent, as we shall see shortly).

A review of the 148 different 'data representation' questions which have been used in at least one of the five annual surveys to date shows the Welsh pupils to be relatively weak across *all* the different types of data representation, including tables, coordinate graphs, Venn diagrams, and charts of various kinds (bar, pie, flow, etc.). The English pupils produced higher mean scores than the pupils in Wales on 85–90 per cent of all the questions (the mean score differences range from a single percentage point to statistically significant amounts of 10 percentage points or more). It is interest-

**Table 4.4**  *'Using graphs, tables and charts'–developmental history 1980–84*

| Survey Year | No. of questions in pool/in survey | | Packaging strategy | Pupils/schools per package | Mean % scores | | |
|---|---|---|---|---|---|---|---|
| | | | | | Eng | Wales | NI |
| 1980 | 54 | 42 | 3 × 14 | 800/110 | 56 | | |
| 1981 | 76 | 28 | 2 × 14 | 800/350 | 57 | 51 | 57 |
| 1982 | 160 | 64 | 4 × 16 | 850/650 | 58 | 51 | 58 |
| 1983 | 179 | 64 | 4 × 16 | 700/600 | 55 | 52 | 55 |
| 1984 | 273 | 90 | 6 × 15 | 510/490 | 66 | 64 | 67 |

ing that this rather general weakness was not apparent among the surveyed 11 year olds. At the earlier age pupils in Wales have shown a relative weakness when handling pie charts, bar charts and coordinate graphs (though not as much as at age 13), but have demonstrated a relative strength when dealing with tabular presentations.

Turning attention now to the performances of boys and girls, Table 4.5 shows that there is no firm evidence of any difference in their performance levels at this age for this subcategory. Where differences in mean scores have appeared these have been small and inconsistent in direction.

This apparent equality in the test achievements of girls and boys when **Using graphs, tables and charts** in practice masks some consistent differences in their relative abilities to handle the different kinds of data representation involved. Analysis of individual question results has produced evidence that boys tend to have more success than girls when dealing with coordinate graphs. Boys produced higher mean scores than girls on around three-quarters of the 45 different graphical questions which have been used in at least one of the five annual surveys. On the other hand, girls produced higher mean scores than boys on about two-thirds of the 100+ questions which featured tables, Venn diagrams or charts of various kinds.

**Table 4.5** *'Using graphs, tables and charts' – the performances of boys and girls*
(Mean per cent scores – weighted population estimates)

| | England | | | Wales | | | Northern Ireland | | |
|---|---|---|---|---|---|---|---|---|---|
| | Boys | Girls | Diff. | Boys | Girls | Diff. | Boys | Girls | Diff. |
| 1980 | 56 | 56 | 0 | | | | | | |
| 1981 | 57 | 58 | −1 | 50 | 53 | −3 | 55 | 60 | −5 |
| 1982 | 59 | 58 | 1 | 51 | 51 | 0 | 57 | 59 | −2 |
| 1983 | 55 | 55 | 0 | 53 | 51 | 2 | 56 | 55 | 1 |
| 1984 | 65 | 67 | −2 | 63 | 64 | −1 | 66 | 68 | −2 |

Although 'higher' here can, as before, range from a slight score difference of one percentage point to statistically significant differences of around 10 or more percentage points, the general pattern is clear. Moreover, these different strengths of boys and girls are already evident at age 11 and persist at age 15 (see Johnson and Murphy, 1986; and the age 15 review, DES, 1988b).

## 4.5  Making and interpreting observations

This subcategory, which is fully described in Chapter 7, is assessed in practical mode with circus administration at all ages. The usual pattern at this age has been to draw a random selection of 45 questions from a relatively small-sized pool, and to distribute these among three test packages or circuses. Trained administrators carry all necessary equipment and other resources to the schools, and organise one or two test sessions in each school. Nine pupils are involved in a test session; the pupils work independently on the tasks, circulating around work benches on which the resources are arranged.

As Chapter 7 shows, the definition of this particular subcategory has caused problems. In consequence there have been changes in the composition of the question pool over the survey period, the greatest of which occurred immediately before the 1984 survey. At this time a restructuring of the pool took place and a number of questions were deleted. The questions which remain now constitute a common pool serving both ages 13 and 15. An associated rationalisation of mark schemes will ensure complete comparability of assessment results between these two ages in the future.

An unfortunate short-term outcome of this rationalisation exercise is seen in Table 4.6 in the clear discontinuity in mean scores between the period 1980–83 and 1984. There are fluctuations in the scores within each country over the first four survey years, but these are all well within sampling limits (the apparent 'trend' downwards in the mean scores for England between 1980 and 1983 is more likely to be associated with the steady increase in pool size over the period than to reflect a real downward movement in pupils' abilities in this area).

It is not possible to comment with any confidence on differences between the performances of pupils in the three countries for this subcategory, since Table 4.6 reveals an inconsistent picture. As anticipated earlier in this chapter, this lack of consistency reflects the inevitably lower level of reliability associated with the estimation of this subcategory, given the rather small numbers of schools which normally participate in the practical exercise (for instance, as noted earlier, just 85 schools in total were involved in this practical testing in 1984, of which about 15 were in Wales and a similar number were in Northern Ireland).

**Table 4.6** *'Making and interpreting observations' – developmental history 1980–84*

| Survey Year | No. of questions in pool/in survey | | Packaging strategy | Pupils/schools per package | Mean % scores | | |
|---|---|---|---|---|---|---|---|
| | | | | | Eng | Wales | NI |
| 1980 | 57 | 45 | 3 × 15 | 800/110 | 52 | | |
| 1981 | 85 | 30 | 2 × 15 | 800/100 | 50 | 52 | 42 |
| 1982 | 118 | 45 | 3 × 15 | 750/100 | 48 | 45 | 47 |
| 1983 | 135 | 45 | 3 × 15 | 750/130 | 47 | 41 | 47 |
| 1984 | 97 | 45 | 3 × 15 | 650/85 | 37 | 37 | 34 |

Table 4.7 presents the performance estimates for boys and girls. This table shows clearly the tendency for girls to produce slightly higher performance scores than boys in this subcategory (only the 1984 difference in Wales reaches statistical significance, however). The same feature has been present in the survey data at age 11 and also at age 15.

**Table 4.7** *'Making and interpreting observations' – the performances of boys and girls*
(Mean per cent scores–weighted population estimates)

| | *England* | | | *Wales* | | | *Northern Ireland* | | |
| | Boys | Girls | Diff. | Boys | Girls | Diff. | Boys | Girls | Diff. |
|---|---|---|---|---|---|---|---|---|---|
| 1980 | 52 | 53 | −1 | | | | | | |
| 1981 | 49 | 51 | −2 | 52 | 53 | −1 | 40 | 44 | −4 |
| 1982 | 40 | 42 | −2 | 45 | 45 | 0 | 43 | 49 | −6 |
| 1983 | 47 | 49 | −2 | 42 | 44 | −2 | 47 | 47 | 0 |
| 1984 | 36 | 37 | −1 | 35 | 38 | −3 | 33 | 35 | −2 |

As was the case with **Using graphs, tables and charts**, there is evidence of differences in the general success rates of boys and girls for particular kinds of questions. Girls have usually produced higher performance scores than boys on questions requiring similarities and differences between objects to be made and recorded. These are often 'biological' in nature, including, for instance, leaf specimens, dead butterflies, insects and so on. Boys on the other hand have frequently produced the higher performance scores on those few questions demanding an explanation of observed events (usually physical science phenomena).

## 4.6 Interpreting presented information

As Chapter 8 illustrates, the information which pupils are asked to 'interpret' in the questions of this subcategory can be presented in any number of forms (tables, graphs, charts as well as prose). Pupils are often simply required to perceive and describe patterns in given data (usually linear relationships between variables), but may in addition or instead be asked to make use of these to explain or predict (by design there is no dependence here on 'taught' science concepts or knowledge). There is, therefore, some overlap with a number of the other subcategories in the assessment framework. For instance, there is an obvious overlap with the subcategory **Using graphs, tables and charts**. But there are also similarities with the 'concept application' subcategories, whose essential difference is that they assume pre-existing knowledge and understanding of 'taught' science concepts.

The developmental history of **Interpreting presented information** is given in Table 4.8. The table reveals a slight downward movement in mean scores over the period 1980–83. This *could* be interpreted as reflecting a real drop in the ability levels of 13 year olds in this 'process skill' area. It is, though, much more likely simply to be an artefact of pool-size change.

Few suitable questions were available for selection in 1980 and 1981; indeed, 'domain-sampling' was not possible in the first survey and of dubious meaning in the second. Partly in consequence test sizes were also rather small. Once the pool had increased sufficiently in size, and in the light of the results of variance analyses conducted in the meantime (see Johnson and Bell, 1985), 'test' size was increased to a more appropriate 60 questions–a strategy adopted at the same time for every 'written test' subcategory.

The severe discontinuity in mean scores between 1983 and 1984 has resulted from the rationalisation exercise referred to earlier–full details of this exercise as it related to this particular subcategory will be found in Chapter 8. In brief, three outcomes as regards the **Interpreting presented information** pool at age 13 were: the deletion of around 20 questions not considered to fit the revised structure; the absorption of around 70 questions from the pool at age 11; and a degree of modification to mark schemes to increase comparability across ages. Among the 90 selected questions administered in the 1984 survey were 48 which were available in the pool prior to 1984. Mean score estimates based on these questions only are 39 per cent, 34 per cent and 39 per cent respectively for England, Wales and Northern Ireland. These are more in line with the figures given in Table 4.8 for 1981–83.

Despite the variations in absolute levels of performance estimate, the picture of relative performance between the three countries is very stable, with Wales once again consistently failing to match the performance scores of England and Northern Ireland. The performance gaps are statistically significant in every year.

**Table 4.8** *'Interpreting presented information' – developmental history 1980–84*

| Survey Year | No. of questions in pool/in survey | | Packaging strategy | Pupils/schools per package | Mean % scores | | |
|---|---|---|---|---|---|---|---|
| | | | | | Eng | Wales | NI |
| 1980 | 34 | 28 | 2×14 | 1000/150 | 41 | | |
| 1981 | 60 | 42 | 3×14 | 800/350 | 39 | 34 | 37 |
| 1982 | 131 | 60 | 4×15 | 900/700 | 37 | 33 | 36 |
| 1983 | 131 | 56 | 4×14 | 700/600 | 32 | 29 | 31 |
| 1984 | 214 | 90 | 6×15 | 510/490 | 43 | 40 | 43 |

The performance score estimates for boys and girls are shown in Table 4.9. As the table reveals, there has been a consistent, though always small, performance difference in favour of boys in England and in Northern Ireland for this subcategory (though only the differences in England in 1981 and in Northern Ireland in 1984 reach statistical significance). In Wales the performance levels of boys and girls have most often been identical.

This tendency for boys to 'outperform' girls slightly but consistently at this age is of particular interest since their performance levels have always been similar at age 11. The reason for the emergence of the performance gap possibly lies in differences in the compositions of the pools at the two ages. In particular, the question pool at age 13 has always contained a higher proportion of questions featuring coordinate graphs than has the pool at age 11. This difference is reflected in the questions actually used in the surveys. In at least one of the five annual surveys at age 11, 117 'interpreting' questions have been administered compared with 148 questions at age 13. Of these, just 6 per cent featured coordinate graphs at the younger age compared with 15 per cent at age 13.

**Table 4.9** *'Interpreting presented information' – the performances of boys and girls*
(Mean per cent scores – weighted population estimates)

|      | England | | | Wales | | | Northern Ireland | | |
|      | Boys | Girls | Diff. | Boys | Girls | Diff. | Boys | Girls | Diff. |
|------|------|-------|-------|------|-------|-------|------|-------|-------|
| 1980 | 41 | 40 | 1 | | | | | | |
| 1981 | 40 | 38 | 2 | 34 | 34 | 0 | 36 | 38 | −2 |
| 1982 | 38 | 36 | 2 | 33 | 33 | 0 | 36 | 35 | 1 |
| 1983 | 32 | 32 | 0 | 29 | 29 | 0 | 31 | 30 | 1 |
| 1984 | 43 | 42 | 1 | 39 | 40 | −1 | 45 | 40 | 5 |

This is important because, as mentioned earlier, boys have shown a greater facility than girls in handling coordinate graphs at all ages. Indeed, it has been suggested that the emergence at age *15* of *statistically significant* performance differences in favour of the boys when **Interpreting presented information** might be attributable to the even greater preponderance of graphical questions in this subcategory at this older age (Johnson and Murphy, 1986). Of the 141 'interpreting' questions administered at least once in the series of surveys at age 15, a full quarter featured coordinate graphs.

## 4.7 Applying biology concepts

As its title suggests, successful performance in this subcategory is heavily dependent on pupils' biological knowledge and, more particularly, on their conceptual understanding. The general nature of the subcategory is described in Chapter 9.

As Table 4.10 shows, there were relatively few questions available for selection in the first two survey years. Half of those available were used in the first survey and three-quarters in the second. The subcategory was not assessed in the 1982 survey (none of the 'concept application' subcategories was), and by 1983 the pool had increased fairly substantially–though it is still not yet at the 'criterion' size. 'Test' size was also increased in 1983 to the more appropriate level indicated by research analyses (Johnson and Bell, 1985).

The mean scores since 1980 have been remarkably stable, with no evidence of change (the three usable data points available for each country would be insufficient to allow comment on trends even if these were present). A noteworthy feature in the performance data given in Table 4.10 is again the pattern of lower scores for pupils in Wales compared with their peers in the other countries.

**Table 4.11** *'Applying biology concepts'–the performances of boys and girls*
(Mean per cent scores–weighted population estimates)

|      | England | | | Wales | | | Northern Ireland | | |
|      | Boys | Girls | Diff. | Boys | Girls | Diff. | Boys | Girls | Diff. |
|------|------|-------|-------|------|-------|-------|------|-------|-------|
| 1980 | 38 | 37 | 1 | | | | | | |
| 1981 | 26 | 26 | 0 | 27 | 22 | 5 | 25 | 25 | 0 |
| 1983 | 25 | 25 | 0 | 25 | 23 | 2 | 25 | 26 | −1 |
| 1984 | 28 | 27 | 1 | 27 | 23 | 4 | 28 | 26 | 2 |

Boys and girls have rarely been shown to differ much in terms of their performance on biology tests. This is true also of the APU survey data for England and Northern Ireland as Table 4.11 shows. The figures for Wales, therefore, are possibly unique, showing as they do a strong consistency in direction, with relatively large differences in performance levels in favour of the boys. Indeed, the performance gaps between the Welsh boys

**Table 4.10** *'Applying biology concepts' – developmental history 1980–84*

| Survey Year | No. of questions in pool/in survey | | Packaging strategy | Pupils/schools per package | Mean % scores | | |
|             |      |      |                |              | Eng | Wales | NI |
|-------------|------|------|----------------|--------------|-----|-------|-----|
| 1980 | 59 | 28 | 2 × 14 | 1000/150 | 37 | | |
| 1981 | 59 | 45 | 3 × 15 | 800/350 | 26 | 24 | 25 |
| 1983 | 100 | 64 | 4 × 16 | 700/600 | 25 | 24 | 25 |
| 1984 | 100 | 64 | 4 × 16 | 510/490 | 27 | 25 | 27 |

**Table 4.12** *'Applying chemistry concepts' – developmental history 1980–84*

| Survey year | No. of questions in pool | in survey | Packaging strategy | Pupils/schools per package | Mean % scores Eng | Wales | NI |
|---|---|---|---|---|---|---|---|
| 1980 | 62 | 28 | 2 × 14 | 1000/150 | 34 | – | – |
| 1981 | 62 | 45 | 3 × 15 | 800/350 | 29 | 27 | 28 |
| 1983 | 101 | 64 | 4 × 16 | 700/600 | 27 | 24 | 27 |
| 1984 | 101 | 64 | 4 × 16 | 510/490 | 28 | 26 | 28 |

and girls are large enough to reach statistical significance in 1981 and 1984.

In fact, the boys in Wales produce similar performance scores to those of the boys in England and Northern Ireland. It is the girls in Wales who perform less well than their counterparts in the other countries, and it is *their* relatively low performance which accounts for the overall difference between the three countries.

It is difficult to attempt a ready interpretation of this particular finding. But perhaps the fact that boys *and* girls in Wales at this age produce poorer performances relative to their peers in England and Northern Ireland when applying chemistry or physics concepts holds a clue. Are many of the boys in Wales more highly motivated in biology than in chemistry and physics perhaps because they expect their occupational future to lie within the strong rural tradition of their country?

A number of survey findings support this conjecture. Firstly, a quarter to a third of the Welsh schools in any survey have described themselves as drawing mainly from rural areas, as opposed to a tenth or so of those in England. A lower proportion of schools in Wales compared with England constrain *all* their 13 year olds to follow the same common science curriculum (60 per cent compared with around 70 per cent). A fifth or so of Welsh schools adopt some other pattern, typically providing separate physics, chemistry and biology courses for the more able pupils and a form of General Science for the average and less able.

It is reasonable to speculate that 'General Science' as taught to the average and less able pupils in Wales at age 13 has a particularly strong biological/rural science component – certainly at the time of testing there was a higher availability of courses in Human Biology and Rural Science during the examination years in the schools of Wales compared with those in England and Northern Ireland. Roughly two-thirds and just under

half, respectively, of the schools in Wales which participated in the 1982 survey at age 15 reported offering such courses – these proportions being about twice those found for the other two countries (DES, 1985a).

## 4.8  Applying chemistry concepts

Table 4.12 reveals the same kind of picture for **Applying chemistry concepts** as was shown in Table 4.9 for **Applying biology concepts**. Pool and test sizes were very small in 1980, test size was increased in 1981, and both pool and test sizes had increased by 1983 (the subcategory was not included in the 1982 survey).

As Table 4.12 shows, the mean scores produced for this subcategory in 1981, 1983 and 1984 fluctuate minimally and arbitrarily, with no evidence of any change in pupils' overall performance levels over the period. The national pattern of performance is also similar to that just discussed for the subcategory **Applying biology concepts**, with the mean scores for Wales falling behind those of England and Northern Ireland in every survey (reaching statistical significance in 1983 and 1984).

**Table 4.13** *'Applying chemistry concepts' – the performances of boys and girls*
(Mean per cent scores – weighted population estimates)

| | England Boys | Girls | Diff. | Wales Boys | Girls | Diff. | Northern Ireland Boys | Girls | Diff. |
|---|---|---|---|---|---|---|---|---|---|
| 1980 | 34 | 33 | 1 | | | | | | |
| 1981 | 28 | 29 | −1 | 27 | 26 | 1 | 29 | 28 | 1 |
| 1983 | 28 | 26 | 2 | 24 | 24 | 0 | 26 | 27 | −1 |
| 1984 | 28 | 28 | 0 | 25 | 27 | −2 | 29 | 28 | 1 |

The pattern of difference between the performance scores of boys and girls is inconsistent as Table 4.13

**Table 4.14** *'Applying physics concepts' – developmental history 1980–84*

| Survey year | No. of questions in pool | in survey | Packaging strategy | Pupils/schools per package | Mean % scores Eng | Wales | NI |
|---|---|---|---|---|---|---|---|
| 1980 | 65 | 28 | 2 × 14 | 1000/150 | 32 | – | – |
| 1981 | 65 | 45 | 3 × 15 | 800/350 | 29 | 28 | 28 |
| 1983 | 126 | 64 | 4 × 16 | 700/600 | 31 | 28 | 29 |
| 1984 | 126 | 64 | 4 × 16 | 510/490 | 29 | 27 | 28 |

reveals. Where score differences have appeared these have usually been small and have varied in direction.

Bearing in mind the strong pattern of performance difference in favour of boys in Wales for **Applying biology concepts**, it is interesting to note that a similar picture has not emerged in the case of chemistry. Both girls *and* boys in Wales have consistently produced lower mean scores on **Applying chemistry concepts** than have their peers in England and Northern Ireland.

## 4.9 Applying physics concepts

Once again we find no evidence that pupils' performance levels on this subcategory have changed over the period of surveys. As Table 4.14 shows, the mean score estimates fluctuate minimally and arbitrarily from year to year in each country. The mean scores for Wales fall significantly behind those for England in 1983 and 1984; the small differences between Wales and Northern Ireland are never large enough to reach statistical significance.

This subcategory is the one for which statistically significant score differences in favour of boys have consistently emerged at all ages and in every survey. Table 4.15 illustrates this strong and stable pattern very well.

In *every* survey in each country the differences in the performance score estimates of 13 year old boys and girls have been about the same size (roughly a quarter of the common standard deviation of raw scores). Moreover the size of the performance gap in these APU surveys is the same as that reported for English 13 year olds in the science surveys conducted in the IEA (International Educational Assessment) programme almost ten years earlier (see Comber and Keeves, 1973).

**Table 4.15** *'Applying physics concepts' — the performances of boys and girls*

(Mean % scores — weighted population estimates)

| | England | | | Wales | | | Northern Ireland | | |
|---|---|---|---|---|---|---|---|---|---|
| | Boys | Girls | Diff. | Boys | Girls | Diff. | Boys | Girls | Diff. |
| 1980 | 34 | 30 | 4 | | | | | | |
| 1981 | 30 | 26 | 4 | 30 | 25 | 5 | 29 | 27 | 2 |
| 1983 | 33 | 29 | 4 | 31 | 24 | 7 | 31 | 27 | 4 |
| 1984 | 31 | 28 | 3 | 29 | 26 | 3 | 31 | 25 | 6 |

There is no discernible change in the size of the performance difference in favour of boys between ages 11 and 13 (see Johnson and Murphy, 1986). Not surprisingly, in view of the different rates of physics uptake by boys and girls at 13+, the performance gap at age 15 is larger (at around half a standard deviation—see Johnson and Murphy, 1986).

A review of individual question statistics reveals electricity and mechanics as conceptual areas which seem to cause girls particular difficulty—at *all* ages surveyed. But there are no 'topics' within the physics question pool at age 13 with which girls cope better than boys; rather they show a pretty general relative weakness in this aspect of science performance. These comments refer to girls *as a group*. It should be stressed that there are, of course, many girls who are very able in physics just as there are very many boys who find difficulty with this subject. It is not the case that all girls are weak in this area and all boys strong. The performance pattern discussed here is based on *average* scores.

The fact that this strong sex-related difference in physics concept application tests is already evident at age 11— and possibly earlier—suggests extra-curricular causes. Plausibly, differences in the leisure-time activities of boys and girls of the kind described in the previous chapter are relevant to a great extent in explaining this feature. Boys and girls do indeed have very different interests in general. Principally, the boys are more interested than the girls in handling and learning about mechanical and electrical objects, and the girls are more interested than boys in biological and domestic activities. Moreover, these clear differences in interests and associated activity among 13 year old boys and girls are already in evidence and are just as strong among 11 year olds (see Johnson and Murphy, 1986).

It is surely reasonable to speculate that the boys' greater mechanical and electrical experience—from the earliest age—could have resulted in their particularly strong superiority when applying learned concepts in just these areas? The absence of any similar areas of superiority for girls in the biological science tests is a little puzzling, but might be explained by the fact that differences among boys and girls in their *degree* of experience in relevant biological activities are smaller than are those differences in their levels of experience of physical science in their hobbies and pastimes.

## 4.10 Summary

There is no evidence in the cumulated survey data of any underlying trends in subcategory performance for 13 year olds over the period of these surveys. For the concept application subcategories, score estimates fluctuate arbitrarily and within sampling limits. In the case of the other subcategories discussed here, sharp discontinuities in mean scores can be related to severe modifications to pool composition.

A consistent feature in the performance data over the period in which surveys were conducted in all three countries (1981—84) is the failure of the sample pupils in Wales to match the performance levels of their peers in England and Northern Ireland in the written tests. This is particularly interesting in view of the fact that no equivalent pattern has emerged in the survey data for 11 year olds; in all three countries pupils at this age have produced very similar levels of performance.

It is tempting to question whether there is something about the education received by pupils at lower secondary level in Wales which might have resulted in their falling behind in science by the age of 13. Plausibly, an explanation might lie in a differential emphasis on physical and biological science in the General Science courses in Wales. Perhaps the stronger influence of the predominantly rural economy of this country means that many of the average and lower ability pupils in Wales study courses with a relatively high biological/rural science component. Certainly, many more of the schools in Wales compared with those in England and Northern Ireland offer examination courses in Human Biology and in Rural Science. A lower emphasis on physical science would also explain to some extent the consistency with which the Welsh pupils fall behind in all written aspects of the assessment framework–these representing the kinds of abilities and skills particularly well-practised in physical sciences.

As far as differences in the performances of boys and girls are concerned, girls have consistently produced slightly higher mean scores than boys for the sub-category **Making and interpreting observations** and boys, on the other hand, have consistently produced significantly higher mean scores than girls for **Applying physics concepts**. There has been a tendency also for boys more often than not to produce the slightly higher scores for **Interpreting presented information**, though these have only occasionally reached statistical significance.

For **Using graphs, tables and charts, Applying biology concepts** and **Applying chemistry concepts** differences have been very small and often variable in direction. The only exception to this is the biology phenomenon in Wales, with the girls consistently producing significantly lower mean scores than boys when **Applying biology concepts**. It is not the case, though, that the girls in Wales are particularly weak in biology. It is rather that the boys here are relatively stronger in this area, to the extent that their performances when **Applying biology concepts** equal those of their counterparts in England and Northern Ireland, whereas for most other aspects of the assessment framework they produce the lowest performance scores. It is reasonable to speculate that motivational factors account for this to some extent, the boys in Wales looking to future occupations within that country's strong rural tradition.

# 5

# Use of graphical and symbolic representation

## 5.1 Introduction

This category of science activity exposes pupils to the more concrete and mechanical aspects of data and information communication skills. That is, it explores the awareness of conventions used in the organisation and the operation of graphs, tables, charts and other standard representations rather than their interpretation. This latter skill of interpretation, which might be thought of as more abstract, or of 'higher order', is assessed by means of questions in the subcategory **Interpreting presented information**. Not surprisingly, these two different categories of questions frequently share similar data in the question stems presented to pupils, while differing in the demand on information processing. While these remarks offer some perspective on the **Use of graphical and symbolic representation**, they should not be interpreted as a diminution of the importance of the operations involved for wider scientific performance. A facility in identifying and manipulating variables must be a prerequisite to exploring and understanding relationships between these variables. In the use of coordinate forms, for example, pupils may be thought of as formalising and reinforcing their understanding of quantified associations between variables. Such an understanding is particularly valued in a 'process' orientation towards science, where pupils are encouraged to formulate and undertake their own investigations.

The global characteristics of performance in this category have been outlined in Chapter 4. Consistently across all surveys and ages assessed, performance estimates within the subcategory **Using graphs, tables and charts** has been higher than in any of the other question domains. Performance has been assessed on a specified range of items using particular scoring criteria. A more detailed analysis of sub-groups of questions within this range should be more illuminative in terms of the skills which pupils appear more or less capable of deploying. Such an analysis will be presented in this chapter.

While in the first two surveys a distinction between **Reading** and **Representing** information was maintained, from 1983, on the basis of the high correlation between the two activities, a single overall performance estimate has been used. In order to explore some of the sub-skills which appear to exist within such an aggregated score, discussion will be structured by reference to five

relatively discrete presentational forms. Section 5.2 will describe these five forms, which will then be treated in detail in sections 5.3–5.7. The other minor subcategory which will be briefly mentioned in this chapter is **Using scientific symbols and conventions**, which is summarised in section 5.8. Since questions in this latter subcategory are concerned with some of the very specific conventions used in science (eg circuit diagrams, section drawings) no attempt is made to aggregate scores into a generalised estimate of performance. The subcategory is treated separately by reference to particular question demands.

## 5.2 Performance on the five question groups

Although question types may overlap to some degree, understanding pupil performance at a more detailed level may be helped by breaking down scores by reference to five identifiable groups of questions. The first three of these are coordinate forms, which may be thought to have more in common than the fourth and fifth groups. The groups which have been nominated are: Tables, Bar Charts, Line Graphs, Pie Charts, and Other Representational forms (Venn diagrams, flow charts, food webs, etc.). A total of 148 questions has been used in surveys, some on more than one occasion. Table 5.1 summarises performance on the total of questions used by reference to the five question groups.

**Table 5.1** *Summary of performance in 'Use of graphical and symbolic representation' by five question groups (1980–1984 data)*

|  | No. of questions used | Mean % score | Range |
|---|---|---|---|
| Tables | 23 | 75 | 51–95 |
| Bar Charts | 30 | 57 | 26–92 |
| Line Graphs | 56 | 63 | 15–91 |
| Pie Charts | 18 | 64 | 27–85 |
| Other forms | 21 | 65 | 27–90 |

The first comment which Table 5.1 provokes concerns the composition of the question bank itself. About three quarters of the questions used to produce the overall performance estimate are concerned with coordinate forms. This reflects the judgement of question writers as to the importance of this form for the age group concerned. More specifically, 38 per cent of questions required pupils to use line graphs (including grids).

The second notable feature of Table 5.1 is that the mean score for tabular questions is much higher than for the other four question groups, where mean scores cluster in the range 57–65 per cent. Furthermore, the range of scores is very much more restricted than is the case in the other question groups. As ever, some caution is required in interpreting these quantitative face-values, bearing in mind the numbers of questions available and the ranges of the scores obtained. The specific nature of demands intrinsic to the five question groups needs to be more closely considered. Some of the explicit and implicit demands will be laid out in the following sections, and where possible, related to pupil performance.

## 5.3   Tables

Data presented in tables may take various forms: numerical, verbal or symbolic. Symbolic data may be representational, verging towards the pictorial, or non-representational and relatively abstract. There may also be combinations of these various forms. The form in which data are presented may affect the volume and density of information which a table is able to convey, and consequently the potential sources of error.

The tabular questions used in the science surveys required pupils either to read from presented data, or to add given information to an incomplete table. Thus, while in practice (for example during a practical investigation) the judgement as to the appropriateness of constructing a table would be the pupil's own, in the questions under consideration here, such decisions are not required. The structure of the tables and their labels were given. Pupils were required to operate within the conventions, using the information given. The logic of table construction consequently permits a certain finite set of operations. For example:

– locating the row or column heading of a particular cell;

– locating a cell, given row and column headings;

– comparing cell values, within a row, a column, or the total matrix.

However, an examination of differential performance levels, by gender for instance, suggests that factors affecting the difficulty level of any given question part go beyond this logical definition of the operations involved. For example, the particular subject matter presented may have some bearing on performance, as discussed in section 5.8 (p. 52). Table 5.2 summarises performance on questions involving the use of tables.

**Table 5.2**  *Summary of performance on tables (1980–1984 data)*

|  | No. of questions used | Mean % score | Range |
|---|---|---|---|
| Reading from tables | 17 | 73 | 56–90 |
| Adding given information to tables | 6 | 79 | 51–95 |
| All tabular questions | 23 | 75 | 51–95 |

Questions involving tabulated data have cross-curricular relevance, as well as a wider social usage than some other aspects of the science assessment repertoire. The representation of questions in the item bank attempts to reflect this wider usage in the content presented to pupils–particularly those tables which require information to be read rather than to be inserted. Those questions which require pupils to add information attempt to reflect the kinds of activities and experiences pupils might be likely to encounter in school, and consequently do not always match the complexity of tables found in published sources.

Table 5.3 summarises performance in the category by reference to the data form. This is a rather rough guide, referring to the nature of the information within each 'cell' of the tabular matrix, whether Pictorial, Verbal or Numerical.

**Table 5.3**  *Summary of performance on tables by reference to data form (1980–1984 data)*

|  | No. of questions used | Mean % score | Range |
|---|---|---|---|
| Verbal | 3 | 85 | 81–88 |
| Pictorial | 8 | 76 | 59–95 |
| Numerical | 12 | 71 | 51–93 |

In view of the small number of questions presented in the verbal mode, and the large range in the means of the other two groups, the patterns of overall mean scores in Table 5.3 must be interpreted with caution. The deliberate heterogeneity of question characteristics within the domain precludes comparisons of matched questions. It remains for a more systematic study to confirm that verbally presented information may be handled most successfully, pictorial data at an intermediate level, with numerical data producing the greatest challenge. Of course, with numerical data, tables frequently call for some operations to be carried out on the cell value, such as multiplication by a constant factor. (See DES, 1986a, Example 3.3, page 22.) The same trend in the effect of the presentational form is more marked when information concerning the overall mean percentage of pupils offering totally correct responses is considered. For verbally presented data, the overall mean for totally correct responses was

71 per cent, for Pictorial information 57 per cent, and Numerical 44 per cent.

Using tables is a relatively discrete skill, and, at first glance, performance appears to be at a high level of scoring in a category within which pupils have relatively more success against the scoring criteria used than is the case in other science activity categories. However, if tables are thought of as straightforward data communication devices, then the scores take on a less favourable aspect. For example, in using a timetable, it might be argued that 100 per cent success is the only reasonable performance criterion to apply, provided no artificially exaggerated complexity has been imposed in the questions. Pupils at the age of 13 are far from meeting this criterion, particularly with numerical data. It might too easily be the case that precisely because of their wide cross-curricular and social application, the responsibility for actually teaching table-reading skills could easily be overlooked.

## 5.4 Bar charts

As with tabular questions, assessment of the skills involved in reading from, and adding information to, bar charts is based on the outcomes of closely specified activities within the questions used. Pupils' own decisions about when to use this data communication form, or how to *interpret* bar charts, are not assessed in this category. Assessment is limited to the mechanical skills and use of conventions. Table 5.4 summarises performance within the four different types of questions which can be identified.

The overall mean scores for reading information from bar charts and representing information in that form are very close. However, when the 'representing' questions are examined as separate groups, there is a clear trend of decreasing levels of performance as the amount of support given within the question decreases.

A partially completed bar chart might typically have called for two or more further bars to be added on the basis of the information given. The scale was provided and labelled, and there were example bars to guide the drawing of the additions. Though the range of performance was wide, depending on factors such as the scale used, the particular values, the requirement for interpolation, etc, the mean score of 66 per cent is the highest of all the bar chart questions. Even the severe criterion of complete success on questions is achieved by 39 per cent of pupils.

When the axes are labelled, but no exemplar bars illustrate the drawing or use of scales, the overall mean performance is 54 per cent of maximum marks. In these circumstances, 24 per cent of pupils offer a perfectly correct response, while a similar proportion had no success.

The most demanding test of bar chart construction requires pupils to construct their own scale, labels and plotting to accommodate the given data. This form of test item is very time-consuming both for pupils and markers but probably represents the closest parallel to science classroom applications. The overall performance estimate is 45 per cent of the maximum, with 10 per cent of pupils managing a 'perfect' response, ie achieving full marks. The construction points which are credited are: appropriate scale, label and units on each axis, consistent bar width and accuracy of plotting. Generally speaking, it was in the area of labelling the axes that otherwise correct responses were likely to show omissions or errors.

Some details of the errors made on two particular questions are outlined in the report of the fourth survey at age 13 (DES, 1986a, pages 26–29). Some of the issues raised in this section will be further elaborated in the next.

## 5.5 Line graphs

Performance on six groups of questions, each placing the burden of demand on a particular feature of graph usage and differing in some way one from another, is

**Table 5.4** *Summary of performance on Bar Chart questions (1980–84)*

|  | No. of questions | Mean % score | Range | % pupils not scoring | % pupils scoring maximum marks |
|---|---|---|---|---|---|
| Reading information from bar charts | 10 | 58 | 29–84 | 13 | 24 |
| Adding information to partially completed bar charts | 7 | 66 | 26–92 | 8 | 39 |
| Constructing bar charts with ready-labelled axes | 8 | 54 | 30–87 | 24 | 24 |
| Constructing entire bar charts using given information | 5 | 45 | 34–63 | 23 | 10 |
| All bar chart questions | 30 | 57 | 26–92 | 16 | 25 |

summarised in Table 5.5. In terms of the division between reading and representing graphical information, performance estimates are approximately equivalent. (Reading, number of questions = 21, overall mean score 55 per cent; representing, number of questions = 35, overall mean score 56 per cent.) Not surprisingly, in view of the shared common skills, pupils' performances with line graphs have much in common with the situation presented for bar charts in the previous section. Some more specific comments are also possible.

The two extreme overall mean scores in Table 5.5 provide an informative contrast in performance on two identifiable and relatively discrete graph construction skills. These questions which require pupils to use grids and coordinates focus on an aspect of plotting, namely the coordination of x and y axes to identify a unique point on the grid. The overall mean score of 83 per cent of maximum partly reflects the fact that interpolation between labelled lines is avoided (see DES, 1986a, example 3.5, page 25). Nevertheless, pupils seem to be demonstrating an understanding of the fundamental organisation of coordinate forms. Seventy-four per cent of pupils, on average across 8 questions, made error-free responses to this type of question. At the other end of the performance range, the overall mean score for naming the variables on the axes was 35 per cent. In this type of question, a verbal description is presented together with a line graph (see DES, 1986a, example 3.10, page 32). Pupils are required to provide labels and units for each axis, the information being drawn from the written question introduction. Some questions additionally ask pupils to say what the graph represents. The requirement in this latter part of the question is that the relationship between the independent and dependent variables should be indicated, in non-technical language. For example 'How long the music box plays for different numbers of turns of the key'. Mean scores were low against all these criteria. Pupils tended to state the *units* of measurement slightly more frequently than they named variables. Expressing the relationship represented by the graph tended to be the least successfully accomplished. Completely correct responses were offered by an overall average of 8 per cent of pupils, while the overall mean rate of failure to score was 41 per cent.

Pupils' apparent relative competence with plotting tends to be confirmed by the mean performance on the four questions requiring them to insert information onto partially completed graphs, though these questions offer considerable support in that they have example points plotted.

The trend of falling mean scores as the level of support within the question decreases is continued in the question type which requires pupils to add information to drawings in which the axes have already been labelled, but no example points have been plotted. The last question type is anomalous as far as the trend of increasing difficulty is concerned. This may be explained by the fact that when required to construct their own scales, pupils are provided with some examples of values which are easier to handle, so that they may engage with the question and deploy other skills which are of interest, relatively unimpeded by this first step. Consequently, the upper end of the range is extended, and the overall mean score is slightly enhanced.

Six questions used in the 1984 survey were subjected to a detailed re-examination, using samples of 200 pupils, (equal numbers of boys and girls) per question. The criteria used and resulting performance characteristics, are described in Table 5.6.

The first five criteria in Table 5.6 refer to performance on *both* axes, and are thus averaged for independent and dependent variables. This does obscure some of the variability in performance attributable to the particular variable, physical quantity, etc, which is the subject of attention within each graph, though it can be seen that some criteria show evidence of a fairly wide range of scores despite the aggregation.

Table 5.5 *Summary of performance on Line Graphs (1980–84 data)*

| | No. of questions used | Mean % score | Range | % pupils not scoring | % pupils scoring maximum marks |
|---|---|---|---|---|---|
| Reading information from Line Graphs | 21 | 55 | 24–80 | 19 | 29 |
| Using grids and co-ordinates | 8 | 83 | 71–91 | 9 | 74 |
| Naming the variables on the axes | 8 | 35 | 15–52 | 41 | 8 |
| Inserting information on partially completed graph | 4 | 68 | 53–78 | 18 | 52 |
| Inserting information with ready-labelled axes | 7 | 43 | 27–52 | 28 | 6 |
| Constructing entire line graphs using given information | 8 | 55 | 29–69 | 20 | 5 |
| All graph questions | 56 | 63 | 15–91 | 22 | 28 |

**Table 5.6** *Summary of performance on six questions requiring pupils to construct complete graphs, expressed as mean per cent scores (1984 data only)*

| | Volume of gas in cm³/ time in minutes | Mass of kitten in g/ time in weeks | Height of sand in cm/ time in minutes | Pendulum length in cm/ number of swings per minute | Elastic length in cm/ number of marbles in pan | Height of bean plant in cm/ time in weeks | Overall |
|---|---|---|---|---|---|---|---|
| **Type of response** | | | | | | | |
| Naming variables | 39 | 22 | 64 | 64 | 64 | 29 | 47 |
| Labelling units | 39 | 53 | 45 | 59 | 50 | 56 | 50 |
| Use of equal-interval scales | 40 | 42 | 65 | 63 | 65 | 70 | 58 |
| Suitable scale | 37 | 42 | 65 | 62 | 64 | 71 | 57 |
| Scale labelling | 61 | 83 | 86 | 83 | 84 | 86 | 81 |
| Plotting | 33 | 69 | 61 | 61 | 73 | 75 | 62 |
| IV on horizontal axis | 44 | 66 | 69 | 34 | 67 | 72 | 59 |
| Points joined | 37 | 53 | 44 | 45 | 53 | 55 | 48 |
| Points joined by curve | 16 | 8 | 12 | 19 | * | 11 | 13 |
| **Type of construction** | | | | | | | |
| Line graph | 37 | 59 | 46 | 45 | 43 | 55 | 48 |
| Points only | 13 | 12 | 28 | 26 | 4 | 12 | 16 |
| Bar lines | 1 | 7 | 1 | 1 | 2 | 6 | 3 |
| Bar chart | 6 | 11 | 16 | 10 | 36 | 17 | 16 |
| Other lines to points | 0 | 1 | 1 | 1 | 2 | 0 | 1 |
| Other | 16 | 6 | 1 | 6 | 5 | 7 | 7 |
| No response | 28 | 5 | 9 | 13 | 9 | 3 | 11 |

* Straight line relationship

Failure to label the variables on each axis may stem from unease or unfamiliarity with the concept represented, as might appear to be the case in 'volume of gas'; it may also be the case that there is a sense of stating the obvious, as when units have been labelled, eg 'seconds'; the variable being considered is self-evidently the passage of time. Other reasons for omitting the name of the variable may include lack of awareness of the convention, or oversight. Similar comments pertain to the use of units, which overall are slightly more likely to be labelled. Unit labelling also calls for more precision. Whereas 'how much gas' could be accepted as a substitute for 'volume', units were required to be accurately specified. Overall about 50 per cent of pupils at age 13 had success with labelling variables and units.

The criterion for use of an equal-interval scale was simply that, for each scale, each division on the graph paper should represent the same value. Success depends to some extent on the complexity of the scale and units used.

The criteria for a 'suitable' scale were very lenient in this instance, being simply that the data should be capable of being accommodated and legibly represented by an equal-interval scale. The best use of the available space on the graph paper provided might be legitimately required in normal practice, but imposes additional computational demands which were not the present focus of interest. The performance levels for the use of equal-interval and suitable scales are very close; those pupils capable of setting up an equal-interval scale had little trouble fitting it on the graph paper.

Scale labelling required that numbers should be attached to divisions, and was credited even where the scale used might have been unsatisfactory in some respects. This mechanical and conventional demand was met by about 90 per cent of pupils who made some response to a question.

In order to avoid dependence on scale construction criteria, 'plotting' was credited where pupils showed evidence of accurate coordination of the scales which they had themselves set up. Treated as a separate skill in this way, levels tend to be equal to or better than the labelling and scale construction requirements.

The placing of the independent variable on the horizontal axis is a convention which requires an understanding of the nature of the relationship represented by a graph. Were it accessible through conversation with children, expression of their understanding might justifiably be regarded as highly predictive of successful performance. In a written response not requiring a justification for the positioning of the axes, success on the stated criterion is achieveable by chance with a 50 per cent probability. Over the six questions, success ranged from 34 per cent to 72 per cent of the sample (39–76 per cent of the sub-sample offering a response) and suggests that a firm and reliable grasp of this understanding cannot be assumed. It is very difficult to see how pupils reached decisions as to which variable to plot on which axis. Order of data presentation or ease of fit may sometimes be deciding considerations.

Almost all those pupils who attempted to draw a line graph also attempted to join the points. Only a minority of the whole sample progressed as far as attempting to join the points which they had plotted with a curve. Even amongst those pupils who attempted a line graph (rather than, for example, a bar chart) no more than 43 per cent managed to draw a curve. Once again, the deployment of this skill was to some extent dependent on whether or not the trend was self-evident within any particular data set.

Overall, about two-thirds of pupils attempted to plot points or line graphs, while about one fifth overall preferred to use bar lines or bar charts. The rates of non-response ranged from 3 per cent to 28 per cent. The four questions having the higher rates on non-response were concerned with gas volume production over time (28 per cent), the rate of swing of a pendulum (13 per cent), the height of sand in a timer (9 per cent) and the stretch in elastic under different loads (9 per cent). The impersonal physical-mechanical content of these questions contrasts with the floral and faunal content of the remaining questions, where non-response rates were 3 per cent and 5 per cent respectively. (All questions except those concerning gas production and the pendulum presented data as whole numbers.)

## 5.6 Pie charts

Pie charts have a relatively minor part to play in data communication in science in comparison with co-ordinate forms. The conventions of presenting descriptive statistics in this graphic form call for a quite separate set of skills. It should be noted at the outset that the questions set avoided the requirement of the geometrical skills associated with pie charts. The assessment of computational aspects of the tasks was also avoided in favour of focussing on the communication skills involved. Table 5.7 summarises performance.

Only four questions have been used to assess the skills involved in reading from pie charts. The precise

demands made included comparisons of pie charts to identify presence or absence of elements, or comparisons of the sizes of various labelled sectors. Three of the questions produced mean scores in the range 81–84 per cent, with up to 5 per cent of pupils scoring no marks. The fourth question produced a markedly different performance. While non-response was at an equivalent level to the other three questions, 30 per cent of pupils made no score, and the overall performance was 66 per cent of maximum. This question presented data concerning the percentages of pupils taking school lunch in various year groups. Although this content might be assumed to be accessible to pupils, another factor which had to be considered was the use of a key, which provided the coding on the various hatchings within sectors of the chart designating different groups. It was the use of a key, as contrasted with directly labelled sectors, which appears to distinguish this question from the other three, in terms of difficulty level.

Fourteen questions required pupils to add given information to complete pie charts. The mean rate of non-response was 9 per cent in these questions, compared with 1.5 per cent in those questions requiring information to be read from pie charts. Fewer pupils scored maximum marks, and more scored no marks at all, when required to add information, rather than read from pie charts.

The question having the highest overall mean score (85 per cent) tested pupils' ability to label all sectors of a pie chart, given a series of values expressed as percentages, and a pie chart drawn with radii defining sectors of appropriate sizes. It is possible to conclude that the majority of pupils at age 13 appear to understand the essential relationship which pie charts represent of quantities expressed as areas. Seventy-three per cent of pupils scored maximum marks on this question.

Ten of the questions requiring information to be added used a format in which a circle was divided by radii into ten equal sectors, and the data given were in percentages. Performance in these questions seemed to be governed by the subdivisions of sectors which had to be drawn. Thus the simplest problem used multiples of ten (mean score 72 per cent); data to the nearest 5 per cent resulted in performances in the range 41–63 per cent. When data were to the nearest one per cent,

**Table 5.7**  *Summary of performance on Pie Charts (1980–84 data)*

|  | No. of questions | Mean % score | Range | % pupils not scoring | % pupils scoring maximum marks |
|---|---|---|---|---|---|
| Reading from pie charts | 4 | 76 | 66–84 | 10 | 60 |
| Adding given information to pie charts | 14 | 60 | 27–85 | 28 | 44 |
| All pie chart questions | 18 | 64 | 27–85 | 24 | 48 |

**Table 5.8** *Summary of performance on Other Representational Forms (Venn Diagrams, Flow Charts, Networks and other diagrams) 1980–84 data*

| | No. of questions used | Mean % score | Range | % pupils not scoring | % pupils scoring maximum marks |
|---|---|---|---|---|---|
| Reading information | 14 | 66 | 36–90 | 14 | 43 |
| Adding information | 7 | 64 | 27–80 | 23 | 47 |
| All questions | 21 | 65 | 27–90 | 17 | 44 |

scores were 51 per cent, 54 per cent and 58 per cent of the maximum. The most difficult problem pupils encountered was how to cope with a pie chart of the constituents of butter, in which the information 'carbohydrate 0 per cent' had to be accommodated. Performance on this question was 27 per cent of maximum.

## 5.7 Other representational forms—Venn diagrams, flow charts, networks and other diagrams

Very little difference in performance between reading information and adding it is apparent through inspection of the overall mean scores (Table 5.8). In fact, as generally tends to be the case in the category as a whole, rates of non-response are much higher in the questions requiring pupils to add information (overall mean 11 per cent, range 3–22 per cent, compared with overall mean 3 per cent, range 1–8 per cent).

When the extremes of the marks are examined, ie percentages of pupils succeeding on none or all of the scoring criteria, the position in the 'representing' group of questions can be seen to be slightly more polarised than is the case in the 'reading' group. That is, there are more pupils having complete success, and more having no success at all, when asked to add information to these forms than is the case with the 'reading' demand. Only 30 per cent of pupils have partial success.

Perhaps the most striking feature of questions within this group is the variability of performance. Even when sub-groups are identified, questions based on Venn diagrams, flow charts, networks and other diagrammatic

representations still show considerable variability. Partly this variability may be a response to particular question content, but it is also true to say that the presentational layout of the questions under consideration may be very variable. For example, the clarity of a flow chart in part may depend on the choice of graphics and other design considerations. Furthermore, all questions in this group may vary in complexity depending on the number of elements and the nature of the relationships between them. Table 5.9 presents the same questions by reference to the four major types which can be identified.

Within each question form, bearing in mind the very small number of questions in each cell, the ranges of performance are quite large, something like 50 percentage points for the first three groups. Despite the variability of mean scores, it is interesting to see the polarisation of performance which tends to occur with Venn diagrams, where, averaged across all questions, 75 per cent of pupils either score full marks, or no marks at all.

## 5.8 Gender-related differences in performance

It was stated in Chapter 4 that when mean scores for all 148 questions used are averaged, performance levels for boys and girls have tended to be roughly equivalent (see Table 4.5, p. 40) but that the aggregation masks some gender differences in the sub-skills involved. The specific nature of these differences will now be considered.

Of the 23 questions which presented data in the form of tables, girls scored higher on 19, boys on 3, with one equivalent (overall mean boys, 74 per cent; overall mean girls, 76 per cent).

**Table 5.9** *Summary of performance on Venn diagrams, Flow charts, Networks and other diagrams*

| | No. of questions used | Mean % score | Range | % pupils not scoring | % pupils scoring maximum marks |
|---|---|---|---|---|---|
| Venn diagrams | 5 | 60 | 27–82 | 26 | 48 |
| Flow charts | 7 | 64 | 41–88 | 14 | 40 |
| Networks | 6 | 56 | 36–87 | 19 | 45 |
| Diagrams | 3 | 77 | 66–90 | 10 | 48 |

Eighty-six questions required pupils to handle information in the form of line graphs, bar charts and other forms of coordinate grid. Girls scored higher than boys on 50 of these questions, boys higher than girls on 28, while eight questions produced equal scores for boys and girls. (The overall mean score is 56 per cent for both boys and girls, though the variance is slightly greater for girls' scores.) Within these graphical questions, it was noticeable that for two Question types, the mean scores of girls were consistently higher than those of boys. In 'Naming the variables on the axes of a graph' (see Table 5.5) the mean scores of girls were slightly ahead of those of boys on all eight questions used (the average mean score for boys was 33 per cent and for girls 36 per cent). On the eight questions in which pupils were required to plot graphs 'from scratch' using the given information, once again girls were consistently ahead of boys on every question (the average of mean scores for boys was 52 per cent and for girls 58 per cent). The gender differences occurring in these two question groups is particularly interesting, as in a sense these questions form the heart of the assessment of coordinate forms. The variable naming group, generally found difficult by pupils, bridges the divide between the simple use of conventions and the *interpretation* of data. The graph construction questions in the second group are the most comprehensive and least supported by contextual question cues of all the items used.

Within the complex of demands and expectations in every question, the particular content or subject matter has been identified as being one factor associated with performance effects (see, for example, Chapter 5 in Age 11 review report–DES, 1988a) and these effects may on occasion be linked to gender. The 148 questions on which the review of performance in data communication was based were broadly divided into four groups on the basis of question content, ie the phenomena providing the data upon which tables, graphs, etc were constructed. The categories used were:

– human/domestic/social
– flora (limited to living material)
– fauna
– physical/inanimate/mechanical

Table 5.10 summarises performance across all questions using these categories.

Several points are of interest. Firstly, questions concerned with flora tend to result in higher perfor-

mance levels than the other groups, for boys and girls. Secondly, girls are equal to, or slightly ahead of, boys on *all* content groups. At age 11, some content appeared to have the effect of depressing girls' performance within this category. There was evidence that invertebrate animals were not favoured by girls at age 11. At age 13 five questions showed a significant difference in performance between the sexes. All were in favour of girls and within the social–flora–fauna Question types. The question producing the greatest performance differences between boys and girls (boys 55 per cent, girls 70 per cent) concerned the rearing in captivity of a praying mantis. The other questions in which girls' performance was significantly higher were: reading information from a food web; interpreting information about an okapi presented on a Venn diagram; adding information about forest tree species to a pie chart; and drawing a bar chart of children's heights.

## 5.9 Using scientific symbols and conventions

The questions within this subcategory assess the knowledge of some very particular conventions associated with apparatus and representations of apparatus. For this reason, aggregated scores are not very useful in terms of suggesting any generalised performance characteristics. As stated in previous reports, the number of questions used is small. However, it is appropriate in this review to summarise what information is available. Table 5.11 (p. 54) describes performance on each of the groups of questions used.

Pupils were relatively successful at matching names to the sectional drawings of apparatus, about 70 per cent overall having at least partial success, 5 per cent having complete failure, and 24 per cent having complete success. The specific items of apparatus represented in the three questions used were: test tube, tube, beaker, gas jar, measuring cylinder, flask, thistle funnel, conical flask, crucible and evaporating basin. The apparatus can be clearly identified within a laboratory context, and many items might be identifiable to the nonspecialist. It might be reasonable to assume that a greater familiarity with the particular items should be associated with a greater facility in naming the various pieces. When required to make a sectional drawing on the basis of a 3-d line drawing, the overall mean score on 5 questions was 32 per cent, with almost half the

**Table 5.10**  *Performance on data communication related to Question Content (1980–84 data)*

|  | Human– social– domestic (41 questions) | Flora (15 questions) | Fauna (29 questions) | Physical/ inanimate mechanical (63 questions) |
|---|---|---|---|---|
| Boys | 61 | 68 | 58 | 60 |
| Girls | 62 | 71 | 59 | 60 |
| All | 61 | 70 | 59 | 60 |

**Table 5.11** *Summary of performance on 'Using scientific symbols and conventions' (1980–84 data)*

| | No. of questions used | Mean % score | Range | % pupils not scoring | % pupils scoring maximum marks |
|---|---|---|---|---|---|
| Matching names to sectional drawings of apparatus | 3 | 64 | 53–73 | 5 | 24 |
| Making a sectional drawing on the basis of a 3-d line drawing of laboratory apparatus | 5 | 32 | 20–42 | 47 | 2 |
| Naming the components presented in a sectional drawing of laboratory apparatus | 6 | 53 | 33–71 | 18 | 18 |
| Drawing a conventional circuit diagram on the basis of a 3-d line drawing | 4 | 24 | 17–31 | 53 | 6 |
| Naming the components of a conventional circuit diagram | 2 | 36 | 24–47 | 40 | 14 |
| Total | 20 | 42 | 17–73 | 35 | 12 |

pupils, on average, achieving no score. Once again, the apparatus presented was typical science laboratory equipment, including, for example, test tubes, beakers, glass tube and corks, bottles, filter funnel, tripod, bunsen burner, crucible and gauze. However, this group of questions poses formal demands and knowledge of conventions which many pupils do not have.

The third group of questions required pupils to label a sectional drawing. Questions differed from the first group described above in that the labels had to be generated by the pupils themselves, though the range of apparatus was almost identical. The burden of having to generate rather than allocate appropriate labels seems to have had the effect of slightly depressing performance on the six questions used. This is particularly evident in the number of pupils making no score.

The last two groups are concerned with electrical circuits. (See Question examples 4 and 5, Gott, R, 1984, page 13.) When asked to translate a 3-d line drawing into a conventional circuit diagram, on average, just over half the 13 year old pupils assessed made no score on the four questions concerned. Pupils appear to have found the labelling of circuit diagrams as represented by the two questions in the last group almost as problematic.

Performance levels for boys were higher than those for girls in 17 of the 20 questions used; the performance differences achieved significance on one question concerned with labelling a conventional circuit diagram.

## 5.10   Summary

This chapter has attempted to indicate something of the sub-structure of demands which exists within the category **Use of graphical and symbolic representation**, and the performance outcomes relating to more or less discrete elements within the whole. Whilst concerned ostensibly with rather mechanical and rote-learned conventions, important parallels can be inferred, particularly amongst the coordinate forms, with a more general variable-based orientation towards science processes. Some of these parallels will be drawn out in more empirical terms in the chapter discussing pupils' performance of whole investigations (see Chapter 11).

As far as teaching intervention is concerned, the discussion of particular scoring criteria raises issues of what is taught, and by whom, since data communication forms have cross-curricular relevance, albeit with differing foci. The skills involved also have wider social relevance, and in some respects, as for example in table reading, raise issues about what constitutes a useful response or level of proficiency, when less than complete accuracy may on occasion lead to gross errors.

# Use of apparatus and measuring instruments

## 6.1 Introduction

Practical work in science is not an end in itself; learning to use measuring instruments with no valid purpose is an activity unlikely to promote pupils' interest in science. In an ideal world the assessment of the use of apparatus and measuring instruments would take place in the context of an investigation designed by the pupil, but there are limitations in such a method. A pupil may choose to use one instrument rather than another (for reasons which may or may not be connected with direct competence with that instrument), so that information about population performance obtained during such investigations will be patchy. It may be that the use of a given instrument presents a hurdle which cannot be cleared by some pupils, and therefore affects their choice of method or even precludes *any* appropriate action during an investigation; thus it appears necessary to focus separately on this limited activity in addition to assessing **Performance of investigations** in a more holistic fashion.

Three distinct components of the use of apparatus and measuring instruments have been identified, and these form the basis of three subcategories:

- Using measuring instruments

- Estimating physical quantities

- Following instructions for practical work

The ability tested in the second of these can be seen simply as necessary for the choice of an instrument of an appropriate range (although pupils of 13 years are seldom offered the opportunity to make such a choice); but such ability also implies the acquisition of an understanding of the nature of the quantity to be estimated and the units associated with it. If pupils estimate that the volume of water filling a beaker is 10 cm, or 100 grams or even 5 cm³ this gives quite important information about their concept of volume.

Following instructions is not, in one sense, an activity to be unduly emphasised in school science: pupils should rather be encouraged to generate and evaluate their own plans of action. However for some purposes, such as learning to use unfamiliar equipment safely or to operate a new technique efficiently, the ability to follow instructions is an advantage. Certainly, it is common practice for science teachers to issue pupils with worksheets, often as a means of allowing individuals or small groups a certain degree of independence.

## 6.2 Nature of the assessment

Considerable thought and trial has been given to ways of asking questions which provide pupils with the *motivation* which might be missing in the absence of self-determined purposes for the tasks involved. In some questions pupils are told indirectly which skill is intended to be the focus of the assessment. This is thought to be particularly important where the ability to 'follow instructions' is being investigated. The introduction to 'Sorting Liquids' (DES, 1984a, page 134) exemplifies the use of both these principles:

> 'The four bottles labelled P, Q, R and S have different liquids in them. The liquids are:
>
> > plain water
> > dilute sulphuric acid
> > dilute nitric acid
> > a solution of Epsom salts
>
> You cannot tell which liquid is which just by looking at them, but you can sort them out by following the instructions for these two tests.'

This introduction is followed by step-by-step instructions, interspersed with diagrams and with labelled grids in which pupils are to record their observations, and ending with a request for the identification of the four liquids. The conclusions themselves are not scored (though they *are* recorded), for the 'score' is intended to represent performance with respect to following instructions. But the request for identification is included to give the pupils a purpose for what would otherwise be a pointless task. The more sharply focused the question, the harder it is likely to be to provide an appropriate 'purpose'. An elaborate suggestion as to why a pupil might want to estimate, say, the area of the top of a plastic sandwich box proves counter-productive by introducing an additional reading load. Similarly if the intention is to discover how well pupils can read common measuring instruments, the best one can do is to translate 'What is the reading on the thermometer?' to 'What is the temperature of the water in the flask?' as in 'Scale Readings' (DES, 1982a, page 24).

The implementation of plans to assess activities such as those described above on a national scale raises problems involving the choice of appropriate *modes of pupil response* and of *modes of marking*. In spite of high cost and logistical problems, the decision was made to allow for pupils to use or inspect real apparatus rather than to provide photographs or illustrations as substitutes. (This alternative has been investigated by a 'probe' which is discussed later.) Various modes of marking are used, according to the particular kinds of tasks set:

(i) In some cases, it is thought reasonable for the pupil to write down a limited response–one or two words or a value–after inspecting an instrument or taking some action; performance is then assessed on the basis of this written response. Such a method is legitimate only if lack of ability to write the response does not override the ability which is the focus of the enquiry; for a small minority of pupils this will inevitably happen. Although administrators are asked to help non-readers by reading the question aloud on request, it is not possible for them to help pupils by writing down spoken answers: there is too much else to do.

(ii) Some tasks are included in which no written response is required. These are of three kinds. In the first, pupils measure out a given quantity of material, which is then checked by the administrator after the test is over. In the second type, pupils follow instructions to set up some equipment, which is marked at once by the administrator who makes a record on a grid provided for the purpose; and in the third type, pupils follow instructions for making a simple product–a kaleidoscope, for example–which they leave behind to be marked.

(iii) It is impossible to assess how well pupils use some types of apparatus, or perform some techniques, without actually watching them at work. It may be true that many pupils can write accounts of what they have done, which correspond loosely with the reality, but they give little information about how *well* the apparatus was used or the technique was applied. 'I used lime water to test for carbon dioxide' may actually mean 'I tipped the lime water on to the white crystals' (see the account of 'Solid P' in DES, 1984a, page 135). For tasks in this class, assessment is made by a science teacher from the pupil's own school who observes the pupil's actions and fills in a simple prepared schedule as in 'Solid P'. Tasks of this kind must necessarily be limited, since it has been found that the teacher can pay attention to no more than one individual pupil at a time.

This category, **Use of apparatus and measuring instruments,** is assessed, then, in a practical mode. In accordance with the need to test as large a number of different aspects as possible with the minimum duplication of apparatus, the practical test is organised as a *circus*,

ie with questions arranged in nine eight-minute stations–one pupil to a station at any one point in time–until each pupil has visited each station. A series of trials was conducted to determine the optimum number of stations taking equal times which would fit into a reasonable assessment period of a little over one hour. Nine stations, with eight minutes spent at each, was found to be most convenient in view of the nature of the tasks considered suitable in this and in the **Observation** category which is assessed in the same circus mode. Thus nine pupils from each school in the relevant sub-sample take the same test, an arrangement which differs from that obtaining with respect to paper and pencil tests where, typically, no more than two pupils of the 27 or so taking part in a given school, receive the same package of questions. Details of the training of administrators, the preparation and distribution of equipment and arrangements for testing within the schools are to be found in DES, 1984a, Appendix 4, and in the report for teachers, 'Practical Testing at Ages 11, 13 and 15' (Welford, Harlen and Schofield, 1985).

*Question selection* for this type of test is not by random sampling from a bank. There are two quite different reasons why this is not appropriate. In the first place, only a limited number of questions can be written to satisfy the condition that scores should reflect primarily the use of apparatus and measuring instruments and not some other ability, such as drawing a graph or writing an account. (Simple changes of value in the quantities to be measured would, of course, give rise to an infinity of questions; but these would not be different in the sense needed, although they may well give rise to different levels of performance.) A second constraint is the need to regulate the cost and, indeed, the weight and the volume of the equipment needed for questions selected. Some apparatus, such as a microscope or even a lever arm balance, is so expensive that its use at more than one station can hardly be justified. (It should be borne in mind that 20 sets of equipment for each circus are required for each survey to equip 20 administrators to cover the sample schools in England, Wales and Northern Ireland during the designated two weeks in June.) Some boxes of equipment needed to supply a single station for up to ten visits are as large and as heavy as a suitcase, and take up more than their fair share of space in the administrator's car. Thus for each survey it is necessary to hand-pick questions for the test from those that were successfully trialled. During the phase of annual science surveys (1980–84) this category was assessed four times; some questions were repeated and some used only once. Since the first year, no overall subcategory scores have been produced; instead, questions have been individually reported. However, for the final year, 1984, a *'Fixed Test'* was constructed common to ages 13 and 15 which included many questions already surveyed. This has several advantages:

– it is possible to ensure that the selected questions cover all aspects of the category;

- it provides a set of questions which define the category for purposes of calculating a category score, enabling comparisons to be made between sub-groups or ages;

- it provides a base line against which future performance can be measured.

In the remainder of this chapter, an account of pupil performances on each of the nine stations of the Fixed Test is given; this includes a comparison of three alternative modes of assessing the ability to read scales of the measuring instruments involved. A station devoted to 'Scale readings' in which real measuring instruments have been used has been included in each of the surveys of Category 2 at age 13.

## 6.3   Scale readings

At this station, pupils were presented with eight different laboratory instruments already set up to measure a given quantity. Pupils were required to record the value and the units of each quantity. The instruments used all carried the name of the relevant unit. In 1984, questions at the station 'Scale readings' were presented in two different orders, the second order beginning halfway through the first but following the same sequence. This arrangement was made so that any possible shortage of time should not always depress performance on the same instrument.

In previous reports of performance at age 13, mean scores have been given which reflect a combination of accuracy and correct use of units. At age 15, a different reporting strategy has been employed in which these two aspects are described separately, and the frequency of choice of different values for a given instrument displayed in addition. (See 'Practical testing at ages 11, 13 and 15', Welford, Harlen and Schofield, 1985.) This has provided useful information about the kinds of error to which pupils are prone, and so a similar strategy has been adopted in this report for 13 year old pupils; mean scores are discussed later in the chapter.

During 1983 and 1984 some specially prepared questions were included in the written packages to test the feasibility and validity of assessing scale reading in the written rather than the practical mode. In 1983 a sample of 571 13 year olds responded to questions using photographs and in 1984 a sample of 407 were given line drawings based on photographs. The results of these two 'probes' have been included in this section. The probe questions are to be found in Appendix 7.

It should be noted that *different* samples of pupils attempted the questions in the three different modes, and this should be borne in mind when the results are compared.

It was not always possible to arrange for the values registered on real instruments to be identical to those shown in the paper and pencil versions. In some cases values had to be set by the administrators after their arrival at the survey school, when time available for adjustment is very short; and in others the pre-set value varied from one set of equipment to another owing to tolerance in the components. The actual values used were, however, recorded by administrators so that although one-to-one correspondence may not always have been achieved, useful comparisons between the three modes of presentation can still be made. Even though the values for the real instruments were in some cases different from those for photographs or line drawings, the instruments themselves were the same. Photographs were taken of the actual instruments used, and the line drawings made from the photographs; these can be seen in the copies of the questions used, which are to be found in Appendix 7, p. 222.

On the histograms which have been drawn to describe performance, only those values given by at least 1 per cent of the sample have been indicated. The scatter of responses was therefore greater than that shown, and the total length of the bars falls short of that which represents 100 per cent of the sample. The pre-set values for the three modes of presentation, even where different, have been arranged at the same horizontal level.

A general pattern across all instruments can be perceived: the scatter of values increases from line drawing to photograph to reality. The reasons for this may sometimes, but not always, be associated with possible variations of the reading in the case of the real instrument. Other interesting patterns occur for a given instrument across all three modes, and these will be discussed as the results are presented. Some anomalies can be associated with particular drawings, photographs or instruments; attention will be drawn to these also.

The descriptions which follow are in the order in which the instruments are presented in the two paper-and-pencil modes, and for half the sample of pupils in the practical mode.

*Measuring cylinder*

The instrument was graduated from 0 to 100 cm³, with smallest scale divisions of 1 cm³, numbered at 10 cm³ intervals.

Only in the case of the line drawings did the greatest proportion of pupils opt for the correct value (Figure 6.1). In all three modes, at least 10 per cent gave the nearest numbered value (50 cm³ or 40 cm³), and for the photographs and the actual instrument, many pupils appear to have counted down, rather than up, from the numbered mark. Some seem to have mistaken the number 40 for 45 and so arrived at the figure 48. This has only occurred in the case of the real instrument;

**Figure 6.1**   *Measuring cylinder*

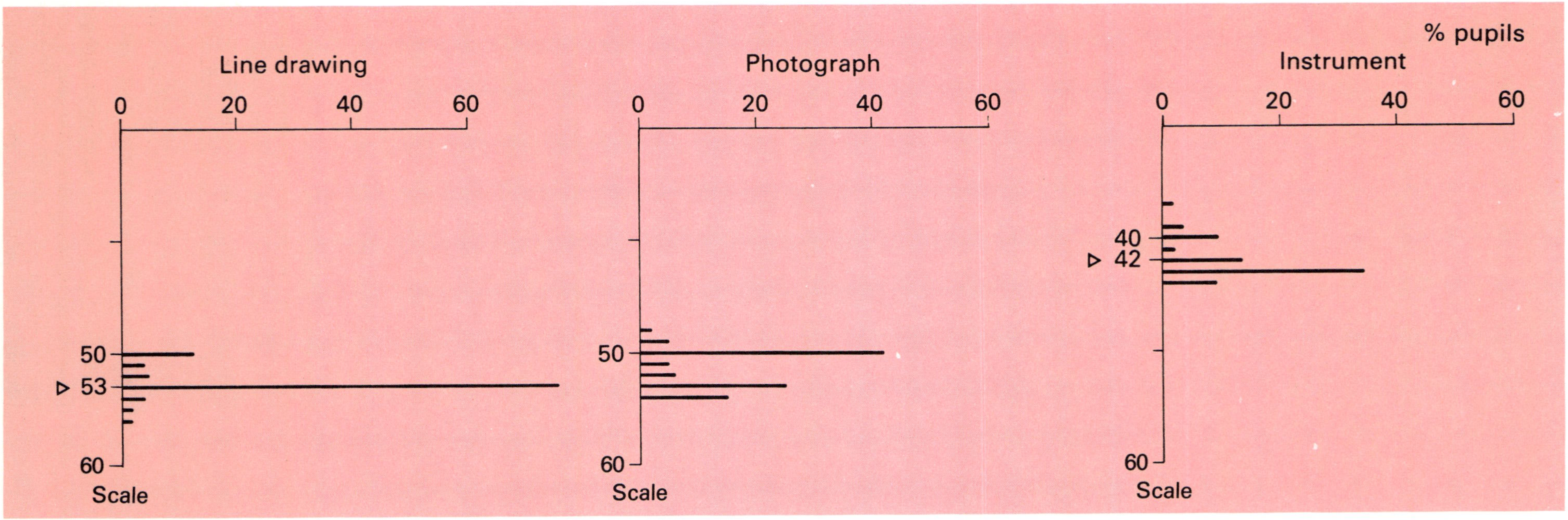

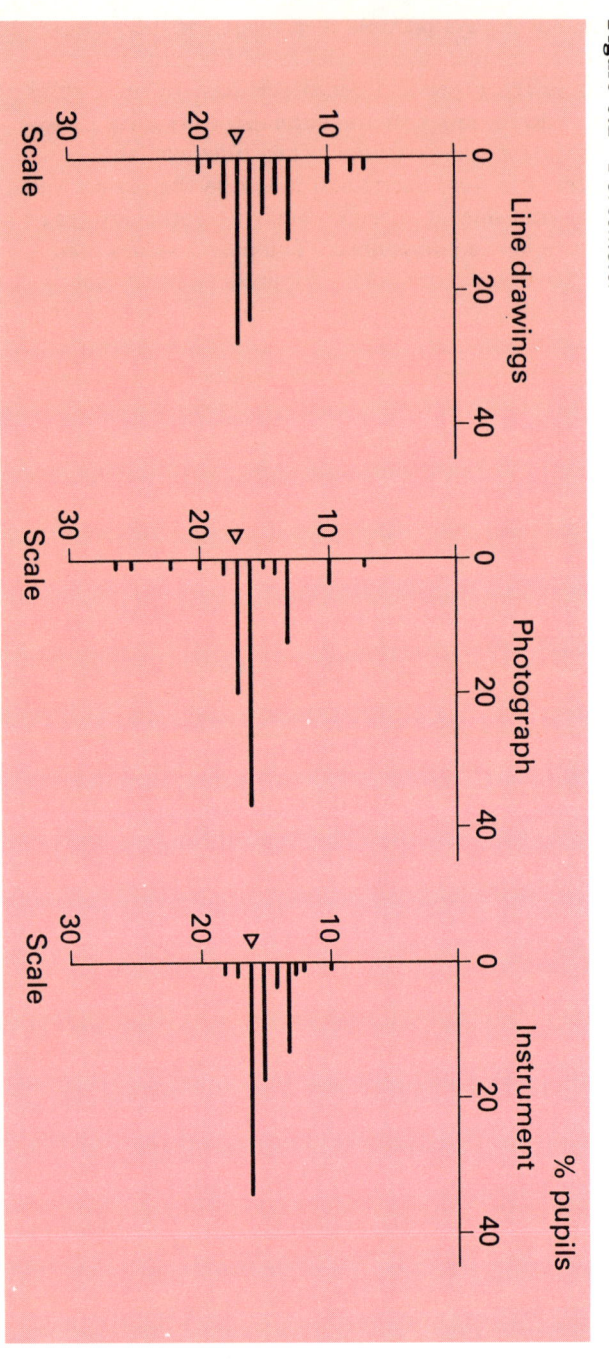

**Figure 6.2**   *Forcemeter*

58

this may be because the figures themselves are not so easy to read as those in the alternative versions.

## Forcemeter

The instrument was graduated from 0–50 newtons, with smallest scale divisions 2 newtons, and numbered at 10 newton intervals. Only part of the scale could be seen at any one time. In the paper versions, the correct reading was 17 N, in the actual instrument, 16 N. Many pupils gave a value 16 instead of 17, perhaps reading to the nearest scale division, but many gave 15 instead of 16 for the real instrument; possibly they were ignoring scale divisions– just estimating a value halfway between 10 and 20, the numbered graduations. In all three cases about 12 per cent of pupils gave 13, which suggests that they were counting each scale division as 1 instead of 2. Some pupils gave 10. In the practical case in Figure 6.2 (p. 58) all values between 10.0 and 10.9 have been included in the bar at 10. However, although a small proportion of pupils gave, or implied, 10.0, around 2 per cent gave each of 10.3, 10.5 and 10.6. These values correspond to the values 13, 15 and 16 already noted above; pupils appear to have counted 10.3 as 13, and so on. This type of error can be detected in pupils' use of other instruments, for example a rule (see below). The value 7, offered by 1 per cent of pupils in both paper versions, could be accounted for in two ways: pupils may have written 7 when they meant 17 (this would entail reading 0 instead of 10) or, a more likely explanation, they may have compounded three errors and counted down 3 divisions from the marked 10 instead of 6 (or 7) up.

## Lever arm balance

The instrument had a single scale from 0–250 grams, with smallest scale division 2 grams, numbered every 50 grams (see drawing in Appendix 7, p. 223).

The paper versions show a value of 116, whereas in the real instrument the mass supplied was 117 grams. The instrument is, of course, subject to a zero error if not on a level surface, but administrators were asked to ensure at the start of each circus that the reading was, in fact, 117 g. The remarkable scatter of values given by pupils which is shown in Figure 6.3 (p. 60) is not, therefore, likely to have been due to such an error, and is in any case replicated to a large extent in the paper versions. In all three versions, fewer pupils gave the correct value than gave some other specific incorrect value. The highest performance was for the line drawing, and even here *only 17 per cent of the pupils give the correct value,* 116. In the practical case, only 3 per cent gave the correct value, 117, but this lay in the middle of a smallest scale division; 16 per cent of the pupils gave a value corresponding to one or other of the adjacent lines. There is again a clear indication that many of the pupils (in this case at least 8 per cent) failed to take account of the fact that the smallest scale division was worth 2 g rather 1 g, thus arriving at too low a value.

## Manometer

The instrument was a glass U-tube half full of coloured water, backed by a vertical wooden board carrying a scale consisting of horizontal lines 1 cm apart (see Appendix 7). In the practical test, the original intention was that the manometer should be set up to measure the gas pressure, which would of course vary from school to school; in practice, it sometimes also varied within a given school, since the pressure was apt to fluctuate according to the use of gas in adjacent laboratories. In addition, there were problems in schools which used bottled gas. For the Fixed Test in 1984, an attempt was made to arrange for a standard reading on the manometer. It proved difficult to find a bung small enough to fit the glass U-tube which would produce an air-tight seal, and so kitchen cling film was used instead. The rubber tubing from the gas was fitted over the cling film, and pupils were again asked 'What is the pressure of the gas at this gas point?'. Administrators were asked to arrange for a difference in level of 18 cm-$H_2O$, with upper and lower levels at 30 and 12 cm respectively. Even where administrators found this possible, fluctuations in room temperature and slow leaks in the system caused variation in these levels and consequently in the value to be recorded by pupils. The histograms in Figure 6.4 (p. 60) show a very great difference in the spread of raw recorded values between paper and pencil version and the practical version. To arrive at a score (discussed later in the chapter), each pupil's value was compared with the administrator's record; the frequency of occurrence of raw values shown on the bar chart is difficult to interpret. However, it is clear from the bar charts relating to the paper versions that in these about 65 per cent of the pupils gave the value of the upper level (36 cm), a few gave the lower level (4 cm), *and only about 6 per cent gave a value for the pressure,* which is represented by the difference in levels. The wording of the question in the paper and pencil versions 'What is the reading on the manometer?' (compared with 'What is the pressure?') may have contributed to this. It is interesting to compare the pattern of performance for this instrument, which is probably not commonly read by pupils of 13 years, with that for a similar requirement–ie the difference between two readings–which occurs when pupils are asked for the length of a rod fixed to a ruler. This is reported towards the end of this section. (See Figure 6.10, p. 64.)

## Thermometer

The instrument had a range of – 10°C to 110°C with smallest scale division of 1°C, numbered every 10 degrees. In the practical test, the thermometer was inserted through a rubber bung closing a vacuum flask so that it was registering the temperature of the water inside. Administrators were asked to adjust this, before the circus began, to 43°C, and it remained reasonably constant for the period of the test. However, in some schools administrators experienced difficulty in adjusting the temperature to, or maintaining it at, the exact value

**Figure 6.3** *Lever arm balance*

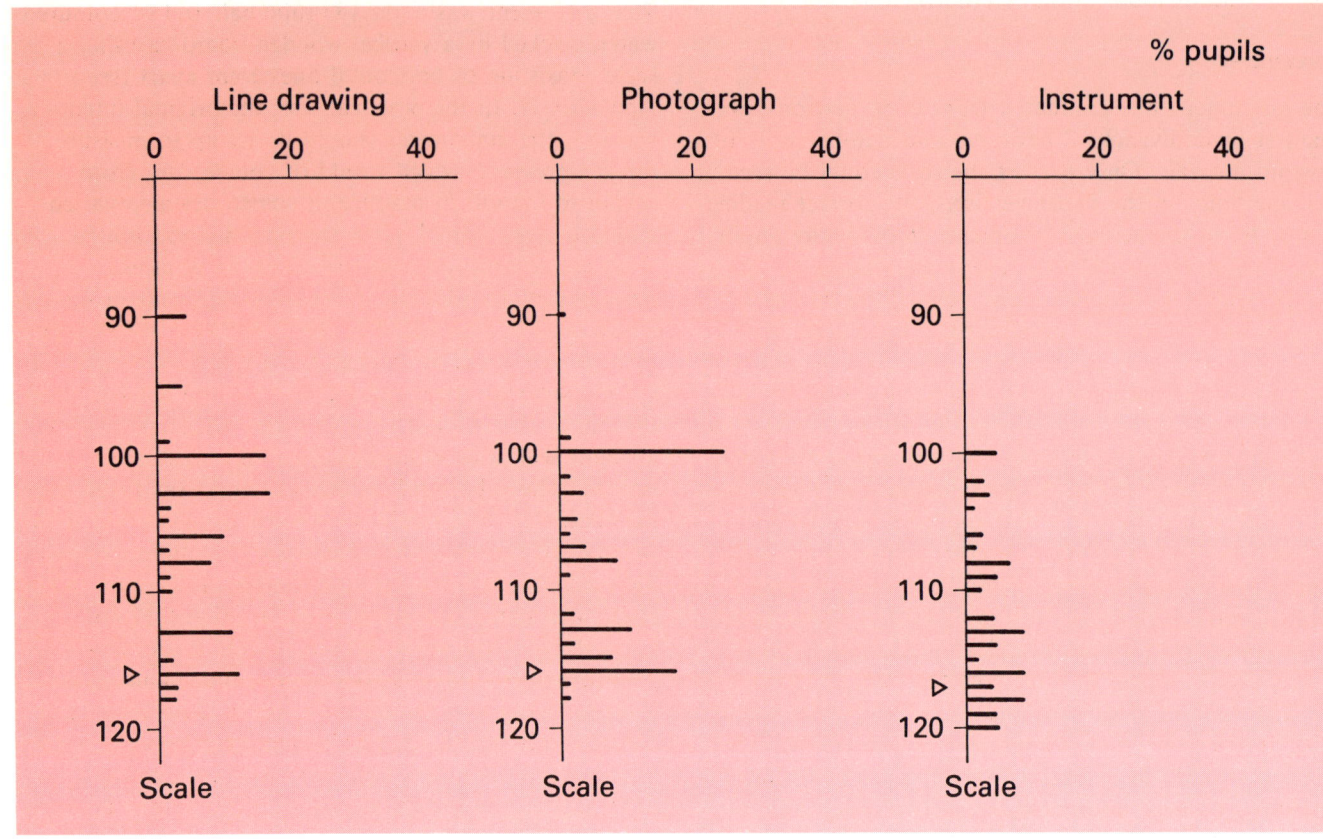

**Figure 6.4** *Manometer*

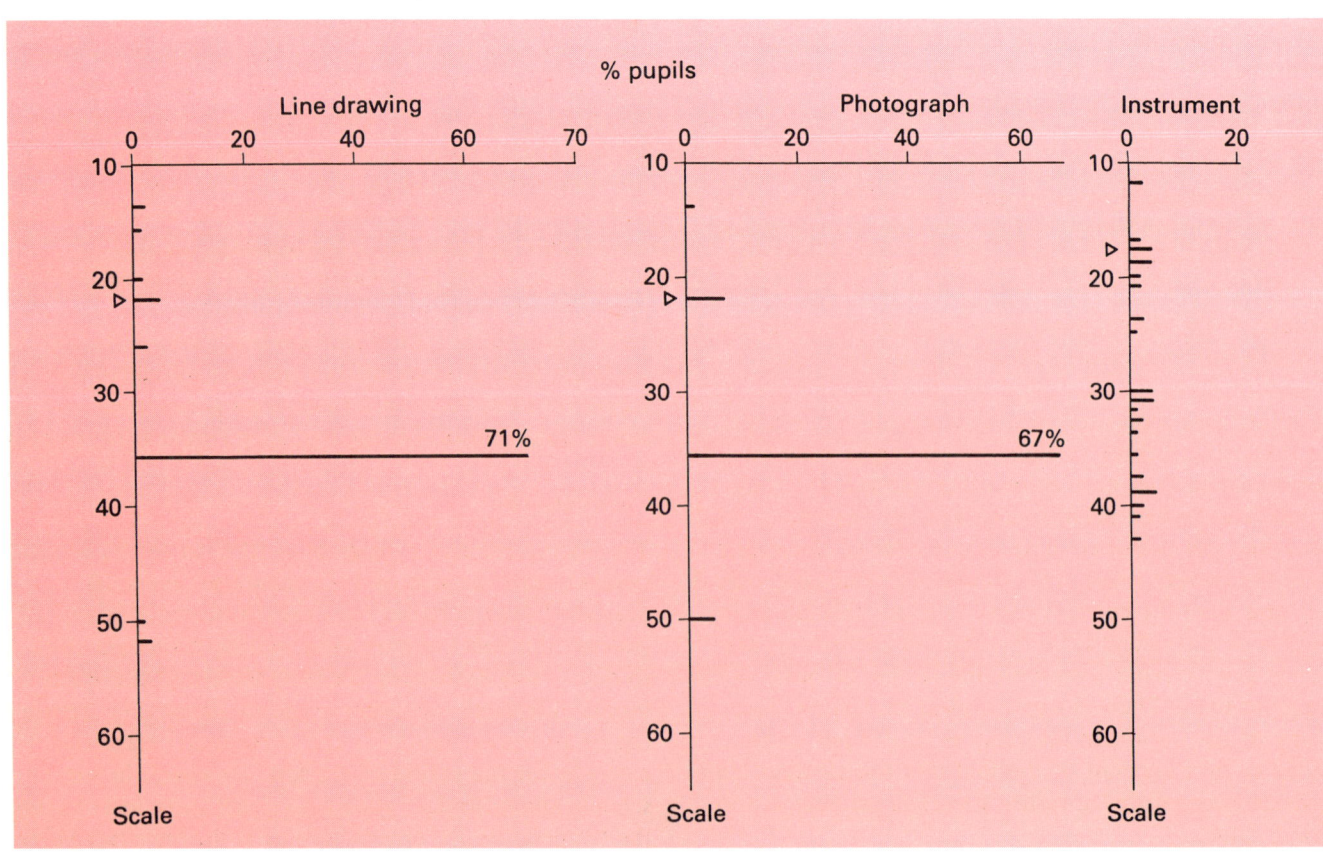

required; for 14 per cent of the pupils, administrators recorded a value outside the range 43 ±1. Thus the apparently lower performance indicated by the scattered responses shown in Figure 6.5 is at least partly due to the fact that different pupils were looking at different readings. Such differences in actual values have been taken account of in arriving at a population score for performance, but not in drawing the histograms such as that in Figure 6.5. While it would be possible to indicate deviations from the correct value (whatever that happened to be for a particular pupil) some advantages of presenting the raw data would be lost in the process; for example the occurrence of peaks at numbered points on the scale might be obscured.

Few pupils made errors in reading the scale using the line drawing. Some, as for other instruments, gave a value corresponding to the numbered line below the reading; and some gave 58 instead of 48. The scatter increased for the photograph, more pupils giving the marked value 40 and some 45, half-way between numbered points. In the case of the actual instrument, some pupils appear to have counted 2 'down' from the numbered line, arriving at a value of 38 instead of 42. Over 2 per cent of pupils gave values 40.2 or 40.3, perhaps by mistake for 42 or 43, a type of error common across many different instruments. About 72 per cent of the pupils gave a value within the range t±1, where t was the value recorded by the administrator.

*Stopclock*

The instrument used is illustrated in Appendix 7 (p. 225). The circular scale was marked every second (or minute) and numbered at 5 second (or 5 minute) intervals. It had separate second and minute hands

sweeping the scale every 60 seconds or 60 minutes. In all three versions, the clock was set at 7 minutes 17 seconds, or 437 seconds. The spread of responses is shown in Figure 6.6, on which values are shown in seconds on the left, and horizontal breaks in the chart indicate discontinuity of scale. In all versions, pupils were asked 'How long had the stopclock been running before it was stopped? (It started at zero)'. Whether pupils answered in seconds or in a mixture of minutes and seconds, answers were converted to seconds for purposes of identifying peaks in the values given.

For all three versions, similar proportions of pupils (just less than a third) gave the correct value either at 437 seconds or as 7 minutes 17 seconds. As for other instruments, responses peaked at certain values, very often the same values for all versions. Possible reasons for the errors are suggested to the right-hand side of Figure 6.6. In many instances, pupils made errors over the minute hand but got the 17 seconds correct. A proportion ignored the minute hand altogether and some—as many as 17 per cent in the line drawing—gave their answer to the nearest minute, ignoring the second hand. It is possible that some of the errors would have been avoided by pupils who were *using* stopclocks rather than just reading them. They would not have been likely to ignore the minute hand, for example, because of the actual time lapse; and the rotation of the second hand might well have alerted them to the need to take note of its position. Since, (in the practical version) about 13 per cent of the pupils appear to have ignored either the minute hand or the second hand, there is a chance that in a real investigation an extra 13 per cent might have arrived at the correct value. This is still *less than half the pupils* in the sample. It would be interesting to compare this performance with the results of an invitation to read the time in hours and minutes on a normal clockface.

**Figure 6.5**  *Thermometer*

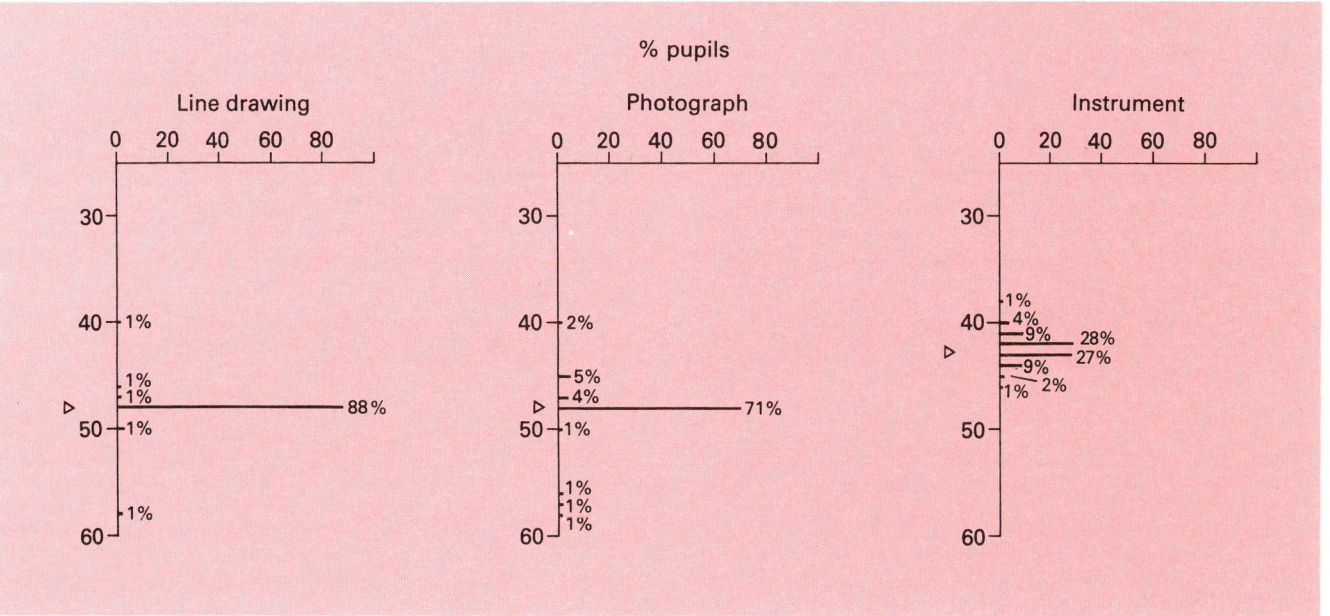

**Figure 6.6**  *Stopclock*

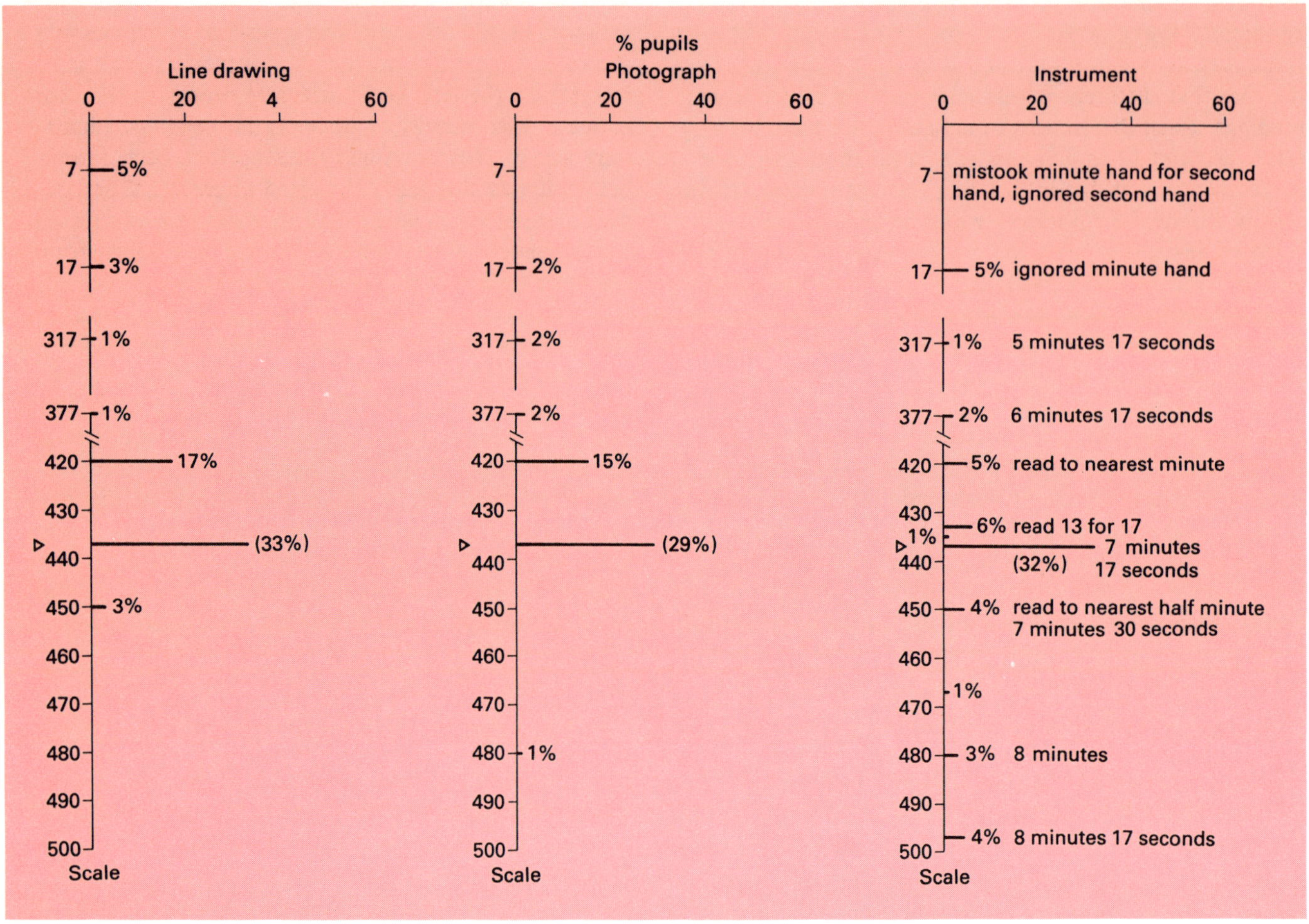

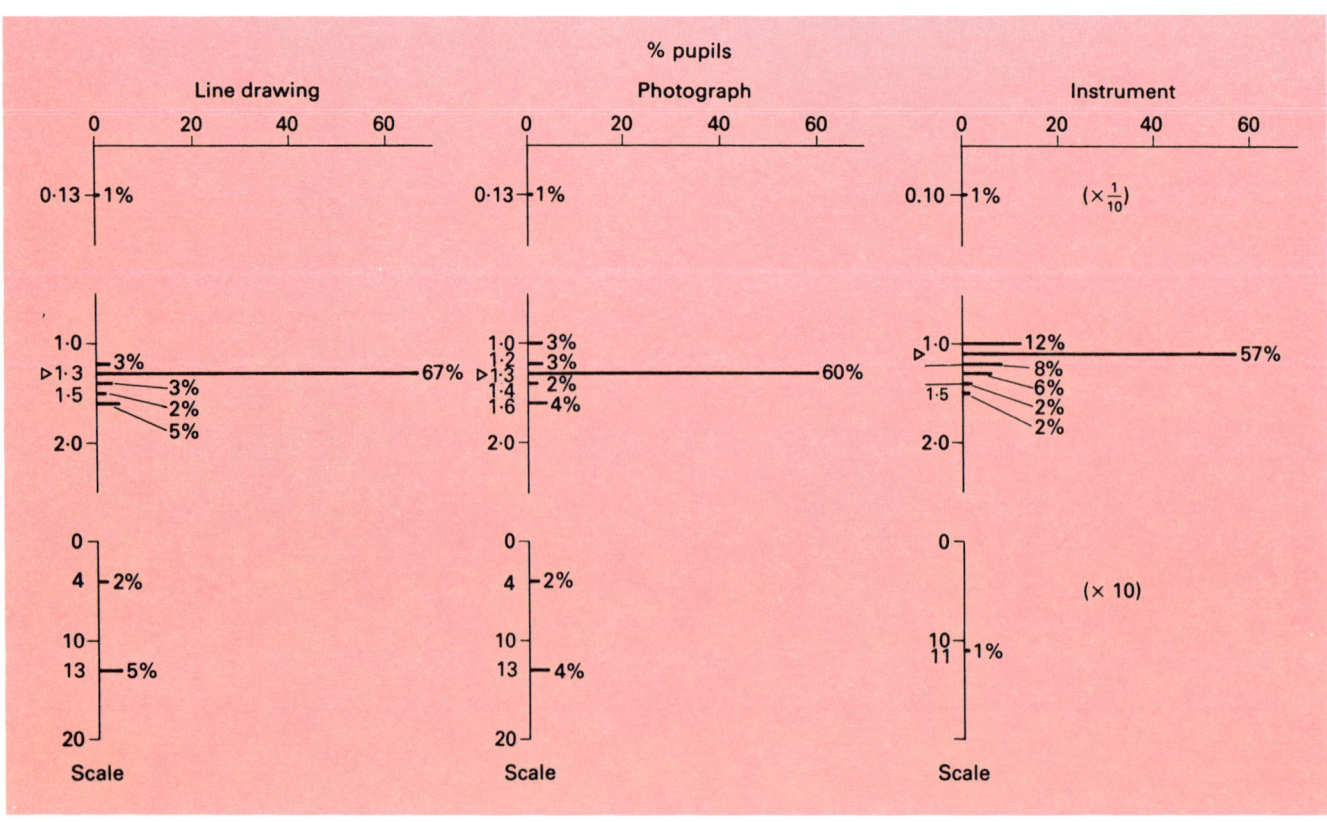

**Figure 6.7**  *Voltmeter*

**Figure 6.8** *Ammeter*

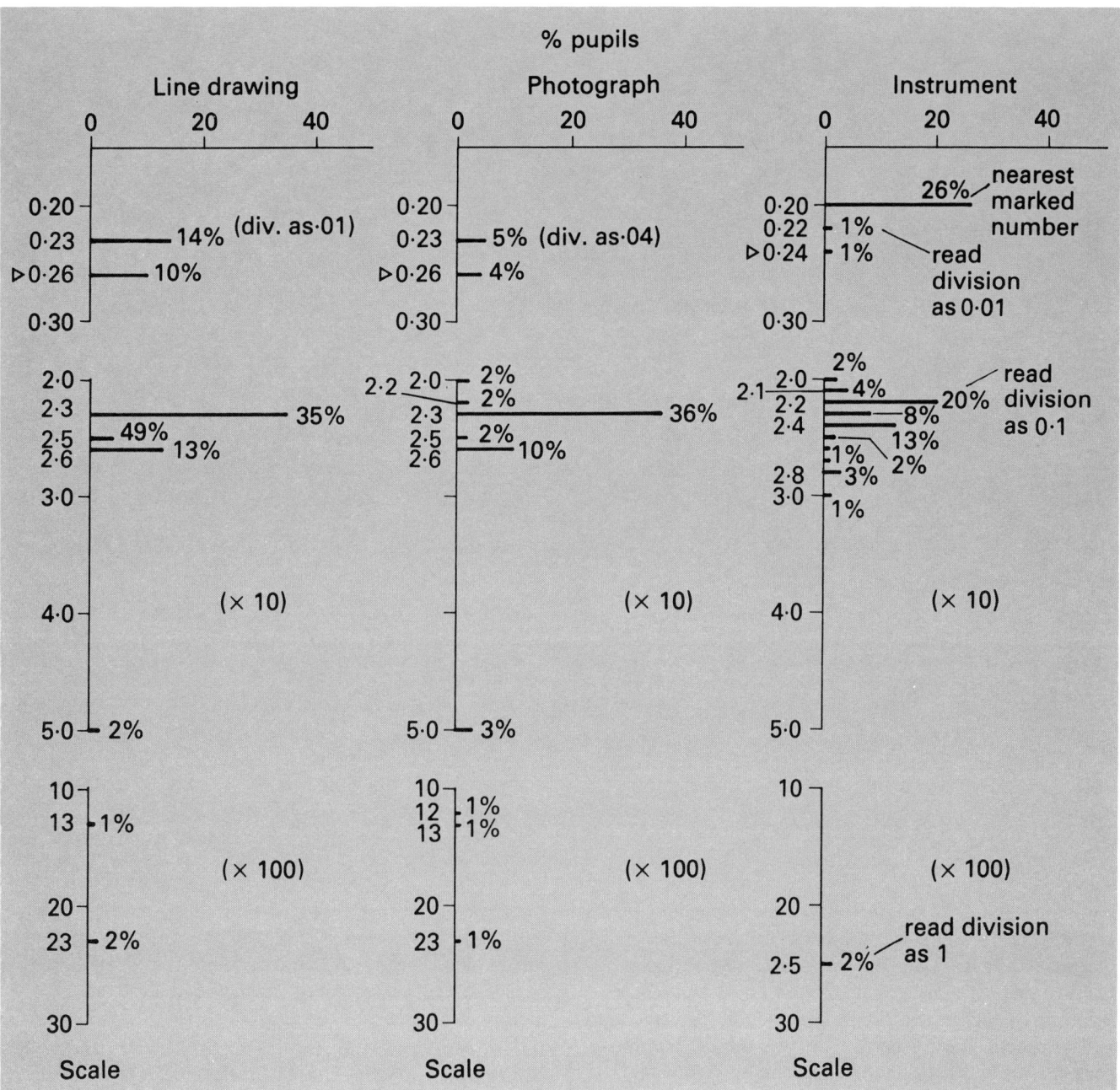

*Voltmeter*

This instrument is not so often in use by pupils of age 13 as an ammeter, but since the scale is usually (as in the survey) easier to read, it is discussed first. The range of the voltmeter used was 0–5 volts, the smallest scale divisions being 0.1 volts, numbered at every volt.

On the two paper versions, the reading was 1.3 volt; but the instrument used in the practical test was part of a simple circuit and gave a reading only when a push button was depressed by the pupil. Variations in resistance in the circuit made it difficult to ensure that the value was, as intended, 1.1 volt, and for some 13 per cent of pupils, administrators reported a value of 1.2 or 1.3. As in the case of the thermometer, raw values have

been used in drawing the histograms in Figure 6.7 (p. 62). When corrections for the deviation of the actual value from 1.1 are made, it turns out that 62 per cent of pupils gave a correct response; this compares with similar proportions for the paper versions. The type of error made is similar for all three versions: about 2 per cent of pupils gave a value ten times too high. This type of error occurs in the ammeter also, and has been noted for age 15 pupils in earlier reports.

*Ammeter*

The range of the ammeter was that in most common use in the school laboratory, 0–1 amp; the smallest scale division was 0.02 amp, and the scale was

63

**Figure 6.9** *Rule–single reading only (actual instrument)*

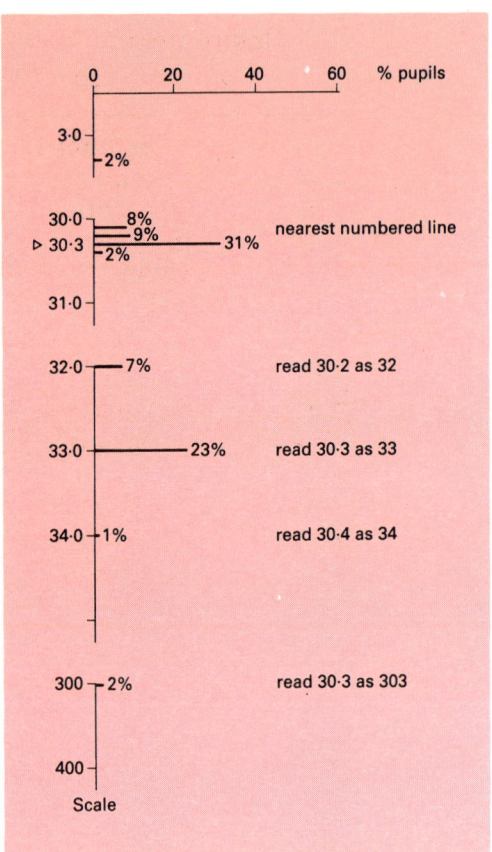

**Figure 6.10** *Ruler–difference in two readings*

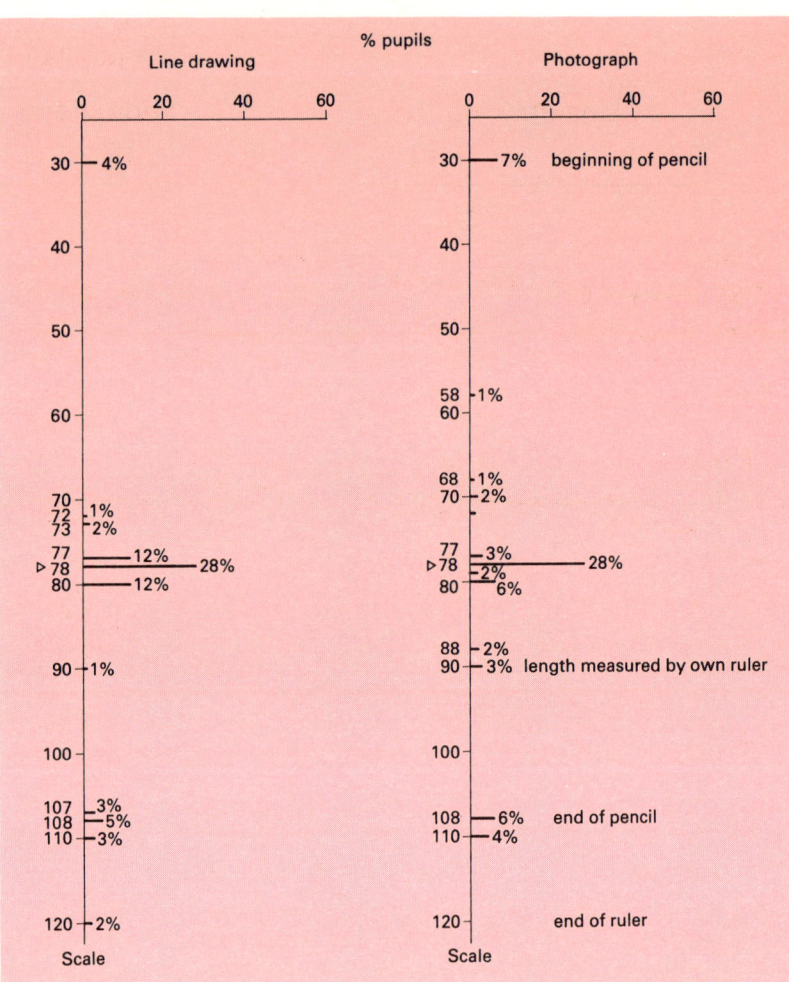

numbered at 0.2 amp intervals. In the paper and pencil versions, the reading was 0.26 amp, while in the practical situation the value was 0.24. The ammeter reading was, like the voltmeter reading, dependent on the components in the circuit of which it formed a part, and in practice, for 6 per cent of the pupils, administrators recorded a value of 0.20. The histogram in Figure 6.8 (p. 63) should be read with this consideration in mind. In all three versions very few pupils gave the correct value (even allowing for the 6 per cent who were correct in giving 0.2). Some pupils took the smallest scale division to have a value of 0.01 rather than 0.02, some were out by a factor of 10, or even 100, and some compounded these errors, as suggested on the right of the figure. In the practical version, 20 per cent of the pupils wrongly gave a value of 0.20, perhaps reading to the nearest numbered line on the scale.

*Ruler*

Discussion of use of the ruler has been left to the end because the task set in the paper versions was essentially different from that in the practical test. In the latter, a thin rod was glued to a half metre rule so that one end was at zero and the other at the point 30.3 cm. Thus, although the question asked was 'What is the length of the stick?', the task involved taking one reading only. In the paper versions, the end of the rod was not fixed at the zero of the scale, and so the difference between two readings was required, as in the case of the manometer discussed earlier.

In the practical task, the half-metre rule had a smallest scale division of 1 mm and was numbered, in cm, every cm. Figure 6.9 shows the distribution of values given by the pupils in the sample. About 42 per cent were within the range 30.3 ±0.1 cm; they were on the right track. Other pupils made errors which were not just of inaccuracy but stemmed from a misunderstanding of the scale. For example, 23 per cent gave a value of 33 instead of 30.3, counting the small scale divisions as centimetres instead of millimetres despite the numbering; others, for the same reason, gave 32 instead of 30.2 and 34 instead of 30.4. Some pupils appeared to make this type of error and then divide by ten; and some gave a value ten times too high; perhaps they were thinking in millimetres but actually writing 'cm'; and as many as 8 per cent gave the value 30, corresponding to the nearest numbered line.

In the paper versions, the ruler was graduated in mm and numbered every 10 mm. In each case the rod

64

**Figure 6.11** *Thin syringe*

Line drawing
% pupils
0
20
40
60
80
0·69
7%
▷0·70
69%
0·71
4%
6·9
2%
7·0
3%
(× 10)
70
3%
71
1%
(× 100)
Scale


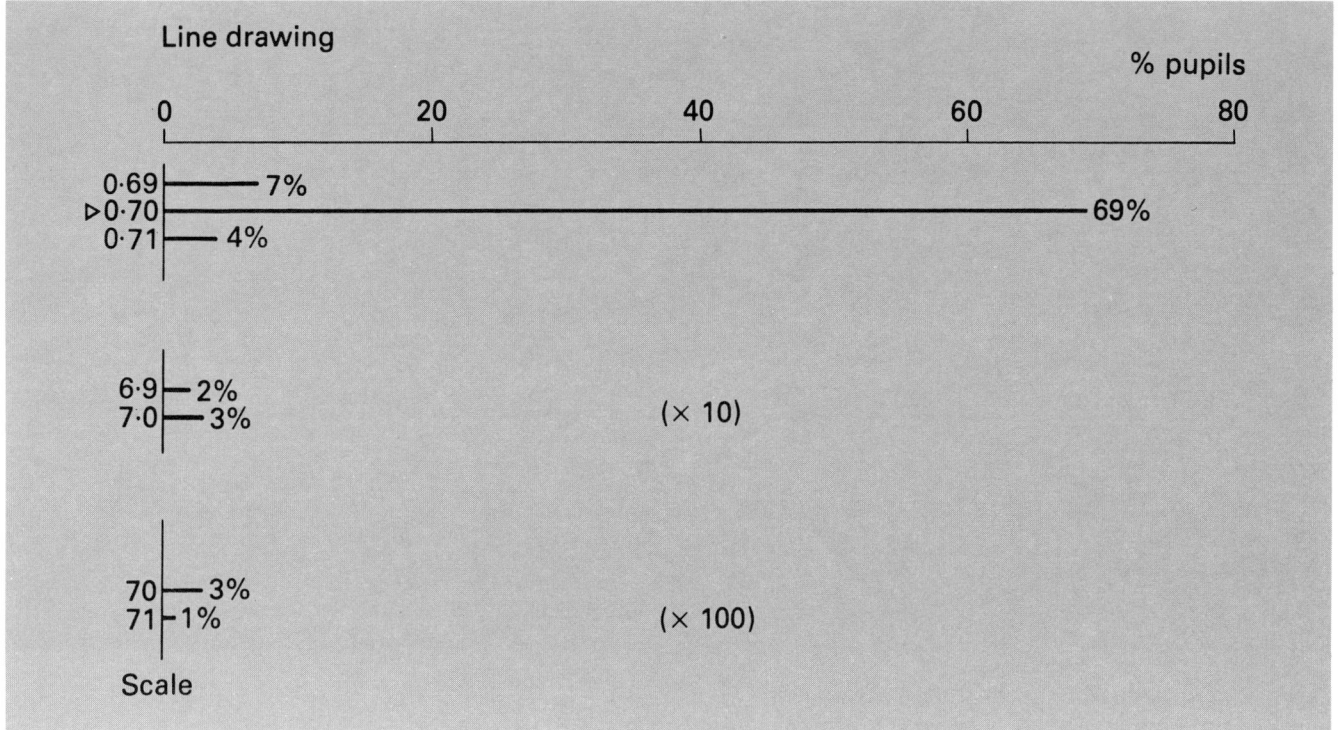

**Figure 6.12** *Fat syringe*

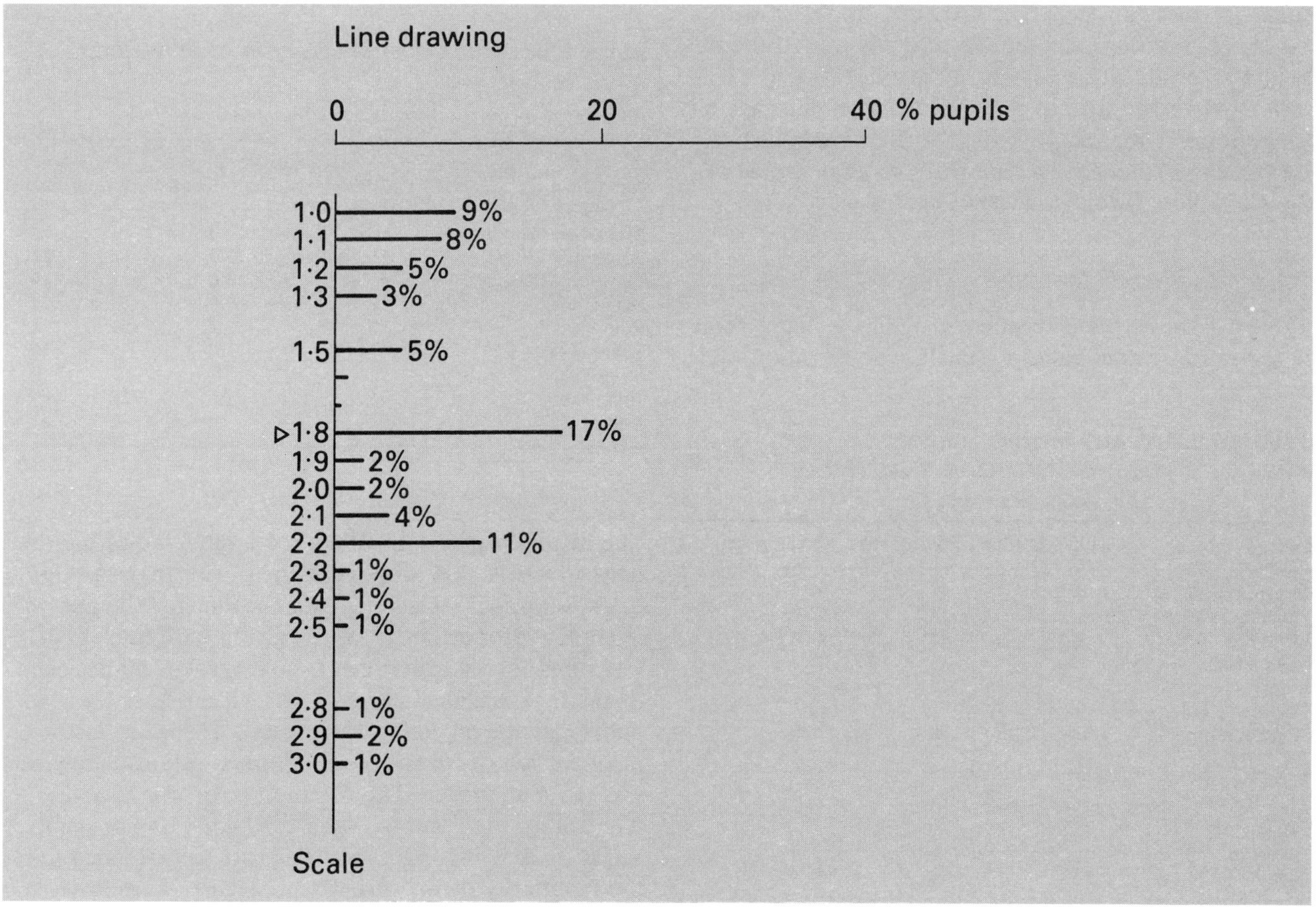

Line drawing
0
20
40 % pupils
1·0
9%
1·1
8%
1·2
5%
1·3
3%
1·5
5%
▷1·8
17%
1·9
2%
2·0
2%
2·1
4%
2·2
11%
2·3
1%
2·4
1%
2·5
1%
2·8
1%
2·9
2%
3·0
1%
Scale

extended from 30 mm to 108 mm, so the correct response was 78 mm. Although different difficulties presented themselves in the two cases, the patterns of response shown in Figure 6.10 share several characteristics. A proportion of pupils gave a value of 30, corresponding to one end of the rod, or 108, corresponding to the other.

Some gave 110 instead of 108, since it was the nearest numbered line on the scale. For the line drawing, 2 per cent gave 120, presumably because this corresponded to the sharply defined end of the ruler. For the photograph, 4 per cent of the pupils gave a value of 90; this corresponds to the length of the rod measured by their own rulers. (The reduction from 90 to 78 between reality and photograph was not duplicated in the line drawing.) The peak of 80 which occurs on both bar charts probably arises through pupils reading the right-hand end of the rod as being at 110 (the nearest numbered line) before subtracting to find its length.

### Syringe

Syringes are not among the measuring instruments included in the practical test at age 13; however, it was of interest to present line drawings of two different types in the probe in order to compare results with those of 15 year olds.

Figure 6.11 (p. 65) shows the distribution of values for the thin syringe; most pupils gave a reasonable value in this case, although a proportion were out by a factor of either ten or a hundred. The increased scatter of values for the 'fat' syringe was almost certainly due to the difficulty of producing a convincing line drawing; it can be seen from Figure 6.12 (p. 65) that many pupils gave a value nearer 1 than 2. It seems that they read the instrument as though the scale were on the far side of the glass tube. (See the question in Appendix 7.)

### Performance levels for scale readings

Table 6.1 shows the percentage of pupils giving a value in the range 'actual value ±1 small scale division', and

**Table 6.1** *Accuracy in scale readings*
(Percentage of pupils within range ±1 small scale division)

| Question order | Line drawing | Photograph | Actual instrument |
|---|---|---|---|
| Measuring cylinder | 82 | 43 | 50 |
| Force meter | 66 | 58 | 62 |
| Lever arm balance | 16 | 28 | 29 |
| Manometer | 5 | 7 | 15 |
| Ruler | 54 | 40 | 43 |
| Thermometer | 90 | 75 | 72 |
| Stopclock | 33 | 30 | 33 |
| Ammeter | 10 | 5 | 6 |
| Voltmeter | 73 | 65 | 83 |
| Thin syringe | 80 | | |
| Fat syringe | 20 | | |
| Number of pupils | 407 | 571 | 842 |

also the percentage of pupils who did not write down a response to the question, for all three versions of each instrument used. In the case of those practical versions where variation in the actual value occurred from pupil to pupil, each pupil value was compared with the corresponding administrator's record so that deviations from the correct value could be computed. For the manometer, since two readings were required, the range of tolerance was doubled.

In the practical mode of testing, the non-response rate was very low for all instruments except the manometer (13 per cent) and the lever arm balance (8 per cent). There was a similar rate for the line drawings but a much higher rate for the photographs, for example 29 per cent for the stopclock and 18 per cent for the manometer.

Pupils were asked to give units in their responses, and these were classified as:

- correct unit, correct abbreviation or name;
- correct unit, appropriate and recognisable abbreviation or name;
- related unit;
- wrong unit;
- no unit.

(Details of this classification can be found in Appendix 7.) Table 6.2 shows the percentage of pupils responding in the four different ways to the request to state units. Only those giving a value are included.

**Table 6.2** *Nature of units given in scale readings (practical version)*
(Percentage of pupils giving indicated response)

| Instrument | Correct | Almost correct | Related | Wrong | None |
|---|---|---|---|---|---|
| Measuring cylinder | 68 | 1 | 0 | 19 | 10 |
| Forcemeter | 43 | 15 | 0 | 11 | 27 |
| Lever arm balance | 66 | 3 | 0 | 5 | 19 |
| Manometer | 1 | 63 | 0 | 0 | 24 |
| Rule | 85 | 1 | 2 | 0 | 8 |
| Thermometer | 67 | 10 | 0 | 3 | 15 |
| Stopclock | 19 | 60 | 0 | 2 | 9 |
| Ammeter | 24 | 9 | 0 | 16 | 49 |
| Voltmeter | 41 | 3 | 0 | 7 | 47 |

The actual instruments all carried a label indicating the units in which they were graduated, with the exception of the stopclock. This does not account for the relatively low proportion of pupils giving (absolutely) correct units for this instrument, however; for 60 per cent of them gave almost correct units—in this case the abbreviated form 'mins.' and 'secs.' The other instrument for which 'almost correct' units were usually given was the manometer. The common error was to give 'cm' rather than 'cm of water'. Whether or not pupils failed to give any units at all appears to be related to the familiarity of the instrument. Figures were lowest for rule, stopclock, measuring cylinder and thermometer, but high for ammeter and voltmeter.

## Summary of results for scale readings

In general, the change in performance from line drawings through photographs to real instruments was similar across all the instruments tried: there was an increase in the scatter of values given by pupils. This is so even when allowance is made for the variation in the correct value itself which occurred in some cases in the practical version. Although the level of performance varied from version to version for any given instrument, the pattern of errors was often quite similar. Thus although paper and pencil tests would give different (usually higher) scores from practical tests, the same errors might well be detected among any group of pupils. However, a different group of pupils answered each of the three versions of the test, so that even where the same errors showed up in all versions, they were not made by the same pupils. Any given pupil might respond differently to different versions of the test, so that reliance on paper and pencil testing for individual assessment might not suffice.

Many types of error are common across a number of different instruments, although performance levels vary considerably from one to another. These errors include the following:

- the nearest numbered line on the scale to the actual value might be given;

- the actual value $\times \frac{1}{10}$, $\times 10$ or $\times 100$ might be given;

- scale divisions worth 2 units might be counted as 1;

- small scale divisions might be counted off in the wrong direction (eg 48 might be called 52);

- there might be confusion between the worth of large and small scale divisions (eg 30.3 might be called 33);

- one or other of two readings might be given when the difference is required.

All these types of error occurred with more than one instrument, and some were common to all. They did not give rise to values which cluster round the correct reading, but to consistent patterns which can usually be observed for all three versions of question-presentation of a given instrument.

An important implication of these findings is that the *particular value* at which the instrument is set, whether in a paper and pencil test or a practical situation, can be expected to affect pupil performance quite markedly. If, for example, a value is within one small scale division of a numbered scale line, many more responses are likely to fall within the range for which full credit is given, and so the mean score will be relatively high. This is an important consideration when comparisons are being made between the performances of different

groups of pupils presented with different values to be read. The effect on performance due to the use of a particular value might over-ride, or at best mask, any which are due to differences in the groups or in their circumstances. Moreover the effects will apply not only in an exercise like Scale readings, but throughout the category **Use of measuring instruments** and, indeed, wherever the reading of scales may be involved. Differences in performance which occur between years or between ages can only be regarded as educationally significant if the examples used are sufficiently varied and numerous to iron out anomalous effects.

## Mean scores for scale readings

The scoring system used in 1984 followed the same general rules as in 1982, when the category was last assessed at age 13; two marks were awarded for values correct to ± one scale division, one mark for values outside this range but within ± three divisions and one mark for suitable units. (Details of unit categorisation are included in Appendix 7.)

**Table 6.3**  *Mean per cent scores for scale readings*

| Instrument | s.s.d. | Value 1982 | Value 1984 | % 1982 | % 1984 |
|---|---|---|---|---|---|
| Measuring cylinder | 1 cm³ | 42 | 42 | 66 | 65 |
| Forcemeter | 2 N | 27 | 16 | 63 | 69 |
| Thermometer | 1 Cdeg | 35 | 43 | 84 | 78 |
| Stopclock | 1 s | 83 | 437 | 53 | 49 |
| Ammeter | 0.02 A | 0.42 | 0.24 | 31 | 23 |
| Voltmeter | 0.1 V | 1.9 | 1.1 | 64 | 68 |
| Manometer | 1 cmH₂O | 30 | 18 | 27 | 11 |
| Balance | 2 g | | 117 | | 48 |
| Rule | 0.1 cm | | 30.3 | | 60 |
| Number of pupils | | | | 916 | 842 |

In general, mean scores for the two years are comparable if the likely effects of the different choice of pre-set values are taken into consideration (Table 6.3). In 1982 the value chosen for the forcemeter (27 N) was midway between two adjacent lines on the scale, and this could well have depressed performance. The value used for the thermometer (35°C) was less likely to be read to the nearest marked division than that (43°C) used in 1984, and this might account for the apparent decrease in performance level. The lower mean score for the stopclock in 1984 is probably due to the change from 1 minute 23 seconds to 7 minutes 17 seconds: in the latter case, those pupils who converted to seconds needed to multiply as well as to add. This probability is supported by the evidence in Figure 6.6 (p. 62). In the case of the ammeter, in 1982 the 'close range' for which full credit was given (0.42 ±0.02) would have included pupil values given to the nearest marked division (0.4); in 1984, because the corresponding range was 0.24 ±0.02, such pupil values would have gained only one mark, not two. Pupils may be more likely to 'round down' to the numbered line below a value than to 'round up'; this seems to be the case, for example, in Figure 6.2 (p. 58). If so, this would account for an increase in the mean score when the voltmeter value was changed from 1.9 to 1.1; certainly among the 77 per cent of the pupils scoring two marks for their value in 1984 were 12 per cent giving a value of 1.0 rather than 1.1.

It appears, therefore, that many of the changes in mean score between 1982 and 1984 might be associated with changes in the values at which the instruments were set. The one instrument for which the value was not changed–the measuring cylinder–was also the one for which there was a negligible change in mean score.

Whichever set of results is considered, there is a remarkable range of mean scores across instruments, as Table 6.3 shows; there appear to be certain characteristics which are likely to cause difficulties. Among the instruments used in 'Scale readings' which exhibit such characteristics are:

— those in which the smallest scale division is a multiple of the basic unit (eg the lever arm balance in which pupils persist in counting in 'ones' instead of 'twos' and so read 156 as 153);

— those in which the smallest scale division is a fraction of the basic unit (eg the ruler, where pupils tend to read 30.2 as 32);

— those in which it is necessary to take account of two readings (eg the stop-clock, where pupils may miss out minutes or seconds);

— those in which it is necessary to find the difference between two readings (eg the manometer or the rule; pupils may ignore one or other reading, or make errors in subtraction).

Familiarity does not appear to have an over-riding effect; for at age 13 the voltmeter is not as often used as either stopclock or balance and yet it is associated with higher performance levels. On the other hand in cases where it is not immediately obvious how a reading should be taken (as in the manometer), repeated use of the instrument would be likely to improve performance.

The general context associated with the instrument does not appear to be a decisive factor; for otherwise there would not be such a great difference in pupil performance in using the ammeter and the voltmeter.

## 6.4  The remainder of the fixed test

A brief description of the remaining eight stations follows, in the same sequence as that in which they were presented to the pupils and using the same question title. The questions themselves are reproduced as Appendix 6. Some of the tasks were very similar, if not identical to, those used in earlier surveys. Where it

seems sensible, in the light of the discussion of the effect of particular choice of value on results, comparisons of performance are made between 1984 and earlier years. For the fixed test itself, the same questions and mark schemes were used at ages 13 and 15; however, comparison across ages is considered in the review report at age 15 (DES, 1988b).

### Results for measuring

The question was in four parts, and can be summarised as follows:

— use a rule to measure the extension of a vertical spring under a load;

— use a forcemeter to find the force needed to hold up a parcel;

— use a measuring cylinder to find the capacity of a beaker which holds more than the maximum scale value of the cylinder;

— use a stop clock to find the duration of a flash of light provided by an electronic unit.

The scoring system was similar to that used for 'Scale readings'. Two marks were given if the response was within ± one small scale division of the expected value; one mark if, although outside this range, it was yet within ± 3 divisions; and a further mark if a suitable unit was used.

**Table 6.4**  *A comparison of results for measuring and for scale readings*
(Per cent mean scores)

| Instrument | Measuring | Scale readings |
|---|---|---|
| Rule | 38 | 60 |
| Forcemeter | 59 | 69 |
| Measuring cylinder | 26 | 65 |
| Stopclock | 73 | 49 |

n = 842

It can be seen that the scores for the use of these four instruments to perform these particular tasks bear little relationship to those for simply reading their scales. Performance is evidently affected by other factors such as the ability to see how to do the job, as in the case of the measuring cylinder, or the manipulative skill required, as for the rule and spring. The flash time was only four seconds, so problems associated with the minute hand did not occur.

### Results for delivery

There were four parts to this task also, but in these pupils were required to use a measuring instrument to measure out a quantity of material; the quantity 'delivered' was checked by the administrator after the circus was over. The tasks were as follows:

— use a half meter rule to cut off 47.3 cm of paper tape;

— use a measuring cylinder to put 55 cm³ into a beaker;

— use a lever arm balance to weigh out 68 g of plasticine;

— put a can on the balance, and then put 82 g of sand into the can.

The scoring system was similar to the one described for 'Measuring', but 3, not 2, marks were awarded for 'deliveries' within the specified narrow range, and there were no marks for units.

**Table 6.5**   *A comparison of results for delivery, 1982 and 1984*

(Per cent mean score)

|  | 1982 | 1984 |
|---|---|---|
| Tape | 60 | 36 |
| Water | 55 | 57 |
| Plasticine | 35 | 60 |
| Sand | 16 | 35 |
| Number of pupils | 459 | 842 |

The values used in this station were the same in 1984 as those used in 1982. However, in 1984 for half the pupils the tasks were presented in a different order, so that pupils who ran out of time did not always miss the same task–'sand'. (This strategy was introduced in 1984 for all stations where possible; its impact on individual mean scores depends on a variety of factors, including average time taken for completion of the particular station.) However, it does not appear to account for the large drop in mean score for 'tape'–from 60 per cent in 1982 to 36 per cent in 1984.

*Results for Tech-check*

Three quite different tasks were presented at this station; the characteristic that they shared was the need for an observer to record on a checklist the techniques pupils actually used in response to the questions. The observers were science teachers from the pupils' own schools, who typically had no more than five minutes in which to familiarise themselves with the checklists and be briefed on other relevant matters by the visiting administrator. The checklists were therefore simple compared to those used in assessing **Performance of investigations**, the tasks being relatively straightforward, and closed rather than open. They were as follows:

— use a thermometer (presented in its plastic case) to measure the temperature (about 64°C) of water in a beaker;

— find the volume of one of 30 marbles given also a 30 cm rule, spring balance, measuring cylinder, and a supply of water;

— find the time of swing of a simple pendulum set up against a background of a card carrying a vertical line.

Credit was given for the way in which the pupils set about the tasks rather than for the results they recorded, and so the mean scores reflect their techniques rather than their numerical results.

**Table 6.6**   *Measuring temperature*

| Action | % pupils |
|---|---|
| Removed thermometer from case | 63 |
| Inserted it the right way up | 91 |
| Read it with the bulb immersed | 74 |
| Waited until the max. temp. was reached | 77 |

n = 842

**Table 6.7**   *Measuring the volume of a marble*

| Action | % pupils |
|---|---|
| Chose to use measuring cylinder | 36 |
| ... in conjunction with water | 32 |
| Added water before marble(s) | 28 |
| Used more than one marble | 5 |
| Read initial water level | 28 |
| Read final water level | 29 |
| Held cylinder upright | 30 |
| Had eye at waterlevel | 24 |

n = 842

**Table 6.8**   *Timing the swing of a pendulum*

| Action | % pupils |
|---|---|
| Initial amplitude less than 10 cm | 22 |
| Direction parallel to card | 84 |
| Bob released, not pushed | 90 |
| Timed between 2 & 5 swings | 11 |
| Timed more than 5 swings | 3 |
| Used the stop clock | 78 |

n = 842

It appears that taking temperatures and timing swings was within the competence of many pupils, but that few of them recalled a displacement method for measuring the volume of a solid. Few pupils availed themselves of the opportunity to use more than one marble or more than one swing in order to improve accuracy.

*Results for lenses*

The tasks at this station were identical to those used in earlier years, the purpose of the exercise being to test the pupils' ability to focus the instruments. The tasks are to identify three groups of four capital letters, the first on card and the last two on slides. The letters are too small to see with the naked eye. In part a) a hand lens is used, in part b) and part c) a microscope; the difference in the last two parts is that in b) the slide is already placed in position on the stage but unfocused, whereas in c) both placing and focusing have to be done by the pupil. In 1984, the mark scheme was changed so that four marks were awarded for each task rather than one—one mark for the recognition of each letter. Because of this, it was now possible for pupils to score a proportion of the marks. This might have caused the increase in the mean score for the hand lens from 68 per cent in 1982 to 77 per cent in 1984.

**Table 6.9** *Responses to lenses*

| Instrument | % pupils scoring | | | | | Mean % scores |
|---|---|---|---|---|---|---|
| | 0 | 1 | 2 | 3 | 4 | |
| Hand lens | 12 | 4 | 13 | 7 | 64 | 77 |
| Microscope | 19 | 0 | 1 | 4 | 76 | 79 |
| Microscope | 22 | 0 | 1 | 1 | 76 | 77 |

n = 842

## Results for Amvocirc

This question had been used previously at age 15, but not at age 13. A cell, two lamps labelled A and B, and a switch are connected in series by 4 mm leads. An ammeter labelled Y, a voltmeter labelled X and six spare leads are provided. Pupils are asked:

— to choose and use a meter to measure the current in the circuit;

— to choose and use a meter to measure the 'voltage' across bulb A.

In each part, four marks could be achieved, one for each action given in Table 6.10.

**Table 6.10** *Responses to Amvocirc*
(Percentage of pupils responding as indicated)

Mean score 27%

| | Point scored | No response |
|---|---|---|
| *Part a)* | | |
| Chose ammeter | 59 | 9 |
| Connected it in series | 20 | 35 |
| Recorded acceptable value | 21 | 37 |
| Gave suitable units | 10 | 37 |
| | | |
| *Part b)* | | |
| Chose voltmeter | 63 | 10 |
| Connected across 'A' | 22 | 41 |
| Recorded acceptable value | 15 | 41 |
| Gave suitable units | 18 | 41 |

n = 842

Table 6.10 shows that slightly more pupils correctly chose the voltmeter in b) than the ammeter in a), probably because the V printed on the voltmeter matched the word voltage in the question. However, fewer pupils connected the voltmeter correctly. Some of the positions in which the meters were wired are shown in Table 6.11.

**Table 6.11** *Positioning of meters in Amvocirc*
(Percentage of pupils connecting meters in positions shown)

| | In series | In parallel across: | | | Cell | Switch |
|---|---|---|---|---|---|---|
| | | Lamp A | Lamp B | Both lamps | | |
| Ammeter | 20* | 11 | 5 | 3 | 12 | 5 |
| Voltmeter | 22 | 14* | 4 | 2 | 6 | 3 |

*Denotes correct positions

n = 842

## Results for mystery liquid

This task was used to find out how well pupils could follow instructions. The motive provided was the identification of one liquid (X) as one of four others (P, Q, R and S) by the addition of one liquid to another in turn, according to instructions. Any observation was to be recorded in boxes in the table of instructions. No recall of specific techniques was required. The liquids were presented in wash bottles and a large supply of chemically clean test tubes was available. Pupils who re-used test tubes, contrary to instructions, incurred penalties since they were liable to get positive results where none should have occurred.

Positive results should have been obtained in four out of ten cases. If, in these cases, responses indicated that the correct action had been taken, two marks were awarded; if positive results were recorded in other cases, marks were deducted. In boxes 2 and 7 the word 'yellow', and in boxes 4 and 8 an indication of a white precipitate, implied that a correct action had been taken.

**Table 6.12** *Positive responses in mystery liquid*
(Percentage of pupils giving the minimum correct response)

| Box number | Minimum response | % of pupils |
|---|---|---|
| 2 | Yellow | 84 |
| 4 | White (ppt) | 39 |
| 7 | Yellow | 28 |
| 8 | White (ppt) | 13 |

n = 842

The mean score for the question was 39 per cent of the maximum. Because of the form of the question, it was difficult to distinguish between those pupils who ran out of time and those who failed to obtain a positive result. However, it seems likely from Table 6.12 that some pupils would have scored more marks had they worked more quickly.

## Results for estimating

Many of the tasks at this section had been set in previous surveys. Pupils were required to make an estimate of the values of eleven different quantities without benefit of any measuring instruments. Values suggested by pupils were divided into four ranges:

**Table 6.13** *Estimating: mean scores, and performance within specified ranges*

| Quantity | Value | % pupils within ranges: | | | | Mean % score |
| | | V. wide | Wide (1 mark) | Medium (2 marks) | Narrow (3 marks) | |
| --- | --- | --- | --- | --- | --- | --- |
| Length of rod | 30 cm | 15 | 21 | 18 | 46 | 65 |
| Time of roll | few s | 25 | 31 | 18 | 26 | 48 |
| Circumf. of circle | 30 cm | 27 | 44 | 12 | 17 | 40 |
| Area of 'disc' | 3 cm² | 49 | 34 | 2 | 14 | 27 |
| Force rub. band | varied | 66 | 22 | 6 | 6 | 17 |
| Temp. in flask | 30°C | 67 | 31 | 5 | 7 | 17 |
| Volume of water | 300 cm³ | 90 | 7 | 2 | 2 | 6 |
| Mass wire ring | 20 g | 72 | 16 | 7 | 5 | 15 |
| Area leaf-shape | 200 cm² | 79 | 16 | 2 | 3 | 10 |
| Mass of block | 5000 g | 87 | 5 | 3 | 5 | 9 |
| Volume of water | 25 cm³ | 74 | 9 | 13 | 4 | 16 |

n = 842

narrow (±10 per cent); medium (±20 per cent); wide (±50 per cent) and very wide. Marks awarded were 3, 2 and 1 for the first three ranges. On this basis mean scores ranged from 6 per cent for the volume of coloured water in a plastic lunch box to 65 per cent for a short length of wooden rod.

Results from similar tasks set in earlier years suggested that pupils are better at estimating length than any other quantity; this is confirmed by figures in Table 6.13, and where values were unchanged mean scores were very similar. Perhaps the most interesting figures in the table are those in the 'very wide' range, in which is shown the percentage of pupils with estimates outside the range ±50 per cent of the actual value. While perhaps there is no great merit in being able to estimate quantities very closely (except in special circumstances in which case the skill can be practised), there is something to be said for getting within 50 per cent; most 13 year olds cannot do this for 7 of the 11 quantities chosen.

*Results for roundabout*

This station also involved estimation, but in a more active sense: pupils were required to leave behind specified quantities of material. Marks were awarded for quantities within ranges defined in the same way as for Estimating.

Performance was very similar to that in 1981, when a similar station was used. But, in the case of mass, although there was no change in the value used, the material itself was changed from sand in 1981 to beans and oats in 1984; mean scores for the last two were similar to one another, but about 10 per cent higher

than that for sand. Beans take up about the same space as the equivalent mass of water, and oats nearly twice as much, while sand takes up less than half the space. Thus it is difficult to see how the change in performance can be accounted for in terms of the change in the density of the materials used.

## 6.5 Summary

Pupils are reported by the administrators to have enjoyed the activities involved in assessing **Use of apparatus and measuring instruments** during the course of the surveys. In general, they have proved quite able to cope with the circus mode of practical testing. However, competence in reading scales and use of instruments is lower than would seem necessary for the successful undertaking of science courses as currently organised. Practical work is often intended to support concept development; for example ammeter readings are used in the derivation of the laws of electrolysis and meter rules in the establishment of Hooke's law. If pupils cannot read the instruments, this method of teaching wastes time and causes frustration and confusion. It is possible that, given a more motivating purpose for the use of the instruments, performance would be enhanced. Evidence from Category 6 suggests, for example, that pupils might 'learn on their feet' through evaluating their own efforts. Nevertheless there are some errors, often associated with particular values, ranges, or scales, which appear to be affecting overall performance; it is possible that the incidence of these errors would be reduced if the attention of teachers and pupils were to be drawn to them.

**Table 6.14** *Roundabout: mean scores, and performance within specified ranges*

| Quantity | Value | % pupils within ranges: | | | | Mean % score |
| | | V. wide | Wide (1 mark) | Medium (2 marks) | Narrow 3 marks) | |
| --- | --- | --- | --- | --- | --- | --- |
| Length (pencil line) | 11 cm | 13 | 24 | 25 | 38 | 63 |
| Volume (water) | 100 cm³ | 15 | 45 | 17 | 23 | 49 |
| Length (tape) | 50 cm | 24 | 35 | 19 | 22 | 47 |
| Mass (beans) | 100 g | 37 | 33 | 14 | 17 | 37 |
| Mass (oats) | 100 g | 36 | 35 | 14 | 15 | 36 |

n = 842

# 7

# Observation

## 7.1 Introduction

**Observation**, defined as a practically based science activity, has had a place in the science assessment framework since its inception. The initial descriptions of the activity to be assessed in this category varied across the three ages surveyed. At age 11 the activity was perceived to be the selection from a set of possible observations those which were relevant. At age 13 the nature of the category was seen to encapsulate three characteristics. These were represented in questions singly or in combination: pupils therefore could be asked to observe using a *range of senses*; to *select* the *relevant* observations and to *use observations* to classify, sequence, explain or predict. At age 15 a more detailed description of *scientific* observation was given, the main feature of which was the statement that observation was *theory-laden*. Thus it was claimed that scientific observation could be distinguished from other types of observation. Each description of the observation activity relied on general terms which allowed considerable latitude in their interpretation.

The structure of the category system reflected an attempt to isolate the 'process' and concept aspects of science. It was felt that Category 3 was principally concerned with the assessment of 'processes'. In practice this meant that pupils' performance on the questions was not dependent on the recall and application of taught science concepts. The chapter describes the development of the category through the questions and mark schemes used, the ones rejected and those remaining.

The chapter is in the following sections:

7.2   History and present position

7.3   Test administration

7.4   Results—overall

7.5   Results—'Making observations'

7.6   Results—'Using observations'

7.7   Discussion

7.8   Implications

## 7.2 History and present position

The category has been included each year in the surveys at age 13. The results are reported in DES, 1982a, 1984a, 1985a, and 1986a. The initial differences expressed at each age concerned the definition of the nature of the category. The differences were reflected in the choice of *content* in the question used. The original age 13 question bank was based on the view that **Observation** was a general skill applicable and relevant across the curriculum. This view was the result of the influence of the cross-curriculum model of assessment (Kay, 1975) adopted by the APU. Observation was regarded as a skill which was not exclusive to science. It was proposed to measure levels and patterns of peformance outside the framework of science as well as within it. As a consequence, questions were written which allowed the 'process' of observation to be applied to everyday content where responses could not be classified as 'scientific'; or to both everyday and scientific content which allowed a variety of response—including those selected observations which could be labelled 'scientific'. Both types of questions are published in the first survey report (DES, 1982a). At age 15 the first survey report included only questions with a scientific content (DES, 1982b). The activity being assessed at age 15 was not perceived to be a general skill but rather *scientific observation*.

The two question banks at ages 13 and 15 had a common structure of Question type, (described in the question descriptors—DES, 1982a), a different selection of question content, and yet very similar mark schemes. The latter point was significant. Whilst there was a clear attempt to look at a wide range of **Observation** skills at age 13, the age 15 position was far from clear-cut. The age 15 strategy was based on the assumption that scientific observation was theory-laden. It was not possible, however, to demand the recall of science concepts and to assess the pupils' performance in relation to their recall. Consequently if a scientific term such as 'spikelet' was used to describe and identify different grasses, then the meaning of the term was illustrated rather than demanded. Similarly, if different beetles were being compared, precise language was not demanded; thus 'mandibles' could be described as 'nippers' or 'claws', etc. There was therefore no distinction made, in terms of the score achieved, for the different theories applied. Exactly the same policy and types of mark schemes were used at the lower two ages for questions with a science content. In addition, at both age 13 and age 15 there were questions in the banks which had a science content and were marked in terms of the *scientifically correct* inferences or explanations derived. For example a question where children had to observe both the smell and the sensation on their skin of different liquids also required them to select the following explanation for their observations: '. . . the change of state from liquid to vapour causes cooling'.

At the time of the first survey there were some differences between the banks at each age, chiefly related to the choice of question content. At each age there was also some difficulty in translating the activity of 'observation' into questions which did not conflict with their position in a 'process' category in an assessment framework where categories were *either* 'process' dependent *or* concept dependent. These difficulties have been the subject of discussion and research by the team since 1980.

In the 1980 survey three sub-categories were assessed: **Using a key; Observing similarities and differences; Interpreting observations**. After the 1980 survey it was agreed that assessing the general skill of observation was not part of the remit of the science assessment. The categories were domain-referenced and it was found not to be possible to generate parallel domains of observation in which performance was defined by non-science content or a science content. The future assessments were therefore to be concerned with scientific observation. The problem was to define *scientific observation*.

An argument was put forward that the distinction between *making* and *using* observations ought to be significant in the debate about what constituted scientific observation. One feature of the 'using' observations bank was the observation of variable-based relationships. The relationships were such that one or more variables had to be linked to another. The relationships had to exist over time and be repeatable. They were not merely features of the particular resource being observed. It was suggested that in defining such a relationship whilst carrying out a task, the focus was automatically on what was scientific and relevant, and hence the observation was 'scientific'. The link with the category **Interpretation** was raised as part of this argument.

The outcome of the discussion was a rejection of the position described in the previous paragraph and an amalgamation of the two early sub-categories, 'making' and 'using' into one category. The argument was that the initial distinction between 'making' and 'interpreting' was artificial and difficult to distinguish for scoring purposes. Whatever the argument, it remained the case and still does, that when pupils were asked to make observations but actually made inferences they failed to score. Similarly when pupils were expected to infer, for example when asked what

they could tell about coloured inks from a chromatogram of them, they failed to score full marks for merely making observations. One consequence of this decision appears to have been a reduced representation of variable-based questions in the bank as the overall bank numbers increased, since these emphasised the separate and distinctive aspect of 'using' which had been rejected.

The position at age 13 in the 1981 survey was described in the following paragraph (DES, 1984a):

'Using observations is an integral part of performing scientific investigations. Pupils have to translate real events into a set of relevant observations and then make further abstractions from the data in order to progress. In Category 2, **Use of apparatus and measuring instruments**, observation is restricted both in context and range. The context is restricted to the instruments and procedures tested. The observations required are focused and dependent almost entirely on sight. Within the context of a scientific investigation, however, observation includes all the senses and is not a passive process. What the pupils observe when confronted with unfamiliar objects and events is determined by the interaction between what is new and their previous experience and understanding. What the pupils bring to the new situation is a pre-existing structure acquired through the pupils' experience both within science and outside it. This pre-existing structure dictates how the pupils perceive the world and hence what they notice and select as relevant. Category 3 focuses on this aspect of science'.

**Observation** was linked to the initial reformulation stage in problem-solving, in which a problem is crystallised from a presented situation. There was now agreement across the ages that scientific observation was theory-laden and that only this kind of observation should be assessed at each age. Unfortunately no practical definition for distinguishing between theory-laden observations and others was advanced. During further discussions in 1982 the key to scientific observation was considered to be the *relevance* of the observations to science. There followed a review of the merged question banks representing **Making and interpreting observations**. The review was to pay particular attention to the notion of scientific relevance.

One outcome of the review was that the 'key' questions from the 1980–81 surveys (DES, 1982a, 1984a) were not to be included in the main category for future surveys. The reason for this was that performance on the 'key' questions was dependent on understanding the working of a key and, more importantly, on understanding, linguistically, the terms used. These two demands functioned as hurdles in the questions, and the observation demand was generally secondary and often trivial.

Two other types of question were rejected. These were, 'match a magnified part of a presented entity to the whole' and 'make a drawing of an object's important features'. The skills applied in these questions were considered to be relevant only to specific contents. In other words the content defined the 'process', and what was being assessed was a particular *representation* of observations rather than the observations themselves. A clear science frame of reference was reflected in the mark schemes for these questions. The questions stood apart from others in the bank in that they did not allow general application across a range of content.

The other Question type rejected was concerned with the 'sequencing of events'. Initially these questions were about observing regularities. This meant they could include observing a set of photographs taken over time of, for example, a group of people walking towards a camera, frogs jumping, birds flying, or plants responding to seasonal changes. It was agreed in 1981 that observing regularities was not of itself scientific; rather, it was the characteristics of the regularity which made it scientifically relevant. The regularity had to occur over time and be repeatable and not an artefact. This meant that a sequence of a candle burning under a beaker, a frog jumping, etc could all be legitimate questions; but it was then decided that the demands of such a question were first and foremost to 'know' in advance the sequence and only then to make observations in order to rearrange the photographs to match the known sequence.

After the review and rationalisation of the banks the position at age 13 prior to the 1984 survey was as follows:

- only scientific observation was to be assessed;

- both everyday and scientific content could be used if the potential for scientifically relevant observation existed;

- some tasks asked of the pupils were regarded as scientific, eg classification, and discerning variable relationships;

- most questions did not require the recall of taught science concepts; their mark schemes reflected a wide range of possible responses;

- some questions required the recall of taught science concepts and were marked accordingly;

- the resource used could be object(s), photographs or events;

- the questions varied in the extent to which they focused on the required observations;

- seven different types of questions were represented in the bank (see Table 7.1, section 7.4).

## 7.3 Test administration

The intention was to produce a domain of observation tasks to represent the activity of scientific observation. The total number of questions developed was significantly lower than that for the other generalisable categories of assessment, because of constraints of time and finance. To trial practical questions and to conduct practical tests in a survey is costly and time-consuming. Apparatus and consumables had to be purchased, trialled and refined along with the question. The development of a resource in this category could require the tracking down of particular shell species or the growing of crystals all with matched specifications. It was essential that the pupils were provided with an identical resource, but it was rare that any suitable resource existed in the quantities required, usually 12–16 matched sets. This had consequences for what the team could achieve in the time available. It also has considerable implications for any classroom-based assessment of such activities. The present joint bank at age 13 and 15 contains 97 questions. Forty-five questions were randomly selected at each age for any one survey test. This constituted three practical test administrations. The variation in performance due to the selection of questions was particularly high in this category. Ideally a much larger number of questions should have been surveyed, but this was not possible because of the cost.

The tests are administered using a circus arrangement details of which are given in the teachers' report 'Practical testing at ages 11, 13 and 15', Welford, Harlen and Schofield, 1985. A typical test would include 15 questions arranged in nine eight-minute stations. The time for each question to be completed could vary from two to eight mintues and questions were combined to produce an eight-minute test slot. The time for each question was derived during the trials and was based on the criterion that the majority of pupils could comfortably complete the task. The intention was to preclude the likelihood of the assessment being a speed test. The tests were administered by science teachers trained over a two-day period. The apparatus was provided in a standard form by Philip Harris Ltd.

## 7.4 Results—overall

The bank in this category, as in others, has changed significantly since it was established in 1980. Initially the changes were due to the inclusion of new questions. Since 1981 the changes have reflected shifts in the definition of the category. It is therefore not useful or helpful to discuss changes over the years in the overall category mean scores. There had been a decrease in overall scores from just over 50 per cent to just over 35 per cent from 1980 to 1984 (see Chapter 4, section 4.5). This decrease is only significant in terms of the questions removed from and added to the bank. Since

1980, questions which allowed observation of everyday content without any particular science frame of reference have been removed. An example of such a question required pupils to select the drawing of a telehone which matched the telephone in a photograph. Most pupils performed well on these questions. Additions to the bank have tended to be based on a science content. The rationalisation and merging of the age 13 and 15 banks has meant that questions from the original age 15 bank are now included in the survey at age 13. Several of these questions have been of the 'structure and function' type which require the recall of taught science concepts; performance on these questions is generally low.

Table 7.1 shows the results for the questions used in the 1984 survey at age 13. The table indicates the different type of questions used, the results for the population and for girls and boys separately, and the range of scores for each Question type.

There are differences in mean scores between the various types of question. However, comparisons are precluded on two counts: firstly there is only a small number of questions within some of the Question types; and secondly the range of scores indicates a considerable difference in performance within type, and an overlap in performance levels across type.

**Table 7.1**  *'Observation': a summary of mean scores on different types of question (1984)*

| Question type | No. of questions | % mean score | | | |
| | | All | Girls | Boys | Range |
| --- | --- | --- | --- | --- | --- |
| (1) Given objects or photographs group objects into self defined classes, or identify the rules used to classify the objects, and add further objects to classes | 6 | 32 | 33 | 30 | 11–60 |
| (2) Given objects, photographs or events describe similarities and differences | 12 | 41 | 43 | 39 | 18–55 |
| (3) Given an event make a record of change | 3 | 31 | 33 | 30 | 18–43 |
| (4) Given an object select the matching drawing from a range of drawings | 5 | 33 | 35 | 32 | 14–53 |
| (5) Given events make a record of observations and either give or select an appropriate explanation | 3 | 31 | 33 | 29 | 11–46 |
| (6) Given objects, photographs or events make a note of differences and make or select a prediction consistent with the observed data | 8 | 40 | 40 | 39 | 26–68 |
| (7) Given events make a record of changes, and either make a prediction consistent with the data or identify a pattern in the observed changes | 8 | 42 | 43 | 41 | 10–80 |

The consistent trend, noted previously, for girls to achieve higher scores is apparent in the table of results. This trend has occurred at each age for each survey. Girls perform at a higher level on the type of questions which are in the majority in the bank, but on many questions (35 per cent) the performance of girls and boys is similar or identical. On five out of 45 questions boys performed at a higher level than girls. These questions included the following contents: screws, electrical circuits and animal alimentary canals. The influence of content on the performance of some boys and girls is noted in Chapters 3 and 11 of this report.

The performance difference between girls and boys in this category cannot be accounted for by content alone. There appears to be a complex interactive effect related to the mode of pupil response, the test context itself and some content influence, both positive and negative. These effects are discussed more fully in Chapter 3.

## 7.5  Results–'Making observations'

To review performance in this category questions have been grouped according to whether they are concerned with making observations or making and using observations. Several different types of questions were used to assess pupils' performance on **Making observations**. They included classification, describing similarities and differences, describing changes in events and matching; these are the first four types listed in Table 7.1.

*(i)  Classification*

The questions used required pupils to *identify* grouping criteria from presented groups; to *generate* their own criteria for grouping and/or explain their choices, and finally to *add* objects to presented groupings and explain their actions. Since 1980 ten different questions of this type have been included in the surveys.

When the content of the questions was 'everyday', performance on the *identification* of grouping criteria was generally high, the mean score being about 60 per cent. Irrespective of the content of the questions, when pupils had to *reclassify*, mean scores dropped by about 20 per cent and the number of pupils failing to respond to this type of demand also increased. This finding did not mean that pupils could not generate classification systems. For example when asked *just* to classify 11 vertebrae from the backbones of 3 different animals the mean score was 63 per cent. A similar question about teeth had a mean score of 60 per cent. The difficulty pupils have in *generating* classification criteria must be considered in relation to the presented resource and the question asked. For the questions which required pupils to both identify and then reclassify a very particular type of pre-selected resource was used. There was in addition a deliberate policy to include redundant distractor variables such as colour and shape. The pupils therefore had to operate within a very closed, pre-modelled system in which both the model and the variables had to be identified. Many of the pupils' reponses indicated a failure to operate within the presented model. For example in a question about grouping 18 different liquids, the samples had been so chosen that the only exclusive reclassification was by colour and opaqueness. The liquids were not labelled or identified, but many pupils classified them by type, eg antiseptics, disinfectants, cleaning things etc.

The pupils in the lower performance bands tended to identify the criterion for two groups but described the third group in terms of a different attribute. More of these pupils also failed to operate within the presented 'assessment model'. This type of error, ie failure to recognise the linguistic and practical cues used by the assessor to denote what has relevance to the task, has distinguished the performance of the lower band of pupils from the top bands in other categories as well. The other finding of note is that more pupils can classify or add additional objects to a presented grouping than can describe their reasons for so doing. The performance of the lower bands indicates that even fewer of these pupils can provide a written explanation for their grouping.

*(ii)   Describing similarities and differences*

The questions used have generally been concerned with the comparison of static objects and in some instances photographs. Some questions allowed data to be collected, or required the comparison of dynamic systems such as ball bearings moving on a track. One major difference between these questions and the ones discussed in the previous section was that pupils were given *no indication* of *what* to *observe* and *no purpose* for their observations. In each survey a large number of this type of question has been included. The general results for these questions indicated that the majority of pupils attempted them and made comparisons. A minority of pupils across all of these questions, ~15 per cent, wrote about at least one attribute of the presented resource without making a comparison between the objects for the same attribute. The most common error was that pupils did not state a comparison but merely implied it. In general few responses were based on recall or unsubstantiated inferences rather than observation (~2 per cent). Pupils found it more difficult to state similarities than to describe differences. This finding occurred across a variety of questions in each survey at age 13, but was not replicated at the older age. Performance was depressed by a failure to identify a sufficient number of differences and similarities. This was the overriding reason for low mean scores on these questions. It was not the case that pupils had insufficient time to do the task, rather they were unable to select any additional relevant observations. The pupils' level of performance was linked to the number of possible observations in the presented resource: the greater the

potential number and the more varied the observations available, then the higher the pupils' performance.

The questions differed in the nature of the resource to be compared, ie whether they were static objects, photographs or dynamic systems. The influence of different types of resource on pupil performance has not been identified in spite of probes carried out at ages 13 and 15. The reason for this appears to be the combined effect of many variables all linked to the type of resource used. A few examples are quoted to exemplify this point. For example, some observations are simply easier to describe than others. More pupils at age 13 are able to describe simple colour differences than are able to describe differences in texture or structure. In addition some observations are far more obvious than others. Differences in appearance related to colour, shine or shape are more obvious than differences or similarities in brittleness, density, or composition.

Obviousness is clearly linked to several other aspects; for example to the degree of 'noise' in the presented resource (ie the number of redundant variables); to the abstract or concrete nature of the differences and similarities; and to the senses to be employed in their observation. In two questions reported in DES, 1985a, pupils had to compare two small vehicle light bulbs and two samples of rock, mica and slate. Performance was lower on the light bulb question, the mean scores being 37 per cent and 46 per cent, respectively. The difference between the presented resources was not in the number of potential correct observations but rather that in the light bulbs there was more to *observe and reject*, and more *detailed* observations to make.

In the 1981 survey report, performance on a static resource was contrasted with performance on a dynamic system. The mean score for comparing tadpoles at different stages of development was 42 per cent. The mean score for comparing the movement of a ball-bearing on three differently shaped tracks was 28 per cent. The abstract nature of many of the observations to be made in the latter question meant that they were both less obvious *and* more difficult to express in writing. In a question where two liquids had to be compared, of the possible observations relating to sound, feel and smell, only smell was reported by a significant number of pupils.

The lack of a defined purpose in the questions must also be remembered, particularly in relation to the resource presented. Without purpose, the pupils have to define and impose their own 'model' of the presented situation. Depending on the pupils' background experience and knowledge, different resources will cue different 'models'. One important consequence will be the resulting perception of what is relevant and noteworthy. Certain overtly scientific resources may well focus the pupils into specific perceptions of relevance with the result that they select the most pertinent observations consistent with their model. These pupils could actually achieve lower scores on mark schemes designed to be atheoretical and which give credit for the *number* of observations made rather than the *type*. This particular point has significance for the following Question type.

### (iii) Describing changes in an event

These questions required pupils to set up and observe events and to record changes in them rather than to make comparisons between similar events. There was a comparison of sorts involved—of the initial, unchanged state with the changed state. In all of these questions there was more indication given of what to observe and a reduction in the number of possible observations. As there was a clear demand for focused observation, the mark schemes used were more stringent than for the previous group of questions. Many of the questions were similar to typical science lesson activities, eg observing swinging pendulum bobs or simple chemical changes. The average mean score for the questions was 30 per cent, with a range from 18 per cent to 43 per cent. The failure to score higher marks was due to the lack of recording sufficient features of the change. Inaccurate observations were relatively infrequent. There was, again, a tendency for pupils to focus on a particular feature of the change. In a question about burning fibres it was the manner of burning which was reported by most pupils. Little attention was paid to the residue or to the characteristic and extremely pungent smells produced by the burning fibres.

It has been mentioned in the 1983 age 15 survey report (DES, 1986b) that pupils in these circumstances may be imposing a purpose on these tasks which is at odds with the actual question demand. It has been suggested that the imposed purpose is related to the school experiences and expectations of the pupils. This argument is particularly persuasive if one considers a common use of practical activities in school, which is to demonstrate phenomena in order to develop or transmit specific concepts. In such activities the teacher deliberately focuses the pupils' attention to achieve their teaching objective. Other variables in the presented activity are labelled as redundant or irrelevant in this context and as such are ignored.

### (iv) Matching

The final type of question used to assess pupils' ability to make observations required pupils to match drawings to real objects or events. Here again the mean scores varied according to the number and difficulty of the observations to be made.

## 7.6  Results—'Using observations'

The questions discussed here required the pupils to **Make and use observations**. They correspond to the last three types listed in Table 7.1. The questions often had an identical format to those in the previous section but always contained additional parts. The main distinguishing feature of this group of questions was that pupils were *expected* to make *focused observations*. In most of the questions the 'use' demanded indicated the type of focus required. The 'uses' included in the assessment were to explain observations or to generalise and/or predict from them.

### (i) Explaining observations

Five questions of this type, listed under 5 in Table 7.1, have been included in the survey since 1980. The total number in the bank was nine. This small number reflects an early uncertainty about the validity of such questions coupled with the difficulty of generating good ones. The uncertainty lay in the obvious contradiction in a 'process' category which included questions requiring pupils to recall specific science concepts. There was one additional conflict; in the same **Observation** test, on questions concerned with 'making' observations, pupils could lose marks for imposing a theory on phenomena rather than faithfully recording all observations of an event. Yet these five questions actually demanded the recall of a theory from a collection of observations of presented phenomena; they were an example of 'guess what's in my mind' assessment.

There was no fundamental contradiction in scientific terms, as these questions clearly represented the links between variable relationships and scientific conceptual development inherent in the APU view of science. However, if the category were to be defined in terms of both 'process' and 'concept', it would be necessary to generate a conceptual 'mirror image' assessment for all the existing questions in the observation bank. One would merely focus on a different dimension of the same activity to do this. It would entail using the same resource but with amended questions which asked for reasons and explanations, or, alternatively, mark schemes which took account of concept-specific observations and inferences only. However, in determining the final structure of the assessment framework it was accepted that a *unidimensional* perspective would prevail in each category. Hence the contradiction which was inherent in these questions and subsequently in the observation bank.

Pupils' performance on these few questions was of interest in itself because of the relationship to performance in Category 4ii, **Applying science concepts**. In this category pupils are cued to a particular concept by the presentation of a general and usually novel situation. In the questions discussed here the concept was cued by a presented phenomenon. The novelty lay in the specific content or apparatus used. Each question required the pupils to focus on specific variables, to relate them and then to explain the relationship. Table 7.2 shows the questions, the variables to be related and the percentage of pupils deriving the correct explanation.

In the question 'Squink' most pupils stated their observations rather than attempting to explain them. About 10 per cent of pupils did suggest that as the ink rose in the chalkstick it separated into different colours. This observation was not, however, related back to the original ink colour. In the question 'Spin-tin' the overwhelming majority of pupils related only two out of the three variables, and so failed to generate a full explanation. On three of the questions boys' performance was significantly higher on the explanation part. The reverse was true for the 'Squink' question. This was interesting as all chromatography questions showed a higher performance by the girls, a finding noted by other researchers (Ebbut, 1981).

**Table 7.2** *Pupils' explanations of their observations*
(Percentage of pupils correctly explaining their observations)

| Question | Variables | Relationship | % pupils |
|---|---|---|---|
| Drops on hand | Smell<br>Evaporation<br>Feel | Change of state liquid – vapour causes cooling | 10 |
| Curdled milk | pH<br>Milk curdling | Curdled milk caused by acids | 37 |
| Polyglass | Material type<br>Temperature<br>Liquid level | Differential expansion of materials | 19 |
| Squink | Ink colour<br>Colour separation | Colour components | 10 |
| Spin-tin | Mass<br>Content of tin<br>Motion | Solid and liquid movement | 3 |

The performance on the questions was lower than the average achieved in the **Applying** category. The performance level appeared to be affected by several factors, including the number of variables focused on, whether they were redundant or not in the relationship, and the difficulty of the underlying concept to be recalled. It would seem, for example, that chromatography is a skill or technique *used* at younger ages but *not understood* conceptually.

*(ii) Generalising and predicting*

The final group of questions had in common the requirement to observe and identify relevant variables and to infer a relationship between them (listed 6 and 7 in Table 7.1). Pupils could be asked to describe the relationships and/or make predictions based on it. Some questions, in addition, demanded the application of a particular concept in order to identify the relevant variables. Questions of the latter type generally concerned the observation of structures and the relationships between them and their functions. They included such content as: fruits' structure related to dispersal,

birds' feet and beaks related to diet and habitat, animal alimentary canals and diet, and skulls related to dentition and diet. The mean scores ranged from 13–50 per cent. The overall mean score masked some significant performance differences. For example, in relating features of birds' feet to their habitat the mean score was 43 per cent, but only 13 per cent of pupils correctly predicted the habitat in all three bird examples. In a similar question about seed dispersal the mean score was 36 per cent, but no pupils successfully predicted the dispersal method for all three fruit examples, and only 13 per cent successfully predicted two. The pupils appeared to be applying recall of specific knowledge rather than applying a general concept to enable them to discern relevant variables and thus to make generalisations about structures and their functions.

Of the other questions surveyed, one in particular required the application of a concept prior to the perception of which variables were relevant. This was again concerned with chromatography. On the basis of a presented chromatogram of various coloured inks, pupils had to predict the chromatogram for a mixture of two of them. The mean score was very low (10 per cent), and girls performed at a higher level than boys.

The remaining questions used in the category did not demand the application of concepts and were all concerned with the identification of variables and the relationships between them. A group of these questions asked the pupils to observe an event and to describe the observed generalisation. Four of these questions are summarised in Table 7.3 with reference to the relevant variables in the events.

**Table 7.3** *Pupil performance on describing generalisations*

| Question | Independent variables | Dependent variables | Mean score % |
|---|---|---|---|
| Wigwag | Mass of block | Speed of movement | 55 |
| Bubble frame | Shape, size | Bubble size and number | 32 |
| Sound pattern | Volume of water | Pitch of note | 46 |
| Tracks | Mass of ball<br>Height of release<br>Speed | Movement of marbles | 37 |

The point has been made that the number of variables, and their confounding, affects pupils' performance. The greater the complexity in terms of the number of variables to be identified and related the lower the performance. This point links with some of the findings referred to in Chapter 11 of this report. In the question 'Wigwag' a simple relationship between two variables had to be observed. Thirty-nine per cent of the pupils gave a full generalisation. Twenty-four per cent identified both mass and motion but did not generalise about them; rather they referred to specific observations of them. Thirty per cent failed to score because they referred only to the dependent variable. In the question 'Bubble frame,' 19 per cent of the pupils generalised correctly about the size of the frame and the size of the bubbles. Twenty seven per cent stated correct observations about the relationship, ie the large square makes larger bubbles. In describing the generalisation between the size of the frame and the number of bubbles only 12 per cent of pupils were successful. This is a marked decrease in performance level from the question 'Wigwag'. It is important to note that not only were there two dependent variables to consider in the 'Bubble frame' question but one variable had no effect, ie the *shape* of the frame had no effect on the size or number of bubbles formed. In addition there was more for the pupils to manipulate.

The effect of the complexity of the event to be observed was noticeable in the performance of pupils on the questions 'Sound pattern' and 'Tracks'. In 'Sound pattern' there was again a simple relationship between two variables and more than 30 per cent of the pupils gave a full, correct generalisation. In the 'Tracks' question only 2 per cent of the pupils described the three independent variables which had an effect on the movement of the marbles. Twenty-four per cent described two variables and 33 per cent only one.

A further group of questions asked the pupils to describe the generalisation and then to make a prediction based on it. The results on the generalisation part of these questions were very similar to those already discussed. For example on a question relating liquid viscosity to the time of fall of ball bearings through the liquid, 47 per cent stated the relationship and 18 per cent gave specific observations incorporating the two variables. In the same question pupils had to relate the *size* of the ball bearings to the time of fall. Forty per cent of the pupils stated the relationship generally, and 20 per cent specified observations. The pupils were generally more successful in making predictions than in describing the generalisations upon which they were based, a finding in common with the **Interpretation** category and one which is clearly linked to pupils' ability to express themselves in this way. In Chapter 11 another aspect of this difficulty is raised, ie the understanding of a scientific relationship, which may explain why there is a consistent proportion of pupils who link the variables but do not generalise about the link across such questions.

Other questions required the pupils to identify variables within an event and record their observations, and then to make a prediction on the basis of the relationship between the variables. For example in one question pupils were required to observe the descent of several paper helicopters and note the relationship between the lengths of the helicopter wings and the rate of the descent; then predict, on the basis of the observation made, how another sample helicopter would fall. Again

across such questions a greater percentage of pupils made an accurate prediction than gave correct observations. It did appear on these questions that the need to predict or to generalise focused the pupils' attention. They progressively paid less attention to the detailed observations demanded having once, as they perceived it, identified the salient points.

Performance on predicting from observations was extremely varied. There was some indication again that performance was affected by the number of variables to be related. Thus when two variables had to be linked in one question the mean score was 80 per cent for prediction. In another where there were three variables the mean score was 70 per cent. Performance also of course depended on the nature of the variables to be observed and the nature of the observations to be made. In a question relating two variables but depending on the senses of sight and sound the mean score on the prediction was 50 per cent.


## 7.7  Discussion

Before discussing performance it should be remembered that generalisations across questions of a given type within this category relate to smaller numbers of questions than for other categories. With this in mind the discussion is restricted to those general features which have emerged consistently over the survey years, from 1980–1984.

The pupils' attitude to this assessment has rarely been commented on. Pupils from all types of schools and backgrounds reported that they enjoyed the questions. It was noteworthy that girls and boys responded in a similar way to questions covering a range of science content, including physical science and biological science. The majority of the pupils perceived the tasks in terms of the actions or demands required rather than the specific content involved. Most pupils, however, expressed less enthusiasm for questions concerned with the observation of static resources, particularly the ones featuring obviously dead animals. These included skulls, crab shells, insect legs and photographs of alimentary canals.

The results for the category showed that about two-thirds of the pupils could identify the rules used to set up a classification provided that the rules were not too obscure. Performance was lower on this demand for questions with an obvious science content. Most pupils could add objects to pre-defined groups but few could explain their reasons for doing it. The disparity between what pupils can do and their ability to express their actions in explicit terms has been noted in many of the other category tests. When pupils had to identify the grouping criteria and then reclassify the same objects into three exclusive groups performance was depressed by about 20 per cent. The reduction in the level of pupil performance seemed to be associated with the constraints of operating within a presented, closed system.

In questions where pupils had to make comparisons and note as many similarities and differences as specified the average mean score was just less than 50 per cent. The most common pupil error was to imply rather than to state the comparison. Performance on describing differences was higher than on describing similarities by about 15 percentage points. The greater the number and the wider the range of possible observations the higher the performance level. Performance on these questions appeared to be affected by the following factors: redundant variables—the more of these present the lower the performance; the type of variable to be compared—the more abstract in nature the lower the performance; the nature of the observations to be made—if the senses to be employed were other than sight the lower the performance. These factors occurred in combination in the questions and therefore no simple direct pattern of their influence has been discernible.

Performance on describing events was lower than that on describing differences and similarities. The depression in performance was due largely to a failure to record the details of the changes. It appeared that pupils focused their attention on particular aspects of the events. This was a common response to activities of this kind.

Pupils' performance on questions which asked them to explain their observations was generally low. The performance level was determined, to an extent, by the complexity of the event to be observed. The complexity was characterised again by the number and nature of the variables involved. In addition it was necessary to recall a specific concept in order to interpret and explain the relationship. Performance was therefore also dependent on pupils being able to recall the concept. The low performance on these questions is not surprising given the dual demands both to use knowledge and to explain the use. For the same reasons the low level of pupil performance on structure and function type questions was in keeping with the similarly strenuous demands.

One point, somewhat tangential to the main discussion, but with wide implications, concerns the introduction in science lessons of techniques and procedures without attention to their underlying concepts. For example introducing chromatography as a technique for purification seems questionable practice when the pupils have no understanding of the manner in which the technique functions.

The ability of pupils, as a group, to observe and discern relationships between variables varied considerably. The performance determinants appeared to be largely the same as those already mentioned. There are interesting

parallels between these question and some of the investigations used in **Performance of investigations** (Category 6). The observation tasks, however, precluded any measurements. The independent variables were often presented as discrete quantities or as pre-modelled entities, for example, the variable 'shape' in 'Bubble frame' was presented to the pupils as a circle, a triangle and a square, thus obviating the need to conceptualise it. The parallels in tasks and pupils' performance are referred to in Chapter 12 of this report. The extent to which pupils could describe generalisations depended in the first instance on whether they were able to observe the relationship in the data. Thus any factors reducing their ability to discern a relationship would also depress their performance on the generalisation. Across all the questions, though, there was a significant proportion of pupils, about 20 per cent, who made accurate observations of the related variables but made no attempt to express them in a general way. This aspect of pupils' performance had much in common with other categories, particularly those of **Interpretation** and **Performance of investigations**. The links with these categories are explored in Chapter 12.

In general pupils were more successful at making predictions than at describing the relationships upon which they were based. Questions which asked pupils to both observe in detail and to use the observations produced a focused response from many pupils. The 'use' demanded seemed to encourage pupils to identify and record only the salient points as they perceived them. An actual or perceived focus of demand had a wide-ranging effect on pupils' performance in the category. If pupils were directed to use a particular sense, then in general they seemed able to do so. Without the direction, the tendency was for them to rely on sight alone. Sounds, smells, 'feel' or weight were all disregarded by the majority of pupils.


## 7.8  Implications

The main implications of the results, both for assessment and teaching, are concerned with the unresolved issue of what constitutes scientific observation. If it is accepted that scientific observation is theory-laden, how is this aspect of the activity to be assessed? This is particularly problematic when the theories are uncued in the questions so that there is scope for many alternative models.

Another important point which emerges from the results concerns the manner in which conceptual understanding is assessed at present, both in this and other assessments. Most teachers would agree that whilst explicit statements of knowledge by pupils have value for learning, attention should also be paid to encouraging pupils to develop use of their knowledge. Practical activities are of particular value here because properly exploited they can provide occasions, within a procedural context, for pupils to deploy and express their scientific understanding in a purposeful way. Thus in observation, the implicit or tacit knowledge that pupils use ought to be a focus of attention so that they can develop their ideas by making them explicit. For any of this to happen, pupils need to be able to engage with the activities in science lessons, and teachers need to understand and share their approach. Phenomena presented by teachers often reflect the teacher's perception and understanding, and may not take account of the pupils' views. In such situations pupils may be concerned with alternative problems, either because they consider the view held by the teacher to be irrelevant, or because they form an incorrect view of what the teacher regards as relevant.

The final points are reflections on the position of **Observation** in the assessment framework and science education generally. **Observation** was regarded as a significant activity of science by most of the educationists consulted during the early stages of the project. Teachers, both at primary and secondary level, claimed that the skill of observing was an important aim of teaching.

One of the first tasks for the team in the pre-survey years, was to review existing test instruments. Very few questions were found, whether in use in schools or in assessment literature, which were suitable; the scarcity was particularly noticeable in the **Observation** category.

The team had to start generating and trialling new questions. Producing good observation tasks was found to take a lot of time, ingenuity and resource. The rewards were however immediate. The questions were well received by both children and teachers alike and were regarded as most closely representing useful and innovative classroom activities.

From this it would appear that the monitoring has produced results of immediate value for teaching. However, the findings discussed in this chapter have highlighted some of the many factors which need to be considered before translating the assessment questions into classroom activities. One important factor is the need to consider the conceptual demands inherent in such activities. This aspect of the research work is only just beginning. What has been exposed is the immense complexity within the activity labelled as **Observation**. The complexity has two clear sources: the multiple nature of the demands and the wide range of purposes for which the skill is deployed.

The existing data provide a starting point for the grading and ordering of tasks in terms of difficulty. If it proves to be possible to derive a description within **Observation** which has an explicit structure, then the teaching implications are obvious. Such a structure could, as in **Performance of investigations**, provide a base from which to generate and test hypotheses about learning sequences in observation, and thus about appropriate teaching.

# 8

# Interpretation

## 8.1 Introduction

In this report, the discussion of Category 4 is split between two chapters: **Interpretation** in this chapter and **Application** in the next. However, the two sections of the category have not always been seen as separable. During the first few months of the monitoring team's existence its members consulted with the Steering Group to establish a list of processes which should be included in the monitoring programme. The proposed list was published in a *consultative paper* (DES, 1977). Most of those processes related to the present Category 4 were included under the headings **Generalisation** and **Explanation and enquiry**; for example:

7.2.1   linking observations with each other to discern patterns;

7.2.2   relating new observations to patterns previously identified, to extend or modify these where appropriate; seeking out individual differences;

7.3.1   explaining different patterns of observations in terms of one another; checking that explanations are consistent with observations as far as they go;

7.3.2   proposing alternative explanations and comparing them in terms of how well they fit observation;

7.3.4   selecting and linking appropriate knowledge and observations to tackle a novel problem; applying previous knowledge in quite new contexts.

After further work, which included the writing of questions to address those processes and attempts to ensure that each could be assigned by different people to the same process, the list relating to Category 4 became more refined and at the same time more limited. The new version was published in a progress report (DES, 1978), as follows:

In these tasks a selection from observations has been made and is presented as data to pupils:

inferring patterns in data;

making predictions based on patterns inferred from data and/or accepted concepts;

suggesting one or more hypotheses consistent with presented data;

assessing the validity of conclusions and/or patterns in relation to presented data.

Further writing and trialling of questions, together with consideration of the need to report usefully on the results and all that this implied in terms of labelling and categorising, gave rise to the decision to divide the questions into two sections: those which required pupils to apply science knowledge and concepts which they were likely to have acquired through school science lessons, and those which did not. A subsequent reorganisation resulted in the present division of the two sections into three and four subcategories respectively. Figure 8.1 indicates the first two stages of their evolution from the proposals in the progress report.

**Figure 8.1**   *Evolution of Category 4*

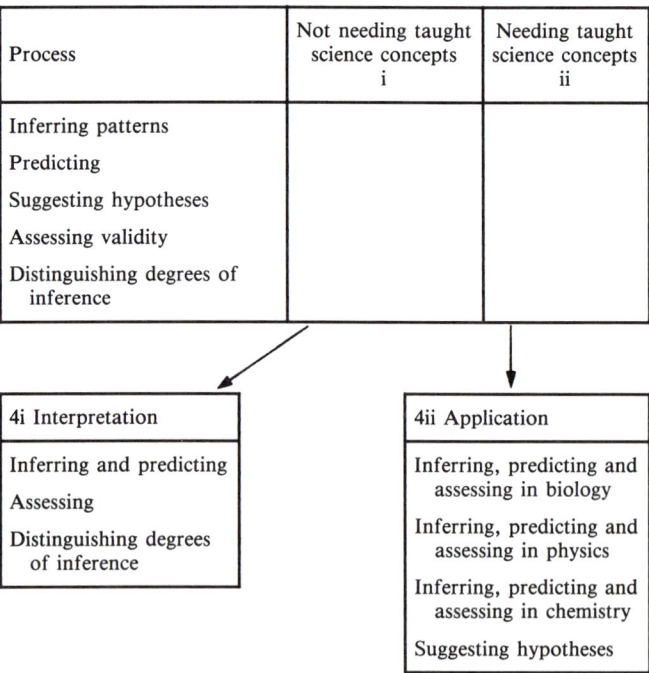

| Process | Not needing taught science concepts i | Needing taught science concepts ii |
|---|---|---|
| Inferring patterns<br>Predicting<br>Suggesting hypotheses<br>Assessing validity<br>Distinguishing degrees of inference | | |

**4i Interpretation**

Inferring and predicting

Assessing

Distinguishing degrees of inference

**4ii Application**

Inferring, predicting and assessing in biology

Inferring, predicting and assessing in physics

Inferring, predicting and assessing in chemistry

Suggesting hypotheses

Meanwhile, the decision was taken to use a system in which the production of equivalent tests is achieved by the random selection of questions from a bank. As with other categories this necessitated the writing of a very large number of questions which were in any case unusual (because of the intention to report by process) and difficult to write. Having written and trialled a range of different types of question for each subcategory, the teams wrote a generalised descriptor for each question type so that it could be used as a template for the production of many more. This was seen at the time as a way of accelerating the building up of a large enough bank, but has since proved useful in at least two other respects: the clarification of boundary lines between categories–that is, the definition of the categories themselves; and the grouping of questions with the same process-related skill (for example, inferring patterns) but different characteristics in other respects.

Initially, at the progress report stage represented at the top of Figure 8.1, question descriptors were common to the two sections of Category 4; experience of writing questions indicated the need for changes, so that although there remain clear links between the sections in this respect they are different in detail. (A list of question descriptors defining the Question types used in this and other categories can be found in Appendix 4.)

As Figure 8.1 shows, **Interpretation**, the subject of this chapter, crystallised into three subcategories; they are described in the assessment framework in section 1.3 (p. 2) as:

**Interpreting presented information**

**Judging the applicability of statements to data**

**Distinguishing degrees of inference**

The first of these is the only one for which an overall subcategory performance level is now computed. The remaining two contain too few questions to be similarly treated. Although reference will be made to them towards the end of this chapter, the intervening sections (8.2–8.9) are devoted to discussion of **Interpreting presented information**.

## 8.2   The nature of the subcategory pool of questions

All the questions in **Interpreting presented information** require pupils to infer a relationship (a regularity or pattern) from information embedding several different pairs of data. Each question falls into one of eight Question types, which can be regarded as the fine structure of the process dimension, already discussed in section 8.1. Questions are set in a wide variety of contexts. In the initial setting up of the subcategory pool of questions, the aim was to arrange for equal representation of the contexts 'Everyday + other school subject', 'Physics', 'Chemistry' and 'Biology'. However, subsequent strategies such as the move towards merging banks from the three different ages, have meant that this distribution is no longer appropriate. In any case the definition of context as perceived by the pupil is problematic; and indications are that it is the specific content of a question, rather than any generalised

context, which affects performance. None of the questions requires the application of science concepts from the published list, which relates to science taught in schools. Since in practice there can be no sharp boundary between concepts acquired in and out of school science lessons, it is often necessary to refer to this list in order to decide whether a question qualifies for inclusion in **Interpreting**, Category 4i, or should in fact be transferred to **Applying science concepts**, Category 4ii.

Because of the wide variety of content and style thought necessary for proper assessment of this subcategory, a number of question characteristics are present which might affect performance. These include the type of relationship to be perceived, the method of presentation of data, and the level of background noise in the information. Questions have now been labelled with respect to these three characteristics, and attempts are made in sections 8.5 to 8.8 to assess the degree to which variations in them affect levels of performance.

As in many questions set to test process skills rather than recall of content, there are language difficulties, not only for the pupils in expressing their response but also for the assessor in framing the question. Partly, perhaps, as a result of this difficulty, pupils often tend to misconstrue the question and then tend to answer in terms of experience or belief. This problem is discussed in section 8.13 in so far as it affects **Interpreting**, but readers will find it recurs throughout the report.

## 8.3   Performance across Question types

As already indicated, all questions present information from which the underlying relationship can be perceived, but demands, or combinations of demands, differ across the eight Question types used. The basic demands involved are:

– describe a perceived relationship

– predict from a perceived relationship

– justify such a prediction

In those Question types in which there is a demand to *select* a prediction or a description, pupils are presented with at least four alternatives from which to choose. The response to such demands is in coded answer form. All other demands require a free and more extended response.

In the report of the first age 13 survey (DES, 1982a) many questions were included, along with the performance levels associated with them, for the purpose of explaining to the reader the meaning of the categories to which they related. They were there in the first place mainly as exemplars which were to help make sense of the performance profiles. However, interest was shown in the results for specific questions, and in the degree to which performance varied systematically with question characteristics, in particular with the demands made by the eight different Question types. In earlier reports there have been tentative suggestions that coded answer questions (or part-questions) tended to have lower non-response rates and higher mean scores, on average, than those needing extended responses; and that pupils were more able to make a prediction than to describe the relationship on which it was based.

In a single survey the number of questions of any one type may be too small for conclusions to be sensibly drawn, since the effect of other factors on performance level is difficult to estimate. Table 8.1 summarises the results for all questions which have been used in the five surveys at age 13. For each Question type, the table shows the number of questions used, the range of mean scores for those questions, and the average value of the mean scores.

The data do not give much support to the view expressed earlier that coded answer responses have higher mean scores than extended responses. Nor is it obvious that pupils find it easier to make predictions than to describe the relationship on which they are based. However, because several of the Question types are composite in terms of both the basic demands and the mode of response this issue needs further exploration.

**Table 8.1** *Mean scores of questions within a given Question type (1980–1984)*

(Ordered as in Appendix 4)

| | Demand(s) of Question types | Abbrev-iation | No. of questions used | Range of % mean scores | Average of % mean scores |
|---|---|---|---|---|---|
| 401 | Describe | D | 26 | 5–73 | 36 |
| 402 | Describe and predict | D + P | 19 | 14–80 | 44 |
| 403 | Describe + Select prediction | D + P$_S$ | 10 | 24–75 | 45 |
| 404 | Predict | P | 22 | 14–87 | 50 |
| 405 | Select prediction | P$_S$ | 10 | 16–68 | 41 |
| 406 | Select description | D$_S$ | 14 | 18–83 | 47 |
| 407 | Predict + Justify | P + J | 7 | 32–49 | 39 |
| 408 | Select prediction + Justify | P$_S$ + J | 12 | 9–59 | 36 |

## 8.4 The effect of context on performance

It seems likely that the context in which a question is set may have considerable effect on performance levels. However, it is difficult to generalise about the size—or even the direction—of this effect, since it appears to vary from pupil to pupil, and from time to time. In a small-scale probe conducted at the time of question trials, pupils were asked to say whether the question reminded them of an out-of-school or within-school

activity, and if within-school, of which subject. The responses were clearly linked to the recent experience of each particular class of pupils, since in one school almost all trial pupils assigned a given question to biology and in another to geography. In yet another class the contexts assigned were very varied, and included 'everyday' (ie out-of-school), and 'mathematics'. The actual demand of the question being posed was to describe the relationship presented in a graph showing the increase in height of barley with time.

Members of the monitoring team have labelled the context of questions used in the surveys; even had they been successful in perceiving the context from a pupil's point of view, rather than their own, the labels could only match the perceptions of *some* of the pupils, not all. Add to this the fact that team members themselves may be subject to the same lack of consistency, and for similar reasons, as the pupils, and it is clear that the value of current labels is limited; it seems unproductive, for example, to attempt to generalise by calculating mean scores for questions with a particular context label and presenting the results as a bar chart. This is not to say that the effect of context cannot be discussed: the issue arises constantly in this and other reports; but it has been found that in general it is the specific content of a question, and not simply the broad label by which context has been classified, which affects the level of performance.

Of all the other characteristics of questions which might affect performance, three have been selected for investigation:

– The type of pattern or relationship involved;

– the way in which variables are presented;

– the level of background noise in the information given.

These three were chosen in the light of results from the first four surveys. The incidence and the effect of these characteristics are discussed in sections 8.5–8.7.

## 8.5 The effect of type of relationship on performance

Questions have here been re-grouped under nine heads with respect to the type of relationship to be perceived from the information presented.

There are normally only two related variables involved, although there may be a third unrelated variable which contributes to the background noise in the information. Sometimes one variable is related simultaneously to two others, and in other cases one quantity remains constant while another varies. The nine types of relationship considered are summarised in Table 8.2 (p. 85).

# Table 8.2  *Type of pattern or relationships to be perceived*

1. Constant value of y for any x
2. Direct trend between x and y
3. Inverse trend between x and y
4. More complex relationship, eg irregular, Gaussian curve, etc.
5. Simultaneous relationship between x and y, z and y (eg height/width and stability)
6. Discontinuous or categorical variables, eg 2×2, or x by y matrix
7. Cyclically repetitive series, eg seasonal order of events
8. Dynamic spatial regularities, eg gears, pulleys
9. Static spatial regularities, eg symmetry

It is usually the case that questions can be assigned to one or other of these nine types of pattern without any ambiguity; however there is a certain amount of overlap in the groups which needs to be resolved by further research. Another difficulty in appreciating the impact of Pattern type on performance levels is the uneven distribution of the nine Pattern types across Question types, leading to a corresponding imbalance in questions selected in surveys. This distribution is illustrated in Table 8.3. In each cell the number of questions used is followed, in parenthesis, by the number available in the bank.

# Table 8.3  *Distribution of Pattern types across Question types*

| Pattern type | Question type: 401 D | 402 D+P | 403 D+P$_S$ | 404 P | 405 P$_S$ | 406 D$_S$ | 407 P+J | 408 P$_S$+J |
|---|---|---|---|---|---|---|---|---|
| 1 | | | 1(1) | | | 1(1) | 2(3) | |
| 2 | 7(12) | 10(12) | 2(8) | 4(5) | 1(3) | 3(6) | 2(8) | 3(4) |
| 3 | 2(8) | 3(5) | 5(5) | 3(4) | 3(5) | 4(9) | 0(2) | 2(3) |
| 4 | 12(14) | 2(2) | 2(2) | 2(3) | 2(3) | 3(7) | | 1(2) |
| 5 | | | | 2(2) | 1(1) | | 1(1) | |
| 6 | 3(3) | 0(2) | | 4(4) | 1(2) | 1(3) | 2(5) | 1(1) |
| 7 | | 2(2) | 0(1) | 2(5) | 1(1) | | | |
| 8 | | | | 4(7) | | 2(2) | 0(2) | 0(2) |
| 9 | 2(4) | 2(2) | 0(4) | 1(4) | 1(2) | | | 5(13) |

An uneven distribution such as that shown in the cells of Table 8.3 occurs also with respect to the characteristics to be considered in the next two Sections. It would, of course, have been impossible to set up a pool of questions balanced across *all* the characteristics against which performance might subsequently be analysed. Indeed for some characteristics, such as 'degree of background noise', even distribution would not have been suitable. However, when the significance of variation in the average values of mean scores of questions within a particular group (such as a particular Pattern type) is being considered, possible effects of the presence or absence of other characteristics must also be kept in mind. Table 8.4 shows the variation of levels of performance with Pattern type.

The number of questions in some Pattern types is too low to allow sensible conclusions to be drawn. How-

# Table 8.4  *Variation of performance levels with Pattern type*

| Pattern type | No. of questions used | Range of mean % scores | Average of % mean scores |
|---|---|---|---|
| 1 | 4 | 18–37 | 32 |
| 2 | 32 | 27–76 | 46 |
| 3 | 22 | 23–75 | 45 |
| 4 | 24 | 5–81 | 32 |
| 5 | 4 | 24–39 | 33 |
| 6 | 12 | 29–78 | 51 |
| 7 | 5 | 14–54 | 31 |
| 8 | 6 | 20–87 | 49 |
| 9 | 11 | 9–80 | 48 |

ever, in the case of types 2, 3 and 4, the numbers appear high enough to support the suggestion that pupils find Pattern types 2 and 3 easier to deal with than 4; that is, the type in which one quantity increases or decreases with the other is found easier than a more complex type in which the direction of the relationship varies. However, although these generalisations may be justified in view of the numbers of questions involved and the differences in mean scores, individual questions may not conform. This is obvious from the range of mean scores, particularly in the case of Pattern type 4. It also seems possible that the mean score for Pattern type 4 is affected by the fact that half the questions which represented it in the surveys came from Question type 401, in which the demand is to describe the pattern.

## 8.6  The effect of presenting variables in different ways

Results obtained in the past suggest that performance may be influenced by the way in which the information is presented; that is according to whether pictures, words, numbers or graphs are used. Consequently all the questions in **Interpretation** have been labelled with respect to 'variable presentation'. In most questions there are two related variables, and for these a label indicating a combination of two methods of presentation is used. A simple hypothesis might suggest that data which are predominantly pictorial tend to be easy to interpret, those which are largely numerical harder, and graphical representation the most difficult. Consequently the labels are listed in order as in Table 8.5.

# Table 8.5  *Variable presentation – the seven labels*

| First variable | Second variable | Label |
|---|---|---|
| Pictorial | Pictorial | P/P |
| Pictorial | Verbal | P/V |
| Pictorial | Numerical | P/N |
| Verbal | Verbal | V/V |
| Verbal | Numerical | V/N |
| Numerical | Numerical | N/N |
| Graphical representation | | G |

The distribution of questions in these seven groups is not balanced since, as explained in the preceding section, the subcategory pool was not set up with this particular grouping in mind. Table 8.6 shows how many questions of each 'variable presentation' group fall within each Question type. The notation used for Question type is as for the corresponding Table 8.3.

**Table 8.6** *Distribution of variable presentation groups across Question types*

| | Question types: | | | | | | | |
|---|---|---|---|---|---|---|---|---|
| Variable presentation | 401 D | 402 D+P | 403 D+$P_S$ | 404 P | 405 $P_S$ | 406 $D_S$ | 407 P+J | 408 $P_S$+J |
| P/P | 3(6) | 2(2) | 0(4) | 4(11) | 1(3) | 2(3) | 0(2) | 4(9) |
| P/V | 4(4) | 1(1) | | 4(5) | 0(1) | 2(2) | 0(1) | 0(1) |
| P/N | 4(10) | 1(2) | 2(2) | 5(7) | 2(2) | 1(1) | 1(4) | 0(2) |
| V/V | | 0(1) | 1(1) | 2(2) | 2(2) | | 1(2) | 1(1) |
| V/N | 3(4) | 1(1) | | 1(2) | | 0(1) | 3(7) | 1(1) |
| N/N | 4(6) | 6(9) | 2(4) | 1(1) | 4(8) | 2(2) | 2(4) | 4(7) |
| G | 8(11) | 8(9) | 5(10) | 5(7) | 1(1) | 7(17) | 0(1) | 2(4) |

In each cell the number of questions used is followed, in parenthesis, by the number available in the bank.

As before, the average value of the mean scores for all the questions which have been used in the five surveys has been found for each of the seven groups; these performance levels are shown in Table 8.7.

**Table 8.7** *Variation of performance levels across variable presentation groups*

| Variable presentation | No. of questions used | Range of mean % scores | Average of % mean scores |
|---|---|---|---|
| Pictorial/pictorial | 16 | 9–87 | 57 |
| Pictorial/verbal | 11 | 18–73 | 49 |
| Pictorial/numerical | 16 | 14–78 | 36 |
| Verbal/verbal | 7 | 37–57 | 45 |
| Verbal/numerical | 9 | 32–48 | 39 |
| Numerical/numerical | 25 | 13–75 | 40 |
| Graphical | 36 | 5–81 | 38 |

Although for some groups the number of questions surveyed is rather low, and for most groups the *range* of mean scores is very large, the results in Table 8.7 support the hypothesis that questions in which information is presented pictorially prove easier, on average, than others; and that if numerical data are included the general level of performance drops whether the numbers are alone, associated with pictorial data, with words or with graphs. However there are other factors which may contribute to this effect. For example, the number of data pairs which can be presented on a sheet of A4 paper in pictorial form is necessarily limited to three or four; whereas a table of figures can extend to cover at least twice as many. It is hard to decide whether it is the pictorial nature of the presentation, or the limited amount of information which can be conveyed, which has the observed effect.

## 8.7 The effect of varying degrees of 'background noise'

Three different factors affecting the level of 'background noise' were distinguished. One was the inclusion of information about an unrelated variable; for example in the question 'Pollen' a table included variations in temperature as well as the related variables humidity and pollen count. The second factor was the disordering of information, and the third the need for pupils to consider figures which had not been 'cleaned up' to fit a relationship exactly; that is, the need to allow for experimental errors, biological variation or too low a sample size, all of which might produce perturbations in an otherwise smooth relationship. The third factor might well have different effects for pupils with different backgrounds. However the number of questions is too few to split further.

Questions were grouped according to the particular combination of the above factors associated with them. The list in Table 8.8 has been ordered according to a view of the degree of noise occurring in the information, starting with the lowest. The assumption has been made that the presence of an unrelated variable is likely to have considerably more effect than either of the other types of disturbance.

**Table 8.8** *Information noise levels*

| | Presented information includes: | | |
|---|---|---|---|
| Noise level | Unrelated variable | Disordered data | Perturbations |
| 1 low | x | x | x |
| 2 | x | x | ✓ |
| 3 | x | ✓ | x |
| 4 | x | ✓ | ✓ |
| 5 | ✓ | x | x |
| 6 | ✓ | x | ✓ |
| 7 | ✓ | ✓ | x |
| 8 high | ✓ | ✓ | ✓ |

If a high level of noise adversely affects performance, then average values of mean scores for questions, taken level by level, might be expected to decrease, all else being equal. However, Table 8.9 shows that, for the

**Table 8.9** *The effect of information noise level on performance*

| Noise level | No. of questions used | Range of mean % scores | Average % mean scores |
|---|---|---|---|
| 1 (low) | 67 | 5–87 | 43 |
| 2 | 10 | 13–78 | 43 |
| 3 | 18 | 9–76 | 45 |
| 4 | 6 | 18–75 | 41 |
| 5 | 12 | 26–53 | 38 |
| 6 | 3 | 28–45 | 37 |
| 7 | 3 | 41–69 | 57 |
| 8 (high) | 1 | | 23 |

**Question examples 8.1: 'Quick ticks' and 8.2: 'Rise and set'**

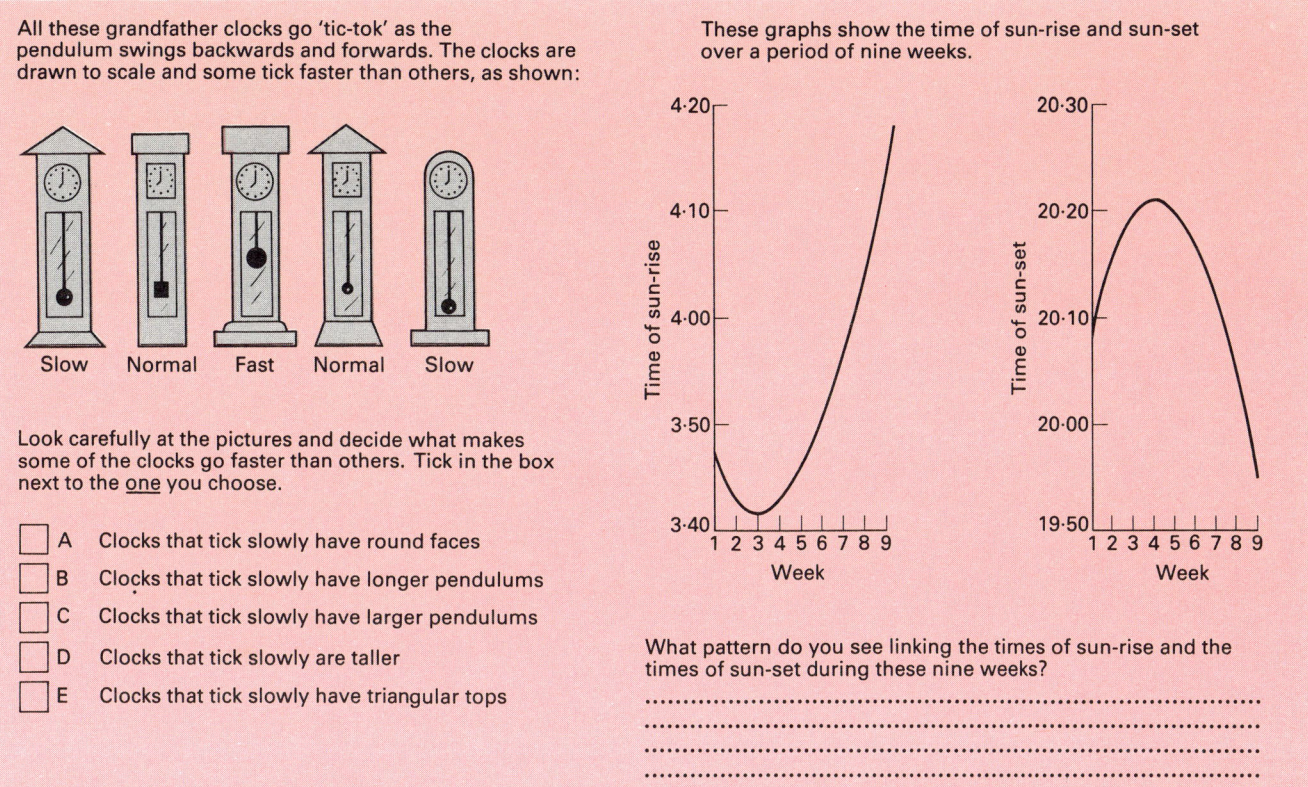

All these grandfather clocks go 'tic-tok' as the pendulum swings backwards and forwards. The clocks are drawn to scale and some tick faster than others, as shown:

Slow   Normal   Fast   Normal   Slow

Look carefully at the pictures and decide what makes some of the clocks go faster than others. Tick in the box next to the <u>one</u> you choose.

☐ A   Clocks that tick slowly have round faces
☐ B   Clocks that tick slowly have longer pendulums
☐ C   Clocks that tick slowly have larger pendulums
☐ D   Clocks that tick slowly are taller
☐ E   Clocks that tick slowly have triangular tops

These graphs show the time of sun-rise and sun-set over a period of nine weeks.

What pattern do you see linking the times of sun-rise and the times of sun-set during these nine weeks?

..............................................................................
..............................................................................
..............................................................................
..............................................................................

questions used in the survey, this does not seem to be the case.

It would also seem that 'noisy' questions involving both an unrelated variable and disordered data (noise level 7) tend to be easier than those involving fewer distractions. However, the number of questions in level 7, and indeed in several others, is too few for any firm conclusions to be drawn. This situation reflects the uneven distribution of questions across levels within the sub-category pool which is shown in Table 8.10.

**Table 8.10** *Distribution of questions with a given noise level across Question types*

| Noise level | 401 D | 402 D+P | 403 D+P$_S$ | 404 P | 405 P$_S$ | 406 D$_S$ | 407 P+J | 408 P$_S$+J |
|---|---|---|---|---|---|---|---|---|
| 1 | 12(15) | 13(14) | 5(11) | 15(24) | 7(10) | 8(15) | 1(8) | 6(11) |
| 2 | 3(9) | 1(2) | 0(1) | 3(5) | 0(2) | 1(2) | 1(1) | 1(3) |
| 3 | 5(11) | 2(4) | 1(5) | 3(5) | 1(1) | 0(1) | 2(6) | 4(10) |
| 4 | 2(2) | | 2(2) | | 1(1) | 1(1) | | |
| 5 | 2(2) | 3(5) | 1(1) | | 1(1) | 3(6) | 2(2) | |
| 6 | 1(1) | | 1(1) | | | | 1(2) | |
| 7 | 1(1) | | | 1(1) | | 1(2) | 0(2) | |
| 8 | | | | | 0(1) | | | 1(1) |

The extent to which questions in the bank load into the lowest 'noise' level, with no unrelated variable, no disordered data and no perturbations to be allowed for, exemplifies the attempt by question writers to produce age-appropriate questions. Trials showed that where the data had not been carefully 'selected from observations'

(to quote the progress report) pupils had much greater difficulty. Questions remaining in the bank at high noise levels tend to have other characteristics which compensate for degree of noise. Compare, for example, the question 'Quick ticks' in noise level 7 with a mean score of 69, with 'Rise and set' in level 1 with a mean score of 12.

The two questions differ in at least four respects:

| | 'Quick ticks' | 'Rise and set' |
|---|---|---|
| Information noise level | 7 (high) | 1 (low) |
| Mean score | 69% | 12% |
| Question demand | Select description (coded answer) | Describe |
| Variable presentation | Pictorial/verbal | Graph |
| Pattern type | 2 (simple direct) | 4 (complex) |

It is clear that although 'Quick ticks' does indeed have a high noise level due to unrelated variables (for example, the size and shape of pendulum bobs) and disordered data, the simplicity of the presentation, and of the Pattern type, together with the coded answer format, far outweigh any difficulty due to the high noise level. The question 'Rise and set', on the other hand, has characteristics outside those considered in sections 8.5 to 8.7 which make it particularly difficult. Nevertheless, a comparison of the two questions illustrates the confounding of the variables considered which makes it difficult to generalise about their effects on performance.

## 8.8   Patterns of performance in 'Interpreting presented information'

In the preceding sections, the effects on performance of a number of question characteristics have been explored in turn; some of the effects are difficult to interpret because of the distribution of questions; in other cases, the effect of one characteristic is masked by the effect of another, as in the two question examples quoted above; but the matter is further confounded by the fact that the characteristics are not always entirely independent. For example, if data are presented as a graph they can hardly be disordered; if presented pictorially the number of data pairs must be limited because of lack of space and therefore the amount of disordering which is possible is also limited. Patterns are more likely to be categorical in chemical and biological contexts than in physics, at any rate in questions suitable for the age range, and these contexts may also influence matters one way or another.

In order to anticipate pupils' performance, it is clear that all possible relevant factors must be considered, and their interactive effects assessed.

It seems probable that performance will be low if a question:

- demands an extended response;

- presents a complex relationship numerically;

- has a high level of background noise.

The use of an adverse context and over-formal language would probably depress performance even further. Both these factors are discussed later in the chapter, with reference to all three subcategories of **Interpretation**.

## 8.9   Differences in performance between boys and girls

There has been a consistent but slight tendency for boys to outperform girls in the subcategory **Interpreting presented information** over the five years of the survey. However, inspection of results for individual questions suggests that there is no particular Question Type, Pattern type, Variable presentation, or Information noise level which favours one gender or the other, with the possible exception of the following:

(a) Pattern type 8 (spatial dynamic) where for four questions out of six, boys had a higher performance, the difference in mean scores being statistically significant at the 5 per cent level for each question.

(b) Pattern type 9 (spatial pattern) where for four questions out of 11, boys had a higher performance.

(c) Variable presentation 1 (pictorial/pictorial) where, for six questions out of 16, boys had a higher performance.

However, all the group (c) questions are included under (a) or (b) and so it may very well be the Pattern type, rather than the 'pictorial' presentation, which is associated with the difference–especially since the presentation is, in these cases, diagrammatic rather than pictorial. Sex-related differences in performance associated with spatial patterns have received comment in earlier reports (for example, DES, 1984a) and indeed a probe was included in the final survey designed to investigate this issue. A report of this set of probe questions (see pp. 92–7) is given in section 8.12; the results support the suggestion that this Pattern type poses particular difficulties for girls. Since it is also one which pupils meet often in the early stages of school physics, this is of particular interest.

Table 8.11 (p. 89) lists all the questions for which girls have a higher performance than boys, and then all those for which boys have the higher performance. The Question type, Pattern type, Information noise level and Variable presentation group are also shown.

One or two other points of interest arise from the data in Table 8.11. The Question type indicates whether the response required is extended, short, or coded; D (describe) and J (justify) are normally extended answers; P (generate a prediction) is shorter while $P_S$ and $D_S$ are coded. Of the eight questions for which girls have the higher performance level, seven require, in part, an extended response; in the 17 for which boys do better, 12 do so. Thus the differences cannot easily be explained in terms of the greater ability of girls to express themselves in writing. In the column which indicates the way in which the two related variables in the data are presented, 7 (G) stands for a graphical representation of the relationship–a line graph or bar chart. Four of the eight questions for which girls do better are of this kind; two are line graphs and two histograms. In only three of the 'boys' group of 17 questions are the variables presented by graphical representation. This is an interesting result, since in general it has been found that boys handle graphs more competently than girls.

Apart from the presence or absence of a relationship expressed as a spatial pattern, there seems, therefore, to be no obvious reason why questions should fall into one or the other group of questions. Probably a number of factors interact to produce the result shown in Table 8.11, including the specific question content, about which it is hard to generalise. None of the 'girls' group of questions has a school science laboratory setting, for example, apart from 'Celery stick'. The other seven questions are about activities or events which takes place out of school–but then so are many of the 'boys' group. It has been suggested that transport is a context favouring boys, and indeed 'Traffic meter'

**Table 8.11** *Questions with gender-related differences in performance\**
(All questions included have a difference in mean score between boys and girls which is statistically significant at the 5% level)

| Name | Question type | Pattern type | Information noise level | Variable presentation | % mean score |
|---|---|---|---|---|---|
| **(Girls higher: 8 questions)** | | | | | |
| Salty water | 401(D) | 6 | 1 (xxx) | 5 (V/N) | 44 |
| Compost heap | 401(D) | 4 | 1 | 7 (G) | 42 |
| Squirrel season | 401(D) | 4 | 1 | 7 (G) | 30 |
| Badger | 402(D + P) | 4 | 1 | 7 (G) | 54 |
| Celery stick | 403(D + P$_S$) | 3 | 4 (x✔✔) | 3 (P/N) | 50 |
| Kim's game | 403(D + P$_S$) | 4 | 1 | 7 (G) | 28 |
| Trainspot | 405(P$_S$) | 7 | 1 | 3 (P/N) | 54 |
| Washing hands | 408(P$_S$ + J) | 6 | 1 | 4 (V/V) | 37 |
| **(Boys higher: 17 questions)** | | | | | |
| Baby pattern | 401(D) | 9 | 1 | 1 (P/P) | 66 |
| Econocorde | 401(D) | 4 | 1 | 7 (G) | 11 |
| Survey | 402(D + P) | 3 | 5 (✔xx) | 6 (N/N) | 49 |
| High tides | 402(D + P) | 7 | 1 | 5 (V/N) | 48 |
| Photophobic worm | 402(D + P) | 9 | 7 (✔✔x) | 1 (P/P) | 66 |
| Fossil layer | 403(D + P$_S$) | 2 | 3 (x/x) | 3 (P/N) | 59 |
| Acid cross | 403(D + P$_S$) | 3 | 1 | 7 (G) | 24 |
| Cotton reels | 404(P) | 8 | 1 | 1 (P/P) | 69 |
| Traffic meter | 404(P) | 8 | 1 | 3 (P/N) | 20 |
| By-pass | 404(P) | 8 | 1 | 3 (P/N) | 20 |
| Wheels wavy | 404(P) | 8 | 1 | 1 (P/P) | 87 |
| Pine needles | 405(P$_S$) | 4 | 1 | 6 (N/N) | 46 |
| Galileo's spheres | 407(P + J) | 1 | 5 (✔xx) | 5 (V/N) | 34 |
| Hilo-cold | 408(P$_S$ + J) | 4 | 1 | 7 (G) | 43 |
| Reflection | 408(P$_S$ + J) | 9 | 3 (x✔x) | 1 (P/P) | 9 |
| Supaball | 408(P$_S$ + J) | 9 | 3 (x✔x) | 1 (P/P) | 14 |
| Shadow | 408(P$_S$ + J) | 3 | 8 (✔✔✔) | 6 (N/N) | 23 |

\*For definitions see Tables 8.1, 8.2, 8.5 and 8.8.

and 'Bypass' come into the transport category; but so does 'Trainspot'. The first two, however, present a plan view and involve the flow of vehicles, being classed as Pattern type 8, whereas 'Trainspot' requires recognition of drawings of four different types of engine and a sequence of times of appearance. It is clear that the power of a question to discriminate between boys and girls depends on a complex interaction of a number of factors, many of which remain to be explored.

## 8.10 Judging the applicability of statements to data

This subcategory now includes two Question types:

| Given | Outcome |
|---|---|
| Equivocal data and a statement (or pair of contradictory statements) | Assess and discuss the validity of presented statement in relation to data |
| Data and a minimum of four statements | Assess the validity of the statements in relation to data and identify those consistent with it |

One question of the first type, 'Mushrooms', was discussed on page 73 of the report of the first survey (DES, 1982a). The following year such questions were included in the subcategory pool for **Interpreting** presented information, in addition to the newly introduced coded answer version. Subsequently both Question types were removed from that pool, which is now restricted to questions concerned with perceiving regularities in data, as described in section 8.2 above. In both Question types in **Judging the applicability of statements to data**, an element of doubt is introduced which is not present in **Interpreting**. In the first the presented data are in some way equivocal. Sometimes they can be seen as supporting two or more incompatible relationships; sometimes the evidence for a relationship is very weak, as, for example, where the results of a survey are very close. Pupils are asked to assess the validity, with respect to these equivocal data, of a statement or pair of opposed statements. The second of the two Question types is rather different. The information presented is not in itself equivocal, and usually takes the form of a set of data pairs in which one or more clear relationships can be perceived. Pupils are then asked to consider five statements and identify those which follow from the presented data and those which do not. The statements may include proposed descriptions of one of the relationships, or predictions based on it, as well as statements tangential to the data, making unwarranted assumptions. One (rather specialised) set of such questions is reported in section 6.4 of Report No 4 at age 13 (DES, 1986a). 'Woodlice choice' (DES, 1984a, page 172) is another example. It has been decided that not only are these questions sufficiently distinct in character to warrant exclusion from **Interpreting**, but also that they are too few in number to justify the production of an overall subcategory score. When Report No 4 was written, this decision had not yet been made; a few questions of both types had been included in the relevant survey and so reference was made to them in the discussion of performance on question elements. (The open-ended and coded answer Question types were then referred to as Ass and Ass$_S$ respectively.) When results from all surveys are included, the average value of mean scores for seven questions of the open-ended type is 21 per cent and that for nine coded answers questions 28 per cent.

As well as a low mean score, there is a relatively high non-response rate for questions of the first type; they require an extended response (always less popular than a coded answer or single phrase response) and in addition the uncertainty of the data, often emphasised by the wording of the question, appears to increase the tendency to pass on to the next item. For example, data may be followed by two contrasting statements attributed to John and Mary respectively. Pupils are asked 'Who do you agree with, John or Mary?', followed by 'Give a reason for your answer'. A similar question, but with the uncertainty removed, would be 'Say why John is wrong'. The indications are that although the mean score would not be very different, the non-response rate would go down. However, this rate is very much lower for questions of the second type, even though pupils do not necessarily respond to all five options. The effect of uncertainty is partially balanced by the attraction of a coded answer response.

## 8.11  Distinguishing degrees of inference

Questions in this group fall outside the subcategory **Interpreting presented information** because there is no pattern to be perceived in the presented information. They are, in fact, closely associated with the **Observation** category, except that the factors of which notice is to be taken have been extracted from reality and presented on paper. Typically, information is presented as a line drawing of an event or situation, followed by five statements relating to that information incorporating varying levels of inference. In a few cases the presented information takes the form of a written account rather than a line drawing. Initially, attempts were made to write questions such that statements could be ranked in order of degree of inference; this proved, perhaps predictably, not to be feasible. As a result of such trials, a single Question type is used, in which pupils are required to select the statement resting on the *least* inference.

Finding a way to explain to pupils what was required of them proved difficult; one solution (in the question 'Sheep', DES, 1982a, page 78) was to ask, after the statements:

'Tick the *one you can be most sure* is true just by looking at the picture'.

In most questions, the statements were claimed to have been made by five different people, and pupils were asked:

'Who sticks closest to what they can see without jumping to conclusions? Put a tick in the box next to the *one* you choose'.

This was the style used in a sub-group of questions in which some of the likely inferences had to do with the sex of persons doing particular jobs in the presented pictures–looking under the bonnet of a car, perhaps, or pushing a pram. (DES, 1986a, page 86.) Mean scores ranged from 21 per cent to 68 per cent, the average being 44 per cent. In 12 questions, girls performed at a slightly higher level than boys, but in only two cases were the differences significant. One was 'Election' (DES, 1982a, page 79) where, from the most recent survey, the mean scores were 40 per cent and 49 per cent for boys and girls respectively; the other, 'Milkman', which has not been reported, had mean scores of 43 per cent and 56 per cent for boys and girls respectively. In the latter case the biggest factor causing the differences in scores seems to have been the abnormally high rate of multiple response (7 per cent) on the part of the boys. The non-response rates were very low throughout, in spite of the unusual demand of the questions; no doubt this was due to their coded answer format. It never rose above 2 per cent and was more often zero.

On the whole pupils appeared to understand the nature of the unfamiliar demand being made of them in these questions. Of course a statement intended to carry the **least** inference can never carry *no* inference and may sometimes have been rejected by pupils on quite legitimate grounds. In the question 'Painters', for example, option A–'Someone is painting an upstairs window'– was deemed to carry least inference; but pupils might consider that the windows were being cleaned, rather than painted, and this thought would then overshadow inferences carried by other statements, like the male sex of the person up the ladder. In many other sub-categories, it has been noted that pupils often respond from belief or experience, rather than evidence put before them in the question. It is therefore encouraging to observe them in this collection of questions, over 40 per cent of the pupils are able to avoid falling into this particular trap.

## 8.12  Interpretation of patterns in space: the spatial probe

Questions in the **Interpreting** bank requiring the perception of patterns in space such as that of reflection–essentially one of symmetry–had proved to have low mean scores and to discriminate sharply between boys and girls. Many of these questions were set in a Physics context. It was not therefore, clear whether the lower mean scores for girls were associated with the nature of the pattern or the physics context; both factors have been suggested as having an adverse effect on girls' performance. An understanding of elementary physics requires the perception and use of this and other spatial patterns, and so it was thought worth while to include in the final survey 12 questions written to probe this area. The intention was to gain information on the following:

– Do pupils find the spatial patterns of physics hard to recognise?

– Do the patterns appear to be harder in some contexts than others?

– Is the difference in performance between boys and girls already noted consistent across all patterns and in all contexts tried?

There were 12 of these probe questions in all, distributed across 12 different packages. They are reproduced on pp. 92–7, and the results summarised in Table 8.12. The first seven required the recognition of *direction of movement* in the coils of a spiral as clockwise or anticlockwise. Four were about coils of wire through which an electric current flowed, two about twining plants, and one about water flowing through pipes. The words 'upright', 'horizontal' and 'random' describe the disposition of the spirals on the page, $P_S$ and D indicate the demand made (select one prediction from a choice of five, describe a pattern). The next three questions were concerned with the equal angle law of reflection at a plane surface, one in an abstract setting, one set in the context of physics with a drawing of a lamp and references to rays of light, and the third in the context of a game of snooker. (In view of the popularity of the programme 'Pot Black' on television, this might be

described as an 'everyday' context.) The final two questions were designed to investigate pupils' ability to perceive the pattern known as the 'left-hand rule'.

It proved exceptionally difficult to write questions in such a way that pupils responded appropriately to the demand 'describe the pattern'. Simply to ask 'what pattern do you see?' or 'what do these things have in common?' allowed too many opportunities for responses unconnected with the regularity to be perceived. In order to make the task clear, it was found necessary to contrast four drawings which conformed to the regularity involved with a fifth which did *not* conform, and then to ask how the first four were similar to one another but different from the fifth. The fact that such a circuitous method of asking the question is necessary itself suggests one reason why performance is generally low – the language needed for efficient communication is lacking. (Of course it is easy to ask pupils to 'spot the odd man out', and give a reason for their choice. But this is a different demand.)

As well as summarising the questions included in the probe, Table 8.12 shows mean scores and non-response rates overall and for boys and girls separately.

*The spiral group*

(i)  Questions 1–4: Coils

In 'Horizontal coils' and 'Random coils' pupils are asked to identify the one coil in which the current flows clockwise, viewed from a specified position. The mean scores for these (41 per cent and 33 per cent respectively) are more than twice those for the corresponding elements 'Select a prediction' of the other two coil questions (15 per cent and 16 per cent). In 'Upright coils' the drawings are identical to those in 'Horizontal coils', but rotated through a right-angle. However the viewing position is not stated directly, but

**Table 8.12**  *The spatial probe – mean scores for question parts and non-response rates*

| Question | % mean score: | | | | | | % non-response rates: | |
|---|---|---|---|---|---|---|---|---|
| | Describe | | | Select a prediction | | | Describe | Select a prediction |
| | All | Boys | Girls | All | Boys | Girls | | |
| 1.  Upright coils | | | | 15 | 13 | 17 | | 2 |
| 2.  Horizontal coils | | | | 41 | 45 | 37 | | 1 |
| 3.  Random coils | | | | 33 | 34 | 32 | | 2 |
| 4.  Coils and coils | 6 | 6 | 6 | 16 | 20 | 12 | 21 | 4 |
| 5.  Upright twiners | | | | 37 | 38 | 35 | | 1 |
| 6.  Twiners and twiners | 2 | 2 | 2 | 9 | 8 | 10 | 13 | 1 |
| 7.  Random pipes | | | | 41 | 42 | 41 | | 3 |
| 8.  Abstract rebound | 9 | 11 | 7 | 20 | 21 | 20 | 23 | 7 |
| 9.  Light rebound | 14 | 19 | 9 | 28 | 35 | 20 | 16 | 6 |
| 10.  Snooker rebound | 17 | 21 | 14 | 23 | 30 | 16 | 7 | 3 |
| 11.  Finger box | | | | 28 | 26 | 30 | | 3 |
| 12.  Finger and thumbs | 15 | 15 | 15 | 33 | 34 | 31 | 20 | 9 |

n = about 500

## Question 1

The drawings show five different coils of wire. They are standing upright on a bench. They are connected to batteries (not shown) so that currents flow through the wire in the directions of the arrows.

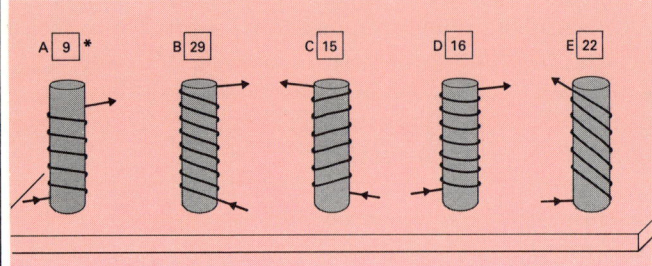

In which of the coils is the current moving upwards in a clockwise direction? Put a tick in the box above the one you choose.

| Upright coils | P 0001 | QD 406 | MARK SCHEME | |
|---|---|---|---|---|
| | | | Score | Code |
| Key C | | | 1 | C |
| | | | 0 | A B D or E |

## Question 2

Look at the drawings of five coils of wire. They are connected to batteries (not shown) so that a current flows through the wires in the direction of the arrows.

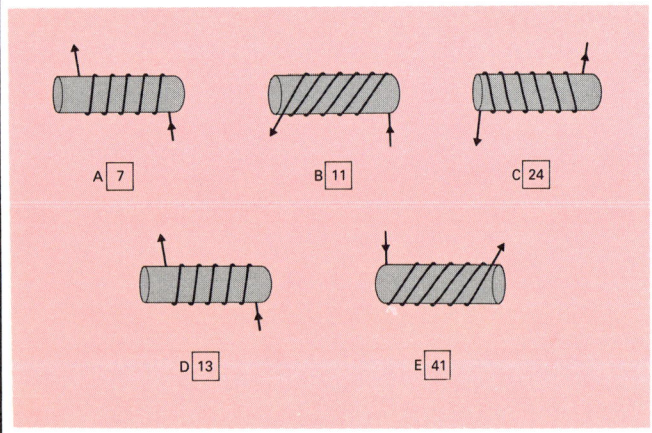

Imagine you are looking at the coils from the right hand side. Which coil has the current flowing in a clockwise direction? Put a tick in the box beside the one you choose.

| Horizontal coils | P 0002 | QD 406 | MARK SCHEME | |
|---|---|---|---|---|
| | | | Score | Code |
| Key E | | | 1 | E |
| | | | 0 | A B C or D |

## Question 3

The drawings show the direction in which an electric current flows through five coils of wire. (The connections to the batteries are not shown).

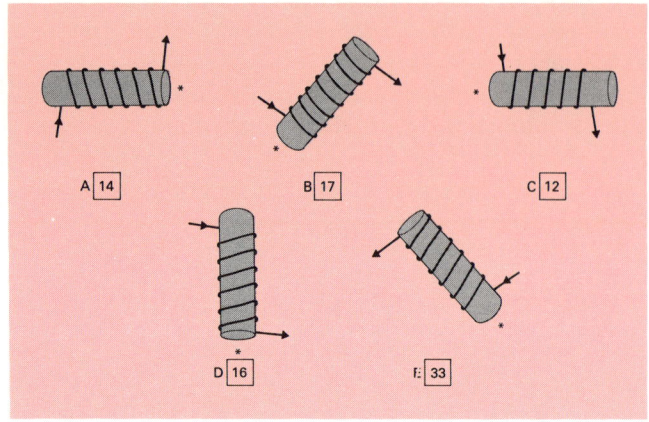

If you were able to look through the coils from the end marked *, in which one would the current be flowing in a clockwise direction? Put a tick in the box beside the one you choose.

| Random coils | P 0003 | QD 406 | MARK SCHEME | |
|---|---|---|---|---|
| | | | Score | Code |
| Key E | | | 1 | E |
| | | | 0 | A B C or D |

## Question 4

The drawings show four different coils of wire; a current flows through each coil in the direction of the arrow. (The connections to the battery are not shown).

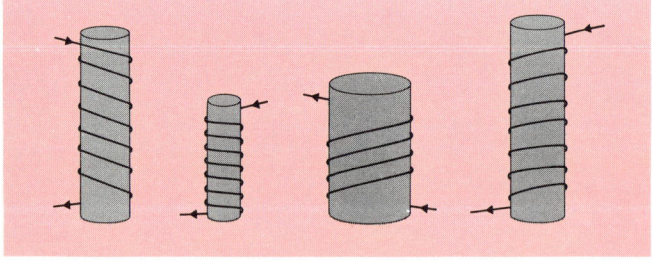

a) What is there similar about the way the current flows at the bottom of these coils, but is different in the one below?

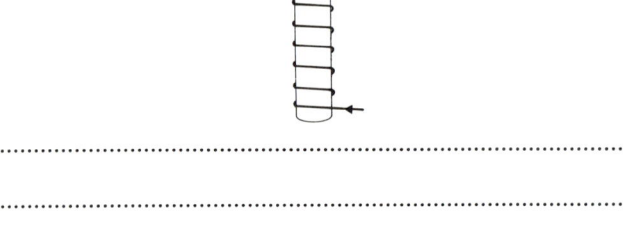

.................................................................................

.................................................................................

.................................................................................

---

*The figures in the boxes (Questions 1–12) indicate the percentage of pupils choosing a particular option or making a given type of response.*

*continued on facing page*

Question 4 (*continued*)

b) Which <u>one</u> of the coils shown below does not fit in with the first four? Put a tick in the box under the <u>one</u> you choose.

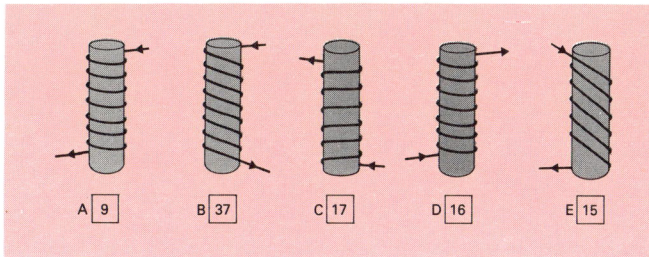

A 9    B 37    C 17    D 16    E 15

| Coils and coils    P 0004    QD 403 | MARK SCHEME | |
|---|---|---|
| | Score | Code |
| a) They are similar because: | | |
| The current flows <u>round</u> the coil in the same direction, ie <u>clockwise</u> if viewed from below (or vice versa). (Current goes clockwise is adequate) | 3 | A  1 |
| The current flows <u>round</u> the coil in the same <u>direction</u> | 2 | B  4 |
| The current goes round the back | 1 | C  8 |
| b) Key D | 1 | D |
| | 0 | A B C E |

implied by the phrase 'current *moving* upwards'. Some pupils may in fact have answered simply by looking for an 'odd man out'.

The fourth question, 'Coils and coils', was an attempt to elicit a description of the pattern without mentioning the words clockwise or anticlockwise. Some pupils unfortunately answered part (a) in terms of whether the current flows across the front instead of behind the back of the cylinder on which the coil is wound. Pupils who described this pattern (8 per cent) rather than that intended (5 per cent) would be likely to have chosen option B, which attracted 37 per cent of the pupils, rather than the intended option D, which collected only 16 per cent of the votes.

(ii)   Questions 5 and 6: Twiners

The intention here was to write questions which were parallel to 'Upright coils' and 'Coils and coils' but with a biological rather than a physics context.

The mean score for 'Upright twiners' was more than twice for 'Upright coils'. The wording was in terms of 'a plant climbing' rather than 'current moving upwards'; it is hard to tell whether the improvement in performance was due to the possibility of using simpler wording in the question, to the more solid-looking drawings, or to the biology context. Whatever the cause of the improvement, it did not operate in 'Twiners and twiners', where the scores for the two question elements 'Describe' and 'Select a prediction' were 2 per cent and 9 per cent, compared with 6 per cent and 16 per cent for 'Coils and coils', the parallel question in the physics

context. There was a very high non-response rate for the 'Describe' element (21 per cent); presumably because a pattern depending on a clockwise or anticlockwise direction of climbing did not suggest itself to pupils. In the 'Select a prediction' element, 50 per cent of the pupils wrongly chose option D, not because it answered the question, which was in terms of 'climbing up', but presumably because the plant had no leaves and was seen as an anomalous case.

Question 5

The drawings show five different plants which climb upwards by twining their stems or stalks round a support, such as a stick.

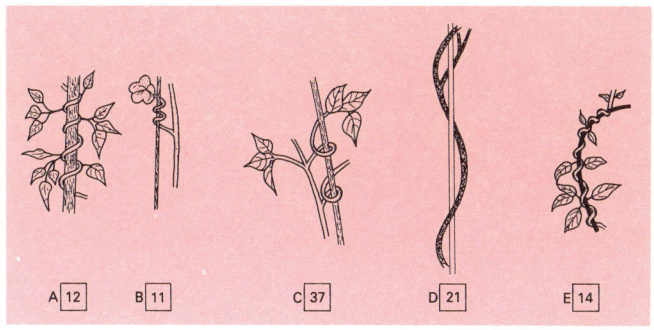

A 12    B 11    C 37    D 21    E 14

Which <u>one</u> of the plants is climbing anti-clockwise? Put a tick in the box under the plant you choose.

| Upright twiners    P 0005    QD 406 | MARK SCHEME | |
|---|---|---|
| | Score | Code |
| Key C | 1 | C |
| | 0 | A B D or E |

Question 6

The drawings show four different plants which climb upwards by twining their stems or stalks around a support, such as a stick.

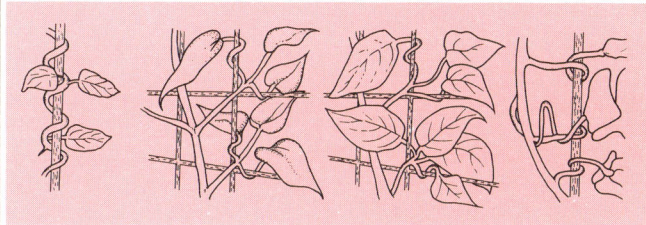

a) How are the four plants climbing up in a similar way to one another but differently from the one below?

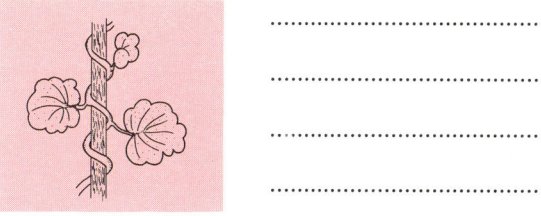

...............................................

...............................................

...............................................

...............................................

*continued overleaf*

93

## Question 6 (continued)

b) Which of the five plants drawn below does not climb up in the same way as the first group? Put a tick in the box under the one you choose.

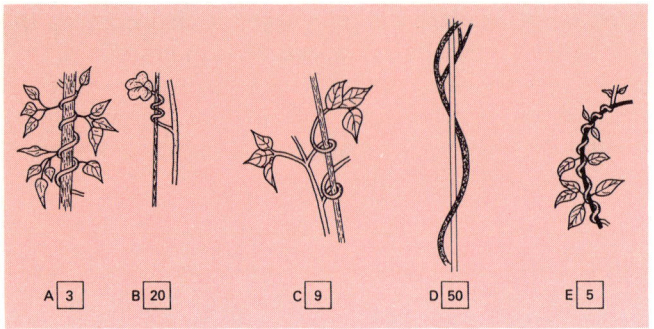

| | | | | |
|---|---|---|---|---|
| A 3 | B 20 | C 9 | D 50 | E 5 |

Twiners & Twiners    P 0006    QD 403    MARK SCHEME

|  | Score | Code |
|---|---|---|
| a) All are going round the stick in the same direction—clockwise | 3 | A  1 |
| (climbing clockwise is adequate) | | |
| All are going round in same direction | 2 | B  1 |
| It climbs in opposite direction | 1 | C  1 |
| b) Key C | 1 | C |
| | 0 | A B D or E |

## Question 7

The arrows in the drawings show the direction in which water flows through part of a pipe in the shape of a coil.

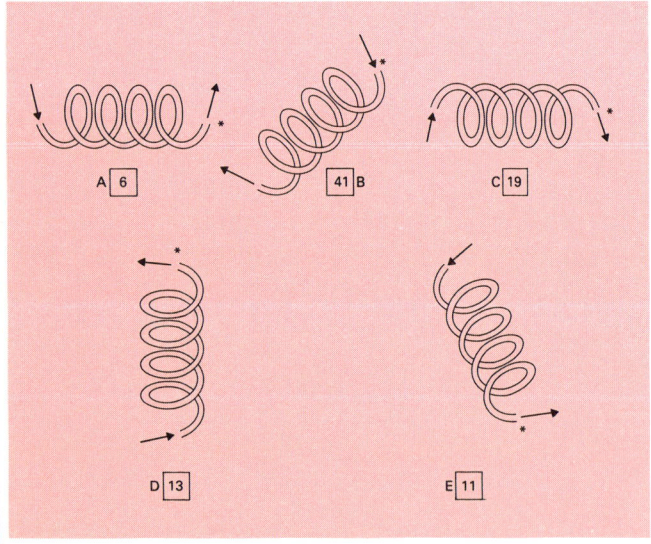

| | | |
|---|---|---|
| A 6 | 41 B | C 19 |
| D 13 | E 11 | |

If you were able to look through the coils from the end marked *, in which one would the water be flowing in a clockwise direction? Put a tick in the box beside the one you choose.

Random pipes    P 0007    QD 406    MARK SCHEME

|  | Score | Code |
|---|---|---|
| Key B | 1 | B |
| | 0 | A C D or E |

## (iii)  Question 7

The question 'Random pipes' was very similar to 'Random coils', but with a different context—perhaps nearer to everyday than to physics. The mean scores for the two, both of which were 'Select a prediction' elements, were 41 per cent and 33 per cent. Possibly the increased score was due not so much to the change of context from physics to everyday as to the more concrete nature of the question content: in some circumstances water can actually be seen to flow.

Boys fared better than girls on only two of the seven questions in this spiral group: 'Horizontal coils' ('Select a prediction', boys 45 per cent, girls 37 per cent) and the corresponding elements of 'Coils and coils' (boys 20 per cent, girls 12 per cent). In the other five cases there was no significant difference in performance.

### The rebound group (questions 8–10)

Each of the three questions in this group was compound, demanding first a description of the pattern and then a coded answer based on the pupil's perception of the pattern. The format of all three questions was similar to that already described for the question 'Coils and coils'; in order to make the task clear to pupils, four examples which fitted the equal angle pattern were contrasted with one which did not. The diagrams were identical in all three questions but in the second two the context was set by an introduction and a drawing, in one case including lamp, beam of light and mirror, and in the other a snooker player, table, and balls. The mean scores for the 'Describe' element were below 20 per cent in all cases, though highest for the snooker setting at 17 per cent and lowest for the abstract setting at 9 per cent. Mean scores were higher for the 'Select a prediction' element, this time with the light context having the highest, 28 per cent, and the abstract setting again lowest, 20 per cent. It is of interest to note that the non-response rate for the 'Describe' element of the abstract version is much higher than that for corresponding elements of the other two contexts. But perhaps the most interesting thing about these questions is the difference in performance of boys and girls; the mean score for boys was very much higher than that for girls in all cases but one—the *coded answer* element of the *abstract* version. The relative non-response rates do not, on the other hand, indicate a strong reaction by girls against the other two contexts when both elements of each question are taken into account.

## Question 8

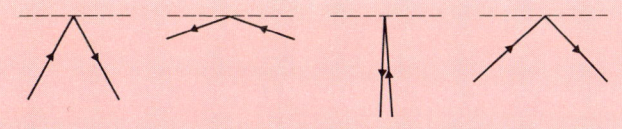

a) How are the four drawings above similar to one another but different from the one below?

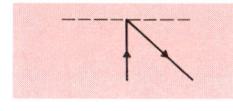

............................................................

............................................................

............................................................

b) Which of the five drawings below does <u>not</u> fit in with the first four?
Put a tick in the box beside the <u>one</u> you choose.

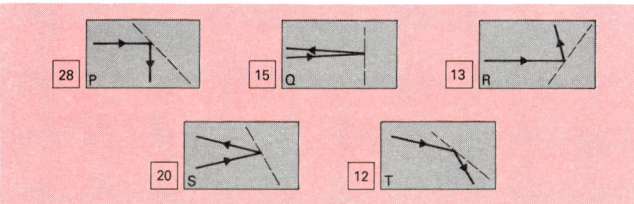

| Abstract rebound | P 0008 | QD 403 | MARK SCHEME | |
|---|---|---|---|---|
| | | | Score | Code |
| a) Angle of incidence is equal to angle of reflection. Angle between arrowed lines (rays) and dotted line is the same | | | 3 | A 4 |
| Diagrams are all symmetrical | | | 3 | B 1 |
| The angles are equal | | | 2 | C 2 |
| All (acute) angles, not straight up or at right angles to dotted line | | | 0 | D 22 |
| Not at 'an angle'–meaning the odd one is not symmetrical or is skewed | | | 1 | E 4 |
| Ones above are reflected off a mirror | | | 3 | F 2 |
| b) Key S | | | 1 | S |
| | | | 0 | P Q R or T |

## Question 9

Mary had a lamp and a mirror, set up like this:

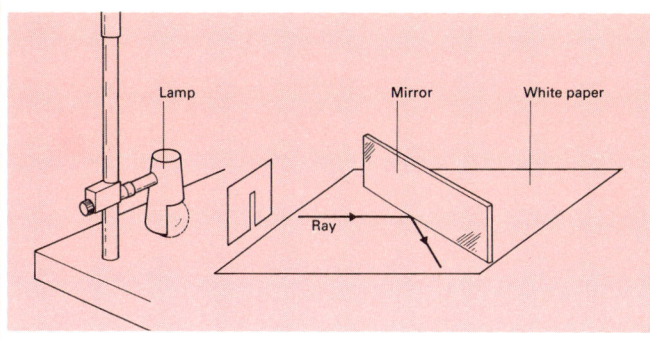

She marked the ray of light on the paper before it hit the mirror and after it was reflected. She did this several times, using a fresh piece of paper and changing the position of the mirror each time.

a) Here are her first four results:

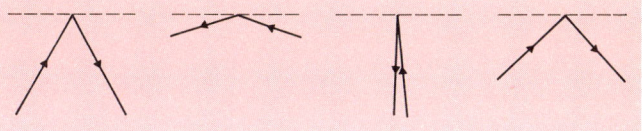

How are they similar to one another but different from the one below?

............................................................

............................................................

............................................................

b) Mary made drawings of five more reflections with the mirror in different positions. But she made a mistake in one of them.
Put a tick in the box next to the <u>one</u> you think is wrong.

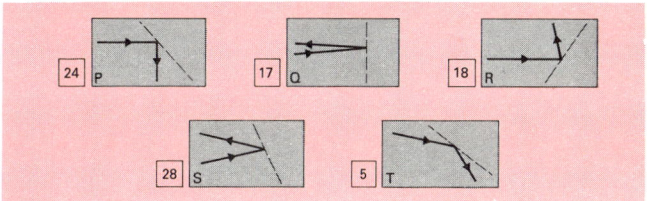

| Light rebound | P 0009 | QD 403 | MARK SCHEME | |
|---|---|---|---|---|
| | | | Score | Code |
| a) Angle of incidence is equal to angle of reflection. Angle between rays and mirror is the same | | | 3 | A 6 |
| Diagrams are symmetrical | | | 3 | B 2 |
| The angles are equal | | | 2 | C 7 |
| All acute angles/not straight up/not at right angles to mirror | | | 0 | D 16 |
| They are not 'at an angle' meaning not skewed or asymmetrical like the odd one | | | 1 | E 4 |
| b) Key S | | | 1 | S |
| | | | 0 | P Q R or T |

## Question 10

Joe was watching his brother, who was practising making a ball rebound from the edge of a snooker table.

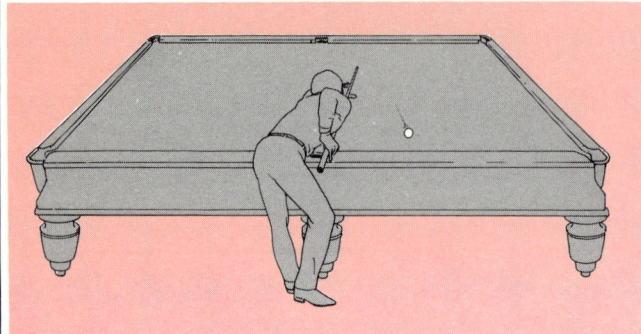

Each time his brother hit the ball, Joe made a drawing showing how it had moved.

a) Here are his first four drawings:

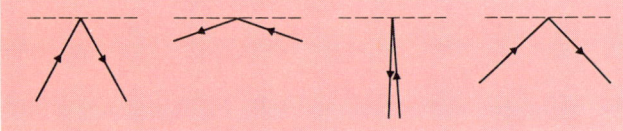

How are they similar to one another but different from the one below?

............................................................

............................................................

............................................................

b) Joe made drawings of five more rebounds from different positions. But he made a mistake in one of them.
Put a tick in the box next to the <u>one</u> you think is wrong.

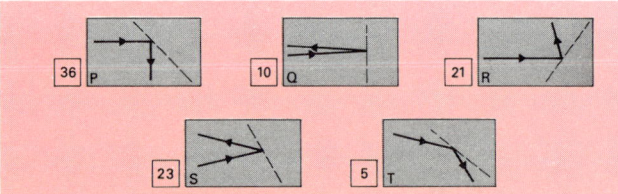

| Snooker rebound | P 0010 | QD 403 | | MARK SCHEME | |
|---|---|---|---|---|---|
| | | | Score | | Code |
| a) Angle of incidence is equal to angle of reflection<br>Angle between paths of ball and edge of table are equal | | | 3 | | A 9 |
| Diagrams are symmetrical | | | 3 | | B 2 |
| The angles are equal | | | 2 | | C 9 |
| Others hit at an angle, not straight up/or at right angles to edge | | | 0 | | D 48 |
| He hit it slower/harder | | | 0 | | E 0 |
| Not a possible shot | | | 0 | | F 2 |
| b) Key S | | | 1 | | S |
| | | | 0 | | P Q R or T |

## The 'Left-hand rule' pair (questions 11 and 12)

The format for the question 'Fingers and thumbs' was again as decribed for 'Coils and coils'. Pupils were invited to describe a pattern by stating how four diagrams were similar to one another but different from a fifth, and then to select the one example from five which did not fit the pattern. Question 11, 'Finger box', presented the same five diagrams as part (b) of question 12, but pupils were asked to pick out the one in which the labelled box did not fit into the left-hand. Mean scores were slightly higher for the 'Select a prediction' element of 'Fingers and thumbs' (33 per cent) than for the 'Finger box' (28 per cent), even though the pattern had first to be inferred.

## Question 11

You can fit the corner of a box in your left hand like this:—

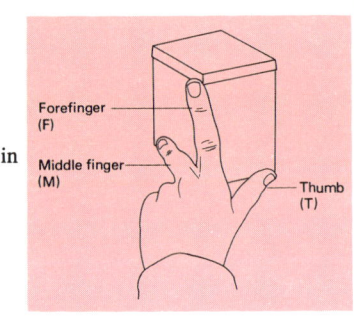

Look at the diagrams below and decide whether you could fit the corners of the boxes in your left hand in the way shown. (T stands for thumb, F for forefinger and M for middle finger).

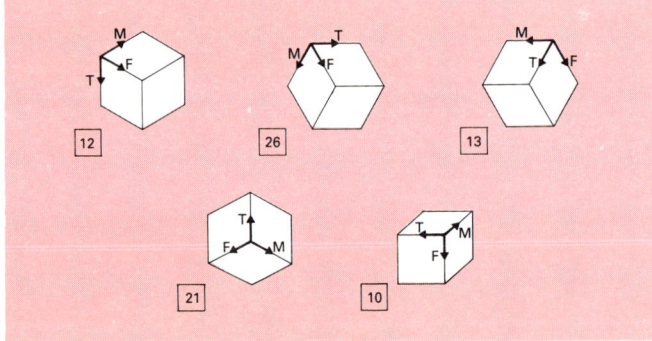

Put a tick in the square beside the <u>one</u> arrangement which is not possible.

| Finger box | P 0011 | QD 406 | | MARK SCHEME | |
|---|---|---|---|---|---|
| | | | Score | | Code |
| (Read squares A B C D E) | | | | | |
| Key B | | | 1 | | B |
| | | | 0 | | A C D or E |

## Question 12

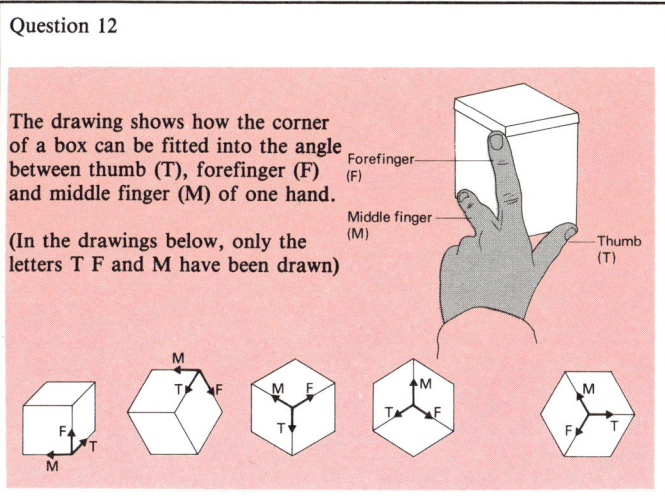

The drawing shows how the corner of a box can be fitted into the angle between thumb (T), forefinger (F) and middle finger (M) of one hand.

(In the drawings below, only the letters T F and M have been drawn)

Forefinger (F)
Middle finger (M)
Thumb (T)

a) How are the first four diagrams similar to one another but different from the last one?

..............................................................................

..............................................................................

..............................................................................

b) Which <u>one</u> of the diagrams below does <u>not</u> fit in with the first four above? Put a tick in the square beside the one you choose.

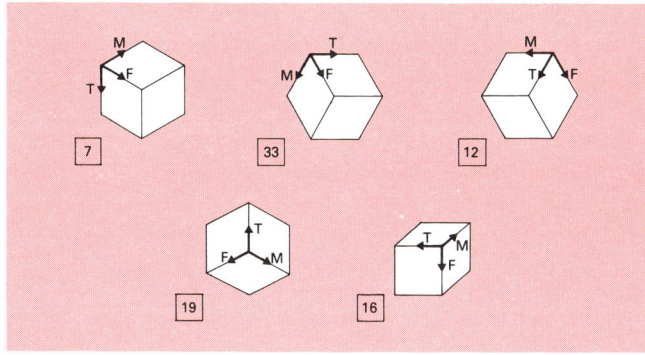

7   33   12

19   16

| Fingers & thumbs | P 0012 | QD 403 | MARK SCHEME | |
|---|---|---|---|---|
| | | Score | | Code |
| a) First four will fit left hand, but the last one needs the right hand | | 3 | | A 6 |
| Last one will not fit left hand | | 2 | | B 2 |
| Last one does not fit/is not possible | | 1 | | C 23 |

b) Read as if   A    B    C
               D    E

| | | | |
|---|---|---|---|
| Key B | | 1 | B |
| | | 0 | A C D or E |

---

*An overall view of the probe questions*

In each compound question, the mean score for the 'Describe' element was lower than for the 'Select a prediction' element. The question with highest performance on the 'Describe' element was 'Snooker rebound' (17 per cent)–an everyday context–but two questions had a mean score of 41 per cent, the highest score for a 'Select a prediction' element: 'Horizontal coils' and 'Random pipes'.

The format for the compound questions was used (in addition to the main purposes of the probe already discussed) to test the hypothesis that girls in particular will make use of a pattern more readily when they have first been required to describe it. This hypothesis is not supported by comparisons between the three relevant pairs of questions–1/4, 5/6 and 11/12. Indeed in the first and last pairs girls fared relatively worse after describing the pattern.

In general, all of three patterns appeared to be hard to describe; the effect of changes in context is difficult to interpret, since effects are not consistent. There appears to be little difference in performance between boys and girls in the 'spiral' and 'left hand rule rule' patterns, but a noticeable difference in the 'rebound' group, with the exception already noted.

## 8.13   Summary

This is a category in which pupils are asked questions which are unfamiliar in kind. They are not asked to recall facts or explanations, or to describe objects or procedures. They are asked to generalise from presented data and make specific use of such generalisations; to assess the validity of statements with respect to given information and to recognise degrees of inference. It is likely that none of these things receives much direct attention in a typical science course, and the level of performance reflects this as well as pupils' ability to operate the processes themselves. Pupils appear to need practice in phrasing their responses–in knowing how much to say. It is no good writing, in response to the question 'Growth rings', for example, 'the number of rings depends on the height of the tree' because there is no sense of direction contained in that statement. Neither does it suffice to say 'the tallest tree has most rings' because this is a specific statement and not a generalisation. Some pupils just do not say enough: 'It gets bigger' might refer to any one of several variables. There is no way of telling whether the pupil who writes this has perceived the pattern or not; certainly it has not been described. At a more precise level, pupils often fail to give sufficient detail about a relationship. Given a graph showing the increase in length of an elastic band with increasing load, many pupils say simply 'the heavier the load the longer the band' without reference to the change in rate of the increase in length. Quite precise use of language is needed if regularities (or, indeed, anomalies) are to be described. Most pupils will need practice before they are able to distinguish between the meaning of 'one thing goes up in proportion to another' and that of 'one thing goes up if another thing goes up'.

Teachers expect many pupils to have difficulty in expressing answers; it is less common for teachers (in their role of examiners) to acknowledge problems in expressing the questions. Yet it appears that pupils frequently misinterpret questions which require them to operate a process other than recall. In this category, **Interpretation**, the only demand which can be simply expressed with a reasonable chance of successful communication is 'predict', which translates to 'what will happen when...' or a similar phrase. When the demand is to describe a regularity there are no readily understood phrases which convey the correct message to the majority of pupils. Ideally it would be preferable to avoid pinpointing the identity of the quantities involved, and to use a phrase such as 'What pattern do you notice in this information?' Unfortunately the word 'pattern' seems to be interpreted by some pupils as a visual pattern, as in a roll of wallpaper. In the question 'Growth rings' (DES, 1984a, page 161), in which the word 'pattern' was used, 6 per cent of 13 year old pupils responded in terms of a *visual* pattern. 'What do you notice?' appears to draw attention to specific peculiarities rather than to regularities. Even when the two variables are identified, problems remain. 'What have they got in common?' or 'What property do they share?' are equally mystifying to most pupils. Questions appear to be better understood if they include a phrase such as 'What do you notice about x and y?' or 'How does x depend on y?'. When such phrases are used, however, the initial stages of the process of pattern perception are not explored, since irrelevant information is already largely discounted. The 'describe' element of the question 'Pollen' (DES, 1985b, page 91) would elicit a very different performance if pollen count and percentage of humidity were identified as the relevant variables. The difficulty of asking for a description of a regularity without 'giving the game away' is illustrated by the circuitous nature of the wording of some of the questions in the probe described in section 8.12.

There are communication difficulties in the other two subcategories, discussed in sections 8.10 and 8.11. It is hard to phrase a question so that pupils can recognise a demand to weigh two statements against the information presented without necessarily voting entirely in favour of one or the other. It is also very difficult to ensure that pupils know that they are to select all statements which *follow from the data* rather than those that they know, from other sources, to be true. When it comes to distinguishing degrees of inference, effective communication is only achieved by the use of the phrase 'Who sticks closest to what they can see without jumping to conclusions?'

A large part of the difficulty is that pupils are seldom required to perceive and describe patterns, assess validity or consider degrees of inference during the normal course of science lessons, except as necessary steps towards the acquisition of specific items of knowledge or concepts. Very often pupils are guided so carefully and so rapidly up these steps that they have no time to operate the processes for themselves, but must take them as read. For many pupils, before a pattern has been perceived, it has been described by someone else, translated into formal language and solidified into a rule or a law to be learnt by heart. Since it is not common practice for teachers to ask pupils to interpret data, the appropriate language for communicating the request has not been established. It seems likely that this lack of the ability to communicate the nature of what is required may be a major factor affecting the performance of young pupils in **Interpretation.**

# 9

# Application

## 9.1  Introduction

An account of the evolution of Category 4 and its eventual split into the two sections **Interpretation** and **Application** has been given in Chapter 8. In **Interpretation** (4i) no recall of taught science is required, while in **Application** (4ii) pupils need to recall and apply concepts and knowledge from an agreed list which is discussed in section 9.2. From an initial list of descriptors which was common to both sections, (see Figure 8.1, p. 82) **Application** came to be defined in terms of four subcategories; the first three are now differentiated by concept region, and each includes the need to infer, to predict, to assess and to explain, while the fourth requires two or more alternative hypotheses to be suggested with no restriction on concept region. As in other categories, after much writing and trialling, the teams wrote general descriptors of those questions that proved effective in assessing the specified qualities.

Initially, Question types closely paralleled those used in **Interpretation**. However, it often proved difficult to write questions of parallel type; for example, if a science pattern was to be inferred from presented data, there was the chance that it would have been taught already to some of the pupils and therefore be recalled rather than inferred from the data. Instead, information was presented which would not be subject to this disadvantage—in which the pattern or regularity was not a 'law' to which pupils would already have been exposed —but such that exposure to scientific nomenclature or to science concepts such as density or reactivity would be a distinct advantage if not an absolute requirement. The distinction between 'application of knowledge and concepts' in this sense and a 'context effect' is bound to be a fine one in some borderline cases: a few questions written for **Interpretation** could almost be classified **Application** and vice versa. In cases of difficulty the matter was decided, question by question, by a consensus among three team members. Other descriptors were modified or acquired alternative forms; for example the demand 'Describe a relationship based on data and accepted concepts and use it to generate predictions', which is broadly parallel to Question type 402 'Describe and predict', was expanded by the addition of the alternative 'Generate predictions giving reasons based on data and accepted concepts'. The change allowed by the alternative form was considerable, for the data did not now have to constitute a pattern. The presented information more

often than not simply described a situation, and pupils were required to recall and apply a 'pattern' from their science lessons in order to make a prediction and then to explain why they had done so. The nature of the demand resembles that in another of the **Interpretation** Question types 407 'Predict and justify', in which pupils are required to justify the prediction they have generated; in the latter case they are intended to use a perceived pattern in the data, not recall or experience, though as noted in Chapter 8 they do not always respond as intended.

The two sections of Category 4 also diverged in relation to the way in which the three demands, (a) to assess, (b) to distinguish degrees of inference, and (c) to suggest hypotheses, were incorporated or omitted. The differences can be seen in Table 8.1. 'Assessing' was included in each of the first three subcategories in **Application** although finally, after much debate, allocated to a separate subcategory under **Interpretation**. The reasons for this have been discussed in Chapter 8. **Distinguishing degrees of inference** was restricted to situations where recall of science concepts was not a prior requirement, and thus came under the heading **Interpretation**, while **Generating alternative hypotheses** was included in Section 4ii because it was found that pupils drew on a variety of concepts in making their suggestions. A list of the Question types which finally emerged and which now help to define **Application** appears in Appendix 4.

## 9.2  The list of science concepts and knowledge

This list is based on suggestions made by the APU Steering Group on Science; it was amended after consultation with teachers from about 100 schools and the scrutiny of school and Examination Board syllabuses. It was published as an Appendix to the 'Science Progress Report' (DES, 1978). The list indicates the Science concept areas to which pupils might be expected to have been exposed at the end of three stages in their school career: the end of the primary stage; the end of the first two years of secondary education; and the end of the following year, after which many pupils discontinue some or all of their science subjects. The list has served several purposes. It has provided a map of the territory within which the extent of science knowledge and concepts demanded by questions in the bank can be limited; it has enabled question writers to spread questions across the whole territory; and it has been used to relate pupil performance to concept areas. Reference to Appendix 5 will show how the list is organised. It is broken down into six areas (labelled A to F), two of which relate to biology, two to physics and two to chemistry. Each of these areas is in turn sub-divided into several numbered sections; each section is further defined by a group of short statements, such as 'All living things respire in order to make use of energy stored in food'.

Although the list of concepts and knowledge indicates the concept areas of which pupils are assumed to have had experience, the emphasis in the questions is not on recall of taught science but on the use which pupils make of what they recall. The situation and the data presented in the questions are intended to be novel as far as the pupils are concerned. Thus it is not likely that the required explanations have been taught in relation to the particular content of the question; ideally, nothing in the question should provide a trigger for a parrot-like response. This does not mean that recall is not valued, but that in this category it is not assessed except in conjunction with the need to apply what has been recalled from memory. In order to reduce the burden on recall, a number of questions were written in which a set of concept statements was presented along with other information; pupils were invited to use any or all of the statements to help them to answer the question. It proved difficult to interpret the results. If pupils picked the wrong statement, then error was obvious; but if they picked the right one and repeated it word for word it was not invariably clear whether they were doing so by intent or by chance. A decision was made not to give credit for an answer which was limited to such repetition unsupported by additional comment, since such an answer did not give evidence of understanding.

## 9.3 The variety of factors which might affect performance

During the course of the surveys, attempts have been made to tease out the relative effects on pupil perform-ance of a number of different factors associated with questions in the subcategories relating to **Applying science concepts**. Since in any given question, several, if not all, of such factors are likely to interact, these attempts have proved inconclusive. The situation is even more complex than in the subcategory **Interpreting presented information**. A list of factors includes:

– the Question type to which the question belongs;

– the particular concept area applicable;

– the way in which information is presented (for example by words, numbers, pictures or graph);

– the level of background noise (as in **Interpretation**);

– the extent of mathematical or linguistic demand;

– the context or specific content of the question.

Particular attention has been paid in previous reports to the first two of these factors, using results from the single survey under consideration. It is possible now to review these findings with the advantage that results from all surveys can be aggregated, thus providing a sounder basis for discussion.

## 9.4 The effect of Question type on performance

The Question types listed in Appendix 4 are numbered 430 to 439. At age 13, no questions fall into type 430, 'Re-order the stages of a sequence', and very few into type 439, 'Select one prediction from two and give a reason'.

For ease of reference in tables and figures, symbolic 'shorthand', similar to that which has appeared in earlier reports, will be used as a reminder of the demand made by the question. The 'shorthand' can be read as follows:

| | |
|---|---|
| $P_s$ | select a prediction from four suggestions |
| P | generate a prediction |
| $Ex_s$ | select an explanation from four suggestions |
| Ex | generate an explanation or reason |
| $Ass_s$ | assess five statements and identify any which are correct |
| Ass | assess the validity of one or more statements |

The number of pupils who have been presented with a given question has varied from survey to survey, but is of the order of several hundred. The score obtained by individual pupils can, of course, vary from 0 per cent to 100 per cent of the maximum, but for each question a mean score has been calculated which represents its facility. A question with a mean score of 80 per cent is easier (or at least has elicited higher performance) than one with a mean score of 30 per cent. This way of describing questions applies to those which have a maxi-mum of 3 marks as well as those multichoice questions which carry only one mark. At age 13, all questions of a given type carry the same maximum; only two types (434 $P_s$ and 437 $Ex_s$) carry a single mark. Table 9.1 (p. 101) shows the average mean scores within Question type for the biology, physics and chemistry concept areas separately and for all three areas together. The numbers of questions used are given in parentheses.

The table is ordered according to the average values of the mean scores for each Question type, taken across all

**Table 9.1** *Mean scores within Question types in 'Application' in order of overall mean scores*

Mean % score

| Question type | | Overall | Biology | Physics | Chemistry |
|---|---|---|---|---|---|
| 434 | $P_S$ | 42 (25) | 51 (6) | 37 (8) | 41 (11) |
| 437 | $Ex_S$ | 40 (37) | 36 (17) | 49 (10) | 36 (10) |
| 432 | P | 40 (25) | 37 (6) | 39 (9) | 43 (10) |
| 438 | $Ass_S$ | 37 (39) | 41 (10) | 36 (19) | 35 (10) |
| 431 | P+Ex | 28 (29) | 27 (10) | 31 (11) | 25 (8) |
| 433 | $P_S$+Ex | 27 (28) | 24 (8) | 27 (9) | 30 (11) |
| 435 | Ex | 19 (52) | 16 (16) | 22 (24) | 17 (12) |
| 436 | Ass | 15 (27) | 15 (11) | 14 (8) | 16 (8) |

three concept areas. (The profiles of performance across Question types are not quite identical for the three concept areas, but they are very similar. The numbers of questions in some Question types are rather low; it is possible that had they been higher, the three profiles would more closely approach a common pattern.) The advantage of aggregating across concept areas is that it provides a large number of questions within each Question type.

Table 9.1 shows that the Question types fall into three groups. Those with the highest average performance levels (with an average mean score of about 40 per cent) are:

434 : select a prediction
437 : select an explanation
432 : generate a prediction
438 : select all correct statements

Of these four, three have coded answer response modes and the other requires only a short answer. The next level of difficulty appears to be related to the following two types:

431 : generate a prediction and give a reason
433 : select a prediction and give a reason

These both have mean scores of about 28 per cent. They are similar to one another in that they each have an 'easy' component (ie one of the first group) coupled with the demand to give a reason–to explain. The remaining two types both require extended responses. They are:

435 : explain
436 : assess the validity of a statement

In the first, pupils need to apply some science concepts and knowledge to a situation likely to be new to them; the second provides an additional element of uncertainty: pupils are not told whether they should support or refute a presented statement, so they have to decide for themselves what it is that they need to explain. The average mean score for these two types is less than 20 per cent.

Thus it seems that the questions in the bank can be arranged in three groups according to average mean scores for their Question types.

| High (around 40 per cent) | coded answer questions requiring the selection of one or more correct predictions or hypotheses, or short answer questions requiring the generation of a prediction |
|---|---|
| Medium (around 28 per cent) | questions in which one of the above demands is linked with that to explain a new event or situation |
| Low (below 20 per cent) | questions which require explanations to be given or discussed as extended responses; some include an element of uncertainty |

The levels of difficulty discussed above are related to Question type rather than 'science process'. A division of questions into those which are about the 'process' of predicting and those which are about the 'process' of explaining does not produce a clear difference in performance level; both 'processes' figure in the highest group of Question types. However, predicting falls *only* within this group, while explaining is associated also with the Question types in the lowest group. The different levels of difficulty seem to be due, at least in part, to the mode of response involved; they may also be associated with the 'processes' of predicting and explaining themselves. In the questions in **Applying science concepts** 'predicting' typically requires pupils to focus on one or more specific events, whereas 'explaining' typically means quoting, or at least referring by implication to, a generalisation.

Whatever the reasons, *on average*, the Question types used in the surveys, taken together with their corresponding mark schemes, appear to be associated with three distinct levels of difficulty. There is a sense in which one can say 'coded answer' questions are easy and 'explain' questions difficult; but this is only true for large groups of questions. The very wide range of mean scores for questions in any given Question type indicates that single questions might be easy or difficult, depending on the particular content of the question.

This is illustrated clearly in Figure 9.1 (p. 102), in which the dots represent the mean scores of individual questions and the arrows, indicate the average value of mean scores within a given Question type. Even for a particular concept area (in this case biology) the range of mean scores for each Question type is wide, and the distribution of questions over this range is irregular. Thus the Question type cannot be used as a predictor of difficulty of any individual question.

## 9.5 Performance levels in different concept areas

During the five years during which surveys have been carried out, the mean per cent scores for biology,

**Figure 9.1** *The mean scores of questions displayed within Question types for the biology concept area*

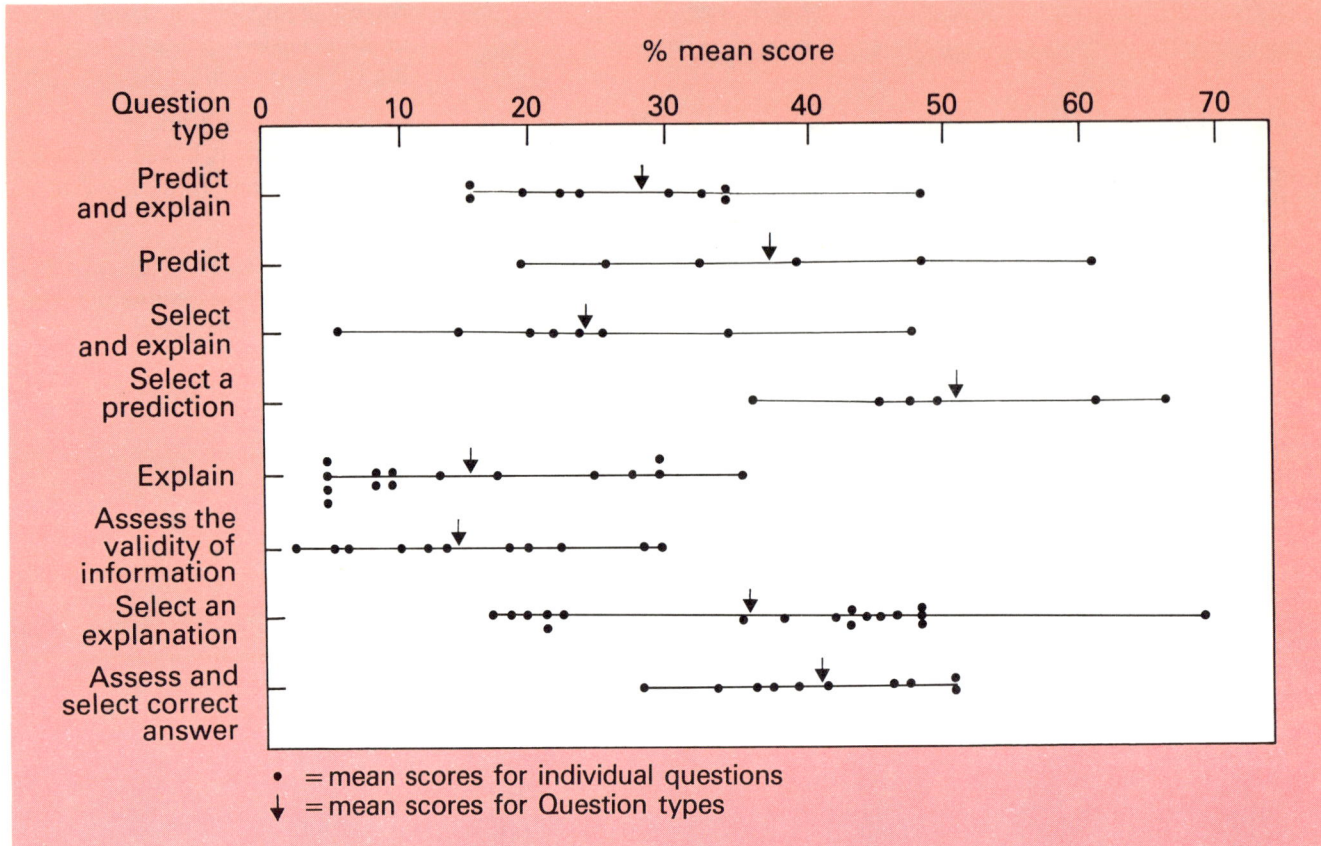

physics and chemistry each decreased after the first year and then remained fairly constant, as described in Chapter 4. In some years one concept area has had a higher mean score than the other two, and in other years another. As Table 4.1 shows, in 1984 performance in the three areas was similar, the mean scores for biology, physics and chemistry being 27 per cent, 29 per cent and 28 per cent respectively.

These global performance levels can be broken down with respect to more limited areas of science concepts, since each question can be related to one of the 26 pages in the 'List of science concepts and knowledge',

the derivation and organisation of which is described in section 9.2. Each page carries a group of statements which help to define the territory to which it refers. The complete list of such statements can be found in Appendix 5. It is of interest to see how performance levels vary across these limited concept areas. Tables 9.2, 9.3 and 9.4 show this variation within biology, physics and chemistry respectively. In each table the average of the mean scores of all questions within the narrow concept area is given, with the range of mean scores and the number of questions concerned.

The numbers of questions within each of these closely defined concept areas is inevitably small and, as can be seen, the range of mean scores across each area is wide; little can therefore be said about relative levels of

**Table 9.2** *Performance levels in different areas of biology*

| Concept areas | No. of questions | Range of mean % scores | Average of mean % scores |
|---|---|---|---|
| **A. Interaction of living things with their environment** | | | |
| 1. Interdependence of living things | 22 | 4–66 | 23 |
| 2. The physical and chemical environment | 10 | 6–61 | 27 |
| 3. Classification of living things | 7 | 10–49 | 31 |
| 4. Physical and chemical principles | 7 | 4–43 | 25 |
| **B. Living things and their life processes** | | | |
| 1. The cell | 3 | 4–61 | 30 |
| 2. Nutrition | 10 | 2–48 | 28 |
| 3. Respiration | 10 | 8–47 | 29 |
| 4. Reproduction | 12 | 21–48 | 32 |
| 5. Sensitivity and movement | 7 | 17–69 | 45 |

**Table 9.3** *Performance levels in different areas of physics*

| Concept areas | No. of questions | Range of mean % scores | Average of mean % scores |
|---|---|---|---|
| **C. Force and field** | | | |
| 1. Movement and deformation | 20 | 9–64 | 35 |
| 2. Properties of matter | 22 | 0–72 | 29 |
| 3. Forces at a distance | 6 | 13–49 | 34 |
| 4. The Earth in space | 8 | 8–67 | 33 |
| **D. Transfer of energy** | | | |
| 1. Work and energy | 26 | 4–57 | 26 |
| 2. Current electricity | 11 | 23–59 | 35 |
| 3. 'Waves' | 10 | 10–64 | 32 |

performance within these areas except, perhaps, that those questions related to area B5 (sensitivity and movement) and to E5 (the periodic table) appear to be easier, *on average*, than those in other areas. However, this statement can only be made with reference to the questions used in the surveys and their corresponding mark schemes. Obviously, the facility of a question will also be affected by its specific content, and by its Question type. Questions used in surveys from a given narrow concept area are not necessarily distributed evenly over Question types. Indeed there may be fewer questions within such a concept area than there are Question types. If Question type *does* have a generalised effect on facility, as discussed in section 9.4, then it is unlikely that anything useful can be said about the relationship of performance to narrow concept area, simply by looking at the averages of mean scores for questions representing them in the surveys.

**Table 9.4** *Performance levels in different areas of chemistry*

| Concept areas | | No. of questions | Range of mean % scores | Average of mean % scores |
|---|---|---|---|---|
| E. | **The classification and structure of matter** | | | |
| 1. | States of matter | 15 | 1–59 | 22 |
| 2. | Pure substance | 8 | 8–39 | 20 |
| 3. | Metals and non-metals | 6 | 3–49 | 32 |
| 4. | Acids and bases | 7 | 19–34 | 28 |
| 5. | Periodic table | 8 | 27–67 | 50 |
| F. | **Chemical interactions** | | | |
| 1. | Solutions | 9 | 6–53 | 28 |
| 2. | Reactivity | 16 | 8–70 | 37 |
| 3. | Properties of chemical reaction | 7 | 10–64 | 30 |
| 4. | Some chemical reactions | 5 | 20–38 | 29 |

In order to explore the effects which Question type may have on performance, questions within each narrow concept area (A1, A2 etc) have been sorted into the three groups High, Medium and Low which are described in section 9.4. Even within such restricted concept areas, the average values of mean scores of the groups show a similar pattern to that described for **Application** overall. When a correction is made for the effect of the different proportions of questions from the groups which occur within each narrow concept area, the mean scores across the different concept areas are remarkably similar, and most of the variation shown in Tables 9.2, 9.3 and 9.4 disappears. The only areas for which the corrected mean score differs by more than 12 per cent of the overall mean from that mean are E1 (states of matter), E2 (pure substance) which have lower means, and E5 (periodic table) which has a higher mean. This lends support to the hypothesis put forward in earlier APU science reports that, for the questions and mark schemes in the bank at age 13, the effects on performance due to Question type override those related to concept area.

## 9.6 Pupils' understanding of particular science concepts

When the framework for assessment was being set up towards the beginning of 1978, a great deal of discussion took place about the interpretability and utility of the survey results which would ensue. One particular area of concern was the degree to which it would be possible to answer questions about the extent of pupils understanding of specific content areas (for example, of the basic principles of heredity). It was suggested at that time that the framework of categories proposed would not allow such questions to be answered without a supplementary programme of some kind. The reason for this suggestion is fairly obvious. If the plan is to provide a large bank of questions for each **Application** subcategory, ranging over all relevant content (that is, any content appropriate to the 26 defined areas of the 'List of concepts and knowledge'), then the number of questions related to a particular concept is likely to be limited. Even allowing 60 questions per subcategory test, there will be only about seven to a concept area as wide as the 'Properties of matter' (C2). Now at age 13 this area includes (as reference to Appendix 5, p. 206, will show) density, pressure, the kinetic theory, diffusion, expansion, displacement and capillarity. Since questions are randomly selected from the bank for use in surveys, there is, of course, no guarantee that they will be evenly spread with respect to those topics. The opportunity to collect information about pupils' understanding of, say, the kinetic theory, has therefore been limited. However it did sometimes happen that over the years a number of related questions were selected by chance, and this allows useful comments to be made about performance with respect to specific concepts, especially since a system of categorising pupil responses, rather than simply awarding a numerical score, was frequently adopted.

Obtaining an insight into pupils' conceptual development is another matter. Not only are more questions needed, concentrated in a particular area of the subcategory framework, but they must be of a particular kind; ideally, they should be open-ended and such that pupils respond to them. Answers to coded answer questions, which have a high response rate, tend to yield little detail; and open-ended questions, or part questions, which lend themselves to category marking of a detailed nature, tend to have a low response rate. The only concept area in which an investigatory probe (an additional package of 'custom-built' questions) has been used at age 13, was in the chemistry area F2: Reactivity. Although several questions were written, trialled and set in the 1981 survey, little additional information was obtained; pupils responded to the 'short answer' parts of the questions but not to the open-ended demands. It has been noted that pupils are more likely to *respond* to questions of the latter sort if they are set in an everyday context rather than a school science context. They seem to be more willing to take a risk in an answer to a question about condensation on jugs of lemonade at a tennis match than in one about condensation on the outside of a beaker of water in the laboratory. Reactivity is not a subject that lends itself readily to this method of encouragement. The very names of metals, salts and acids appear to have an adverse affect on response rate, except when a coded answer or a simple listing of elements is all that is required. Scattered results of interest have surfaced, but they act as a spur to further in-depth research rather than a basis for considered evaluation at this stage.

The assessment framework was not designed to produce differentiated tests, such that all pupils could expect a fair measure of success, but simply to enable the pattern of performance across domains to be charted. The exercise called for a variety of questions ranging from very easy to very hard. Even where questions have a very low mean score, there may be a few pupils who score highly on them. The consequence is that it is easier to point to what thirteen year olds cannot do than to what they can do; easier to itemise common errors than to list successes. In the next few paragraphs attention is drawn again to some of these common errors, most of which have received comment in earlier reports.

*Common errors and tendencies*

- Pupils of this age find it difficult to handle more than one idea at a time; when asked about respiration in animals, they may show that they know the names of the gases involved and which is absorbed and which produced. A smaller proportion have a clear idea of the gaseous exchanges which take place during photosynthesis, though most know that plants need sunlight to 'stay healthy'. However, when required to consider a situation where both processes (as well, of course, as respiration in plants) occur together, very few pupils sustain a clear line of argument.

- Acceleration is understood in a qualitative sense, as 'getting faster'; speed also is dealt with in a satisfactory way as long as nothing quantitative is required. Indeed the need to quantify lowers performance throughout the category, especially where numerical values are not whole numbers.

- Magnetic and electrostatic effects are commonly confused; balloons and combs become 'magnetised' and magnets charged. Attention is focused on the concrete—the magnets—and the concept of a magnetic field appears not to be grasped.

- Pupils appear to understand how the spin of the earth on its axis can account for day and night, but not at all how its revolution in an orbit round the sun accounts for seasonal changes.

- Materials are considered intrinsically 'hot' or 'cold' (metals are 'cold'); how they will feel to the touch is not seen as a function of their temperature and conductivity, but as a recalled experience.

- Objects are visible because we look at them, not because they emit or reflect light; pupils argue in terms of 'line of sight' rather than in terms of rectilinear propagation. Sound 'does not travel in a vacuum' but to most pupils a vacuum is an enclosed space, like a bell jar, rather than space itself.

- There is a great deal of confusion about condensation and evaporation, the words often being used almost interchangeably, or as substitutes for 'water' or for 'water vapour'. Although the factors affecting evaporation appear to be understood in a general way, the fact that evaporation causes cooling is not; many pupils think of water as intrinsically 'cold'—as for example, in wet socks.

- Pupils recognise metals by their physical rather than chemical properties, although they can perceive and use patterns in presented (limited) sections of the periodic table. They can handle the idea of 'an acid' more easily than that of 'acids'; and they think in terms of a substance being an acid, an alkali or neutral rather than of its degree of acidity. The word 'reactive' is associated with a 'violent' reaction, but not necessarily with displacement. Gases and vapours are not seen as contributing to the mass of reactants, and rusting is associated with the presence of water but not of oxygen.

Overall, the impression is of a group of pupils who think in specific terms rather than generalities; who do not engage in quantification; who relate situations to themselves and who rely for their answers as much on experiences gained outside school science as on those gained in the laboratory.

## 9.7 Gender differences in 'Application'

Reference was made in Chapter 4 to gender-related differences in performance within the subcategory of **Applying science concepts**. Boys and girls do not differ much in performance with respect to the biology concept area (except in Wales), and there has been no consistent difference over the 5 years of the surveys with respect to chemistry; but in every survey there has been an overall difference, in favour of boys, in the physics concept area. As already noted, the difference varies from question to question; indeed for a few questions girls do better than boys. In Table 9.5 (p. 105) an indication is given of the number of questions within each Question type that show performance differences which are statistically significant at the 5 per cent level, and of whether the difference is in favour of boys or girls. For example in Question type 435, in the biology concept area, there were two questions in which boys did better than girls and four in which girls did better than boys.

The balance within concept areas (over all Question types) contributes to the separate subcategory results, the greatest inbalance occuring in the physics concept area (boys 43: girls 3). There is also some lack of balance within Question types, though effects are not always consistent across concept areas, and the numbers involved are small.

## Table 9.5 *Gender differences in 'Application'*

(Number of questions within Question types with statistically significant differences in mean scores. The number of questions used altogether is shown in parentheses)

| Question type | | Biology B:G | | Physics B:G | | Chemistry B:G | | Science overall B:G | |
|---|---|---|---|---|---|---|---|---|---|
| 431 | P + Ex | 1:1 | (10) | 4:1 | (11) | 1:1 | (8) | 6:4 | (29) |
| 432 | $P_S$ + Ex | 3:0 | (6) | 7:0 | (9) | 3:2 | (10) | 13:2 | (25) |
| 433 | P | 2:2 | (8) | 6:0 | (9) | 3:3 | (11) | 11:5 | (28) |
| 434 | $P_S$ | 1:0 | (6) | 2:0 | (8) | 0:2 | (11) | 3:2 | (25) |
| 435 | Ex | 2:4 | (16) | 13:0 | (24) | 4:3 | (12) | 19:7 | (52) |
| 436 | Ass | 7:1 | (11) | 3:1 | (8) | 2:1 | (8) | 12:3 | (27) |
| 437 | $Ex_S$ | 2:2 | (17) | 5:0 | (10) | 2:0 | (10) | 9:2 | (37) |
| 438 | $Ass_S$ | 4:0 | (10) | 3:1 | (19) | 2:1 | (10) | 9:2 | (39) |
| All Question types | | 22:10 | (84) | 43:3 | (98) | 17:13 | (80) | 82:26 | (262) |

Although, for each question, any difference in performance was statistically significant, the actual difference in mean scores varied. In some cases it was not, considered alone, of great *educational* significance. However, the complete group of questions was inspected in an attempt to identify characteristics which elicit a difference in performance between boys and girls. The characteristics considered were:

– Context: biology, chemistry, physics, other school lesson, or everyday.

– Narrow concept area: A1 to F4, as described in section 9.2.

– Mathematical content: none, whole numbers, decimals.

– Question length: short, medium (= half a page of prose), long.

– Question style: diagram, line graph, food web, table, prose.

– Response style: coded answer, single phrase, extended writing.

All the questions noted in Table 9.6 have been inspected to see whether any particular characteristic or pattern of characteristics can be associated with either group of questions–those in which boys do significantly better ('B' questions) or those in which girls do significantly better ('G' questions). Of course it is not possible to tell for a question in which, say, boys do better than girls, whether this is because boys perform better than usual or girls worse than usual on that question. It may be that boys are motivated by the content, or girls are dis-

couraged by it, or both. It is also important to bear in mind, during the discussion which follows, that questions selected for use in the survey are not necessarily evenly distributed across any of the characteristics.

## Table 9.6 *Gender differences within narrow concept sections*

(Only those questions with statistically significant differences in mean scores are included. The number of questions used altogether is shown in parentheses)

| Narrow concept section | | B:G | |
|---|---|---|---|
| A1 | Interdependence of living things | 11:0 | (21) |
| A2 | Physical and chemical environment | 1:2 | (10) |
| A3 | Classification of living things | 0:3 | (7) |
| A4 | Physical and Chemical principles to interpret life phenomena | 2:1 | (7) |
| B1 | The cell | 0:0 | (3) |
| B2 | Nutrition | 0:1 | (10) |
| B3 | Respiration | 3:1 | (10) |
| B4 | Reproduction | 2:2 | (11) |
| B5 | Sensitivity and movement | 3:0 | (5) |
| Biology overall | | 22:10 | (84) |
| C1 | Movement and deformation | 11:1 | (19) |
| C2 | Properties of matter | 7:1 | (21) |
| C3 | Forces at a distance | 1:0 | (6) |
| C4 | The Earth in space | 3:1 | (8) |
| D1 | Work and energy | 8:0 | (23) |
| D2 | Current electricity | 5:0 | (11) |
| D3 | 'Waves' | 8:0 | (10) |
| Physics overall | | 43:3 | (98) |
| E1 | States of matter | 7:1 | (15) |
| E2 | Pure substance | 2:1 | (8) |
| E3 | Metals and non-metals | 0:0 | (6) |
| E4 | Acids and bases | 0:0 | (7) |
| E5 | Periodic table | 0:5 | (8) |
| F1 | Solutions | 1:3 | (9) |
| F2 | Reactivity | 3:3 | (15) |
| F3 | Properties of a chemical reaction | 2:0 | (7) |
| F4 | Some chemical reactions | 2:0 | (5) |
| Chemistry overall | | 17:13 | (13) |

Table 9.6 shows the distribution of the group of questions under consideration across the 25 sections of the Concept List. In biology, the 'girls' questions were evenly spread, while half the 'boys' questions were from section A1 (interdependence of living things). In fact half the questions used from that section turned out to be 'boys' questions. In physics, 'boys' questions came from all sections of the concept region, but loaded most heavily into section C1 (movement and deformation) and section D3 (waves). In chemistry, 'boys' questions loaded into section E1 (states of matter), while girls did better in the section E5 (periodic table), where five of the eight questions used are 'girls' questions.

No very firm conclusions about the relationship of gender differences in performance to particular narrow concept areas can be drawn because of the probable interaction effects of other characteristics, such as Question type. Further work is needed to investigate the trends outlined above.

No clear patterns emerged as a result of inspection of the other question characteristics listed. Six of the 30 'girls' questions (20 per cent) and 19 of the 83 'boys' questions (23 per cent) required a coded answer response. In none of the 'girls' questions was a line graph used in presenting the data, while 8 per cent of the 'boys' questions involved a line graph.

## 9.8 Generating alternative hypotheses

Questions in this subcategory describe, in words or otherwise, an event or situation for which there is no obvious single explanation; pupils are asked to suggest hypotheses (or explanations) which are consistent with the data and with accepted science concepts and knowledge. Pupils of age 13 often think of everyday explanations which include no science which can be located on the agreed 'List of concepts and knowledge'; since they are usually invited to give three different suggestions. There is also the possibility that, for any given question, some suggestions will relate to the biology area, some to physics and some to chemistry. Consequently although questions were initially labelled with respect to the narrow concept area of the list as described for **Applying science concepts**, it makes little sense to try to relate performance to these labels. In addition, since each question appears to test something unique to itself, there is no attempt to generalise across them. The number of questions set in this subcategory has therefore been fairly limited. Questions which have been included in the surveys have been reported individually and at length (Reports No. 1, 2, DES, 1982a, and 1984a). They were set in widely different contexts and gave opportunities for the application of ideas about situations as diverse as growth of shrubs, rate of chemical reactions, density, population curves, and weathering of stone.

Two characteristics which responses to all questions had in common were:

– a decrease in response rate which occurred as pupils were required to propose a second and third hypothesis;

– a corresponding fall in score across the three parts as suggestions became less acceptable or repetitive.

Pupils tended to be more *confident*, though not necessarily more *successful*, when the situation described was in an everyday rather than a school science setting. For example, a question about pupils collecting hydrogen from the action of an acid on magnesium had the very high non-response rate of 21 per cent, rising to 44 per cent by the time pupils came to offer their third alternative (DES, 1984a, page 211). A question about the rose bushes growing near the garden fence had a more usual non-response rate (for the subcategory) of 5 per cent, although the conceptual difficulties were as great and the success rate not much higher (DES, 1984a, page 217). An everyday context provides pupils with the opportunity to make wrong suggestions, whereas a strong school science context, in this connection, appears to inhibit pupils' attempts.

## 9.9 Summary

The **Application** subcategories were set up to provide a picture of performance when pupils are called upon to apply science concepts and knowledge to make sense of new information. To do this, it was necessary to arrange for a spread of questions across the whole range of concept areas included in the agreed list, and across an equally wide range of question content and mode of presentation. The major dimensions considered in setting up the framework of the subcategories were *concept area* (labelled sub-divisions of the agreed list) and *Question type* (a combination of the process required and the response mode). It is to these two dimensions that performance has been related.

When questions from all concept areas are considered together, and performance related to Question type, a pattern of performance emerges which suggests that a significant difference in facility exists between three groups of Question types. This is only true if each type is represented by a large number of questions. The three groups are described as high, medium and low in section 9.4. The group of Question types having relatively high facility includes those requiring coded answers or predictions to be made. The group with low facility included types requiring extended explanations or discussion, while in the intermediate group were questions demanding some combination of the two kinds of response, for example a coded answer followed by an explanation.

No difference in performance, in terms either of mean subcategory scores or the profile of performance across Question types, appears to exist between biology, physics and chemistry. When these wide concept areas are divided further, the number of questions within subdivisions are often rather few for any conclusions to be drawn, considering the range of concepts still included and the varying levels of application which might be required. When a correction is made for the effect of the different proportions of questions from the high, medium and low groups of Question types which occur within each narrow concept area, mean scores are remarkably uniform from area to area.

Because of the nature of the assessment framework it is difficult to comment in depth on pupils' understanding of particular concepts, since responses are available from too few relevant questions. However, a number of common errors have arisen, described in section 9.6, which suggest where further research might prove profitable.

# Planning of investigations

## 10.1 Introduction

In the discussions that accompanied the establishment of the assessment framework for science it was agreed that the careful planning of investigations was a fundamental aspect of scientific activity. The category labelled 'Design of investigations' was included in the assessment framework at the three ages in order to assess the general principles involved in such planning. In the year preceding the first science survey, the framework underwent a process of external validation by a number of experts involved at all levels in education. This validation exercise confirmed the view that planning was a significant aspect of school science. Subsequently the term 'design', used in the description of the category, was regarded as insufficiently representative of the general principles involved in the generation of an overall strategy for carrying out investigations in science. The title was therefore changed to that of **Planning of investigations.**

During the initial five-year monitoring phase the team's ideas about the activity of **Planning** changed. The ideas developed as a result of a two-way process which involved reflecting on the work already carried out and, at the same time, looking at what the pupils did when faced with the questions. The chapter will describe the results of this process in two phases. The first reviews the theoretical development of the category. The second is a detailed review of the questions used to assess pupil performance and the pupils' responses to them.

The chapter is organised in the following sections:

10.2 Historical background
10.3 1983–84
Performance review–by type of question
10.4 Assessing testable statements
10.5 Planning parts of investigations
10.6 Planning entire investigations
10.7 Performance by Question type and ability
10.8 Discussion
10.9 Implications

## 10.2 Historical background

This section and the one following it describes the theoretical development of a category of the assessment

framework: **Planning of investigations.** To appreciate the developments in a category it is necessary to keep in mind the scale of the *whole* exercise (see Chapter 1 for discussion). The need to produce domain-referenced pools of questions meant that progress within a category was necessarily slow. Consequently in the first survey (DES, 1982a) the pools were small and only partially representative of a domain. An incremental advance in the development of the domain in one category had the potential to influence the work carried out in others. In some senses the review of the assessment exercise has required the teams to paint a picture of a web of interconnections. The web is only partially formed and in some instances only partially perceived and understood.

The discussion of the background to the category will focus on two theoretical issues pivotal to the definition of the category and its subsequent translation into questions and mark schemes. These are the view of the *purpose* of scientific activity in schools and the understanding of the *nature* of scientific investigations. In the first years of monitoring at ages 13 and 15 the following abbreviated description of **Planning** was developed. For a list of specific question descriptors and a more complete description of the category see DES, 1982a, Chapter 6, Tables 6.15, 6.16 and 6.17.

**Table 10.1** *Abbreviated description of the 'Planning' bank (1980)*

| | |
|---|---|
| Step One | **Assessing testable statements.** This aspect took into account the need, prior to the development of a design for an experiment, for a problem or hypothesis to be framed in such a way that it is open to empirical investigation. |
| Step Two | **Assessing experimental procedures.** This aspect was concerned with the status of particular variables within a presented problem situation. The following variables were highlighted:<br>Those to be:  varied<br>               controlled<br>               or judged irrelevant |
| Step Three | **Sequencing procedures** |

Other specific aspects included in the category were the identification of the status or function of different activities or pieces of apparatus within a particular experiment and finally the recognition of the problem or of the hypothesis being tested in a given experimental design.

Step One was assessed by a group of questions forming a subcategory. The assessment of Steps Two and Three together constituted another subcategory of questions. A question in this subcategory could include a single aspect of one step or a mixture spanning both. In the assessment of Steps One to Three, the type of question response demanded varied; the pupils were required either to select or to generate an answer and, less frequently, to criticise a given design.

The final feature of the category was represented in questions which asked pupils to undertake **Planning entire investigations;** this was the third subcategory. These questions required an extended response and took an average of fifteen minutes to complete. The marking of these questions reflected the structure implicit in Steps One to Three outlined in Table 10.1.

When reflecting on the composition of the **Planning** question banks after the first survey, the impression gained was that the overriding purpose of carrying out scientific investigations in school was the accumulation of a body of scientific knowledge which could be used to explain phenomena. One important way in which such a purpose can be achieved is to demonstrate phenomena to pupils in order to exemplify theories. The use of such theories to explain and predict observable phenomena was the focus of the assessment in another category of the science framework, **Applying science concepts.** Thus one could discern a close link between the categories of **Planning** and **Application.**

Consideration of the bank structure described in Table 10.1 suggests that an investigation tended to be seen as concerned essentially with the setting-up of the conditions by which phenomena could be observed. There was therefore a focus on experimental set-ups which took account of the independent variable (that which has to be varied systematically) and control variables (those whose effect must be held constant). Measurement strategies were generally given in the question, to describe the method of data collection. There were no questions in which the focus of the demand was the dependent variable or its measurement.

The emphasis in the early banks of questions was consistent with the demands of typical school science laboratory experiments. Many experiments in Physics, Chemistry and Biology require the observation of outcomes rather than any measurement of them. In those experiments where this is not the case, the dependent variable and the measurement procedure are usually given. Commonly, in experiments of this kind, the difficulty is seen to be in the interpretation of the results rather than the carrying out of measurements to obtain them. However, in the APU surveys, the inter-pretation of experimental results was assessed in the category **Interpretation** and not in **Planning.** At this stage in the general view of **Planning** measurement was not considered to be either a significant element or a hurdle to pupils in carrying out scientific investigations. Nevertheless there were assessment questions in the bank which indicated that hurdles to successful planning did exist; for example in the need to know standard procedures or techniques such as filtration or chromatography.

The picture that emerges from a review of the early bank of questions in the category can be interpreted as follows: scientific activity has a purpose which places emphasis on the accumulation and development of scientific concepts. Practical investigations enable this process, by allowing pupils to observe phenomena directly and thus to gain understanding of the theories used to explain them. Implicit in this overall picture is the need to know in advance of the hypotheses to be tested and of the stepwise algorithm to be recalled in order to carry out the investigation. This, coupled with knowledge of the variables in the experimental set-up and any relevant standard procedures, will enable pupils to plan investigations across different contexts and contents, in science and outside of it.

Part of the general assessment brief for the APU project was a commitment to consider pupils' ability to use their science *outside* school. Questions written to assess this aspect of performance often included an everyday content and were set in a context outside the science laboratory. These questions tended to be concerned with open-ended problems. The main demand in these questions was to arrive at a way of solving them. It was also significant that, given a more open-ended problem, there were generally several alternative plans of equal adequacy for its solution. Thus a focus on standard techniques and on an algorithmic approach could be potentially limiting in these problem situations.

In problems of this type, measurement becomes a fundamental element for planning consideration as it tends to distinguish an appropriate scientific plan from the more everyday solutions frequently suggested by the pupils. In 1980 there was therefore some ambivalence in the bank of questions designed to assess pupils' ability to plan, and a failure to recognise the full gamut of planning procedures pupils had to be competent in. The next section discusses the further development of the category.

## 10.3   1983–1984

In 1980 a different category, **Performance of investigations,** was undergoing development and trials. Two important outcomes of this work affected the **Planning** category. Crucially, investigations were not considered to be solely vehicles for the demonstration of phenomena. Here importance was placed on activities where *both* scientific procedures and concepts had to be used by pupils of all abilities to solve problems and make sense of new information. The shift was therefore one of purpose rather than of anything else. The end-point of the assessed investigations was the method of their solution, ie the development and deployment of a problem-solving strategy in order to collect data and to interpret it in the light of the problem set and the strategy used. There was no requirement to explain or predict on the basis of the data collected. Moreover a problem was only considered to be a problem if there was no well defined and predetermined solution for it. A significant part of the solution is therefore now concerned not with the recall of a single method of solution but with the application of procedures to the selection and development of what is, to the pupil, a novel method. Thus the teams moved away from a step-wise previously known method of solution, with the particular purpose of gathering data for explanations, towards the model of cyclical activity discussed in DES, 1984a, 1984b, and the teachers' report, *Science at age 13* (Murphy and Schofield, 1984).

Scientific investigations are regarded here as a dynamic process whereby the problem-solving strategy changes as the scientific knowledge drawn on is utilised. There is therefore a relationship between the general procedures and the specific scientific knowledge demanded to investigate any particular issue. Within this view there is also an acceptance of individual choice, as the investigator makes a selection of the procedures and knowledge that seem to be appropriate.

This expansion of the perception of the purpose of scientific activities, coupled with an alternative strategies approach to investigations, led to a review of the **Planning** bank. It was seen that there were important aspects of planning procedures missing, and some aspects included which related more closely to recall of specific content. This was particularly the case in the sequencing of standard techniques. An across-age review was carried out in 1982 with the intention of establishing a new bank structure for the 1983 survey and a bank of questions to represent it.

The overall structure for the **Planning** category:

> **Assessing testable statements,**
> **Planning parts of investigations,** and
> **Planning entire investigations**

was retained but the focus for the assessment moved to the latter two subcategories. Table 10.2 represents the present bank structure for **Planning parts of investigations** and the position of the questions within it (see section 10.5 for discussion).

*Performance review*

The present assessment structure in **Planning** has been implemented twice, in the surveys of 1983 and 1984. The review of performance which follows in sections 10.4, 10.5 and 10.6 takes each subcategory in turn and where appropriate discusses each type of question used. In some instances reference is made to additional questions which were specially written to probe particular issues. These questions helped the interpretation of the assessment results, but did not contribute to the subcategory scores as they were selected by hand and not at random from the bank. The discussion considers both how pupils succeed and how they fail, and raises questions about the category, the manner of its assessment and possible ways forward for future work.

**Table 10.2** *Structure of the bank 'Planning parts of investigations' 1983–1984*

| Question focus: | Question demand: | Performance review section |
|---|---|---|
| **Within an experimental design, or prior to it, identification of** | | |
| −how to vary the independent variable (I) systematically | Select or describe the procedure necessary to vary (I) | 10.5 (i) |
| | Criticise an experimental set-up with respect to the test of (I) | |
| −those variables which must be controlled | Select or generate some variables requiring control | 10.5 (ii) |
| | Criticise an experimental set-up with respect to controls | |
| −what to measure to allow a judgement of the dependent variable (D) | Select or describe the measurement procedures | 10.5 (iii) |
| **Within an experimental design identification of** | | |
| −those variables which must be taken into account to ensure a valid test of (I) and measurement of (D) | Describe or criticise experimental details including scale; range and number of readings; repetition; measurement techniques | 10.5 (iv) |
| −what to vary−the independent variable (I) and what to judge−the dependent variable (D) | Select in relation to a given experimental design that problem which can be solved | 10.5 (v) |
| −use of judgements/measurements in solving a problem | Describe how the measurements taken can be used to solve the problem | 10.5 (vi) |

## 10.4 Assessing testable statements

Two types of question were used in this subcategory, asking pupils to identify a testable statement or to rephrase a general statement into a testable form (see DES, 1982a, 1982b and 1984a, for a discussion of results and question examples).

### Identifying a testable statement

An example of this type of question asked the pupils to consider five statements about two competing washing powders and to decide which statement could not be empirically tested. In the first survey questions of this type were awarded marks. In general the mean scores were in the range 20 per cent to 60 per cent. The crux of these problems was the understanding that the vagueness of such terms as 'better than' precludes empirical investigation.

Questions of the type described here, but with a science content and set in a science context, had much lower mean scores than those with an everyday content. It was noticeable also that the non-response rate was higher. It seemed to be the case that the easier it was to imagine the actual experiment needed (a feature of many of the questions with an everyday content and context), the easier it was to judge whether the hypothesis was testable. The point to note here is that originally these questions were regarded as assessing the *first* step in a plan, and yet for many pupils it is clear that to respond to them an overall picture of the 'problem' has to be visualised in the first instance.

### Rephrasing a general statement

An example of this type of question gave the pupils a proposition such as 'feathers are lighter than lead' and asked them to rephrase the statement into a testable form. The questions on 'rephrasing into a testable statement' were marked in 1980 but not in 1981. The marking difficulty that arose here was in dealing with responses of equivalent adequacy but of a quite different nature. In the 1981 survey it was decided to use descriptive categories of responses, ie to code different responses rather than just give a mark. The overall findings for the questions were as follows:

- pupils either rephrased the statement by generating a reformulation including a testable hypothesis and some specified controls;

- or, more commonly, pupils rephrased the statement into a test which may or may not have included controls and in which the reformulation was implicit.

The other common categories of response (which do *not* answer the question asked) included the one in which pupils tried to 'explain' the presented statement. This type of response was common across the bank of questions in **Planning** and is discussed later in section

10.9. The tendency to explain was more common in everyday settings, an aspect of pupil performance noted in other categories in the framework. Another error was to treat the question out of context and to rephrase the statement in a grammatical rather than a scientific sense, a response which indicates the novelty of these questions for some pupils. The consequence of this novelty is that the pupils have actually to define the task for themselves, a point picked up later as a general performance influence.

In conclusion, after extensive interviews had been carried out with pupils across the three ages, it was decided that an actual problem situation had to be presented to the pupils and alternative problem definitions considered by them. Setting up this assessment situation effectively in a paper-and-pencil test mode met with little success.

## 10.5 Planning parts of investigations

Table 10.2 above shows the structure of the bank of questions for **Planning parts of investigations**. The structure highlights six different planning foci for the questions in the bank. These are discussed in turn in the following section.

It is important, prior to considering performance in this part of the category, to keep in mind the reasons for certain questions being present in the bank. The developments in the category **Performance of investigations** led to the inclusion of particular questions related to measurement tactics and strategies. However, **Performance of investigations** had another influence. In the discussion in Chapter 11 in this report several possible hurdles to pupils' success in practical problem-solving are posited, one of these being the failure of pupils to sustain an overall strategic view of the problem. Thus they often tend to do less well in the latter part of the investigative process. It was decided to consider this hypothesised hurdle in the assessment of **Planning investigations**. One is immediately aware here of the constraint of trying to look in depth at planning issues using paper-and-pencil tests, when it is the planning of *practical* investigations rather than *theoretical* ones, which is under consideration. It is, however, necessary to use a written test mode in order to cover the wide range of questions and planning features. These points will be referred to more fully in later sections of this chapter, when implications are discussed.

### (i) Identification of the independent variable

This type of question focused on the pupils' ability to recognise the object or the variable to be systematically varied (see Examples 10.1–10.4, pp. 111–2). Questions of this type were distinguished by the amount of experimental detail included. In some questions the

## Example 10.1   *'Shadow'*

Aamir was looking at the shadow formed by a ping pong ball when it was placed in front of a torch.

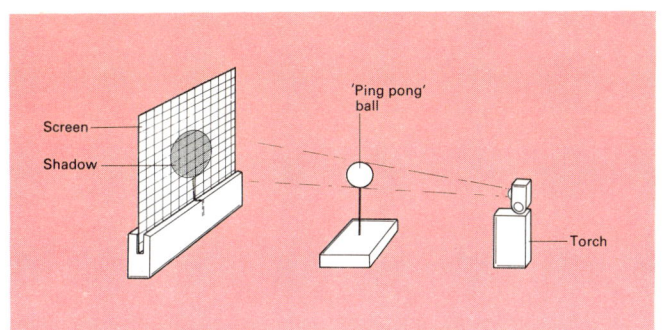

He noticed that the size of the shadow changed when he moved the ball and the torch.

He wanted to find out if <u>the position of the torch made any difference to the size of the shadow.</u>

a)  To find this out, what things should he be sure to keep the <u>same</u>?

..................................................................................

..................................................................................

..................................................................................

b)  What must he be sure to <u>change</u> to find out the answer?

..................................................................................

..................................................................................

| Shadow | B 5195<br>C 2177 | QD 512 | MARK SCHEME | |
|---|---|---|---|---|
| | | | Score | Code |

a)  Score 1 for any acceptable variable that
    needs to be controlled

    eg  Position of the screen
        Position of the pingpong ball
        Intensity/position of additional lighting
          in the room
        Characteristics of torch affecting
          intensity of light produced (eg battery,
          bulb) etc.           2

b)  Position of the torch       1

                        Maximum   ③

## Example 10.2   *'Celery'*

Kelly noticed that when celery stalks were put in coloured ink, the ink travelled up the stems and could be seen in the veins of the leaves.

## Example 10.2   *(continued)*

She wanted to find out if <u>the thickness of the celery stalks made a difference to how quickly the ink travelled up the stem.</u>

a)  To find this out, what things should she be sure to keep the <u>same</u>?

..................................................................................

..................................................................................

..................................................................................

b)  What must she be sure to <u>change</u> in order to find out the answer?

..................................................................................

..................................................................................

| Celery | B 5190<br>C 2069 | QD 512 | MARK SCHEME | |
|---|---|---|---|---|
| | | | Score | Code |

a)  Score 1 for any acceptable variable that
    needs to be controlled to a maximum of 2
    marks.

    eg  Temperature of ink solution
        Concentration of ink solution
        Type of ink
        Temperature of environment
        Humidity of environment
        Air movements in environment
        Amount of leaves on celery
        Maturity of leaves/celery
        Height of celery to leaves
        Type of celery etc.       2

b)  The thickness of the celery stalk     1

                        Maximum   ③

## Example 10.3   *'Springload'*

Semra had a collection of springs she was investigating. When she hung a load on the end of a spring and let go it bobbed up and down.

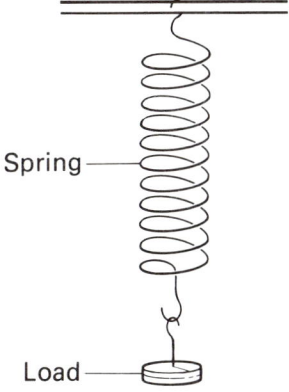

She noticed that some springs bobbed up and down faster than others. She wanted to find out if <u>the position of the spring made any difference to how quickly the load bobbed up and down.</u>

a)  To find this out, what things should she be sure to keep the <u>same</u>?

..................................................................................

..................................................................................

..................................................................................

b)  What must she be sure to <u>change</u> to find out the answer?

..................................................................................

..................................................................................

*continued overleaf*

**Example 10.3**  *'Springload' (continued)*

| Springload | B 5197<br>C 2180 | QD 512 | MARK SCHEME |
|---|---|---|---|
| | | | Score |

a) Score 1 for any acceptable variable that
   needs to be controlled to a maximum of 2
   marks

   eg diameter/width of the spring load on
      the spring
      method of release of load (pull/drop)
      gauge of wire spring made from method
         of fixing spring
      number of turns per unit length
      type of wire

                                          etc.    2

b) the length of spring                            1

                              Maximum        ③

---

**Example 10.4**  *'Dirty 'T' shirt'*

The people who make a washing powder say it washes things as well
in cold water as it does in hot water.

To find out if this is true Alex sets up five different tests shown
below.

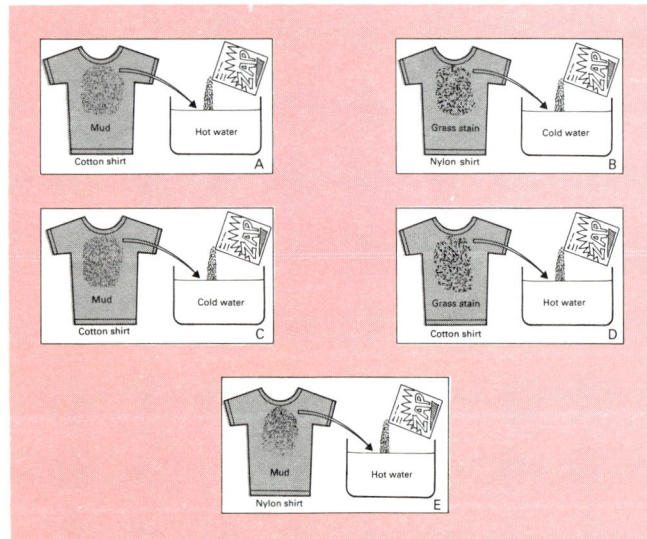

Alex only needs to compare two of the 'T' shirts to find out the
answer.
Put a tick in the box by the two tests he needs to do.
Put a cross next to the ones that would not tell him the answer.

☐  A    A and C

☐  B    A and D

☐  C    B and D

☐  D    C and E

☐  E    D and E

---

**Example 10.4**  *(continued)*

| Dirty 'T' shirt | B5021<br>C0369 | QD 516 | MARK SCHEME |
|---|---|---|---|

|  | Score | Code |
|---|---|---|
| ✔ | 1 | |
| X | 1 | |
| X | 1 | |
| X | 1 | |
| X | 1 | |
| Maximum score | | ⑤ |

Scaling:

| | |
|---|---|
| 5 | 3 |
| 4 | 2 |
| 3 | 1 |
| 2 | |
| 1 | |
| 0 | 0 |

pupils were presented with a problem without any detail
about how to carry out the investigation. In other
questions, in addition to a statement of the problem,
pupils were given, in very general terms, a plan of how
to vary the independent variable and how to judge the
dependent variable. (Question Example 10.2 is
representative of the first group of questions described
and Example 10.4 of the second group.) In both groups
the pupils had either to generate the independent
variable and control variables, or else to select them in
a coded answer response. In a small number of cases
the pupils had to criticise the experimental set-up with
respect to the independent variable.

The average mean score for these questions was 40 per
cent and the range was from 2 per cent to 64 per cent.

In the early survey reports suggestions were made about
possible factors affecting performance on these
questions. In 1980 at age 15 (DES, 1982b) it was noted
that performance dropped with increasing dependence
on *taught science concepts*. In the 1981 discussion of
performance at age 13 (DES, 1984a) the *nature* of the
independent variable was raised as a possible influence
on performance. This point was noted again in the
report of the 1983 survey. In addition it was suggested
that low performance was also related to the effect of
increasing the amount of *experimental detail* presented
in the question.

In the discussion about the nature of the independent
variable it was indicated that a discrete or discontinuous
variable was easier for the pupils to handle than a continuous one, as the requirement to conceptualise the
variables prior to identification had been removed.
Moreover, it was hypothesised that a question became
more difficult if more than one variable was embedded
within a single representation; for example when the

variables, width and length, were determined by the dimensions of a single piece of wood. Increasing the amount of presented experimental detail appeared to increase the demand to handle information in the abstract, and consequently depressed performance. If one considers the three question examples presented earlier–'Shadow' (Example 10.1), 'Celery' (Example 10.2) and 'Springload' (Example 10.3)–the proportions of pupils identifying the independent variable were 60 per cent, 40 per cent and 20 per cent respectively and the mean scores were 48 per cent, 27 per cent and 37 per cent. One can see that the set-up of the independent variable is much more visually apparent in the question 'Shadows', the illustration effectively presenting a 'minds eye view' of the investigation. In the question 'Celery' the 'thickness' of the sticks are perhaps easier to imagine in abstract than the 'length' of the springs; this seems to be a more conceptually difficult variable. However, the controls in the 'Celery' question are more dependent on specific science concepts and also less obvious within the presented situation.

It is apparent that isolating the amount of experimental detail presented in the question as an influence on performance is too coarse a consideration to be useful. It is the *effect* of the experimental detail and the *manner* of its presentation which appear to be the significant influences on performance. Both may either increase or decrease the ability to imagine and abstract the whole investigation. So, for example, it is worth noting that experimental detail presented in the manner exemplified by the question 'Dirty 'T' shirts' (Example 10.4) does depress pupil performance. In this question the pupils are presented with several alternative strategies in which a *combination* of variables is given. They have to isolate the strategy in which the independent variable is tested and the other presented variables are controlled. Only 26 per cent of pupils selected the correct pair of tests.

Given the many ways in which questions vary, it is hard to attribute performance fluctuations directly to any one factor such as the nature of the independent variable. It is the case that *selecting* the answers from a range offered, rather than *generating* them, increases the performance level achieved irrespective of the experimental detail included or the type of independent variable considered. Pupils' performance appears to be more varied on both 'select' and 'generate' questions when they have to take account of the detail of someone else's plan.

The difficulty of isolating any particular effect due to the independent variable is increased by the possibility of pupils scoring marks for controlling variables only (see Table 10.3). The variables to be controlled are not only specific to the problem situation both in number and nature but are also dependent on the application of specific science concepts. This point is exemplified in the mark schemes for 'Shadow' and 'Celery'. The problem situation presented in the question determines the number and type of variables which have to be held constant. One can also see at a glance that the concepts

which have to be understood to know that the amount of leaves on the celery has an effect are quite different to those underlying the understanding of the effect of the type of ink or the intensity of light. Consequently performance appears to be task-dependent. In the 1984 survey some attempt was made to isolate those pupils who achieved marks and correctly identified the independent variable from those who achieved marks for controlling variables only. Table 10.3 shows the results for the ten questions considered in this way.

**Table 10.3** *Proportion of pupils in the sample who correctly identified the independent variable and/or control variables by question example*

| Question example | For the same question | |
| --- | --- | --- |
| | % pupils who correctly identified the independent variable and control variables | % pupils who correctly identified control variables only |
| 1 | 60 | 11 |
| 2 | 54 | 20 |
| 3 | 42 | 22 |
| 4 | 40 | 16 |
| 5 | 37 | 34 |
| 6 | 26 | 45 |
| 7 | 23 | 51 |
| 8 | 20 | 60 |
| 9 | 11 | 41 |
| 10 | 7 | 56 |

The proportions of pupils correctly identifying the independent variable vary considerably across the questions. Consideration of the characteristics of each question and the pupils' performance on the questions does not provide any simple insight into what affects pupils' performance on this aspect of planning. The difficulties pupils experience seem to relate to their ability to imagine both the experimental set-up and the independent variable within it. In addition, the number and obviousness of the variables to be controlled, and whether the pupils know the effects of those variables, appear to affect performance.

Several questions were set in the 1984 survey not only to consider if pupils could identify the independent variable but also to see if they knew how to set up a test of it. (See Example A8.1 in Appendix 8, p. 227.) These questions did not contribute to the overall subcategory score, as they were selected to probe a particular aspect of performance. The mean score for Example A8.1 was 30 per cent, and about 14 per cent of pupils suggested both taking a sufficient number of readings and covering the range. A further 10 per cent indicated the need for several readings in order to get a reliable answer. Forty per cent of pupils mentioned taking more than three readings.

As the range was mentioned by so few pupils an attempt was made to focus on this aspect alone. In order to do this pupils were presented with a complete strategy for an investigation, which included an inadequate cover of the range. They were asked to comment on the measurements taken (see Example A8.2 in Appendix 8). This type of question is very difficult to ask in a paper-and-pencil test but the results are interesting in that they confirm common error responses and some of the suspected influences on pupils' responses in this category. In Example A8.2, 41 per cent of the pupils explained the answer, 18 per cent found the experiment satisfactory, and 15 per cent criticised other aspects of the set-up, such as the need to control the independent variable. Interestingly, 10 per cent of pupils interpreted 'how quickly' as duration rather than rate; this has been an error for a proportion of pupils in all problems concerning rate. Tables A8.1–A8.3 in Appendix 8 give some results for other questions of the same type as that exemplified by question A8.2.

### (ii) What to control

In these questions pupils have to identify *only* those variables which must be kept constant in order to avoid invalidating the set-up of the independent variable or the judgement of the dependent variable.

In previous surveys the mean scores obtained for this type of question have been generally high—around 70 per cent. The range of mean scores in the last two surveys has been from 10 per cent to 74 per cent, showing a considerable variation in performance level. Table 10.4 lists several factors which seem, from the results, to exert an influence on performance on these questions along with the general direction of their hypothesised influences.

In any given question, a combination of some of these factors exists. Thus it was noted in the 1983 probe (see Chapter 7, DES, 1986a) that, for questions concerned with identifying variables to be controlled, those set in an everyday context rather than a scientific context usually had lower mean scores. However, in the questions included in the probe the use of an everyday context was also accompanied by an increase in the amount of irrelevant information presented to the pupils, which provided additional scope for error.

None of the factors listed in Table 10.4 exists independently and neither do their effects occur independently. It is the case that in writing questions about realistic investigations (ie ones that are both probable and possible) one cannot 'control' for the interactive effects on performance of many factors.

In the 1984 survey two factors were looked at in more detail. These were the dependence on taught science and the manner of question presentation. Nine selected questions were set which specifically focused on the need for taught science concepts (see Examples 'Ice shape' and 'Cars' in Appendix 8). The mean scores for the questions were in the range 3 per cent to 40 per cent. Performance did appear to depend on the pupils'

conceptualisation of the variable. In fact the question responses when considered in detail proved to be very informative with regard to pupils' conceptual understanding. (See Table A8.4 in Appendix 8 for typical pupil responses to 'Ice shape'.)

**Table 10.4** *Possible influences on performance on control of variables*

| Factor | Performance effect |
|---|---|
| Question demand: generate | ↓ |
| select | ↑ |
| criticise | ↓ |
| Number of potential variables: few | ↓ |
| many | ↑ |
| Amount of irrelevant information: a little | ↑ |
| a lot | ↓ |
| Dependent on taught science concepts | ↓ |
| Obviousness of variables | ↑ |
| Amount of experimental detail to be visualised: a little | ↑ |
| a lot | ↓ |
| Ease of visualising 'whole' investigation | ↑ |
| Context: everyday | ↓ |
| scientific | ↑ |

Key: General direction of effect in relation to the average mean score for the Question type: elevated performance ↑ depressed performance ↓

In 'Cars' 31 per cent of the pupils stated the independent variables (mass of the car) as a control variable. This finding relates to the discussion in DES, 1986a, which suggested that in examples presented in the manner of 'Cars', many pupils respond to the *problem situation* rather than to the specific investigation. The specific investigation quoted in DES, 1986a, was 'find out the effect of surface area on the rate of dissolving of a jelly'. It appears that pupils respond to the problem situation, ie a dissolving jelly, rather than the actual investigation highlighted. The question demand the pupils appear to be answering is to generate as many potentially relevant variables *irrespective of their status*. A valid answer to this demand would include both the independent and dependent variable. It was suggested that questions asked in this way artificially raised performance on this element of planning. Other questions used to assess pupils' ability to control variables actually presented the pupils with a problem and someone else's plan for its solution. The pupils had then to consider the status of the presented variables; to identify those which needed control or criticise an identified variable in those terms. Such a question is quite a different exercise from the one presented in 'Cars'.

As quite different results were obtained, depending on the manner of presentation, it was decided to reconsider the control of variables in the **Planning** category. Questions were written with the same content and

**Example 10.5** *Survival controls*

Imagine you are stranded on a mountainside in cold, dry, windy weather. You can choose a jacket made from either a blanket or from plastic.

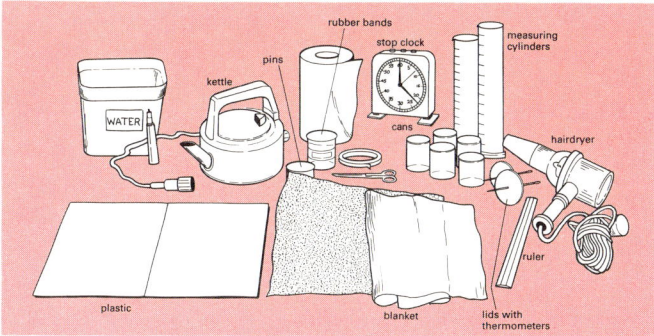

You have to think of a way to find out:

> Which fabric would
> keep you warmer?

You could use any of the things shown in the picture for your experiment.

If it is to be a fair test, do you think it is important to keep some things exactly the same? Explain your answer by giving an example.

..................................................................................
..................................................................................
..................................................................................
..................................................................................
..................................................................................

manner of presentation as used in **Performing** and **Planning entire investigations**. Thus each question included the problem and the apparatus available for its solution, and the question demand was fairly open (see Example 10.5 Survival controls). However, pupils were asked to consider fair test conditions and to suggest what things should be kept the 'same', as in the questions exemplified by 'Cars'.

The percentage of pupils scoring marks for stating controls was between 12 per cent and 48 per cent on these questions, in comparison with a range of 66 per cent to 95 per cent for questions with a presentation like 'Cars'.

The types of response to the example 'Survival controls' are given in Table 10.5. They help to illustrate both the nature of **Planning** on paper and pupils' performance on control of variables. Ten per cent of pupils actually stated correct variables to be controlled. A further 12 per cent described an adequate experiment to carry out the investigation without mentioning controls. Sixteen per cent defined a different problem, 10 per cent of these being concerned with 'survival conditions' in a much broader sense. Other responses were similar to previous findings (DES, 1986a) and are discussed in section 10.9 on 'Implications'. This method of presentation

**Table 10.5** *Survival controls: Pupil responses*

| Type of response | % pupils providing response |
|---|---|
| Correctly suggested a variable which needed to be kept constant | 10 |
| Suggested variables requiring control but for an investigation of the waterproof potential of the materials | 2 |
| Described a suitable experiment including the independent and dependent variables but without specifying control variables | 12 |
| Described an adequate experiment but concerned with the waterproofing properties of the materials | 4 |
| Suggested an alternative problem, focusing on survival on a mountainside | 9 |
| Stated procedures which had to be kept the same | 8 |
| Agreed with the need to keep things the same but failed to specify what | 7 |
| Focused on the need to 'change' things rather than control | 3 |
| Stated the answer to the problem | 13 |
| Disagreed that any variable had to be controlled | 13 |
| No response given | 19 |

appears to focus the pupils on an investigation rather than on a general problem situation. The pupils either consider the actual investigation posed or else generate an alternative one. The tendency to generate an alternative investigation is linked to the type of content and context used as well as to the pupils themselves (see Chapter 11 for further discussion on this). The trend in questions with this type of presentation is for the pupils to generate an overall plan for their investigation in which controls are either explicitly stated or implicit in what they write. The performance on 'controls' in these questions is much lower than that obtained for those presented as in the 'Cars' example or in the practical version in **Performance of investigations**. The results are consistent with the low performance found for control of variables in the context of **Planning entire investigations** for questions with an identical presentation and content.

### (iii) *What to judge*

It was mentioned in the discussion of the background of the category that the dependent variable (what to judge in order to determine the effect of the independent variable) was not a question focus in the pre-1982 bank. Since then it has featured as an important aspect of planning; both the identification of the variable to be judged and the manner in which it is judged have been considered.

The mean scores for this group of questions are in the range from 13 per cent to 53 per cent. The average mean score for the Question type is significantly lower (at the 1 per cent significance level) than the average for the two Question types discussed earlier. The findings described in DES, 1986a, have been reinforced by the 1984 survey results on this aspect of **Planning**. In general, performance on these questions was low, usually with less than half the pupils obtaining any marks.

Those who gained marks either mentioned in very general terms the method of measurement such as 'count the bounces' for the rate of bobbing of a spring, or 'count the woodlice' for a survey of woodlice preference. In all questions of this type there was a tendency for pupils to give only a single measurement even if a comparison was required. Usually only a final reading was mentioned. Measurement tactics concerning for example numbers of readings, range of readings and the manner in which the range was to be covered were not mentioned by over 90 per cent of the pupils.

The variation in mean scores for these questions suggests two hurdles to pupils' success, irrespective of a general tendency to give insufficient detail. Firstly there is the ability to conceptualise the variable itself prior to deciding how to measure it. It would appear, for example, that *rate* for some pupils is equivalent to *duration*. This conceptualisation of rate has featured across several different physical quantities in both planning and investigating. For many 13 year olds the rate of bobbing of a spring appears to be more difficult to conceptualise than a rate of cooling. In interviews with pupils at age 13 in which an attempt was made to help them with this difficulty it seemed that there was a need for some analogous experience to facilitate the conceptualisation of the variable. Observation of a rate of cooling is a common everyday mealtime experience. It would appear that many pupils have no analogous experience for the rate of bobbing of a spring. The majority of 13 and 15 year olds can only use an anthropomorphic view of animals and consequently they fail to set up correctly a measure of animal behaviour in investigations dependent on this conceptualisation. Understanding the meaning of 'hold' in the context of paper towels mopping up water seemed to give little difficulty to 13 or 15 year olds and yet a substantial number of 11 year olds failed to understand the term in order to be able to define a measurement strategy for it. It would appear, then, that in order to develop a measurement strategy one must first be able to conceptualise the dependent variable. The difficulty inherent in this varies from problem to problem and affects different children at different ages.

The second hurdle relates to the nature of the judgement necessary to solve the problem. For example, a qualitative method is easier for pupils to describe than a quantitative one. A quantitative method requiring a comparison of two single measurements appears to be easier than one requiring a series of measurements. The overall difficulty of the latter type of question has been discussed in detail in previous reports. In particular the need to hold another person's problem in one's head, and to then identify the relevant variables and understand the type of data necessary for a solution, requires a great deal of abstract mental processing which constitutes an inherently difficult task. When this type of question was presented in a similar manner to that described in the 'Survival controls' example (ie with the problem and the apparatus but no experimental details)

the pupils tended to write a whole plan and their performance was somewhat higher on the measurement component. Not enough questions have been asked in this way to say whether the difference is meaningful. If it *is* a valid difference, this reinforces the suggestions made in DES, 1986a, that pupils' ability to develop a strategy for an investigation is facilitated by mediation either through actions or through words when developing a plan.

(iv) *What other factors to consider?*

The questions concerned here are extremely varied. They cover all those other issues which may affect the validity of the test of the independent variable or the measurement of the dependent variable. All the questions used present pupils with a problem and an inadequate strategy for its solution. The pupils then have to criticise particular aspects of the design. The mean scores for this group of questions were in the range from 21 per cent to 43 per cent. For this type of question, the average mean score is lower than for those already discussed, and the difference is significant at the 1 per cent level. This suggests that it is one of the most difficult in the subcategory. An extended range of questions was used in 1984 and in many cases the results of 1983 were repeated.

Questions to do with the range of readings or the scale of a physical quantity that it is appropriate to use, considering the types of data necessary, all had very low scores. Those questions which required consideration of the error involved due to the variation between living things had mean scores well below 20 per cent. Many pupils found nothing to criticise in a presented plan, or else focused on another issue. Alternatively they proposed an answer to the problem. In many cases over 90 per cent of pupils failed to score on this type of question.

In 1984 some questions were included about alternative experimental designs. In particular, pupils were asked to choose between a factorial design and a sequential one, ie between a design which considered the potential interaction between variables and one concerned with the main effect of variables separately. About 12 per cent of pupils were able to say that a factorial design was both more efficient and more informative, when looking at the effect of several variables, which is commonly necessary in biological and chemical investigations.

The results for this group of questions are consistent with a *general* lack of refinement in pupils' plans. The results suggest that pupils do not use such planning refinements because they are unaware of them. These results have been confirmed in interviews with pupils at age 13.

(v) *What's the problem?*

In these questions pupils are presented with a complete and adequate experiment from which they must select the characteristic of the event or object that is being tested. A typical example provides an illustrated design for dissolving powdered and granular coffee in a fixed volume of water at a specified temperature. The method of measurement is also included. The pupil then has to decide which one of five propositions the design will test. These questions have mean scores in the range 20 per cent to 63 per cent. It is difficult to comment on what affects performance as it is generally the case that the pupils respond to the specific content in the question. It would appear that if the situation is an everyday one and the variables to be identified are not dependent on taught science concepts, then over half the pupils can deal with the question demand as a data translation and interpretation task. If, however, the situation is dependent on science concepts or set in an area or topic where the pupils' beliefs operate, then the question demand becomes a quite different one. In these cases pupils attempt to apply their knowledge to the situation, often inappropriately, and performance is consequently depressed.

### (vi) *How to use the results?*

In a sense these questions relate to the end point of planning. However, the need to 'know' the type and form of the data necessary to solve the problems influences many, if not all, aspects of the plan. It was mentioned in DES, 1986a, that the failure to see the whole problem in these terms often resulted in an inadequate measurement strategy being planned. The questions set to assess pupils' understanding of how to interpret experimental results actually focus on the procedures of data handling. The pupils are presented with a complete, adequate experimental design including details of the measurement strategy. The question asks them to describe how they would 'use' the results obtained. The mean scores for these questions are in the range of 3 per cent to 22 per cent. The average mean score for these questions was similar, statistically, to that obtained for the questions about 'other factors'. About three quarters of the pupils failed to obtain scores. Those who scored did so by making very general statements; for example they suggested comparing x with y or even more rarely plotting x against y. Fewer than 5 per cent of the pupils described any computation necessary, or what to look for once the data had been translated.

## 10.6 Planning entire investigations

Questions of this kind have been administered in surveys since 1980, with an in-depth probe in years 1982 and 1983. In the first reports at ages 13 and 15 (DES, 1982a, 1982b) the summary of performance on this part of the category suggested that about a third of pupils gave a sensible method whilst about half gave very short general responses without any detail. The remainder of

the pupils gave the important points but in a random manner rather than in a coherent sequence. The main omissions in the plans of those pupils who gave a sensible method were the failure to state controls and to explain how to work out the results. At age 13 the variety of methods offered was noted; these were often of a creative rather than a scientific nature, as in the quoted example of throwing a fish into an unknown liquid to identify the composition of the liquid upon the demise of the unfortunate fish. In DES, 1984a, the failure of pupils to include control of variables in their plans was referred to. In the same 1981 survey five such planning questions were set to the same pupils. In reviewing performance across these questions, it was noted that the same pupils achieve very different levels of performance on different questions even though mark schemes with a common structure were applied. These results suggested that pupils tend to develop a plan within a particular problem situation rather than by recalling and applying a general problem-solving strategy.

In the 1982 survey questions were administered which mirrored the content and presentation used to assess pupils' ability to perform investigations. A sample of pupils was asked to plan practical investigations on paper (see DES, 1985a). Two types of question were used: those with a picture of the presented apparatus (the pictorial version) and those without (the prose version). It was found that the more obvious the science context was made by inclusion of apparatus clues, the more 'scientific' the pupils' plan. In the prose questions a greater divergence of overall approach was noticeable. Some pupils placed their assistants in freezers to judge the thermal conduction of a particular material by noting the drop in body temperature; others placed an animal sample such as mice in a refrigerator and timed how long they took to die. The lack of practical clues also appeared to affect the pupils' perception of the problem, so that many more described alternative investigations. Without the constraints of presented equipment the pupils' designs were often much more creative, if somewhat unpractical or even impossible to carry out. The number of pupils adopting a quantitative approach was greater for questions in which apparatus clues included measuring instruments. However, little detail concerning the carrying out of the measurement was included in the pupils' plans; at most they mentioned a final reading only. More pupils stated variables to be controlled in the pictorial version than in the prose one but the percentage was still below 50 per cent.

When performance on **Planning parts of investigations** is contrasted with that on **Planning entire investigations**, it is seen to be generally lower on all aspects. An exception to this is the control of variables in questions administered between 1980 and 1983 in **Planning parts of investigations**. However, the questions set in 1984 which duplicated the presentation used in the **Planning entire investigations** shows lower performance levels than those obtained for the overall planning. Although not many such questions have been set, they have mirrored both the content and the presentation of those used in **Planning entire investigations**, so the comparison is a valid one.

## 10.7   Performance by Question type and ability

In section 10.5 reference has been made to the range of mean scores achieved within any one type of question. A total of 116 questions spanning the Question types has been administered in the subcategory **Planning parts of investigations**. Figure 10.1 shows the distribution of mean scores within a Question type.

The first three distributions shown are for the questions concerned with the identification of the independent variable and/or control variables. There is a tendency for the scores on those questions in which experimental details are included to spread to the lower end of the scale. However, in the text it was suggested that this was just one influence on performance and that within this type of question there were many other interactive factors affecting pupil performance. This is borne out when the distributions are considered for statistical significance. Performance on the top four groups of questions in Figure 10.1 is not significantly different at the

1 per cent level. The distribution of mean scores obtained for group five (ie for the questions about the judgement of the dependent variable) is significantly different to that for the previous groups of questions and the average mean score is significantly lower. In the text it has been noted that all pupils tend to give incomplete measurement procedures. The distribution of mean scores for groups six and seven is for those questions to do with measurement details, such as choice of scale or range of readings, and with how to use the results of the experiment to determine the outcome for the investigation. The number of questions used in the two groups is very different but both distributions lie towards the lower end of the scale. Pupil performance on these two types of question is not significantly different, but it is significantly lower (at the 1 per cent level) than that for the other Questions types in the subcategory.

For all the questions monitored between 1983 and 1984, performance band data have been established. To do this, each pupil's score on a test package (ie 16 planning questions) was noted and placed in one of five performance bands; for example the 20 per cent with the highest scores fell into Band One. The scores obtained on each question were then analysed by performance band, ie the mean scores obtained by each band of pupils was calculated. The top band of performers (20 per cent of the sample) did significantly better than others *across all Question types*. In addition, these

**Figure 10.1**   *The mean scores of questions displayed within Question types for 'Planning parts of investigations'*

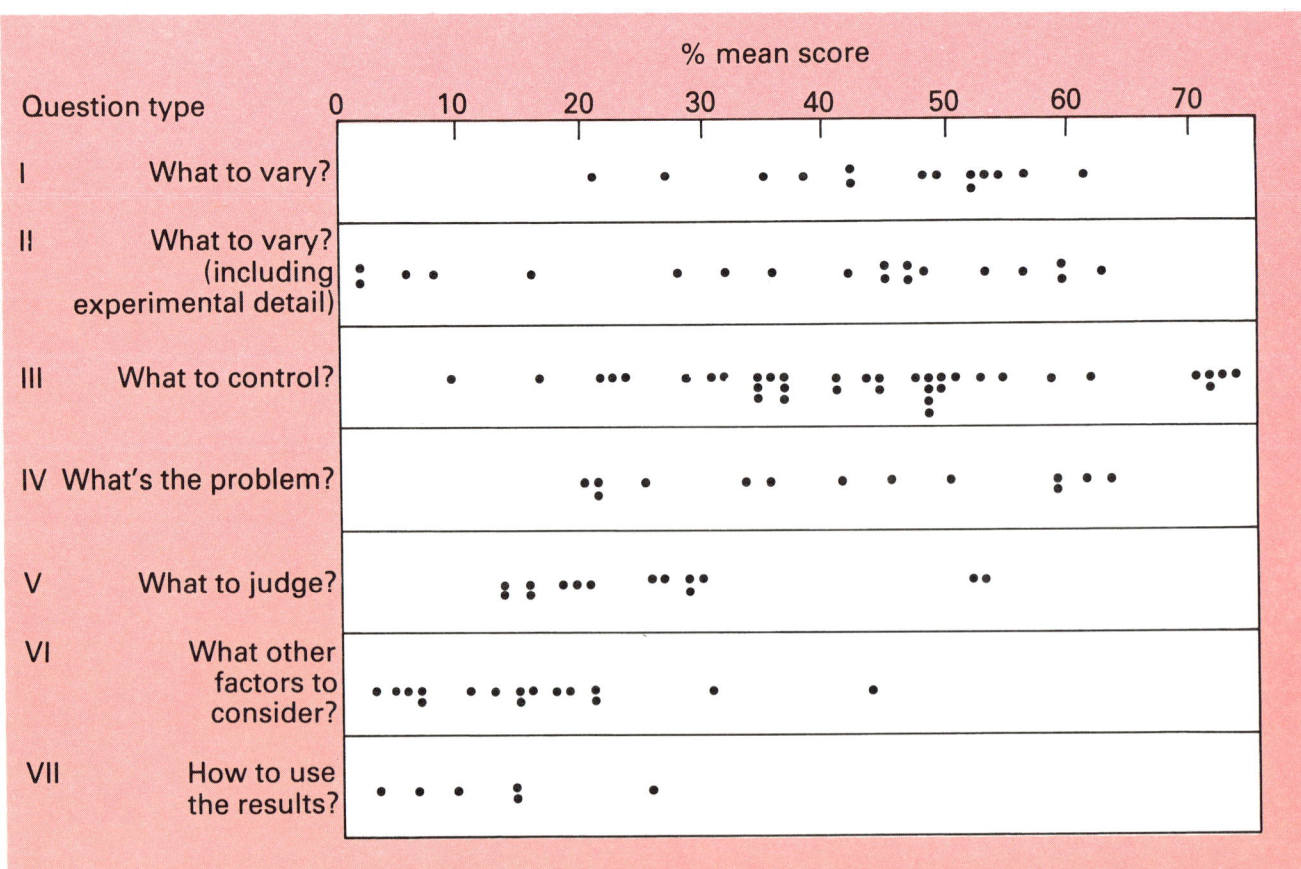

pupils were more likely to attempt the questions. The bottom band of pupils more often failed to distinguish between the independent and control variables. The performance of this group of pupils was generally significantly lower than that of the remaining 80 per cent of pupils when describing measurement procedures. However, in the Question types concerned with how to use results and how to discern the problem the performance of the bottom 40 per cent and often 60 per cent of the sample was essentially similar in terms of the low performance levels obtained.

## 10.8 Discussion

The category **Planning of investigations** has always been considered to represent an important science activity since the framework was first conceived. The significance of the activity has not been challenged in the five-year monitoring phase, but the nature of the category and its role in the assessment has undergone a great deal of change. The major change in the category was a consequence of the development in the category **Performance of investigations**. In this category the view of a problem was one without an immediately obvious method of solution. The analysis of the procedural demands of the practical investigations led to the present structure of the **Planning parts of investigations** bank, and to the present mark schemes for **Planning entire investigations**.

The model of planning changed from a step-wise progress through a known route to that discussed in detail in DES, 1986a. Briefly, in planning whole investigations, pupils are presented with a problem situation in prose or with apparatus clues. To develop a plan for an investigation pupils must first be able to perceive that there is a problem to be solved. To do this pupils have to be able to define the status of the variables in a problem situation. They have first to conceptualise correctly both what to vary (the independent variable) and what to judge (the dependent variable). Secondly, the variables which will affect the investigation if not held constant have to be identified. If the pupils are successful in conceptualising the problem in these terms, they must then recall those procedures necessary to collect the type of data needed. These procedures concern how to test the independent variable; this is determined by its nature, be it continuous or discrete. Secondly, pupils must understand the nature of the measurements needed to judge the effect on the independent variable. This will vary from a single measurement (eg the amount of water held by a paper towel) to a series of connected measurements (eg those needed to judge the rate of cooling of a can of hot water).

The decision about the nature of the measurement necessary, along with the understanding of the type of data to be collected, will involve the pupils in further decisions about the choice of measurement instruments, magnitude of quantities, and number of readings. Pupils therefore need to use their understanding of particular scientific concepts in conjunction with their understanding of the procedures necessary to collect suitable data. Thus in order to describe a plan the pupils must be able to carry out *'thought investigations'* which are very difficult exercises.

In **Planning parts of investigations** the focus is on the specific parts of a planned strategy. The questions were written with two aims, firstly to establish if pupils could plan a specific part when presented with the problem alone, and secondly to see if they could plan a specific part when presented with a problem and an incomplete design for its solution. The first, in theory, is a planning exercise, the second is more closely related to an assessment of recall of procedures. The pupil has to generate or select that procedure which is missing from another person's plan. The two demands are not entirely unconnected in their relevance to planning competence, but their different nature needs to be remembered.

## 10.9 Implications

*Implications for assessment*

The model developed to describe the demands in the **Planning** category has two possible functions: as a generative tool and an analytical tool. In the first instance it can be used for writing questions which target particular elements within planning, and in the second it can be used for developing appropriate mark schemes. In this section several aspects highlighted in the description of the model for assessing pupils' response to planning questions will be discussed in more detail.

*Concept dependency*

The dependence of the planning procedures on the *understanding of taught scientific concepts and other concepts* has been recognised. These include length, width and rate, for example, which need to be known in abstract prior to setting up an investigation involving them, and which cannot be said to be everyday concepts. The effect of the conceptual dependency of planning has been noted throughout this chapter, but as it has not been a feature for scoring (except in a few cases in the probe questions used in 1984) the effect is not well researched. One aspect of future work will be an attempt to illuminate further the interactive role of concepts and procedures within the context of planning.

*Question presentation*

Many of the questions in the bank present the pupils with someone else's incomplete plan and ask them to suggest the missing part. This is one form of question presentation. A second form of presentation used in questions to test planning ability gives the pupils a problem with or without an illustration of apparatus to be used and asks them to generate a plan of either a part of or an entire investigation. Irrespective of the specific demand to keep things the same, to identify what to test or what to measure, or to judge whether a statement is testable, many pupils respond by writing an *entire* plan. This suggests that for many pupils planning is not a simple recall of procedures (assumed to an extent in the first form of presentation mentioned). Rather it is a dynamic situation where it is necessary for the pupils to develop a whole plan through the act of writing and subsequently to establish the component parts of their plan retrospectively. Very few pupils at age 13 can visualise a whole plan in abstract and select the correct component required to answer the question. Questions with this second form of presentation in common show a decrease in performance from **Planning entire investigations** to **Planning parts**. When the parts of planning are assessed in the manner described first, by presenting an incomplete or inadequate strategy (thus requiring the pupils to take on someone else's plan rather than developing their own), performance tends to be depressed even further except for the case discussed, earlier in the chapter, on 'Control of variables'.

In **Planning entire investigations** the addition of apparatus clues in the question presentation reduces the diversity of approach and increases the number of scientifically appropriate plans. Any lack of clues increases the likelihood that pupils will define alternative problems, and the wider the context the more likely this is to occur.

## Context

The context of questions has been raised throughout the category system tests as a possible influence on pupil performance. The direction of the influence has been difficult to disentangle because of the vagueness of the term 'context'. At ages 13 and 15, three contexts have been defined and used to label questions: 'school science', 'other school subject' and 'everyday'. The context is decided by looking at the particular content in a question. There are many question contents which cannot be assigned unambiguously to one or other of these contexts, so the definition is far from watertight. It is also important to note that the assessor decides the context rather than the pupil, whose perception might be quite different.

In **Planning entire investigations** in an everyday situation pupils often choose to use a qualitative approach without controls. In **Planning parts of investigations** the context effect differs from Question type to Question type. In the control of variables an everyday context tends to depress performance. It has been noted from interviews that everyday contexts are often regarded by pupils as not appropriate for scientific testing, and therefore controls do not feature in their plans; it is

also the case that in many instances in an everyday context there are more redundant variables, a factor known to depress performance by increasing the scope for errors. In other questions a known scientific content can cue the pupils to attempt to apply their knowledge inappropriately, and in these questions performance is depressed.

## Other issues

On reviewing pupils' performance on the planning questions it appears that the majority of 13 year olds and 15 year olds treat each of the questions as independent units. Consequently the strategy developed to tackle an investigation is determined by the particular content and problem given. What this means in practice is that pupils do not have a general procedural strategy which they apply across investigations. The failure to have a general, transferable approach to planning investigations in science is apparent in some of the common error responses given by the pupils.

For example a presented plan with a missing procedure which the pupils have to identify is often not understood by them to be a planning question. Rather the pupils impose on the question a purpose of their own which clearly seems both more relevant and more closely associated with their experience in science. Typically they *explain the outcome* of the presented investigation irrespective of the question asked. This response has been suggested to be indicative of their perception of the overriding purpose of science activity in schools (see DES, 1986a). Alternatively they comment on other features in the question content which appear more relevant to the presented problem situation, as for example in 'Survival controls' where they comment on the pointlessness of the investigation given that there is no electricity up a mountainside. In some situations, particularly those set in a wide context but also in many others, pupils will focus on the question content rather than the presented problem and define their own problem. Pupils' decisions to define their own investigations have been considered in interviews and in the classroom situation. The results of this work suggest that the difficulty is not one of language but rather one of individual interest and perception.

Another associated issue concerns the use of specific words in the planning questions. These words are used to convey the meaning of what is being asked to the pupils. In questions used at ages 13 and 15 it is not appropriate to use precise terms such as 'control variables' or 'dependent variables'. Rather we have to say 'what will you keep the same?' or 'should you keep anything the same?'; 'what will you measure?' or 'what measurements will you take?'. Very often pupils' understanding of these words at age 13 and 15 is fragile or particularly constrained. Thus, for example, measurements are equated with units or with instruments only. The term used in a question will cue a particular conceptual understanding and an associated response from the pupils. Some responses include mention of the specific instrument or the units of measurement alone. Pupils with this type of understanding score very low on questions concerned with measurement strategy, and yet in practice they may well be able to *carry out* a measurement during an investigation.

*Implications for teaching*

The APU definition for what constitutes a problem suggests that pupils are not expected to know in advance a well defined and predetermined solution to an investigation. Consequently **Planning an investigation** assumes the need to select and apply procedures appropriate to a specific problem situation. The planning elements for consideration include:

– the nature and status of the significant variables;

– the type of data necessary to solve the problem satisfactorily;

– the type of resource, equipment, and instrumentation available to carry it out;

– the purpose of the particular investigation.

The focus of corresponding planning exercises in the classroom are therefore concerned essentially with the understanding of scientific procedures. The overall strategy that a pupil develops will be a synthesis of the above elements. In order to develop overall strategies for investigating, pupils need to build up practical experience of different investigations which reflect the planning elements outlined above in a variety of ways. From this experience they can begin to develop an understanding of *general* investigative procedures which are explicitly related to the demands of specific investigations. It is the understanding of the interdependence of the general and the particular features of an investigation which will enable pupils to plan investigations across different contents.

In the types of activity outlined in this chapter the demands placed on pupils are complex and intrinsically difficult. It is important for teachers to recognise the complexity of these demands prior to determining what will constitute useful learning situations. It is a premise underlying much of the work of the APU that pupils demonstrate their knowledge and understanding (i) in the way they set about tackling investigations or problems which they find motivating, and (ii) in the way they *talk* about what they are doing. It is also clear that pupils learn from such tasks, so the same activity provides both a vehicle for learning and a means of assessment.

Pupils clearly lack the ability to make explicit formulations of planning procedures; there are many aspects of this lack which need to be considered by teachers. For some pupils the use of common terms, such as measurement, does not reflect a common understanding of them. Those pupils who understand

measurement as a noun–a distance or a time, perhaps–will not see it as a procedure, an activity with a particular application. It is worth considering what understanding pupils have of particular terms in science in order to establish the kinds of experiences that will be beneficial to them.

We make many assumptions about the pre-existing knowledge that pupils bring to lessons. We may assume it to be adequate in some cases, or irrelevant to the investigation in others. However, it has been pointed out in this chapter that one cannot develop a strategy for an investigation which takes account of how to vary the independent variable or how to measure the dependent variable without first conceptualising these variables *beyond* a descriptive everyday type of understanding. The fact that very often in textbooks, in worksheets, and in APU items we present variables organised in advance (as, for example, the type of paper towel represented as 3 given samples of different towels) reduces the need for pupils to conceptualise the variable. But if the aim of teaching investigative skills is to enable a broader application to new situations–outside school, in jobs or at home–then the pupil needs to be given experience and practice in understanding a variety of different variables. The teacher can help by analysing in advance the conceptual demands within any one investigation and taking note of those pupils who have difficulties such as those mentioned earlier; for example, in the understanding of the concept of rate. Different difficulties require different teaching strategies; the failure to conceptualise a variable needs a different learning situation to, say, failure to recall a particular procedure. Therefore it is important to diagnose correctly the nature of the pupil's failure.

It is worth noting that the effective control of variables is also dependent on the pupil's conceptual understanding of the effect of the variable. Thus in the 'Survival controls' example, in order to judge whether both the size and the material of the cans should be held constant, it is necessary to understand specific and quite different scientific concepts. It is also helpful to question whether pupils keep things the same because they actually understand the effect of variables or whether it is a consequence of some other tactic. An example of this was the pupil who appeared to control the volume of water in the cans in 'Survival' but was, in fact, controlling the air above the water and its insulating properties rather than the heat source.

It has been suggested that the manner of presentation of investigations can often unwittingly prevent pupils from gaining the necessary experience to become competent investigators across a variety of contexts and contents. The manner of presentation affects both the conceptual demands and the procedural demands within a problem. The failure of most pupils to provide details about how an independent variable should be tested or a dependent variable measured has been commented on in this chapter. Yet often in the school laboratory the number of readings to be taken and range of readings to be covered for an independent variable are given, rather than arrived at by a discussion of the type of variable and the nature of the problem posed. Pupils need to know which variables require a series of readings and which need single measurement comparisons. They also need to know how to determine the appropriate range for a particular set of measurements and what factors in the problem situation have to be taken into account in order to make such a decision.

In the previous section an argument has been advanced for three things:

- greater analysis of the demands within any investigation by the teacher prior to setting it as a classroom activity;

- greater flexibility in approach and presentation of an investigation;

- increased discussion with accompanying activities prior to starting an investigation and throughout the course of it.

It is recognised that these are both time-consuming and resource-consuming suggestions. It is, however, encouraging that pupils' common sense attitudes favourably dispose them towards making particular decisions which are scientifically appropriate. What is needed is to make the intuitions held by pupils explicitly understood by them and subsequently more generally useful. Thus such complex issues as the type of data necessary can be approached from a common sense view: if you want to get an initial idea first then perhaps testing just the

extremes of a continuous variable is the most efficient way forward. If, however, the purpose of the investigations is to be able to predict quite accurately the likely outcome under certain specified conditions, then a more thorough investigation of the variable relationship is needed.

The *purpose* of the investigation is a useful point for starting and continuing discussions and for evaluating the adequacy of the investigation carried out. All too often, however, the purpose is unclear or missing for the pupil. The pupils would benefit from a broader appreciation of the utility of their science and the sorts of purposes it can serve. Some pupils are constrained by their experience to believe in a single purpose for science activity, ie to learn an explanation given by someone else. This belief often limits their ability to solve problems set with a different purpose. Similarly some pupils have the view that science can only be applied to particular contents. This limits their potential to use their science knowledge to make sense of new information.

A final point, which is discussed in detail in Chapter 11, is to remember the significance of the *entire* task to the pupils' ability to plan a part or an entire investigation. Classroom discussion will inevitably focus on the *elements* of planning and investigating, but it is important to remind the pupils of how these are functions of a holistic view which they hold. Such an approach allows the pupils to understand the significance of their investigative strategy for each decision made about their tactics.

# 11

# Performance of investigations

## 11.1  Introduction

This category was first assessed in the 1980 survey at age 11. The first discussion of results was therefore in the report of this survey (DES, 1981). The purpose of the category as described in this report was 'to find out how practical problems were tackled by pupils'. In the same report the whole category system was described as an analysis of 'scientific-performance' and Category 6 was seen to be the putting together of the component activities. As such, Category 6 was considered to be a reflection of the overall view of scientific performance at age 11.

The need to know the extent to which pupils could put together component activities in carrying out a whole investigation was regarded as particularly relevant at age 11, 'in order to give an adequate picture of pupils science performance'. There were two aspects to this perceived relevance. Firstly, that the interdependence of thinking and doing was particularly important for young children, and, secondly, that the results would be less dependent upon reading and writing skills. Consequently the development of assessment questions and methods of data collection began at age 11. The first survey of the category was conducted and reported in the 1980 age 11 survey.

In the first reports at ages 13 and 15 the only rationale given for the category was that it formed a synthesis of the component activities. It was also affirmed that pupil performance was expected to be affected by the demands of *synthesised* activity. There was, however, across the ages, a shared commitment to a view of science (see Chapter 1) judged to be appropriate for pupils of all abilities from primary through to secondary education.

The relationship between the category **Performance of investigations** and the rest of the assessment framework was initially not well understood. The accretion of annual survey results and research findings has provided a much deeper understanding of this relationship. It has also highlighted the tension which exists between the aim of producing reliable survey results and the need to ensure that the results are educationally valid and interpretable.

The category title, **Performance of investigations**, covers a very wide variety of activities. The category is also the

most time consuming and expensive activity to assess. This has meant that development in the category has had to be slow. For this reason the team had to make careful decisions about the direction the work would take. Some attempt is made in this chapter to indicate the nature of, and reasons for, these decisions. It is important to note that different information would have been obtained if the teams had adopted a different view of the direction for development.

This chapter will attempt to describe the developments in the category, the results which indicate what children do and do not do, and the circumstances which appear to affect their performance. The general influences on pupils' performance are identified and the nature of the influences is discussed. Where these influences have been tested, the results are given.

Finally, the lessons learnt are discussed and some implications for assessment and teaching posited. The chapter is organised in the following sections:

11.2  Historical background
11.3  1981−Position reached and first survey results
11.4  Further developments and results of the surveys 1982 – 1983
11.5  Position prior to the 1984 survey
11.6  The 1984 survey and results
11.7  Discussion
11.8  Summary
11.9  Implications

## 11.2  Historical background

It has been mentioned that the development work in this category started at age 11. The premise on which the development work was based was that in order to know how children tackle problems they had to be allowed to do them and the assessor had to observe what they did. The assessment situation adopted was therefore a practical one with one pupil observed by one tester. The choice of a one-to-one test situation had a two-fold purpose. It was to allow the collection of behavioural data and also, perhaps more importantly, to allow a tester to explain a question orally, and with the equipment, to a child.

The aims and methods of the assessment in the category **Performance of investigations** were both innovative and exploratory. For the first survey at age 11 checklists were developed which attempted to sum pupils' behaviours, their intentions and attitudes (see DES, 1981, 1983, 1984c). There was also a strategy of 'prompting' to enable pupils to 'see' the problem. In addition to checklists of pupils' performance there was some collection of verbal and written data; usually this concerned in the first instance pupils' intentions and secondly their treatment of results.

In 1980, at ages 13 and 15, trials in the category were started. The trials were both of the questions and the assessment methods. They involved watching and interviewing pupils during and after carrying out an investigation. The effect of the age 11 work on these trials was considerable. In addition, the work in the **Planning of investigations** category at ages 13 and 15, was well advanced and exerted an influence. To an extent these influences conflicted. The influence that different categories had on each other has been mentioned in some detail in Chapter 10. The original checklists, like those used at age 11, summed behaviours in single checkpoints. There was however no attempt to check intentions or to provide prompts. The initial view of investigations assumed that what to test and what to judge was clearly specified by the way in which the problem was presented. As such, decisions about these aspects were not demanded from the pupils. This not unreasonable view was however in conflict with the alternative definition of a problem, that is, a 'task for which the pupil cannot immediately see an answer or recall a routine method for finding it' (see teachers' report, 'Assessing investigations in science at ages 13 and 15', Gott and Murphy, 1987). For investigations to have this attribute they have to be posed in a relatively open-ended manner. The perception of what to test and what to judge then becomes a major aspect of the problem-solving demands for many pupils. Only investigations with this attribute have been included in the surveys at age 13.

The developments in the category at age 11 are described in detail in the age 11 review report (DES, 1988a). At ages 13 and 15, the first round of trials established the manner and procedures for the testing. The investigations were to be presented orally and in writing with one tester to one pupil. A range of apparatus was provided which was described and its use demonstrated, where this was appropriate. Help was given with reading, writing and manipulation of apparatus where this was judged to be necessary. The average test time allowed was 30 minutes per investigation. Full details of the test administration are in the teachers' report, 'Practical testing at ages 11, 13 and 15' (Welford, Harlen and Schofield, 1985).

Decisions about the types of investigations to use were more difficult to resolve. The types used were finally selected by a process of elimination. For example a question about the effect of different surfaces on the speed of movement of a snail was rejected, because it

was not possible to carry out a scientific investigation, within the constraints of the testing system, given the vagaries of snail movements. Any intention to carry out a carefully quantified investigation was thwarted in practice by variables outside the pupils' control. A question concerning the effect of the shape and size of windmill sails on the effectiveness of the windmill was also rejected but for quite different reasons. Here the difficulty was the manner of presentation of the investigation. It was found necessary to give the pupils a variety of pre-cut sails which varied systematically in terms of size and shape. The pupil could therefore only investigate the effect of the presented shapes: thus the independent and control variables had been modelled in advance. The pupil could either deal with the problem algorithmically or attempt to discern the 'problem' in the assessor's head. A third type of question rejected is illustrated by the example 'Metal plates'. In this investigation the pupils had to determine which pair out of a set of pairs of metal plates allowed the largest current through when in contact with dilute sulphuric acid. Many 15 year olds and the majority of 13 year olds were prevented from tackling the investigations by the need to understand an electric circuit.

The aim of the first round of surveys in this category was to establish a base line of performance. Little was known about pupils' performance on practical activities in general; it was decided initially to use investigations which would provide a lot of information about the scientific procedures involved in practical investigations. For these reasons the questions selected were procedurally-based practical tasks usually concerned with the relationship between variables and their effects. The conceptual understanding required in the tasks selected was limited to a level at which all pupils could be expected to make an attempt at devising an experimental set-up. The analysis of the trial questions and results led to the understanding that the conceptual and procedural demands of questions could be manipulated and consequently increased, reduced or changed. It was understood even at this early stage that without some conceptual understanding any problem to be investigated would have no meaning. A detailed description of the types and characteristics of the investigations considered suitable for the assessment is given in the teachers' report, 'Assessing investigations in science at ages 13 and 15' (Gott and Murphy, 1987).

The trials of questions were used also to establish and develop the most suitable methods of data collection. The initial trial checklists were single summary checkpoints of behaviours. However, it became apparent very quickly that it was not just at the younger age that thinking and doing were interdependent activities. Whilst carrying out the investigations children were obviously refining their approach to the problem and developing a more complete understanding of it at the same time as developing an appropriate strategy for its solution. This dynamic aspect of the children's problem-solving activity seemed to be as important as any other observable outcome. It was therefore decided to create checklists which did not sum behaviours but recorded single activities in a time sequence. A picture of the pupils' whole investigation could be discerned retrospectively from such a checklist. Thus any changes in strategy would be recorded. Full details of how the checklists were developed are included in the teachers' report, 'Science at age 13', Murphy and Schofield, 1984, and the 1981 age 13 survey report, DES, 1984a.

## 11.3  1981–Position reached and first survey results

To summarise the position reached in the category, the test situation was to be open-ended with the pupils being told the problem to be investigated and what was generally expected of them, eg practical work. The apparatus provided was to act as an aid and not to inhibit them. They were also told to do whatever they chose to do and to change their minds whenever they thought it was necessary. An example of a typical problem script is included in Appendix 9.

A definite policy regarding the type of investigation to be assessed had also been decided. The investigation had to allow the opportunities for a 'scientific' investigation and, if quantification was potentially valid, it had to be practically possible. The strategy for solving the problem could not be a recalled algorithm; thus any particular type of variable relationship had to be expressed in a 'novel' setting. The investigations were to be rich in procedural demands but the conceptual understanding required was not to constitute a barrier to the overwhelming majority of pupils tackling them. For the 1981 survey the investigations chosen varied in the complexity and type of procedures necessary to solve them. They also had different purposes, contents and settings. For example one question was about different types of kitchen paper towels:

- The *purpose* was to decide which of several different paper towels would hold the most water.

- The *nature* of the investigation was the requirement to take a single measurement of the 'amount' of water held and to repeat this for each towel.

- The *content* of the task included the three paper towels, the apparatus, a lever arm balance, measuring cylinders, petri dishes, beakers, stopclocks etc.

- The *context* was regarded as everyday in nature because the question was about usage of materials in a kitchen.

- The *conceptual understanding* required concerned interpretation of the term 'to hold' and knowledge

of the effect of variables such as paper thickness and size.

- The *procedural understanding* required involved the initial and fundamental understanding of the nature of scientific evidence, a pre-requisite of any scientific investigation. It extends to the development of a measurement strategy, eg knowing what to measure and the selection of an appropriate scale, eg the size of each paper towel to use, given the sensitivity of the available measuring instruments.

An extended description of the above definitions is included in the teachers' report, 'Assessing investigations in science at ages 13 and 15 (Gott and Murphy, 1987). The other questions used in the 1981 survey are briefly set out under similar descriptive headings in Table 11.1 (p. 127).

The checklists for each question were designed to collect behavioural data *only*. For example a checkpoint might record whether a pupil did or did not use a measuring cylinder. Thus they were 'activity' checklists. Pupils' intentions were considered in their oral responses to a short structured interview. The two sets of data collected were regarded as qualitatively different. The checklists had to embody both the problem characteristics and the pupil response characteristics. As such they had to take into account the different pathways taken by pupils to solve problems. The development of both the checklists and of the manner in which the data were to be analysed had to an extent to occur in conjunction. The analysis features identified during trials included the pupils *in situ* modifications, the different strategies adopted to solve the same problem and the gradation of adequacy of the strategies. In addition to these features there appeared to be a number of identifiable stages common to the scientific solution. These stages could be identified across the different strategies within a problem and between problems. A general mark scheme which took account of the stages in a procedurally-based solution to an investigation was developed. The scheme was restricted to the procedural activities as these were thought to be the main demands within the investigations set. As such it was a unidimensional view of pupil performance. In the scheme the activities which had to occur were incorporated in an iterative, cyclical model (DES, 1984a, 1984b ; see also Figure 11.1, p. 126).

The model was to function as a general heuristic in that it represented a strategy, independent of question content, that helps scientific problem-solvers to approach and organise their resources in solving problems. It is a prescriptive model based on an 'ideal type'. It enables generalisations to be made about scientific procedures for alternative problems, strategies and solutions. What cannot be shown in a 2-D presentation, but which better represents the understanding of practical investigative behaviour, are the dynamics of the pupils' problem-solving activities. To

**Figure 11.1** *General model*

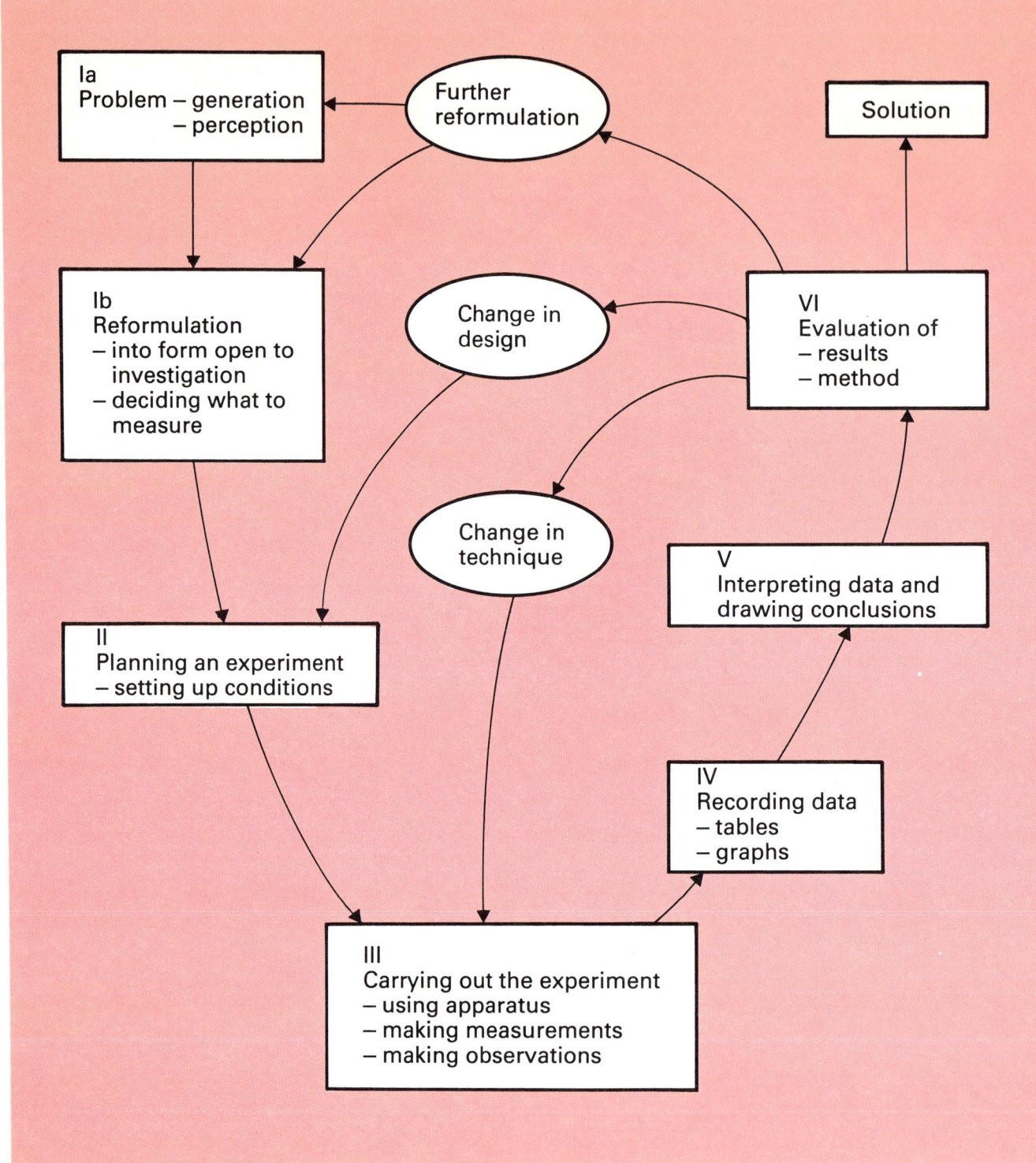

represent the model in action it is necessary to conceive of a spiral of activities. In each loop of the spiral all of the stages, or a selection of them, are involved in a variety of ways as children make decisions, refine their perception of the problem and collect and evaluate sensory input and data. Of course having said this, it must also be recognised that some children will not engage at all with certain activities. For other pupils there is apparently a single line or route to the solution. The model was devised because it appeared to make it possible to generalise across tasks. Perhaps more

importantly, without some coherent logical framework within which to conceptualise pupils' responses it would not be possible to perceive the idiosyncracies that had not been catered for.

In summary, pupil performance was to be considered in terms of what they did and contrasted with a 'scientific' view of expected performance. The scientific view matched each problem's individual characteristics to the general stages within the mark scheme model.

**Table 11.1** *A summary of the individual investigations used in 1981 and 1982*

| Investigation and purpose | The variable to be varied systematically, ie the independent variable | The variable to be measured, ie the dependent variable | Context | Procedural understanding |
|---|---|---|---|---|
| **1981**<br>**Survival:** Which fabric would keep you warmer? | Material (×2) | Thermal conduction | Science | Developing a measurement strategy |
| **Cars:** If all the cars are given the same chance, which one will travel furthest? | Cars (×3) | Distance travelled | Science | Setting up the apparatus. Identifying those variables which will affect the dependent variable |
| **Woodlice:** If woodlice are given a choice of the four places below, which one do they choose to live in? A place which is: DAMP AND DARK or DRY AND DARK or DAMP AND LIGHT or DRY AND LIGHT | Dampness Darkness | Woodlice preference | Science | Setting up the apparatus in such a way as to allow for a measurement of the dependent variable for all four combinations of the two independent variables |
| **Hot wash:** Does this washing powder wash dirty cloth as clean in cold water as it does in hot water? | Cloth dirt Water temperature | Cleanness | Everyday | Setting up four combinations of the independent variables |
| **Flooring:** Which one of the floor coverings do you think is the most suitable for a kitchen floor? | Floor covering (×4) | Suitability | Everyday | Reformulating the problem Defining the dependent variable |
| **1981 and 1982**<br>**Paper towel:** Which kind of paper will hold the most water? | Paper (×3) | Water held | Everyday | Developing a measurement strategy |
| **1982**<br>**Swingboard:** What difference does changing the length (or width) of the board make to how quickly it swings? | Length and width of boards | Period of oscillation | Science | Identifying the two independent variables and developing a strategy for sequencing measurements within that strategy |

The activity checklists embodied the alternative perceptions, strategies and techniques used by pupils. They represented a limited selection of behaviours but were designed to handle the majority of pupils' activities. For the main elements in the cyclical model the checklists allowed for a grading of adequacy of performance. The analysis of the results involved the application of a 'strategy' sieve. A fine mesh was applied first in which all aspects of the ideal strategy were looked for, so that only the pupils who met these requirements fell through. This was followed by a systematic relaxation of the specifications. The application of each gauge of mesh allowed more and more pupils to fall through until all pupils were taken into account. In this way a full description of pupils' performance was achieved. This then allowed an attempt to be made at the much more difficult task of judging the criterion for adequacy between groups of pupils using different strategies.

The six questions used in the 1981 survey at age 13 are shown in Table 11.1. The structure of the analysis included consideration of the following:

**Problem perception**
defining the status of:
— the independent variable, ie that to be varied systematically
— the dependent variable, ie that to be judged

**Problem reformulation**
— how to vary the independent variable
— how to judge the dependent variable
— identification of variables whose effect must be kept constant (control variables)

**Planning and carrying out**
Setting up:
— the test of the independent variable
— the measurement of the dependent variable
— the control of other variables
Taking account of:
— scale for the quantities of variables
— range of readings
(both of which depend on the nature of the variables, the type of answer necessary and the measuring instruments available)

**Recording and interpreting**
— developing a strategy for sifting complex multivariate data
— transforming data from one form to another (here account has to be taken of the whole task and the type of solution appropriate to it)

**Evaluation**
— assessing the data against the demands of the question and the answer to be derived
— assessing the method (the experimental strategy or tactics therein)

Whilst the dynamics of pupils' problem-solving behaviour may well be represented by a spiral of activities, the method of analysis described here involves a static view of a single cycle. The 1981 survey results are summarised in three main sections below. (A detailed account can be found in DES, 1984a.)

### Perception and reformulation of the problem–the approach adopted

On this aspect of the task the pupils had to decide what they thought the problem was about. This was indicated in their experimental set-up by the independent and dependent variables they identified. In 'Survival', 'Paper towel', 'Flooring', and 'Cars', the single independent variable was presented and translated for the pupil. For example in 'Paper towel' 'type of towel' is presented as three different kitchen towels, and in 'Survival' 'which material' was reduced to a selection of two, blanket and plastic. The majority of pupils successfully set up a test of independent variables presented in this manner, 93 per cent, 96 per cent, 95 per cent and 97 per cent for the four investigations respectively.

In the 'Woodlice' question the position was quite different. There were two independent variables, dampness and darkness, and the pupils had to set up four conditions systematically varying the two. Although the conditions were specified, a third of the pupils failed to set them up in a systematic way. These pupils confounded the test of the two variables by setting up damp-light and dry-dark conditions only, or some other limited sets of combinations. In 'Hotwash', as in 'Woodlice', there were two independent variables, water temperature and cloth dirt. Again the onus was on the pupil to establish the conditions in which the variables could be tested. Seventy per cent of the pupils were successful in this. Fourteen per cent, however, set up a test in which the two variables were confounded.

It can be argued that the difference in performance between 'Woodlice' and 'Hotwash' compared to the other investigations is due to having to handle two as opposed to one independent variable. Alternatively or in addition, it could be argued that presenting the variables translated into actual concrete representations, as in the other questions removes the need to conceptualise the variables. From our survey evidence it is noteworthy that for a significant number of 13 year olds the requirement to manipulate for themselves abstract variables such as temperature when developing an experimental design goes beyond their conceptual ability.

Turning now to the dependent variable, ie what to judge in order to determine the effect of the independent variable, this variable was never presented to the pupils as a ready-made measurement procedure. It therefore had to be conceptualised in the first instance. In 'Survival' 82 per cent successfully identified thermal conduction as the variable to be judged. Seven per cent

considered thermal capacity and a further 8 per cent concerned themselves with the porosity or water repellence of the materials. On the 'Paper towel' question about 10 per cent failed to translate the term 'hold' into the quantity of water. Only 4 per cent of the children attempting the 'Flooring' question failed to reformulate 'suitable' into some appropriate variable to be judged. A similar proportion failed in the 'Cars' question. In 'Hotwash' the dependent variable 'cleanliness' was unproblematic for the pupils. Performance on this aspect in 'Woodlice' varied as a consequence of the pupils alternative ways of conceptualising 'woodlice preference'. Approximately three quarters of the pupils considered human patterns of behaviour to interpret the meaning of 'preference'. These alternative perceptions of the dependent variable affected the whole of the pupils' subsequent experimental design. Thus in spite of over 50 per cent of the pupils successfully identifying the four conditions to be tested, only about 20 per cent set them up in such a way that woodlice preference could be judged.

The two aspects are now considered in conjunction, ie the identification and setting up of the minimum requirements for an experiment in terms of the independent and dependent variables–the approach. The results for the 1981 questions are given in Table 11.2.

**Table 11.2** *Performance on problem reformulation (1981 survey)*

| Question | % pupils with an adequate approach |
|---|---|
| Survival | 70 |
| Paper towel | 89 |
| Flooring | 72 |
| Cars | 90 |
| Woodlice | 22 |
| Hot wash | 70 |

In setting up the minimum requirements for an experimental design, account had also to be taken of those variables whose effect had to be controlled. The results on this aspect of pupil performance are included in Appendix 9 (Table A9.1). As the table clearly demonstrates, pupil performance is extremely varied both within and between different investigations. It is apparent that even at the young ages of 11 and 13 children do attempt to apply the procedure of control of variables. Their performance is however affected by their overall view of the problem and the manner in which they model it. Thus not only must the effect of the variable be understood in conceptual terms, its effect must also be understood within the pupils' overall model of the problem. For these reasons pupils can fail to control, for example, the volume of water put into cans which are insulated by blanket and plastic in 'Survival' if they are unaware of the relationship between the heat source and the dependent variable-thermal conduction. Similarly pupils who fail to control the amount of material in 'Survival', wrapping it haphazardly around the sides of the cans but carefully covering the top, are functioning consistently within their model of heat loss by steam transfer only. At age 13, pupils did not hold 'all' things constant but did have a tendency to 'control' variables which were 'obvious'. They did this by default as part of the process of carefully carrying out a scientific investigation, and they consciously controlled those variables whose effects were known to them. In addition, the better the pupils' overall experiment by other criteria the more likely they were to have taken extraneous variables into account.

### Planning and carrying out the experiment

The performance issues raised here include the range and number of readings needed to set up adequately the test of the independent variables and the judgement of the effect on the dependent variable. Also considered are how other variables are controlled and the choice of instrumentation and scale. The latter choices are concerned with judgements about the size of associated error in relation to the answer sought.

In all the questions used in 1981 the issues of range and number of readings relating to the independent variables were largely circumvented by the nature of the variables involved and the manner of their presentation (see Table 11.1). The decision about the quantities of independent variables to use affected 20 per cent of the pupils in the 'Paper towel' question. These pupils chose an inappropriate amount of paper, ie too little, given the instrumentation provided. In the 'Woodlice' question most pupils were unaware of the need to use a sufficient number of woodlice to take into account the error associated with variation in animal behaviour.

In this stage of the analysis the manner in which the pupils made measurements is considered. For the two questions 'Flooring' and 'Hotwash' it was only possible to make qualitative judgements about the effect on the dependent variable. In 'Cars' and 'Paper towel' a quantitative judgement was necessary; in fact it was arranged to be so in the 'Cars' question. It was considered essential, if pupil performance was to be assessed in terms of a quantified strategic approach, to ensure that quantification was both possible and necessary. In both of these questions three single measures of either the 'distance' or the 'water held' had to be taken. Twenty-two per cent of the pupils failed to take any measurements in the 'Cars' investigation, and 23 per cent in the 'Paper towel' question. A further 10 per cent of the pupils on this latter question took a final measurement only, so that no effective comparison of the three towels could be made.

In 'Woodlice' and 'Survival' similar decisions had to be made about the time for which to leave the woodlice or the cans of water. In 'Survival' only 7 per cent of the pupils allowed a time interval of more than five minutes to judge the rate of change in temperature. Sixty per cent of the pupils chose a time interval of less than two minutes. Similarly in 'Woodlice' the overwhelming majority of pupils used a time interval of between one and two minutes. In the 'Survival' question it was necessary to take a range of readings but again as in 'Paper towel' 30 per cent of the pupils took a final reading only. Three per cent took the temperature at regular intervals and only 5 per cent made more than two records.

The use of instrumentation to effect the control of variables was difficult to disentangle because of the variation in the nature of the variables to be controlled. There was a general tendency for 13 year olds not to choose the most accurate of the instruments available, but the better the overall performance of pupils on other aspects of a problem the more likely they were to use the most appropriate instruments. The measurement techniques employed by the majority of pupils suggest that they have little experience in this area of problem-solving. In addition, the general tendency was for 13 year olds not to repeat measurements. The pupils know, on the whole, what to measure but the procedures which affect the validity and accuracy of the measurements are generally unknown at this age.

The understanding of the nature of scientific evidence underpins successful practical investigative work. The development of a strategy for an investigation has to take account of the nature and manner of measurements necessary for judging or operating the independent, dependent and control variables. To develop a strategy like this in advance requires that pupils have a sophisticated understanding of scientific investigations. The understanding has not only to be applied generally, it has to be understood particularly in respect of the nature of variables within any one investigation. In addition it has to be applied advisedly in the context of the type of problem solution required. Viewed in this light the pupils' actual performance is best summarised as a series of tactical moves, albeit accurate, lacking either refinement or integration within an overall strategic view.

### Recording and interpreting information

Table 11.3 (p.130) shows the style of record made by pupils for the investigations used in the 1981 survey.

It would seem that different investigations and results do not affect the style of record pupils consider to be appropriate. On average about 6 per cent of the pupils at age 13 made a tabulated record of their results.

**Table 11.3** *Style of written record*

| Style | Question and % pupils | | | | | |
|---|---|---|---|---|---|---|
| | Paper towel | Survival | Woodlice | Cars | Hotwash | Flooring |
| Tabulated | 5 | 8 | 5 | 9 | 2 | 8 |
| Ordered | 65 | 63 | 60 | 64 | 59 | 67 |
| Random | 27 | 27 | 33 | 26 | 36 | 23 |
| No record | 3 | 2 | 2 | 1 | 3 | 2 |

Any attempt to judge pupils' ability to interpret data in the context of this test is made difficult by the variation in the data available to them. To an extent interpretation within an investigation can be considered as featuring early on in the development of a strategy. It is necessary to hypothesise about the type of data needed and the manner of its organisation prior to refining a view of a problem. Both 'Survival' and 'Paper towel' require some level of *a priori* interpretation. In 'Survival' the failure of any 13 year olds to attempt to produce a graph and the fact that only 5 per cent take more than two readings indicates a limited interpretation of the relationship involved. Similarly in 'Paper towel' the single, final measurement taken by a significant proportion of pupils indicates an interpretation based on specific instances rather than on comparisons and relationships.

*Evaluation*

The evaluation considered here is that which could be discerned from the pupils' actions. The judgement of pupils' inclination to evaluate collected data and their experimental methods assumes a time-scale which was not available for some of the investigations used. In 'Flooring' the evaluative procedures which can be discerned from the pupils' actions include the elimination of some floor coverings. In the course of the investigation 26 per cent of the pupils did this. For the remaining four questions the results for pupils' changes to their investigations are given in Table 11.4.

The 'Cars' investigation had the shortest time-scale for completion and this is reflected in the results in the Table. It was also easier for the pupils to recognise error in procedure.

**Table 11.4** *The changes pupils made in their investigations (1981 survey)*

| Change | Question and % pupils | | | |
|---|---|---|---|---|
| | Survival | Paper towel | Cars | Woodlice |
| Change of approach | 8 | 2 | 19 | 3 |
| Qualitative→Quantitative | 5 | 3 | 26 | 2 |
| Change of method | 7 | 3 | 24 | 4 |
| Repeat complete experiment | 0 | 2 | 90 | 5 |

## 11.4 Further developments and results of the surveys 1982–1983

The results of the 1981 survey of **Performance of investigations** indicated a higher success rate on some aspects of scientific activity than had been recorded in other categories of the assessment framework. The success and confidence with which children tackled the investigations was noteworthy and perhaps surprising given the assessment situation used. This involved the pupils being closely observed whilst handling a complex interaction of demands. Both the demands and the situation were uncommon features in school science lessons. There were some notable exceptions to the pupils' successful performance on investigations. It was clearly necessary to question further both the nature of the successes and the difficulties pupils experienced in the category. The issues considered during the 1982 and 1983 surveys covered the following questions:

— what effect did a *practical test context* have on the pupils' performance?

— what effect did an *action response* rather than a written response have?

— what effect did dealing with a *whole task* have on pupils' performance?

The questions and results used to illuminate these issues are reported in detail in DES, 1985a, and the teachers' report, 'Assessing investigations in science at ages 13 and 15' (Gott and Murphy, 1987).

The use of a practical context raises two factors: first, it provides clues for the pupil and secondly it allows direct interaction and feedback. The effects of the practical context were tested by setting the same problems in different test contexts (paper-and-pencil, with or without pictures of the apparatus, and practical). The results showed that more pupils produced better solutions to investigations when given access to practical apparatus clues. The best performances were elicited in the practical context where both clues and interaction were available and possible.

The contrast between pupils' written responses and action responses was also reported. The written plans of pupils prior to action were less adequate than their action responses in terms of the measurement procedures and techniques that were specified. It was also rare that any control variables were mentioned in the pupils' plans. The pupils' written accounts after carrying out the practical investigation were however reasonable representations of what they did (judging the content rather than the quality of the pupils' writing). It would seem that the process of writing is not in itself an obstacle; rather it is the need in a non-practical context to carry out 'thought' experiments without any form of feedback to stimulate further thought.

In the practical investigations there was some evidence that many pupils were unable to develop a full strategy and/or retain it. It was thought possible that too much was being given to the pupils to handle in the course of an investigation. To consider this further, short questions focusing on aspects of each of the investigation tasks were set in a written context and included in the 1983 survey. The main finding is that performance on the structured investigations is lower on every aspect identified in the analysis. It seems that the ability to 'see' the whole task and to obtain concrete feedback reduces the demand on the pupils to retain a strategic view in their head. Thus paper-and-pencil questions on aspects of investigations increase rather than decrease the demand to have an abstract, strategic view for tackling variable-based problems. This is surprising because a structured question form provides many clues and cues that are not there in an open form: the fact that these do not appear to help confirms again that it is the overall strategy, rather than detailed tactics, which is critical.

An additional practical investigation 'Swingboard' was surveyed in 1982. It was used to collect further specific information about pupils' performance on practical investigations. It was hoped that it would illuminate the effect of the number and manner of presentation of the independent variables, and the effect of the need to conceptualise the variables prior to establishing a design in which they are adequately tested.

In 'Swingboard' the two independent variables, length and width, were presented as pre-cut boards representing a range of combinations of length and width (see DES, 1985a). The investigation was to determine the effect of the length and width of a piece of pegboard on the rate of swinging of the piece. Sixty-three per cent of the pupils set up an adequate test of the two independent variables. This figure was a little lower than the percentages in 'Woodlice' and 'Hotwash', 67 per cent, 70 per cent, respectively. The variables in 'Swingboard' were quantitative in nature but the manner of presentation effectively reduced them to the same type as in 'Woodlice' and 'Hotwash', ie a set of specified conditions. The slight depression in performance on this investigation appeared to be the result of some pupils *not* holding a 'concept' of the variables necessary to abstract them from their embedded form in the pre-cut boards. In addition, the consequence of one variable, the length, having a major effect influenced, *in situ*, the pupils' perception of the problem. Turning to the dependent variable, 31 per cent of the pupils failed to deal with the variable 'rate'. This required them to consider the change in two variables, the *oscillation* and the *time*. These pupils operationalised the variable 'rate' by controlling one of the two variables by considering the duration of swing of the boards. In this investigation a qualitative judgement of the dependent variable was adequate, ie making a direct comparison between the boards. Consequently not much new information was created

about the effect of measurement procedures on overall performance; but that was not the intention in designing the problem.

The performance on control of variables is included in Appendix 9 (Table A9.1). The results reaffirm some earlier speculation. The pupils who controlled the amplitude did so in a deliberate fashion and not by default or intuition. The style of record keeping again was completely in tune with the findings for the other investigations. Only 7 per cent of the pupils kept a tabulated record of their results.

## 11.5  Position prior to the 1984 survey

It was decided not to include the category **Performance of investigations** in the 1983 survey at each age. This decision was made to allow time for further reflection on the existing data. One outcome of the earlier work was the apparent fluctuation in pupils' performance across investigations: investigations which appeared to have similar procedural demands.

Individual investigation profiles were established on the basis of three general criteria:

– approach:     both independent (I) and dependent (D) variables identified;

– set-up:       all the variables which might invalidate the test of (I) and the measurement of (D) identified and measured;

– measurement: an initial and final measurement made.

This was done to illuminate the possible source of significant variation between investigations. The profiles included only the data that it was appropriate to analyse. Thus, for example, the qualitative judgements of the dependent variable in 'Hotwash' and 'Flooring' precluded analysis on the criterion of measurement. The profiles for the investigations surveyed in 1981–1982 are shown in Figure 11.2 (p.132).

Looking at the profile results two things were not clear. These were:

– whether a competent problem-solver in one situation would behave in this way for all situations;

– whether the large number of pupils who failed to deploy an adequate strategy all failed for the same reasons.

These questions could not be addressed by the existing data. It was also impractical to attempt to answer them in a survey with all the practical logistical constraints that this imposed.

Two additional limitations in the existing data were identified. Firstly, that existing interpretations of the

**Figure 11.2** *Investigation profiles–percentage of pupils meeting defined criteria at age 13*

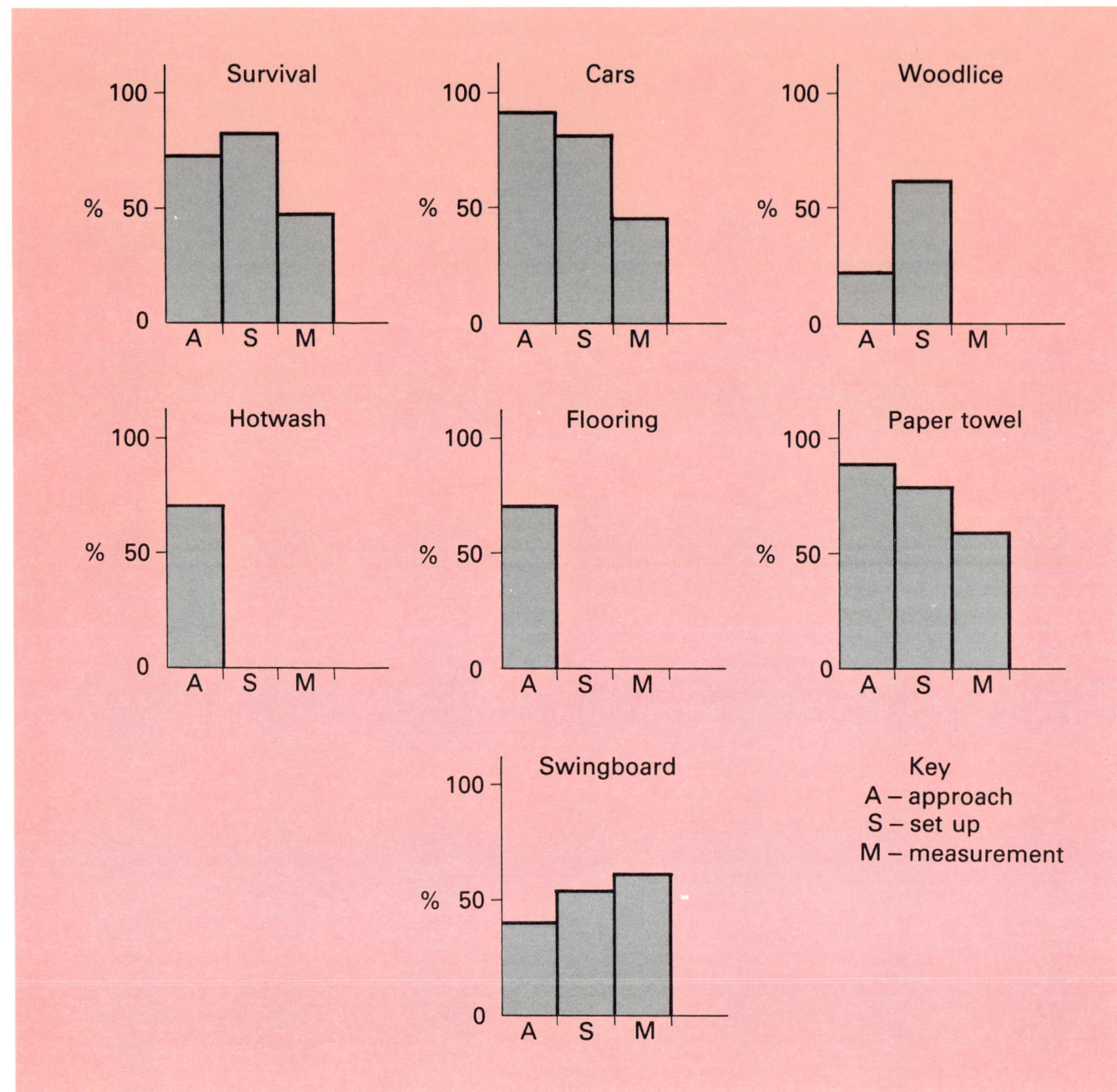

pupils' actions and words did not take account of the pupils' own perceptions of the tasks and the selections they made as a consequence. Secondly, the demands of the individual investigations had been considered from a unidimensional viewpoint only–that of performance on procedures.

A new set of data collection was initiated, starting with discussions with pupils about their experiments across a range of problems. This work was small in scale. The aim of it was to illuminate and explore the influences on pupils' problem-solving activities. The profiles of performance for the investigation served as a focus in this work and guided the observations made and questions asked of the pupils. In addition, investigations

previously rejected were used to better understand pupils' difficulties with them. From this round of in-depth work a set of hypotheses emerged about a general model of pupil response. The scale and method of data collection and the detailed results are reported elsewhere (DES, 1989). The main findings of the work are sum-marised here as they affect the subsequent structure and analysis of the 1984 survey at age 13. The evidence for these findings is not presented here.

An initial aim of the APU survey in this category, men-tioned previously, was to reduce the requirement to recall specific science concepts in the practical investi-gations. The idea of a concept-free problem is in practice not a reality. However the reduction in the overt conceptual demands in the investigations enabled the more subtle, often assumed, general conceptual characteristics of a practical investigation to emerge. These characteristics constitute aspects of the overall demands made on pupils. It is possible to identify and independently label aspects of the demands of investigations as in section 11.3. However, the consequence of the interaction of these objectively defined demands on the pupil has not been identified or described yet. It is this interaction which constitutes the actual demand the pupil has to deal with. The interview work with pupils attempted to consider the interactive effects in order to more fairly represent what the pupils could and could not do.

The interaction of demands is best viewed as the 'model' of the problem the pupil has to generate and then operate within. The content and context within which the assessment investigation is presented act as significant cues to the pupils. It is the pupils' existing conceptual framework and personal experience which determine the effect of the cues and subsequently affect the pupils' behaviours and the decisions they make. It is difficult to describe the alternative 'models' perceived by pupils which are consequent upon their differential responses to, and interpretation of, presented cues. Some examples only will be quoted. Live animals, mountain sides, and metal springs all feature as aspects of presented content in the survey investigations. The live animals cue most children to an anthropomorphic view of animal behaviour. This view affects their 'model' of the problem, including their decisions about how to make judgements and even their apparent ability to control variables. The pupils are however functioning consistently within the 'model' they perceive. Thus one 'knows' things about animals from the animals' expressions and 'moods'. Similarly pupils made decisions not to subject animals to the scientific demands of control of variables so as not to 'upset them', 'depress them' or generally cause them distress. The mountainside setting in 'Survival' evoked the more dominant notion of general human survival for some pupils. Their model of the problem included such variables as food and general protection and was not limited to 'material type' as demanded by the assessor. The metal springs in one investigation recalled Hooke's Law for some pupils. Therefore, irrespective of the actual demand, they were concerned with the extension of the springs and not the rate of bobbing.

The general context of the question, ie overtly everyday or scientific, was reported by some pupils to affect their decisions. A question in an everyday context was seen not to require a 'scientific' investigation. As such, controls and measurements were not carried out rigorously. There were particular context and content influences which affected boys and girls differently in some cases. These are mentioned in Chapter 3 of this report.

The potential to define their own model of the problem seemed to contribute to the pupils' apparent confidence and initial success in the assessment situation. A sense of control over their own ideas and subsequent decisions pervaded the comments pupils made about their liking for the investigations. This was true of pupils of all abilities and in spite of the requirement for them to work on their own under scrutiny. It was also the case that the vast majority of pupils showed considerable commitment to their investigations and worked for extended periods of time, generally longer than twenty minutes. In the assessment it was stressed that what the pupils chose to do was of interest to the testers; thus there was no 'challenge' to their models. In a teaching situation this can clearly not be the case, but perhaps the need to perceive and adopt other perceptions which may be located in a world parallel to one's own could erode pupils' confidence and their potential for successful interaction with a problem.

The model of the problem generated by pupils is significant in that it affects the whole of their subsequent performance and experimental design. In the experimental designs set up by the pupils across investigations, it was observed and sometimes reported that they had difficulty manipulating the *independent variable*. The difficulty was sometimes to do with the conceptual nature of the variable. The pupils often only understood the variable descriptively as a label or a noun such as a length or a temperature, eg 'hot', which did not enable them to set up a design in which it was manipulated in an abstracted form along a scaled continuum. The *number* of variables to be tested could also have an effect on the pupils' performance. Sometimes this was because one variable would exert a major effect which subsequently led some pupils to redefine the problem in terms of that variable alone. The *nature* of the independent variable and the manner in which it had to be varied systematically caused many pupils problems. The difficulty for the pupils was that they were unaware of the need to treat particular types of variables differently. Their lack of understanding seemed to be associated with a lack of experience of the role of quantified data within a scientific enquiry.

When carrying out scientific investigations pupils are expected to understand measurement as a *strategy* for determining the relationships between variables. However, pupils' understanding of measurement generally covered a wide range. For some pupils the term 'measurement' was only understood as a specific procedure, often a procedure recalled by a particular instrument. Thus to measure was 'to weigh' or 'to use a ruler'. For many other pupils at age 13 measurement was more generally understood. Whilst these pupils would often 'know' what to measure, their way of knowing appeared to be closely related to their being able to recall some analogous experience. Consequently understanding of the rate of cooling or rate of dissolving, albeit a complex derivation of two variables, was adequately demonstrated and reported by most pupils. This seemed not to be the case for other 'rate' measures where the related experience was not obvious or could not be recalled.

The pupils' performance on control of variables was affected, as has been mentioned, by their 'model' of the problem and whether it was perceived to be scientific in nature. In addition the variable had to have an effect within the pupil's model. The effect then had to be known or obvious to the pupil.

The previous survey results available for a population on a few problems had now been supplemented by results at the individual pupil level across a range of problems. The speculations about pupils' problem-solving behaviours and the influences on them were used to construct a set of hypotheses. A sub-set of these were selected for consideration in the 1984 survey.

## 11.6   The 1984 survey and results

The following issues were considered in the survey:

— the model of the problem—conceptual influences
                              —context influences
                              —practical cues

— independent variable      —nature
                              —number
                              —presentation

— measurement               —nature
                              —manner of

A round of extensive trials of ten new problems was carried out in 1983–1984. On the basis of these trials four were selected: these four, 'Sweets', 'Chemical', 'Springload' and 'Waterlevel' with their apparatus layout are in Appendix 9. A brief description of them is given in Table 11.5. 'Sweets' and 'Waterlevel' were administered to the same sample of pupils as were 'Chemical' and 'Springload'.

Two of the questions, 'Sweets' and 'Chemical', were included to better understand the effect, if any, of the content and context on the whole investigation. They varied in the content presented in that 'Sweets' was

intended to be *everyday* and 'Chemical' *scientific*. Therefore in 'Sweets' the investigation concerned a common readily available sweet, plastic cups, measuring jugs and teaspoons. These were replaced in 'Chemical' by beakers, cylinders, spatulas and a 'chemical' which was a well known cleaner for false teeth but not presented as such (see Appendix 9). Another feature considered in the two investigations was the manipulation of two independent variables, surface area and temperature.

Springload was a replicate of the 1982 'Swingboard' question in that nine wire springs rather than boards were presented and the same independent variables, length and width, were to be investigated. The dependent variable was 'rate', but of bobbing rather than swinging. The question was included to consider the influence on the pupils' performance of the presentation of the independent variable. It was also hoped to gain more insights into the pupils' performance on measurement and the effect of this on the whole problem.

The development of the 'Waterlevel' question provided important research findings in itself. The question was set to find out how children dealt with a continuous independent variable. As this was regarded as particularly difficult the demands of measurement and controls were reduced as much as possible. This was not done by altering one question but by trialling several possible questions in the hope of finding a 'real' investigation with the hoped for characteristics. 'Waterlevel' was selected by this process.

Each of these four questions had behavioural checklists which were accompanied by a structured set of prompts. Thus if the pupil failed to start, help would be given with the independent variable followed by the dependent variable and so on. The nature and manner of the prompts were varied according to the problem and were only administered if, and when, the pupils had come to a complete halt. If the prompt was given, the nature of it was recorded on the script and on the checklist of subsequent actions. After the investigation an interview was administered, again following all the pertinent issues within the problem. The nature of the questioning was, to take the pupils' actions and to ask them to discuss them. The pupils' ideas would then be used to

**Table 11.5**   *1984 survey investigations*

| Investigation | The variable to be varied systematically, ie the independent variable | The variable to be measured, ie the dependent variable | Procedural focus |
|---|---|---|---|
| Sweets | Surface area Temperature | Rate of reaction/solution | Identifying the two independent variables Developing a measurement strategy |
| Chemical | Surface area Temperature | Rate of reaction/solution | Identifying the two independent variables Developing a measurement strategy |
| Springload | Length and diameter of springs | Rate of bobbing | Identifying the two independent variables and developing a strategy for sequencing measurements |
| Waterlevel | Water level | Rate of flow | Setting up the test of the independent variable |

continue the questioning. A structured interview with a script, and example questions and a script for prompts were provided for each pupil. The testers were trained in their use for two days. An overall strategy for the presentation and use of each aspect of the administration was given in writing and demonstrated in practice. The testers then worked with some children in their own schools before carrying out the actual survey. The results for these four questions are summarised here. (The tables referred to are in Appendix 9.)

The two 1981 questions 'Survival' and 'Woodlice' were re-run because of their clear additional science concept demand. Thus whilst a general case has been made about the need for a conceptual model of the variables this had been irrespective of the need for specific recall of science concepts. However in 'Survival', setting up a measure of the dependent variable 'thermal conduction' does require a learnt science concept. Similarly in 'Woodlice', setting up an 'animal behaviour' experiment requires some recall of biological concepts. The administration of these two investigations was now quite different to that used before. It involved a gradual increase in cues starting with no apparatus and leading up to actual interaction with the apparatus. The children talked about their experiments and were interviewed about both the procedures and concepts underlying their plans and actions.

The testing and data collection methods used were more extensive, innovative and complex than previously. What follows is a first report of the results, already comparable in scale with that of previous surveys. To be further analysed are the relationships between the pupils' oral responses and their actual performance; pupil performance across investigations; the effect of practical cues on performance; and the effect of pupils' conceptual understanding on performance.

*Results for 'Sweets' and 'Chemical'*

The two questions 'Sweets' and 'Chemical' were designed to consider the influence of context on pupils' performance. The designs were constructed to have procedural demands which spread across the stages in the model but which were not particularly burdensome in any one area. There was, however, a decision to include two independent variables. Both of the variables, surface area and temperature, were quantitative in theory but it was difficult, and in the circumstances not appropriate, to attempt an extended investigation of the relationship. The children could only attempt to crush or break into halves etc, the sweets or the 'chemical' (both provided in lozenge form). Any attempt made to manipulate the demands in a problem is limited by the need to maintain a real and probable investigation. Thus whilst keeping many things the same between the questions the choice of the type of chemical and sweet affected the size of the observable effects. In the 'Sweets' question the two variables had similar-sized effects on the dependent

variable. This was not the case in the 'Chemical' question where the effect of temperature was so large and spectacular that one could not fail to notice it.

**Table 11.6**  *Summary of number of readings for the independent variables*

| Independent variable | Group | Number of readings | % pupils | |
| --- | --- | --- | --- | --- |
| | | | Sweets | Chemical |
| Surface area | (1) | 3 out of 4 | 11 | 7 |
| | (2) | 2 | 76 | 72 |
| | (3) | 0 | 13 | 21 |
| Temperature | (1) | 3 out of 4 | 29 | 34 |
| | (2) | 2 | 67 | 65 |
| | (3) | 0 | 4 | 2 |

If Tables 11.6, and Tables A9.2 and A9.3 are considered one can see that fewer pupils test surface area in 'Chemical' than in 'Sweets'. During the children's interviews it was apparent that this failure was not due to a lack of awareness but a definite redefinition of the problem. Consequently 87 per cent of the pupils set up the minimum experimental design in terms of the two independent variables in 'Sweets', compared with 78 per cent in 'Chemical' because in the latter temperature was seen as the major effect (see Tables A9.4 and A9.5). Only a few pupils (3 per cent) in 'Sweets' and none in 'Chemical' when discussing their experiment appeared to have confounded the two variables. A further proportion of pupils, 4 per cent and 7 per cent respectively, indicated they were varying mass as part of their investigation. The everyday context does not appear to influence pupils' performance on this aspect of their investigation.

The fact that fewer pupils tested the effect of surface area in the 'Chemical' investigation must be borne in mind when considering the results in Table 11.7. In Table 11.7 controls of three variables, volume of water, mass of solid and stirring, are considered across the test of both independent variables. Thus the figures refer to 87 per cent of the pupils in 'Sweets' and 78 per cent in 'Chemical'. There is a tendency in the context of the 'Chemical' question for pupils to carry out more effective control of variables.

**Table 11.7**  *Percentage of pupils controlling variables*

| Variables controlled | Sweets | Chemical |
| --- | --- | --- |
| Volume of water, mass of solid, stirring | 31 | 40 |
| Volume of water and mass of solid | 11 | 16 |
| Volume of water only | 2 | 0 |
| Mass only | 46 | 21 |

Table 11.8 (p.136) shows pupils' performance on *setting up* both independent variables. The criteria for performance on this stage are determined by consideration of

the controls, the critical control-mass and the minimum volume of water necessary.

**Table 11.8**  *Setting up the test of both the independent variables*
(Percentage of pupils meeting defined criteria)

| Set-up stage-level | Description | % pupils | |
|---|---|---|---|
| | | Sweets | Chemical |
| 1 | Controlled volume and mass for both variables and used more than 25 cm³ of water | 42 | 53 |
| 2 | Controlled mass but not volume of water and used >25 cm³ of water | 36 | 19 |
| 3 | Controlled mass only and used <25 cm³ of water | 10 | 5 |
| 4 | No control of mass or volume and used <25 cm³ of water | 12 | 23 |
| Number of pupils | | 257 | 248 |

There are more pupils in the top and bottom groups in the Chemical question when pupils' performance on setting up the test of the variables is analysed. For both questions identical proportions of those pupils who have carried out control in practice reported orally that the variables had an effect. The consistency between actual behaviour and reported behaviour on the control of volume and mass was high for both questions.

A similar proportion of pupils in 'Sweets' and 'Chemical', 39 per cent and 41 per cent, reported that amount of water used mattered and explained why. This is much lower than the number who took this into account in practice. It may well be that the judgement of an appropriate volume with respect to mass can be, and is, done intuitively by the pupils and is a common everyday judgement.

In the measurement of the dependent variable the majority of pupils opted for a *quantitative* judgement. A slightly higher proportion of pupils chose a quantitative method in 'Chemical' than in 'Sweets' (86 per cent and 74 per cent respectively: see Table A9.6). The manner of measurement was looked at in terms of the instrumentation used and the judgement of the end point. More pupils, 54 per cent compared with 26 per cent, used the clock accurately and made an accurate judgement of the dependent variable in the 'Chemical' question. Slightly more pupils, 24 per cent in 'Sweets' compared with 14 per cent in 'Chemical', judged the effect on the dependent variable qualitatively. Table 11.9 gives the full results for pupils' performance on this stage.

Table A9.7 displays the percentages keeping different types of record. The results are again very similar, with 5 per cent in 'Sweets' and 4 per cent in 'Chemical' keeping a tabulated record. Slightly more pupils in

**Table 11.9**  *Manner of measurement*
(Percentage of pupils meeting defined criteria)

| Measurement stage-level | Description | % pupils | |
|---|---|---|---|
| | | Sweets | Chemical |
| 1 | Timed until all dissolved used the clock accurately | 26 | 54 |
| 2 | Timed accurately but failed to use an accurate end point of measurement | 24 | 23 |
| 3 | Clock not used accurately end point judgement inaccurate | 24 | 9 |
| 4 | Qualitative judgement of end point | 24 | 14 |
| | No apparent judgement | 2 | – |
| Number of pupils | | 257 | 248 |

'Chemical', 59 per cent, compared with 40 per cent in 'Sweets', made an ordered quantified record but this is in keeping with their overall performance, ie more pupils used a quantified method in the 'Chemical' investigation. The results of the pupils' evaluation are given in Table A9.8 along with the proportion of pupils given 'prompts' and the effects of these.

The type of generalisations given by the pupils to describe their findings were very similar for both samples; see Table 11.10. Any noticeable differences make sense in terms of the overall performance differences which have already been mentioned. For example, more children described the relationship between the temperature and rate of change in 'Chemical' than in 'Sweets'.

**Table 11.10**  *Type of generalisation given by pupils*

| Pupils' written response | % pupils | |
|---|---|---|
| | Sweets | Chemical |
| Relationship expressed correctly: | | |
|   for both variables | 23 | 29 |
|   for temperature only | 12 | 22 |
|   surface area only | 5 | 5 |
| No relationship expressed: | | |
|   specific results described not related | 14 | 6 |
| Statement that both variables make a difference | 7 | 7 |
| Temperature only specified | 9 | 8 |
| Optimum conditions stated for both variables | 11 | 5 |
| Number of pupils | 257 | 248 |

The hypothesis that the tighter and more scientific the context the more likely pupils were to behave in a scientific manner is borne out to an extent by these question results. The particular aspects of performance thought to be affected were the rigour the pupils used in controlling variables and making measurements. Again these specific issues do seem to be affected.

Although the scale of the test is limited the results do seem to confirm this hypothesis. It is also important to rememberthe influence of the change in content on the variables to be investigated. It must also be noted that the performance of the two samples of pupils was very similar in many respects, particularly so in their oral responses to why they carried out certain actions. For example, of the pupils taking two or less than two readings, 41 per cent in both 'Chemical' and 'Sweets' thought the number of readings taken mattered. When subsequently asked if more readings would improve the results, 29 per cent in 'Chemical' and 27 per cent in 'Sweets' agreed.

## Results for 'Springload'

The question 'Springload' was written to replicate the earlier investigation 'Swingboard' also used at age 13. It was again designed to have particular characteristics. These included two independent variables, length of spring and diameter of the coil, quantified in nature but actually presented in specific quantities which could not be altered by the pupils—unlike 'Sweets' and 'Chemical'. The two variables had a similar-sized effect which was not the case in 'Swingboard' where the length had a major effect. Another difference to 'Swingboard' which was purposely included in the problem was the need for quantification. The springs were made to have a particular rate of bobbing (see the results for the springs shown in the Appendix Table A9.9). These characteristics were developed not by manipulating one investigation but rather by trialling several similar types of questions and evaluating their demands.

It should be noted that the same investigation was used in the age 15 survey in 1984 (DES, 1988b) but with significant differences. In the presentation to the pupils the two independent variables were not stressed. There was not a strategy of structured 'prompts' or a follow up interview where the pupils' actions and ideas were used to determine the questions asked. In addition the springs used at age 15 were different. The differences do not allow *direct* comparisons to be made. The results at age 13 are summarised here and some comparisons with 'Swingboard' made.

In 'Springload' 84 per cent of the pupils set up the minimum requirements for a test of the two independent variables (see Tables 11.11 and A9.10). In 'Swingboard' with an identical presentation the figure was 63 per cent. In 'Springload' some pupils tested length (6 per cent) and diameter (6 per cent) alone. This compares with 17 per cent and 7 per cent in 'Swingboard'. The major effect of length and the minimal effect of width in 'Swingboard' could account in some way for this difference. Eight per cent of the pupils in 'Springload' were given help with understanding the variables to be tested by repeating the question and demonstrating the lengths and diameter of the springs. This help was given after the pupils failed to start the investigation. These two effects in

combination would account for the differences in the total succeeding on this stage of the investigation in 'Springload' and 'Swingboard'.

**Table 11.11** *Summary of the number of readings for the independent variables*

| | Group | Number of readings | % pupils |
|---|---|---|---|
| Length | (1) | 9 | 42 |
| | (2) | 3 or more | 38 |
| | (3) | 2 | 11 |
| | (4) | less than 2 | 9 |
| Diameter | (1) | 9 | 42 |
| | (2) | 3 or more | 40 |
| | (3) | 2 | 12 |
| | (4) | less than 2 | 6 |
| Number of pupils | | | 243 |

In pupils' oral reports there was a marked consistency between the pupils' actions and what they said they had done. However, 8 per cent varied the length of the spring but called it the diameter of the coil and 5 per cent did the reverse. This was a similar proportion to that found in 'Swingboard' and to an extent indicates the level of conceptual difficulty for some of the pupils in disembedding variables presented in this way. The comments pupils made about their investigations in 'Swingboard' raised this feature of presentation as a possible difficulty to be considered in the 'Springload' analysis. Four per cent of the pupils confounded the test of the two variables and their oral reports confirmed this.

In setting up the test of the two variables it was necessary to control the load used. Eleven per cent of the pupils actually varied the load and measured the extension of the springs rather than the rate of bobbing. The analogy between the springs and Hooke's Law experiments was too strong for these pupils who modelled their problem on it. The load was the critical variable and was taken into account by 79 per cent of the pupils. In their verbal reports 72 per cent of the pupils said it mattered; of these 35 per cent attempted to explain the effect on the rate of bobbing. The pupils' performance on the setting up stage in 'Springload' is summarised in Table 11.12 (p.138).

The dependent variable in 'Springload' was again a *rate* measure; 68 per cent of the pupils were successful in carrying out a measure of the dependent variable in which both the variables, time and spring oscillation, were reformulated. This compares with 70 per cent in 'Survival', though of these successful pupils 30 per cent took a single reading only. In 'Swingboard' the figure was 66 per cent, of which 42 per cent used a qualitative judgement, which was appropriate in the circumstances. Fourteen per cent of the pupils in 'Springload' reformulated the two variables by holding in effect one

**Table 11.12** *Setting up the test of the independent variables*

(Percentage of pupils meeting defined criteria)

| Set-up stage-level | Description | % pupils |
|---|---|---|
| 1. | Load, method and position of release controlled across both variables | 51 |
| 2. | Load controlled but method and/or position of release not consistent | 28 |
| 3. | Load not controlled, method and position of release not consistent | 21 |
| Number of pupils | | 243 |

variable constant—thus the time was measured until the end of bobbing; whilst in 'Swingboard' the proportion doing this was 31 per cent.

It should be noted that 9 per cent of the pupils in 'Springload' could not understand what they had to judge and 8 per cent required a demonstration of 'bobbing'. Four per cent were then able to carry out the investigation. It would appear that help can be given to some pupils to visualise the 'measurement' needed. It is also apparent that a large proportion of pupils at age 13 will take measurements where these seem to be necessary, given the content and nature of the investigation posed. It is the quality of the measurements taken by pupils which appears to be the problem and which discriminates the performance of 13 year olds from 15 year olds. About 20 per cent of pupils, across a range of investigations requiring a quantified judgement of the dependent variable, chose to make qualitative measurements.

The results for the overall manner in which the pupils carried out their measurements are given in Table A9.11 and Table 11.13 below. Thirty-four per cent of the pupils used a quantified method and chose an appropriate range in terms of the time and number of oscillations. The range was determined by considering the size of the measurement error in relation to the judgements which had to be made between the individual springs. These pupils also used the clock accurately. A

**Table 11.13** *Manner of measurement across the springs*

(Percentage of pupils meeting defined criteria)

| Measurement stage-level | Description | % pupils |
|---|---|---|
| 1 | Quantitative using an appropriate number of bounces or set time. Clock used accurately | 34 |
| 2 | Quantitative method. Reduced number of bounces or set time used—increased measurement error | 34 |
| 3 | Qualitative judgement of rate | 16 |
| 4 | No apparent judgement, or a judgement of duration, not rate | 16 |
| Number of pupils | | 243 |

further 34 per cent used a less appropriate range and so increased the potential for measurement error.

Table A9.12 shows the types of record kept by the pupils for both 'Springload' and 'Swingboard'. The results for each are very similar. The manner in which the pupils expressed their generalisations are shown in Table 11.14.

**Table 11.14** *Type of generalisation given by pupils*

| Pupils' written response | % pupils | |
|---|---|---|
| | Springload | Swingboard |
| Relationship expressed correctly | | |
| for both variables | 29 | 28 |
| for length only | 8 | 25 |
| for diameter/width only | 8 | – |
| No relationship expressed (either specific statements or explanations given) | 54 | 40 |
| Number of pupils | 243 | 523 |

These are similar except that more pupils in 'Springload' wrote specific statements which were non-directional, eg 'the length makes a difference' (10 per cent), or 'the diameter makes a difference' (15 per cent). Comparative figures for 'Swingboard' are 2 per cent and 1 per cent respectively. The size of variable effects appears to have an influence here. More pupils expressed a generalisation between length and rate in 'Swingboard', 25 per cent compared with 8 per cent in 'Springload'. In addition, the fact that more pupils considered a bivariate rather than a trivariate relationship in 'Swingboard' could account for their increased ability to express the generalisation. This general point is considered further in Chapter 12 of the report.

### Results for 'Waterlevel'

The 'Waterlevel' investigation was written to find out if pupils at age 13 could handle a *continuous* independent variable. During trials the question met with little success as the majority of pupils could not understand the problem presented, ie what difference does the level of the water inside the container make to how quickly the water comes out of the jet? It was not until an everyday situation had been thought of, in which the problem could be visualised by the pupils, that any success was met with. The identical problem accompanied by an analogy with a tea urn was readily accepted by the overwhelming majority of pupils. This result does go some way to indicate the significance of the need to model a problem prior to being able to conceive of an experimental design for it.

The equipment provided for this investigation was a simple model tea urn made from a clear plastic lemonade bottle. The pupils had a tray, a clock, a cylinder, a beaker and a ruler for measuring. They had in addition water-soluble ink pens for marking the urn. Graph paper was also provided for the pupils. The focus of the question demands was to be on the setting up of the test of the independent variable, 'Waterlevel'. There were no variables as such to be controlled. The nature of the investigation made measurement essential, and in an obvious way. The characteristic of the investigation was therefore an inherent difficulty associated with the independent variable but a reduced measurement demand as a consequence of focusing on it.

In this question it was possible to consider the number and range of readings used by pupils to set up a test of the independent variable (see Table 11.15).

**Table 11.15**  *Independent variable measurement*
(Percentage of pupils meeting defined criteria)

| Group | No of readings | Range covered | % pupils |
|---|---|---|---|
| (1) | 5–9 | >600–1500 cm³ (with systematic cover) | 18 |
| (1) | 3 or more | >600–1500 cm³ (with systematic cover) | 40 |
| (3) | 3 or more 2 | >250 cm³–<600 cm³ >600 cm³ | 28 |
| (4) | 2 or less | <250 cm³ | 14 |
| Number of pupils | | | 249 |

Fifty-eight per cent of the pupils took three or more readings and systematically covered a range exceeding 600 cm³. The other pupils generally failed to appreciate the significance of the range covered by the readings. Consequently they reduced the time scale within which to make their judgements from approximately 20 seconds to between two and five seconds.

Of the pupils who took two or less readings, over 50 per cent felt that the number of readings did not matter and more readings would not improve their results. Similarly, 60 per cent of the pupils who used an inadequate range stated that it was not a relevant issue. Only 17 per cent thought that a wide range would alter their results for the better. Of these pupils few were able to express the nature of the envisaged improvement.

The way in which the pupils set up the independent variable measures is described in Table 11.16.

Again the fairly small proportion of pupils (17 per cent) at age 13 who choose the most accurate measurement instrument available is noticeable. Other pupils (19 per cent) used the beaker and marked and measured the distance from the jet. Perhaps discussions about choice of instrumentation are rarely entered into in the science lesson and pupils use that which they are directed to, without understanding the significance of the choice.

**Table 11.16**  *Setting up the test of the independent variables*
(Percentage of pupils meeting defined criteria)

| Set-up stage-level | Description | % pupils |
|---|---|---|
| 1 | Water added to the container. Cylinder or beaker used and initial level and distance marked | 36 |
| 2 | Water added by beaker and volume measured. No other measurement taken | 55 |
| 3 | Water volume/height judged by eye | 10 |
| Number of pupils | | 249 |

It was deliberately arranged that quantification would be necessary for a pupil attempting an empirical investigation of this question. It was also hoped that the set-up would ensure that the clock became an obvious and helpful instrument. As in the 'Chemical' question a very high proportion of pupils did use the clock and attempted a quantified method (91 per cent). The number using a qualitative approach was reduced from the general level of approximately 20 per cent to 6 per cent. The majority of pupils, 74 per cent, considered rate of flow by reformulating the two variables, volume/level of water and time in conjunction. The figure is close to that found in the 'Survival' question and a little higher than that found in 'Springload'. Again a proportion of pupils had difficulty deriving the rate measurement. These pupils generally held the time constant. The full results for 'Waterlevel' are shown in Table A9.14 and Table 11.17.

**Table 11.17**  *Manner of measurement*
(Percentage of pupils meeting defined criteria)

| Measurement stage-level | Description | % pupils |
|---|---|---|
| 1 | Quantified approach with a measurable end point. Clock used accurately. Levels/volumes noted accurately | 83 |
| 2 | As above but levels not noted accurately | 9 |
| 3 | Either the initial or end point measurement judged qualitatively. Levels/volumes not noted accurately | 4 |
| 4 | Both the initial and final measurements of the volume or level inaccurate, or no apparent measurement | 5 |
| Number of pupils | | 249 |

The issue of the role of quantitative approaches in investigations in science has been raised several times in the chapter. It does appear that whilst many 13 year olds consider taking measurements, a full understanding of the usefulness of quantified data for producing a reliable and readily interpretable solution to a problem is held by only a small proportion, about 10 per cent. This minority of pupils at age 13 apply a quantified

**Figure 11.3** *The relationships between some activities in the 'Waterlevel' investigation*

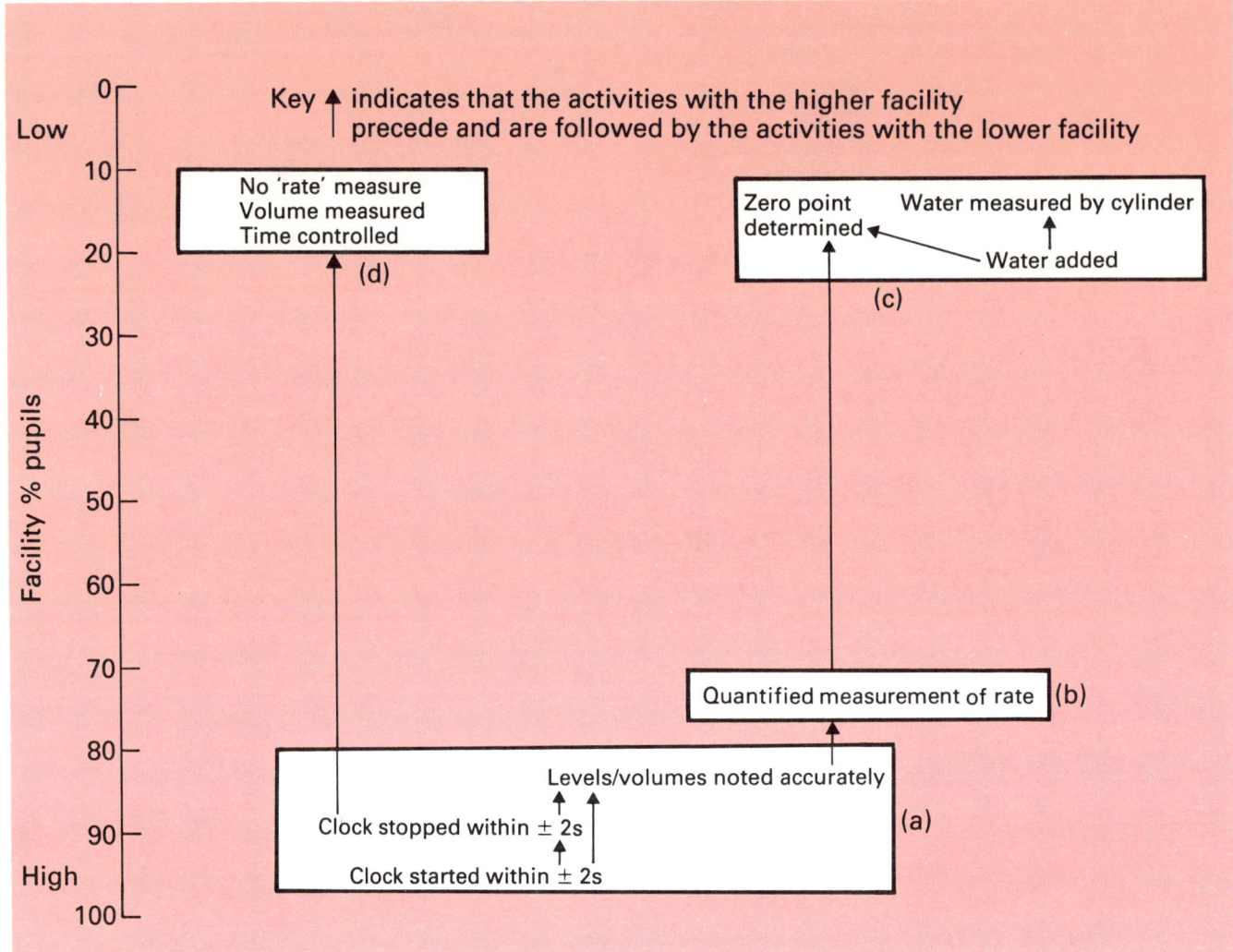

approach across all the stages in their strategy. Thus they are more likely to use instruments of appropriate range in both setting up the independent variables and measuring the dependent variable. Consequently their measurements are more accurate and carefully made. In addition these pupils take a larger number of readings and attempt to produce a graph of their results. The association between the checkpoints which demonstrate the links between the measurement of the dependent and the independent variable is shown in Figure 11.3.

The figure shows that the sub-group of pupils who attempt to set up a quantified test of the independent variable (c) also conceptualise the dependent variable correctly (b), ie as a derivation of two variables, volume and time, whereas those who do not achieve stage (b), will only measure volumes without measuring the independent variable (d).

Turning to the analysis and interpretation of results, 15 per cent of the pupils drew a graph–of these 11 per cent produced a line graph. The remaining pupils were asked about the helpfulness of graphs. Forty-nine per cent thought a graph would be helpful–of those, only 7

per cent were able to say why. Twenty per cent of the pupils who thought it would help, also thought they had a sufficient number of readings. These pupils were asked what a sufficient number would be. Half of them mentioned between four and seven readings; the other pupils tended to think either a very large number was necessary or that one or two would suffice!

The question presentation focused upon the measurement of the dependent variable and consequently the demands placed on the pupils were reduced. For this reason some attention was paid to the difficult task of working out the relationship between the volume of water and the time of flow. The pupils were asked how they worked out their results and were also asked on their record sheet to *explain* how they worked them out. Forty-six per cent of the pupils described a correct quantitative attempt to interpret the results. However, 33 per cent described a qualitative interpretation. Some of these pupils ignored their results and a total of 11 per cent did not use their results at all to help their interpretation. The pupils were cued into taking measurements to an extent, but clearly many did not know how to move from the results to an interpretation of the relationship.

In their written explanations 37 per cent of the pupils when asked how they worked out their results described the method of their experiment or repeated their results. It is clear that a large proportion of 13 year olds have difficulty not just with the interpretation but also with knowing what is expected of them after measurements have been collected. It appeared when talking to pupils that the results were often seen to be the end point for them. Perhaps they are used to a general class conclusion being drawn irrespective of individual results; in which case their results would indeed be the end point of their personal involvement in a science task. Thirty-seven per cent of the pupils explained their working out correctly, which is an impressive number given the difficulty of the relationship. Ten per cent gave an explanation which was incorrect.

Ninety-two per cent of the pupils made a record of their results. The details of these are given in Table A9.15. There is some noticeable consistency here, with 49 per cent of the pupils making a tabulated or ordered quantitative record and 46 per cent describing a correct quantitative attempt to work out the relationship. More pupils in 'Waterlevel' than in 'Sweets' and 'Chemical' specified the correct units for time, 37 per cent compared with 19 per cent. This is interesting, as in 'Waterlevel' the pupils were dealing only in seconds but in 'Sweets' and 'Chemical' it was minutes and seconds. The same pupils and testers were involved with both 'Waterlevel' and 'Sweets'.

*Overall levels of performance*

Throughout the discussion of the results *three stages* of performance have been summarised:

(a) the ways in which pupils systematically varied the independent variables;

(b) the way they set up the apparatus to do this and to eliminate the effect of variables which would invalidate their experiment;

(c) the method and manner in which they measured the effect on the dependent variable.

The summary of performance was based on a detailed breakdown of pupil performance. Within each stage in the checklists the optimum performance level was defined by listing all the activities which had to be carried out to arrive at an accurate and appropriate solution to the investigation. Successive lower levels were defined by systematically relaxing the specifications of the 'ideal' strategy. In addition, levels reflecting alternative approaches to the problem or idiosyncratic errors were established so that a full description of the sample's activities was recorded. The detailed levels for each stage, (a), (b) and (c), are given in Figures A9.1, A9.2 and A9.3 at the end of Appendix 9.

In summarising the stage-levels across the investigations similar criteria were used but the individual characteristics and detail within any one investigation had also to be taken into account. The criteria used to distinguish different levels of performance in each stage were as follows:

(a) For the *Independent variable* (I), the following general distinctions were made:

(I) level 1    sufficient readings taken to give an accurate relationship in the circumstances

(I) level 2    the minimum number of readings necessary to test the variable effect

(I) level 3    failure to test the variable/s

It was possible to extend the description between the top and middle levels as described if the potential number of readings in an investigation was greater than three. Thus for 'Springload' and 'Waterlevel' four (I) levels were established.

(b) In the *Set-up levels* (S), attention was paid to the scale of quantities used, to the error associated with this and to the critical controls. The summary levels included the following distinctions:

(S) level 1    controls, scale and instrumentation taken into account

(S) level 2    relaxation of less critical controls

(S) level 3    failure to take account of critical controls and scale

If the problem had several variables to be considered, ie more than one was critical, then again the middle level could be sub-divided. (See 'Sweets' and 'Chemical'.)

(c) In summarising the *Measurement levels* (M) account was taken of the reformulation of the dependent variable, the choice and use of instruments and the range of readings taken. The distinctions between levels were as follows:

(M) level 1    a correct reformulation of the dependent variable, accurate use of instruments and an appropriate range of readings

(M) level 2    a reduced range of readings and/or accuracy of use of instruments and/or end point measurement

(M) level 3    a qualitative measurement of the dependent variable (if this is inappropriate) or no apparent judgement of it

In investigations where each of the specifications listed in (M) level 2 were in operation then two rather than one intermediate levels were established. The summary stage-levels for the four investigations, 'Waterlevel', 'Springload', 'Sweets' and 'Chemical', are shown in Figures A9.1, A9.2 and A9.3.

The next step in describing pupils' performance is to consider it *across* the stages within any one investigation. A pupil's overall level of performance is derived from the summary stage-levels. Again it is necessary to adopt some rules for summing pupils' behaviours across stages. To describe every combination of stage-levels is neither useful or readily communicable. However, there are difficulties in summarising behaviours across stages. Within each stage it is possible to specify criteria which have some validity as they relate logically to the demands of the individual investigation. Thus it is possible to determine the effect of various control variables and different scale values on the accuracy of the measurements made and make judgements accordingly. In going across stages, decisions have to be made about the *value of each stage* within the whole solution. Are they of equal value or are there criteria which function as hurdles? The structure of the 1984 survey included investigations which were expected to have hurdle-elements as in 'Waterlevel'.

To look as pupils' overall performance a simple rule was used. To achieve the top level of performance the performance in each stage had to be at the highest level specified. The next overall level, 2, is achieved by any pupil who has no level less than 2 for any stage.

The overall levels defined in this way are shown in Table 11.18 for 'Waterlevel'.

**Table 11.18**  *Overall performance on 'Waterlevel'*

| Overall level | Stage | Description of overall performance | % pupils |
|---|---|---|---|
| 1 | I | 5–9 readings, range covered >600 cm$^3$ | 9 |
|   | S | Accurate judgement of levels/volumes, using a cylinder or a beaker plus level measured by a ruler | |
|   | M | Quantified judgement made. Accurate use of the clock | |
| 2 | I | 3–4 readings, range >600 cm$^3$ | 41 |
|   | S | Water added by beaker, ie used as container | |
|   | M | Quantified judgement | |
| 3 | I | 3–4 readings, range >250–<500 cm$^3$ or 2 readings range >600 cm$^3$ | 36 |
|   | S | and/or water judged by eye | |
|   | M | and/or qualitative judgements of flow | |
| 4 | I | Less than 2 readings or 2 readings and a range <200 cm$^3$ | 15 |
|   | S | Water not measured and/or | |
|   | M | No measurement of flow | |
| Number of pupils | | | 249 |

All the combinations of pupils' performance across stages were considered in order to determine the effect of the rule. They showed that no pupils dropped out of overall level 1 because of the way in which they set up the experiment or made measurements. Pupils were in level 2 either because the number of readings taken was smaller than in level 1, or the values of the independent variable were not measured. For all the performances in level 3 there was both a reduction in the number of readings or the range covered and a failure to measure

quantities. Level 4 represents in practice a failure to test the independent variable. The mismatch that gives rise to some concern is for the 6 per cent of pupils who either used a reduced range, or took only 2 readings across a wide range but carried out a careful experiment in all other respects. These pupils, because of their performance on the test of the independent variable, fall into overall level 3. A decision to put these pupils into level 2 has to be made on the basis of a value judgement that their solution would be as good as those pupils in level 2. However this is not the case in the context of the investigation: two data points alone reduces the relationship to a direct comparison of extreme effects. Therefore the only way to place a higher value on the performance of these pupils would be to create a new level intermediate between 2 and 3. Any decision to produce a set of overall levels is in recognition of the need for a readily communicable description of pupil performance. To create more levels is to move in the opposite direction to this.

The relationship between the overall levels and the separate stage-levels was considered next. There was a strong relationship between the overall level and the independent variable stage-level. This adds weight to the view that the test of the independent variable constitutes a hurdle in this investigation. If performance on the independent variable alone is used to judge pupils the sample distribution shifts slightly. Three-quarters of the pupils remain at the same level. The remaining 25 per cent fail in the setting-up and/or the measurement and so would move to a higher overall level if the independent variable alone was considered.

The overall levels for 'Springload' are given in Table 11.19. These were established in the same way.

**Table 11.19**  *Overall performance on 'Springload'*

| Overall level | Stage | Description of overall performance | % pupils |
|---|---|---|---|
| 1 | I | Nine readings for both length and diameter | 10 |
|   | S | Load, position and method of release controlled | |
|   | M | Quantitative judgement. Accurate use of clock. Appropriate range used | |
| 2 | I | Three or more readings for both length and diameter | 41 |
|   | S | Load controlled | |
|   | M | Quantitative judgement. Clock used but less adequate range chosen | |
| 3 | I | Two readings for both length and diameter | 29 |
|   | S | and/or load not controlled | |
|   | M | and/or qualitative judgement | |
| 4 | I | One or both variables not tested | 20 |
|   | S | No controls | |
|   | M | and/or no apparent judgement of the dependent variable | |
| Number of pupils | | | 243 |

The levels established were compared with the pupils' actual performance. Two groups of pupils appeared to be misplaced. Six per cent of the pupils fell into level 2 only on the basis of taking less than 9 readings. In every other respect these pupils performed in the manner specified in level 1. Again to consider how to value these pupils' performance requires consideration of the whole investigation. There is no doubt that their performance is less adequate than level 1 but it is also more adequate than level 2. Logically one can only regard these pupils as a sub-set. Most pupils are in level 2 because their judgement of the dependent variable was less accurate than required. The other group (3 per cent) were in level 3 for taking 2 readings only. These pupils did control the load and made a quantitative judgement of the dependent variable.

When the relationship between the stage-levels and the overall levels were looked at it was strong only in the case of the stage-level 'measurement'. The presentation of the two independent variables, length and diameter, in a pre-modelled form and one single critical control variable may indicate that measurement is acting, to an extent, as a hurdle in this investigation. If this is accepted to be the case then one may well consider moving the pupils, mentioned earlier, up a level. However on the same basis one would leave the pupils in the 'Waterlevel' question in the performance levels into which they originally fell.

Turning to the 'Sweets' and 'Chemical' investigation the overall performance of pupils is shown in Table 11.20.

Pupils fell into level 2 because of both a reduction in readings and a less accurate judgement of the dependent variable.

**Table 11.20** *Overall performance on 'Sweets' and 'Chemical'*

| Overall level | Stage | Description of overall performance | Sweets | Chemical |
|---|---|---|---|---|
| 1 | I | Three or more readings for temperature | 4 | 8 |
| | S | Volume mass controlled. Scale >25 cm$^3$ of water. | | |
| | M | Quantitative judgement. Accurate end-point and use of clock. | | |
| 2 | I | Two readings for both temperature and surface area. | 37 | 50 |
| | S | Mass controlled. Scale >25 cm$^3$. | | |
| | M | Quantitative judgement. Use of clock and/or end point inaccurate. | | |
| 3 | I | Two readings for both variables | 29 | 13 |
| | S | Mass controlled. Scale <25 cm$^3$. | | |
| | M | Qualitative judgement used. | | |
| 4 | I | One or both variables not tested | 29 | 29 |
| | M | and/or no apparent judgement of the dependent variable. | | |
| Number of pupils | | | 257 | 248 |

The pupils in level 3 either failed to control any variables and used an inadequate scale or failed in the judgement of the dependent variables.

Level 4 pupils failed either to test the independent or the dependent variables. The difference in pupils' performance in 'Sweets' and 'Chemical' have been discussed earlier.

Across the four investigations there are some noticeable differences in the performances of the bottom two bands. The spread of pupils in 'Waterlevel' and 'Springload' looks very similar. However, the 15 per cent of pupils in the lower level for 'Waterlevel' failed to test the independent variable. A slightly higher proportion of pupils fall into this level for 'Springload' because some fail to test the two independent variables and others fail to set up a measurement of 'rate'.

In 'Sweets' and 'Chemical' there are more pupils falling into the lowest level of performance than for the previous two investigations. These figures represent a combination of effects. For example, a failure to make any judgement of the dependent variable caused most pupils in 'Sweets' to fall into level 4. In 'Chemical', pupils fell into the lowest level as a consequence of failing to test the two independent variables. One could hypothesise that if the size of the individual variables effects in 'Chemical' were more equal, then a different spread of pupils would have been observed. It is probable that in these circumstances pupils would have moved from level 4 to level 3. This distribution would have more closely represented the spread of pupils obtained in 'Springload'.

## 11.7 Discussion

The results in this category are based on investigations concerned with simple relationships between variables. The main types of investigation used were 'decide which product is best for...'; 'decide which circumstance/condition is best preferred...'; and 'find the effect of...'. All the investigations used have been deliberately selected so as to require little in the way of recall of taught science concepts. The pupils' performance has consequently been assessed in terms of the perceived procedural demands alone. Interpretations of their performance, however, reflect both the procedural and conceptual aspects inherent in any investigation. The development of conceptual mark schemes to assess pupils' problem-solving behaviours in addition to the procedural mark scheme is a research issue being addressed at present.

The view of problem-solving exposed in this chapter and elsewhere is referred to in some detail in Chapter 10 of this report. Some fundamental attributes of this view will be mentioned briefly here. The activities labelled as problem-solving in this chapter are in the main characterised by the mutual dependency of scientific-procedural and conceptual understanding. Pupils are regarded as having to access the pool of knowledge available to them in order to first develop a 'model' of the problem–that is, in order to perceive that there is indeed a 'problem' for them. A procedural strategy has then to be developed, but the pupils' particular conceptualisation of the problem is the link which determines the procedures that are understood to be appropriate in the problem situation. There is, then, the additional demand that the pupil has the procedural understanding needed to develop an appropriate strategy. There is a basic premise operating here that prior to having procedural understanding one must hold a concept of the procedure.

This general view allows several useful ways of conceptualising pupils' responses. The problem features themselves can be analysed both in terms of their objective demands to recall specific concepts and procedures and in their effect on pupils' ability to access their own knowledge and procedures through cues and clues. The conceptual and procedural features are not independent and have to be viewed as embedded within the pupils' perceptions of the whole task.

Across all of the investigations there was a small percentage of pupils (<5 per cent) who could not engage with or identify a problem. The majority of pupils did, however, consider that there was a problem for them to solve. The ability of pupils to perceive a problem is affected by the method of presentation of the investigation. The content of the investigation, ie the apparatus, words and illustrations, must evoke some previous experience which will allow the pupils to construct 'meaning' in the task. This effect is generally removed by judicious selection of the tasks during the development trials. Examples of this effect have been described with particular reference to the 'Waterlevel' investigation. Once meaning has been established the pupils can access their knowledge to try and recall the concepts which underlie both the independent and dependent variables. The perception of these two main variables forms the nucleus of the problem. Another feature which facilitates this perception is the manner of presentation of the variables. If the variable quantities are represented for the pupils in concrete terms as in 'Survival' and 'Paper Towel', then about 95 per cent will *see* them.

The specific content and general setting of the investigation can affect pupils' ability or willingness to deal with the problem; as such, access is blocked by the pupils themselves. This feature of pupil behaviour has been noted, for some girls with particular science contents, for example electricity, and for some boys, with a domestic content such as floor surfaces. The girls reject the problem from an expressed belief that the necessary knowledge is not available to them. The boys reject it from a belief that the knowledge they do have,

labelled as 'science', cannot usefully be applied to the problem as they perceive it.

There are aspects of the presented investigation which evoke *alternative* problems for the pupils. Assessors attempt to provide the right cues to evoke in the pupils the same task perception that they themselves hold. However, cues will function in a pupil-specific way. Examples of this effect have been given in this Chapter in section 11.5.

An overtly everyday setting allows some pupils to feel an initial sense of competence and control in the problem situation. This facilitates their initial interaction with the investigation. For others with a different view of the role of science knowledge it can constitute a barrier, or cue *selective* access of their knowledge, ie only to that which they think is appropriate in the situation. The results for the 'Sweets' investigation demonstrate the effect of this selective access.

Pupils who perceive a problem have then to translate their knowledge and understanding into an appropriate procedural strategy. To establish a test of the independent variable the pupils have to have an abstract concept of it in the first place. Presentation in particular ways will obviate the need for this. Most 13 year olds can deal with two independent variables if they can be treated as discontinuous variables, ie in specific quantities hot/cold; whole/halves. If on the other hand the variables have to be manipulated to establish conditions in which both are varied systematically, then about 20–30 per cent of pupils at age 13 have conceptual difficulties. A continuous independent variable appears to be harder than other types to conceptualise and hence understand for 13 year old pupils. If a suitable related experience within which to imagine the variable can be found, then approximately 50 per cent of pupils take 3 or more readings for it without assistance. There is a general tendency for 13 year old pupils not to measure the quantities of the independent variable. Any judgements that are made are cursory.

The identification of the dependent variable requires the pupil to interpret the meaning of the terms used in a question. For example the meaning of 'warmer' or 'holding water' in relation to material properties, 'preference' in relation to animal behaviour, 'quickly' in relation to swinging boards, bobbing springs or reacting chemicals. Some children do not understand the meaning of these terms or have an understanding which conflicts with the scientifically acceptable one. Whatever their understanding, the identification of the variable determines how the pupils develop a measurement strategy. About 20 per cent of pupils, across investigations, do not see the advantage or need for measurements. Most 13 year olds, in practice, reduce a necessary measurement strategy to a comparison of extremes or of single measurements. There appear to be two sources of pupil failure which relate to the same issue, ie understanding the need for *quantified evidence* in a science investigation and the meaning and implications of a scientific *relationship*. Most 13 year olds seem to understand a 'fair test' and to appreciate the purpose of comparing different quantities. However, for a significant proportion of pupils this understanding appears to be their general approach to any investigation, irrespective of the actual solution required.

Few 13 year olds have a general understanding of error in relation to measurements. This is not surprising given their lack of appreciation of the purpose of measurements. Consequently they tend not to use the most appropriate instruments available or, for some pupils, take account of scale in their designs. Most pupils do attempt to control variables whose effects they understand. This procedure seems to be available to the majority of 13 year olds.

The pupils' record keeping and interpretation of collected data reflect several of the findings already mentioned. It is, for example, essential to understand the meaning of a scientific relationship in order to appreciate the need for quantification and hence the role of graphs as a useful data representation. The majority of 13 year olds do not understand the usefulness of graphs and do not attempt to draw them. There is also a significant proportion who see the results, the collected data, as the end point of their investigations. The understanding of a relationship underpins the assumption that a generalisation can be drawn. About 50 per cent of the pupils can describe their findings as a generalisation for an investigation of variable effects. It is clear that there are language difficulties which hinder many pupils in their ability to express themselves in a general way. Added to this, pupils' actions indicate an understanding of variable effects in terms of simple comparisons or specifics rather than as a continuum. Thus they establish that the variable has an effect or not. Alternatively they attempt to consider magnitude specifically, ie it is a large effect, rather than identifying the *nature* of the relationship. Their strategy for solving the problem, then, is reflected in the manner in which they express their conclusions.

## 11.8  Summary

The trials and development work in this category up to, and including, the 1981 survey results established the following:

— a definition of a practical problem-solving activity;

— a description of science investigations concerned with simple relationships between variables;

— a method of collecting behavioural data from 'activity' checklists based on scientific-procedures;

— a model for the analysis of data concerning scientific-procedures;

— a description of pupils' performance on investigations which varied in content, context and procedural demand.

The results showed a higher success rate for the investigative problems than for some other forms of assessment used in the survey. There were some noteable exceptions to this success which led to the identification of possible sources of error. These included:

— the number of independent variables;

— understanding the meaning of the dependent variable;

— a tactical rather than a strategic approach to measurement.

The 1982 and 1983 surveys confirmed four aspects of pupils' success. These were:

— the interaction in a practical context with apparatus clues;

— a response in action;

— the interaction with a whole task;

— the interaction within a 'personal model' of a problem.

In addition, the survey results exposed further, potential sources of variation in performance. These included:

— the manner of presentation of the independent variable;

— the size of effect of the independent variable;

— the conceptual demand implicit in the understanding of the main variables.

The individual investigation profiles in Figure 11.2 could be discussed in the light of these suspected sources of variation. However, the existing data were collected from a unidimensional perspective which took account of procedural demands only. This meant that interpretations were limited and many issues remained unexamined.

The work carried out in 1983 and 1984 opened a new perspective on the investigation tasks. It was now considered essential to reflect on the demands of an investigation in terms of the conceptual and procedural demands; *and* the content and context influences in order to interpret pupils' performance. Investigation profiles for the four investigations are given in Figures 11.4, 11.5 and 11.6 (p.146). As in Figure 11.2 the three criteria used are the approach, ie the identification of the independent and dependent variables; the set-up to eliminate the effect of variables which would invalidate the experiment; and the method of measurement.

Some of the results of the 1984 survey which have been presented confirm the effect of these other dimensions. For example the context difference between 'Sweets'

**Figure 11.4** *Investigation profiles–'Sweets' and 'Chemical'*
(Percentage of pupils meeting defined criteria)

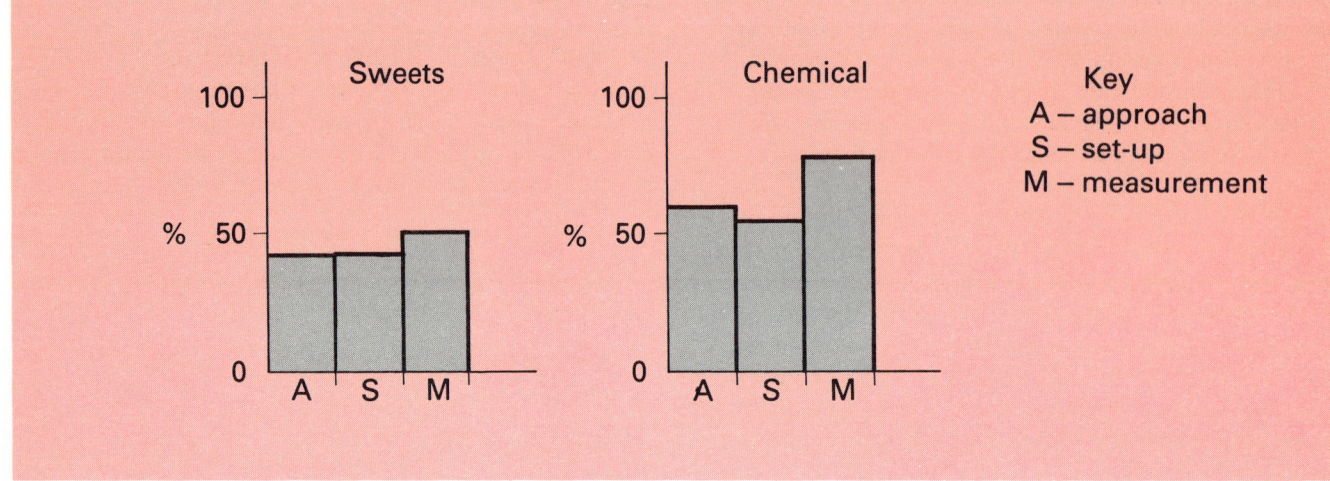

**Figure 11.5** *Investigation profile—'Swingboard' and 'Springload*
(Percentage of pupils meeting defined criteria)

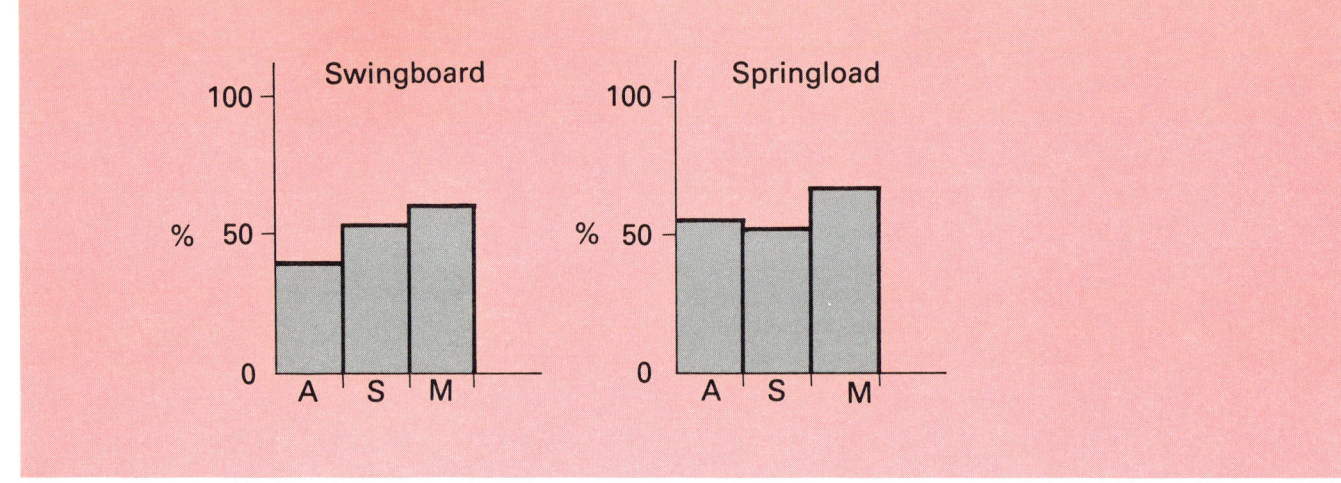

**Figure 11.6** *Investigation profile–'Waterlevel'*
(Percentage of pupils meeting defined criteria)

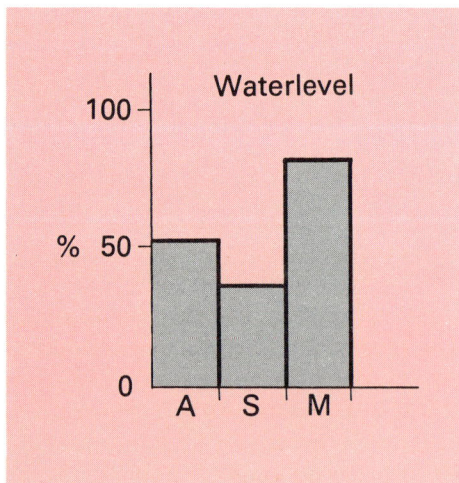

'Sweets' investigation because it featured an everyday context. Figure 11.4 demonstrates the outcomes for the two investigations.

In addition, the results confirmed the influence on some pupils' performance of the size of the effect of an independent variable. This effect depressed the criterion performance levels in 'Chemical' on both the approach and the setting-up. Overall, it can now be seen that whilst the similarity of these two profiles can be understood in terms of the matched nature of the two investigations, the differences between them and particularly the higher overall level in 'Chemical' can also be understood in terms of the effect of context.

This influence was again noted in the performance levels of 'Swingboard' and 'Springload' shown in Figure 11.5.

'Swingboard' and 'Springload' are two investigations which are also similar in underlying structure. The differences between the investigation profiles can be understood in terms of the proposed effects of the content differences on pupils' response. Fewer pupils in

and 'Chemical', was expected to affect pupils' performance on controlling variables and carrying out measurements. Consequently pupils' performance across the investigation profiles would be depressed on the

146

'Springload' investigated only one variable and because the dependent variable seems more easy to appreciate, and has a larger effect, in the case of 'Springload' this gives an enhanced score on approach.

The higher score on measurement is probably due to differences in the perceptual effects of swinging rather than bobbing. The tendency to avoid measurement if a cruder observation will suffice may be reinforced more by the discrete nature of the slower and heavily damped pendulum swing than by the rapid and lightly damped spring oscillation.

The 'Waterlevel' results confirmed the influence that the nature of the independent variable had on pupils' performance. The continuous variable in this investigation did prove more difficult to conceptualise and manipulate than other variables which were presented discontinuously.

The analysis of this investigation was extended to consider the effect of setting up a test of a quantified independent variable. This aspect had not featured in previous surveys at age 13. It is shown in Figure 11.6 that the inclusion of this feature in an investigation depressed performance on the setting-up stage. Thus in this case, the result, that this profile has a lower level on 'set-up' than any in Figures 11.1, 11.4 or 11.5, can be explained as an outcome of the particular stress laid on quantifying an independent variable.

The influence of pupils' conceptual science understanding has not been demonstrated by the results reported here. The data exist but the analysis methods are continuing to be developed. Overall, these results show how profiles such as those in Figure 11.2 can be understood through the more complex models of pupil response that were explored using the 1984 tasks.

The present position in the category is that we have a more adequately complex rationale to inform:

— the selection of tasks;

— the manner of presentation to pupils;

— the analysis of tasks.

Foundations have been laid from which it is hoped rapid progress can be made.

## 11.9   Implications

*Implications for assessment*

The implications for assessment depend on two issues: whether it is survey- or classroom-based assessment and whether the assessment is formative or summative. In terms of the survey assessment we are only at the beginning in terms of our understanding of this assess-

ment category. It will be necessary to consider other types of investigations and different modes of pupil-response including both theoretical and practical problem-solving. The difficult task of exploring pupils' conceptual models in problem-situations needs to be developed and taken further. This work will give insights into the ways in which children hold and deploy their science knowledge. Information of this kind will further our understanding of the 'meaning' of the problems we set. A third area requiring work is the description of the performance criteria. This is particularly necessary at the older ages, and will probably result in an extension of the criteria already used to include further aspects of measurement and data interpretation.

Classroom assessment is a very different issue. There is a limit to which the methodology discussed in this chapter has relevance in the classroom given the different circumstances, resources and time available. The move at the school level to criterion-referenced assessment does mean that many of the findings are pertinent. Performance criteria have been described in this chapter which refer both to general features of scientific investigative behaviour and to specific problem demands. These should inform the general debate about what to assess and how to assess, both for the purpose of diagnosis and for summarising pupils' scientific achievement. The source of pupils' failures and difficulties is an important feature of any assessment which attempts to consider pupils' potential in relation to their achievements. In this situation the individual problem demands, both procedural and conceptual, and the 'models' developed by pupils when presented with different sets of cues have to be taken into account.

For summative assessment the establishment of overall levels of performance becomes an important aim. The question to be addressed for this purpose is the *value* which is to be placed within the summation process on each aspect of demand in a presented problem. This is a difficult question to answer and any decisions concerning it will have a critical influence, particularly if the assessment relies on only a few instances of practical assessment. The pupils' perception of tasks and the resulting meanings that they construe could be regarded as irrelevant in an assessment concerned with pupils' 'scientific' achievement. However if the scores are to be criterion-referenced then the question of whether to avoid or to deliberately measure pupils' performance in influential contexts needs to be answered. In addition the use of investigations with 'hurdle' demands as a means of simplifying and focusing classroom assessment methods requires some careful thought. The development and confirmation of more adequate models to understand pupil responses as outlined in section 11.8, could be of particular importance here.

*Implications for teachers*

There are obvious implications for teaching in this chapter, some of which can be addressed in the short term. Others such as building up an understanding of the nature of scientific evidence and the meaning of relationships, can only be dealt with slowly over time. The more immediate issues which the chapter highlights include:

- the need to think carefully about what, and how, investigations are presented to pupils.

If in certain situations a particular aspect of science activity is to be focused on, how can this be cued for the majority of pupils? Other clear messages are:

- the need for pupils to act and plan in conjunction *and* in the context of the whole task.

For example, if the focus of an activity is on what and how to judge which metal is the best bender, then pupils need to think about what to measure as they explore and bend different pieces of metal. In the same way if the investigation is about whether snails prefer particular colours, then deciding what to test is best done by going and selecting different pieces of card, etc.

- the need for group discussions followed by a class discussion during the course of practical activity.

In this way matters such as quantities of the independent variable or which variables should be controlled will arise as pupils reflect on their own and others' choices.

- the need to develop in pupils an awareness of the role of measurement in science.

This can be done with most pupils by establishing the need to communicate findings to others, especially if the purpose for the communication is one which the pupils recognise and value.

- the need to recognise the inherent difficulty of matters of scale and associated errors.

Such matters are better left as discussion points after pupils have made their choices and collected some results. An abstract discussion of errors is not possible for most 13 year olds. However, evaluating the results collected by the class during discussion will allow the issue to surface gradually as the pupils consider the reasons for differences. Pupils will only begin to understand the difficult concept of 'error' when they are able to criticise their own performance in those terms.

# 12

# Across-category performance issues

## 12.1 Introduction

The assessment framework was described, in the preface to the first survey report at age 13, as an innovatory system which separated the variety of activities contributing to scientific performance. This separation into component activities was regarded as a necessary step in order to provide information which could be reported in a useful way; that is, to indicate the general spread and level of response of pupils of all abilities to a set of common questions. The perceived aim of the assessment was to draw up a profile report of the population. Given this aim it may seem contradictory to have a chapter entitled 'Across-category performance issues'.

In establishing the categories for assessment, activities were identified which were educationally significant and which it was expected could be translated into a coherent group of questions. There was some doubt expressed about whether each category or subcategory represented a 'simple skill'. Moreover in the first reports, no claim was made that the categories represented fully validated constructs. An external validation exercise had been carried out but it was concerned with the educational significance and meaning of the category definitions. The data were not yet available to carry out a statistical validation of the framework. It was also recognised that the categories were not independent of each other. The boundaries established between the categories were to some extent arbitrary and artificial, defined to serve the dual purposes of assessment and reporting. Moreover, some categories have some mutual dependence by nature of the way they are defined.

This point was made particularly clear in Category 1, **Use of graphical and symbolic representation,** and Category 2, **Use of apparatus and measuring instruments.** It was stated in the 1980 survey report at age 13 (DES, 1982a) that the questions in Category 1 were designed to determine the extent to which the use of symbolic representations constituted a barrier to communication in science and therefore a hurdle to success in more complex activities. The examples cited of other activities in which the skills of *representation* were embedded, included the ability to make predictions from tabulated information; investigations which depended on the setting up of apparatus in accordance with a conventionally drawn diagram; and investigations which depended on the production of a 'smooth' graph

in order to determine the outcome. Similarly in Category 2 the practical skills of using measuring instruments, handling equipment and following instructions were considered possible contributors to pupils' failure with more complex activities. Thus Categories 1 and 2 were labelled as hurdle skills or *enabling skills* and as such were so defined that they were bound to *overlap* with the other categories. Category 6, **Performance of investigations,** was defined as the putting together of the component activities within science performance, hence an overlap with other categories was assumed. For the remaining categories the relationships were not so clear cut. Category 5, **Planning of investigations,** was defined, ultimately, to have very close structural links with Category 6, **Performance of investigations.** Consequently it was assumed to involve a significant array of scientific activities, including many which featured in other categories. **Application** was distinguished from **Interpretation** by the objective requirement to recall and apply taught science concepts. The types of question asked were however very similar except for the important demand *to explain*.

It was possible, therefore, to view the assessment framework of component activities in terms of their potential 'skills' overlap. However, in establishing category definitions questions were written to *fit* one category only. The degree of *fit* was established during the external validation exercise carried out by groups of experts in the education field. The criterion of fit used was the *burden* of the given question's demand, i.e. its ultimate loading in terms of the demands made on the pupils. Questions which failed to fit the category they were designed for were rejected or rewritten. If this criterion was met then what might be overlap in principle would in practice have little effect on performance score correlations.

This position might imply that there was little to be gained in reviewing performance links *across* the categories. However, the identification of enabling skills in two categories of the framework suggests that the possible effect of these on pupils' performance in other science activities requires consideration. Furthermore it had become apparent, in the reporting of the five years of survey results, that many of the questions made demands on pupils other than those specified in the definition of the Question type. The Question type was seen to represent the major demand of a question but the subsidiary demands also appeared to influence pupils' performance. Many of these subsidiary demands occur in several categories of the assessment framework.

This Chapter summarises briefly:

– the particular issues which indicate an overlap or link between categories.

  12.2–The enabling skills
  12.3–Those issues across categories deliberately included in the assessment, ie the links between planning and performing and representing and interpreting data.

– the findings which suggest some important underlying question demands which arise across the categories.

  12.4–Variable identification
  12.5–Relationships and generalisations
  12.6–Conceptual influences.

– other across-category influences on performance.

  12.7–Other influences

It must be remembered that the assessment was set up to produce quite different results, that is results based on the individual categories. Consequently this chapter is of necessity brief and to an extent speculative. The speculations will be restricted to those features described independently within one category of performance which have also been noted in the responses of pupils in other categories. When mean scores are referred to they represent average mean scores for a group of similar questions. The feature which is considered to be in common between the groups of questions compared is described, but the questions themselves are often quite different in presentation and in the manner in which the pupils are asked to respond to them. Thus the comparisons are not quantitative in nature but are used as a device to draw attention to the possibility of considering pupils' successes and failures from a different perspective to that commonly used. The adoption of an alternative perspective has provided further insights into the complex nature of the demands placed on children when carrying out activities in science.

## 12.2  Enabling skills?

It has been noted in the introduction to this Chapter that Categories 1 and 2 were labelled as enabling skills. Chapter 5 of this report reviews performance in Category 1 at age 13. In this Chapter (section 5.1) two statements have been made which are relevant to this discussion of links between categories. The first suggested that the ability to identify and manipulate variables, ie Category 1, is a *prerequisite* to understanding relationships between the variables, ie Category 4. The second considered that the *use* of coordinate forms established a base for the understanding of the variable-

based investigatory paradigm. The second statement appeared to follow logically from the first. The findings discussed here shed further light on this.

One of the chief problems that has to be faced when comparing performance across categories concerns the lack of representation of similar features of question demand. The focus of the assessment is different for each category of the framework. This is reflected in the questions selected to represent a category. In Category 1, **Use of graphical and symbolic representation,** for example, the *form* of data representation used was referred to in the discussion of pupils' performance. This aspect of the questions was specified in the definitions of the Question types. The other category most closely associated with Category 1, in terms of question demand, was **Interpretation.** In this category the *type* of data rather than the representational form was a chosen focus for the discussion.

### Data representation

The results in Category 1 showed a fairly high performance level across all forms of data representation, the highest performance being achieved for the reading and presenting of information in tables. The results suggested that pupils were competent at using and, by implication, understanding a variety of coordinate forms. The ability to use different forms of data representation cannot, however, be equated with an understanding of the function and utility of data representation forms. The results in the practical category **Performing investigations** cast some light on this issue. In this category, irrespective of the type of investigation being carried out, on average only 6 per cent of 13 year olds recorded their data in a tabular form. This figure did not increase even when both variables under consideration were quantitative. The proportion of pupils generating tables of quantitative results, by choice, did not increase significantly between the ages of 13 and 15. In a study (DES, 1985a) where a sub-sample of pupils was required to make a written plan prior to carrying out an investigation, the only significant, positive, difference in their subsequent practical performance was in the proportion, about 20 per cent, who made a tabulated record. The increase was noted at age 15 only. It appeared that in these instances tables were recalled as a necessary aspect of organised classwork which evoked the sequence of method, results and conclusion.

Thus pupils can use tables but do not use them of their own account for systematising data.

### Type of data

In the Category 1 chapter, attention was paid to the type of data to be represented, thus allowing a comparison with performance in the **Interpretation 4i** subcategory. For data representation, the lowest level of performance in Category 1 was associated with numerical data. This finding was reinforced by the results for **Interpretation 4i**. The proportion of pupils gaining full marks on the reading and representing of numerical data was 44 per cent. The nature of the difficulties pupils experienced was not pin-pointed in either category, due to the influence of many other factors. However, the associated need for *numerical operations,* when dealing with numerical data, was raised as a possible reason for the low performance in Category 1.

*Mathematical demand*

The requirement to *quantify* resulted in lower performance throughout the **Application** category particularly where the numerical values were not whole numbers. This result is linked with pupils' difficulties with scales in both Category 1, **Use of graphical and symbolic representation** and Category 2, **Use of apparatus and measuring instruments.** It also relates to the general lack of appreciation or facility with measurement noted in the pupils' performance on investigations in science.

The results in Category 1 also showed that pupils could plot points on line graphs. If the pupils were given an example point already plotted, the average mean score for further plotting was 68 per cent. This figure dropped to 43 per cent if no example point was plotted. The pupils' performance on constructing entire line graphs without any prompts or cues was on average 55 per cent. Fifty-one per cent of the pupils at age 13 scored full marks on these questions and 20 per cent no marks. These results warranted comparison with performance on the practical investigations. Only two investigations have been surveyed at age 13 where a graph was either helpful or necessary. In the first, 'Survival', where production of a graph would have indicated a deeper understanding of the type of relationship to be considered, no pupils *chose* to plot a graph. The second, 'Waterlevel', required a graph as the most efficient way of interpreting the relationship. Eleven per cent of 13 year olds plotted a line graph and 5 per cent a bar chart. Of the remaining 85 per cent only half thought a graph would be helpful, of which a low 7 per cent could indicate why.

Another weakness noted in pupils' performance on line graphs was to do with plotting points. Performance dropped when the points failed to coincide with the marked divisions on the axes. This performance difficulty also affected scores in Category 2 for reading measuring instruments and is discussed later in the section.

*Identifying and relating variables*

When pupils' performance on constructing line graphs was considered in detail, one difficulty that was much in evidence was their inability to label axes. In these questions pupils had to derive the variable from a presented verbal description of it. This aspect of performance was closely related to that in **Planning parts of investigations** in Category 5. The average score in Category 1 for identifying variables presented in this way was 35 per cent, which compared with 40 per cent for a similar demand in Category 5. The range of scores was 15–52 per cent and 2–64 per cent, respectively. The requirement to identify, ie conceptualise a variable in abstract, underlies data representation activities and practical investigations as defined in Category 6. It was regarded as noteworthy that data representation often appeared to make many of the very real demands of practical problem-solving. Teachers will not be able to increase 13 year old pupils' use of coordinate forms of data representation if pupils are experiencing underlying conceptual difficulties with relationships between variables.

Difficulties appeared in data representation when the question demand was to describe the relationship between an independent and dependent variable represented in a graph. The scores were very low for this demand even though these technical terms were not used in the question. A low 8 per cent of pupils scored full marks and 41 per cent no marks. Many pupils stated units rather than variables, which corresponded to a finding in **Planning parts of investigations** (DES, 1986a). This finding raises doubts about what pupils understand by a graph, which are discussed in greater detail in sections 12.4 and 12.5.

The section started with a question mark in the title. It appeared to be clear from the initial definition of the category that data representation was considered to be a basic skill to be used as an algorithm by pupils. The speculations across categories suggested that in some instances pupils may well be applying the algorithm when directed to do so. However, the fundamental conceptual understanding which would allow the algorithm to be applied without direction, and transferred, may well be missing for most pupils. It would appear that such underlying concepts need addressing if pupils are to have the ability to interpret data in a variety of forms when they need to do so. A similar point was made in Chapter 7 of this report with reference to the use of techniques such as chromatography without attention being paid to the pupils' understanding of the manner in which the technique functions.

*Use of apparatus and measuring instruments*

In comparing the performance of pupils in Category 2 **Use of apparatus and measuring instruments** with other categories, it was necessary to distinguish between quantification and reading instruments, the latter being subsumed in the former. However, the relationship between the two proved to be very complex for a population of 13 year olds. Again, as in Category 1, the performance (on reading instruments) was quite high although this depended on the type of instrument used, the operation and scale involved and the task set. For example reading a thermometer had a score of 78 per cent and a stop-clock 49 per cent. The factor which overrode all others was the particular value at which an instrument was set to be read. If it was within one small scale division of a numbered scale line many more responses fell into the range for which credit was given. This mirrors an influence on pupils' apparent ability to plot additional points on a line graph. The proportion of pupils not responding to tasks was low (less than 5 per cent) and was clearly related to the instrument to be read.

It was interesting to compare pupils' performance in Category 2 with their performance in Category 5, **Planning** and Category 6, **Performance of investigations.** There were however substantial differences between the demands of the categories. In Category 2 pupils were presented with the instrument and the quantity and directed to take measurements. None of these cues could be present in the **Planning** questions. In the practical investigations the apparatus cues *alone* were present. This meant that in Category 2 there was no requirement for the pupils to consider what was to be measured or to determine if measurements were necessary or what type was appropriate given the task in hand. It must also be said that in Category 2 there was no obvious *purpose* to the measurements except in the instances where the end product has to be delivered and judged. Perceived purpose has been raised as an important aspect of pupils' engagement with questions in all of the categories of the assessment. In Category 2 performance was higher on reading instruments when the pupils were actually involved in using the instrument. In addition they more often gave the correct units in these circumstances.

The low proportion of pupils failing to respond to Category 2 tasks can perhaps be contrasted with the 20 per cent who generally failed to see the need for any measurements in the practical test in spite of presented instruments. Removing the practical cue caused performance on this aspect to be depressed even further.

In the use of the stopclock in Category 2 just less than a third give the correct value. Nineteen per cent gave the correct units and 60 per cent nearly correct units for a time including minutes and seconds. A common error was for the pupils to ignore either the minute or second hand. A much higher mean score (73 per cent) was obtained when the set time considered was in seconds only. These results can be compared with pupils using a stopclock in the course of an investigation. The same sample of pupils performed the 'Waterlevel' and 'Sweets' investigations reported in Chapter 11. The two questions were also administered by the same tester. In 'Waterlevel' only seconds had to be dealt with, and 37 per cent of the pupils gave the correct units compared with 19 per cent in 'Sweets', where both minutes and seconds were called for.

The use of a thermometer in Category 2 was affected considerably when presented in the plastic protective case. Over one third of 13 year olds and a quarter of 15 year olds failed to remove the instrument from the case. This part of the activity was done for them in Category 6. The mean score was 78 per cent in Category 2, which compared with over 70 per cent correctly using a thermometer in Category 6. Of the pupils reading a thermometer, 61 per cent gave the correct units, which rose to 79 per cent if the pupils were using, rather than reading off a pre-set value from, the thermometer.

Some questions used in the Category 2 test were concerned with standard techniques, and to an extent these linked more closely with the demands in the practical investigations in Category 6. One example asked the pupils to find the time of swing of a pendulum bob. Performance on this was contrasted with performance on the investigation to determine the effect of variables on the rate of swing of different boards (DES, 1985a). As the need to conceptualise the variable was removed in the Category 2 task there was no comparable group of pupils measuring duration of swing rather than rate of swing on the Category 2 question. In the Category 6 investigation 67 per cent of the pupils attempted to determine rate; of these 24 per cent used a quantified method involving two or more swings. This compared with 14 per cent in the Category 2 test. The overwhelming majority of pupils on the Category 2 question (64 per cent) attempted to time one swing only. This compared with one per cent in the Category 6 investigation. Twenty-two per cent of the pupils took no measurements in Category 2, compared with 42 per cent in the practical investigation. In the latter case, however, this was an appropriate strategy, but it was not suitable for determining the time of the swing for the pendulum bob.

The instructions given in the Category 2 tasks about the measurements to take did not seem to exert as much influence on pupils' performance as the need, in the Category 6 investigations, to derive a solution to a problem. The practical problem-solving context led many pupils to evaluate critically their results and performance and consequently to refine their measurement strategies. The actual instruction given to find the time of swing may have precluded the possibility of pupils conceptualising the measurement in context. This was essential in translating the problem posed in Category 6 into an investigation in which the pupil had decided *how* to measure the dependent variable.

Many pupils were able to read instruments but this did not appear to enable them to handle the higher order demand of measuring variable effects. The combination of a purpose and a practical context seemed to exert more of an enabling influence on this complex activity. In fact, as demonstrated in both the **Planning** and **Performance** categories, decontextualised use of instruments can prove to be detrimental to pupils' scientific performance for two reasons. Firstly, pupils' facility to use and read instruments in this way may mask conceptual and procedural difficulties they experience in understanding when and how to deploy instruments in context. Secondly, if pupils experience measurement in the context of instrument use alone, they actually understand measurement only as a specific procedure rather than as a general strategy for use in science.

## 12.3 Across-category probes

The results discussed here arose from the deliberate testing of demands between categories which were perceived to be similar. As these results have been reported in detail elsewhere only brief reference will be made to them.

In the **Planning** and **Performance** probe the same investigations were set to pupils in which they could respond in action or in writing. In addition, the written response questions included either an illustration of the practical apparatus or none at all. Finally, written response questions which isolated specific demands within the investigations were set to the pupils.

The results for all of the investigations included in the survey showed the same performance trends. The comparison between the pupils' responses in action and in writing are exemplified by reference to one investigation concerning how much water was held by a number of different kitchen paper towels. Some typical results are shown in Table 12.1, taken from the teachers' report, 'Assessing investigations in science at ages 13 and 15' (Gott and Murphy, 1987).

Pupils' written responses were generally less adequate than their practical response. The main differences were in the lack of measurement detail given and the failure to include the control of variables. Increasing the availability of measuring instruments resulted in their being used or referred to more often.

In the absence of apparatus clues, performance on the written questions was even lower; more alternative problems were perceived by the pupils and more impractical methods employed. It was the case that the size of the difference in performance varied according to the nature of the practical problem. Some questions were much more dependent on particular scientific skills of design and measurement technique than others, and in such cases apparatus clues had more significance.

Another way of presenting the investigations was to break them up into their component parts. A series of short structured questions on each of the investigations was presented to a sample of pupils. The main feature distinguishing performance on the structured questions was that performance was lower on the structured questions than on the practical investigation for every aspect of the investigations considered (see DES, 1985a, and the teachers' report, Gott and Murphy, 1987). The

**Table 12.1** *'Paper towel'–comparison of pupil performance in 'Planning' and 'Performance of investigations'*

| | | % pupils (age 13) | | |
| | | Written | | Practical |
| Level | Description | Without apparatus | Picture of apparatus | |
| --- | --- | --- | --- | --- |
| 1 | An accurate quantitative measurement method | 12 | 24 | 43 |
| 2 | A rather less accurate method but still capable of discriminating between the towels | 3 | 8 | 5 |
| 3 | Either 1 or 2 but with no restriction on size of towel used | 13 | 14 | 19 |
| 4 | Here, only a final measurement was made in those approaches where this is not sufficient | 1 | 3 | 10 |
| 5 | Qualitative measurements only or no measurement either taken in the practical or mentioned in the written versions | 71 | 51 | 23 |

important characteristics facilitating pupils' successful performance were identified as the practical cues available, the influence of the whole task and the practical response allowing concrete feedback to the pupils. Many other factors were also identified and are discussed in the next four sections along with the results from other categories.

The other probe set to consider across-category performance looked at the hurdle element of data representation within questions requiring pupils to interpret presented data. As performance was much higher on reading information from a variety of representations than for further interpretation of the information, it was suggested that the barrier lay in the process of perceiving and using the relationship presented. The results of the probe were inconclusive. They showed that reading information was not a problem for the majority of 13 year olds. Performance was lower overall on the *description* of the relationship and on *predictions* based on it. However, factors other than the requirement to describe or predict clearly affected pupils' performance as indicated by the range of scores obtained. These factors included the nature of the variables and the amount of redundant information present; they are discussed in the following sections.

## 12.4 Variable identification

From the results across the categories it appeared possible to identify some performance determinants related to the pupils' ability to identify variables. The results generally concerned the identification of the independent and the dependent variables only. The results featured only in those categories where either the skill was assessed in isolation or the analysis of pupils' error responses was considered in terms of the skill. In the Category 1 results discussed previously, the difficulty that pupils had in identifying a variable from a verbal description of it has already been noted. A similar finding occurred in the Category 5 test for **Planning parts of investigations.**

It was suggested that performance in Category 5, **Planning**, was affected by pupils' ability to imagine the variable. It was noted in the same category that a variable could be made more accessible either by the use of a simple illustration of the variable in operation or by its representation in three-dimensional, tangible forms. The more real the variable the higher the performance.

The results in the practical test of investigations suggested a similar influence. Over 90 per cent of pupils were able to identify a discontinuous variable, such as 'type' of towel, presented in the form of three *'actual'* kitchen towels. Pupils' performance was similarly increased when a continuous variable was presented discontinuously; for example when the 'length' of board was presented as three pre-set quantities: long, medium and short.

The need to derive conditions by manipulating two different independent variables caused performance to drop in the practical investigations. This same finding was noted in the Category 5 performance as well.

Some of the questions set in the **Observation** tests were very similar to the whole investigations used in Category 6. The main differences between the questions were that for the **Observation** tasks the independent variable was always presented and often cued and the dependent variable had to be observed rather than measured. One example quoted in Chapter 7, section 7.6, 'Wigwag', involved the observation of a simple bivariate relationship between mass and period of oscillation. The question was similar in this respect to the 'Paper Towel' investigation. Sixty-three per cent of the pupils identified the independent variable in 'Wigwag' compared with over 90 per cent in 'Paper Towel'. In 'Wigwag' 90 per cent identified the dependent variable in their written response. This compared with 70 per cent in 'Paper Towel'. The single dependent variable in the observation question was cued and very visible. The translation of the term 'hold' to mean quantity of water in the 'Paper Towel' investigation, however, required an abstract conceptualisation of the term.

In both Categories 3 and 6 at age 13 the number and nature of the variables to be identified were noted as affecting performance. The requirement to identify and manipulate a trivariate relationship depressed pupils' performance by approximately 20 per cent in these categories.

In the chapter concerned with the interpretation of presented data at age 15 (DES, 1988b) a similar performance influence was identified. If was noted that pupils who appeared readily able to generalise a two-variable relationship did not appear to want to undertake the manipulation of trivariate data. The general trend noted across categories was: the more variables to be manipulated the lower the performance; and the more obscure the variables to be identified the lower the performance.

The complexity of the presented data or event has been found to influence performance in most categories. The presence of redundant information, ie information unrelated to the variable relationship, depressed performance in the identification of all the main variables including control variables, in the **Planning** questions. It also appeared to reduce pupils' success in identifying relationships in data in the categories concerned with **Observation** and **Interpretation.**

## 12.5   Relationships and generalisations

In the practical investigations surveyed in 1984, particular attention was paid to pupils' performance on describing and interpreting the relationships in their collected data. There was a tendency for pupils to consider comparisons between variables rather than to attempt to look at an extended relationship between them. They did not consider the possibility or desirability of extending the rule to cover further cases of the relationship. This was apparent in the number of readings they considered appropriate and in their failure to appreciate the use of graphical representations. There was a significant proportion of pupils across the investigations who saw the collected data as the end point itself.

About 50 per cent of the pupils did not describe their practical findings as a generalisation. This is not an unexpected result if pupils are indeed not concerning themselves with a generalised relationship. The fact that a significant proportion of pupils express their answers as specific observed statements backs up this suggestion. In the age 11 review report (DES, 1988a) the low level of performance on this aspect of pupils' practical investigations was also noted. In that report it was suggested that the low performance was related to an inability to grasp the nature of a relationship rather than a matter of poor vocabulary or writing skills.

This aspect of pupil performance is particularly complex, as the results just mentioned indicate. It is difficult to interpret the cause of pupils' failure. For example, is it the failure to take measurements which leaves the pupils without the necessary data to generalise from, or is it the failure to appreciate a scientific relationship which limits the pupils' perception of the measurements they need to take? The results from the **Planning** category throw some light on this.

In the report of the 1983 survey (DES, 1986a), performance on the Question type concerned with how to use experimental results was very low (3–22 per cent). Very few pupils described any computation to describe what to look for in results. Even rarer was the response of 'plot x against y'. In the same survey it was noted that the better the pupils' performance on describing the measurements they would take, then the more likely these pupils were to include a description of how to use the results obtained. This happened irrespective of any requirement in the questions to describe the use of experimental results. This would suggest that the two features are interdependent aspects of scientific performance. Pupils' vagueness about appropriate data collection makes it impossible for them to envisage what data will emerge and what use it might be.

In the questions used in the **Observation** category the proportion generalising from observed data was approximately 40 per cent for a bivariate relationship. In this category about 20 per cent of pupils failed to generalise and instead recorded correct observations in which the two variables were linked. This is similar to the response given by a significant proportion of pupils in the Category 6 investigations when asked to describe what they had found out.

It has been suggested that pupils' failure to generalise is related to their failure to appreciate the nature of scientific relationships. It has, however, also been noted that the problem may be linked to pupils' inadequate linguistic skills. Other survey results which illuminate this issue further come from the **Interpretation** category. Four questions were included in the 1983 survey at age 13 (DES, 1986a) where a relationship of the type $y = mx + c$ was presented graphically. The pupils had to select the statements which described the relationship. The mean scores for the questions were similar (31 per cent). It was concluded that pupils were unable to recognise which descriptions of the relationship were correct unless they were at a very vague and superficial level. An example of such a description was given as 'If x increases so does y'.

Another description of pupils' failure to interpret data as generalised information was given in the age 15 review report Chapter 8 (DES, 1988b). It was suggested there that in spite of having the technical skills to extract data pupils may be unable to translate the data fully into a *verbal expression* of such a relationship.

To summarise, underlying the requirement to describe data as generalised information appear to be three interlinked factors which depress pupils' performance:

— inadequate understanding of a scientific relationship;

— inadequate understanding of measurement techniques;

— inadequate verbal expression.

## 12.6 Conceptual influences

Pupils' performance on the **Observation** questions and on the practical investigations has been characterised, in this report, by the need to 'model' the presented task. The pupils' existing conceptual framework and personal experience determine the 'model' they construct. The pupils' model of a task affects the whole of their subsequent performance on that task. From this perspective, concepts have a fundamental influence on the pupils' performance across the categories of assessment.

In Category 6, pupils have to reformulate problems in terms of the main variables. To do this successfully requires them to hold an abstract concept of the variables to be manipulated, unless the need to do so is obviated by the manner of presentation of the variables.

It was noted in the discussion of pupils' practical investigations that the dependent variable always had to be conceptualised in the first instance. Pupils' success at this depended very much on the particular variable under consideration. For example a group of pupils understood 'rate' in terms of 'duration'. This finding was also noted for pupils' performance in **Planning parts of investigations.** In another investigation concerned with the judgement of thermal conduction it was apparent that some pupils regarded materials as intrinsically 'hot' or 'cold'. The response of pupils to questions in the **Application** category indicated a similar understanding (see Chapter 9, section 9.6).

The ability to control variables in the tests of both **Planning** and **Performance** depended upon the pupils knowing the effects of the variables in question.

Another fundamental point influencing performance in every category of the assessment was the need to understand procedures and techniques conceptually if they were to have any general use across contexts.

Only in a few instances has there been a direct assessment of scientific conceptual understanding across categories. This has occurred to a small extent in the **Observation** tests and was the main assessment focus for the **Application** category. In spite of the modest numbers of questions used, very similar results were obtained. They indicated that pupils at age 13 usually deal with one idea at a time and recall specific terms rather than generalities. For example, in the review of performance in the **Application** category it was noted that pupils understood 'an acid' more easily than 'acids'. Moreover, general concepts such as 'degree of acidity' were not understood by the overwhelming majority of 13 year olds. This quoted example reflected a general trend in performance. The performance of pupils on 'structure and function' questions set in the **Observation** tests suggested very similar findings. The pupils tended to recall specific aspects related to the content of the resource rather than the global features linking structures with their functions. It is the global features which have broad application.

There appeared to be two very significant points arising from the consideration of the influence of concepts across categories. These included firstly the erroneous assumption that many questions did not make conceptual demands of pupils. This was clearly not the case and this was made even more apparent by assessing procedures across a range of contents and contexts. The ability to understand a procedure to the extent that it is transferable across contents assumes a conceptual understanding of both the procedure and of any of the variables to be manipulated within it. Secondly, the fact that pupils' conceptual understanding is limited to the recall of specifics makes it of very limited use to them. These two points suggest that attention needs to be paid, as mentioned in Chapter 7, to how we assess and teach conceptual understanding in science.

## 12.7    Other influences

There were many issues which could have been addressed in this section. Of these only two will be mentioned. These have been commented on consistently across categories and for each of the surveys conducted.

The first relates to the demand in all assessment that the pupils perceive the same task as the assessor intended. The assessor provides cues, usually linguistic ones, to enable the pupil to construct the same meaning in the task that they themselves hold. The analysis of error responses in each category of the assessment framework suggested that this was the point of failure for many pupils.

In the category, **Performance of investigations** it was reported that some pupils perceived alternative problems or alternative demands which resulted in a reduction in the level of their overall performance. Particular contents used in the **Planning** questions, usually those within the experience of the pupils, led many to redefine the question demands as demands concerned with generating explanations. On different questions in the same test, other pupils faced with a novel demand failed to understand it. These pupils redefined the task in terms of the observable features which they regarded as most salient.

In the **Interpretation** category it was reported that pupil errors were often associated with the perception of alternative question demands. The tendency was for pupils to consider a much broader demand than that intended by the assessor. One feature of the difficulty appears to lie in the mistaken belief that, in the assessment, content would function as a vehicle. As such it was perceived to have a narrowly defined effect.

Similar error responses were noted in pupils' performance in **Observation.** In test situations where a closed system was presented to the pupils, within which it was expected they would function, many failed to do so. Again, the content of the question exerted an influence on pupils' responses.

The finding directly related to this general influence on performance concerns the difference in performance of the top band of pupils from the lowest band. The ability to perceive the 'assessment model' intended, and to function within it, distinguished the performance of these two groups. Thus the top performers generally and consistently avoid the errors summarised here. This finding has been reported at each age and across the different categories of performance.

The context of the question is the other influence considered worthy of inclusion in this chapter. The context is defined as the general setting of the question and is determined *objectively* by the specific content used. The influence of a question's context has been noted in most categories in each survey. The 1984 results have provided more readily interpretable data concerning this influence.

In the **Observation** tests it has been noted that performance was depressed when pupils had to classify scientific content. An everyday context was found to elevate pupils' performance on the **Application** questions as well. Here it was noted that pupils seemed to be more prepared to take a risk and attempt such questions. This same type of influence was found for some pupils in the performance of practical investigations. An everyday context encouraged them to engage with the investigation and so increased the likelihood of a successful, initial interaction. On the other hand, in **Planning**, pupils' performance on control of variables was higher in a science context. It was suggested that this was as much to do with the removal of redundant information as a measure of a context influence.

The results for the 'Sweets' and 'Chemical' investigations are of particular significance here. A deliberate attempt was made in these questions to determine the influence of context on performance. The hypothesis that the tighter and more scientific the context the more likely pupils were to behave in a scientific manner, was borne out to an extent by these results. More pupils in the scientific context rigorously controlled variables and made measurements.

## 12.8    Discussion

The location of a question in a particular category was determined by a consensus view of the criterion of fit. If the criterion of fit was indeed, as intended, the burden of a question's demand then the subcategories would represent independent constructs. However, the findings selected for discussion in this chapter suggest that the subcategory activities are not independent. Several aspects of commonality or interdependence have been identified; they include:

– *the evidence of 'enabling skills'*;

– the evidence of ***cross-category*** demands;

– the evidence of ***overarching*** links between categories.

The question that arises from this is how to treat these findings. The aim in developing the assessment framework was to identify and separate out important activities in science performance. Throughout the survey years, results have been reflected on in an attempt to better understand and document the meaning of the activities. It now appears that there are identifiable *'demand' structures* within the subcategories. These structures are apparent but require further research and validation. The findings discussed in this chapter point to ways in which we can consider variation in scores on category performance. This work forms a part of the research phase, the rationale for which is precisely to better understand and describe the assessment framework and pupils' performance against it.

Some teaching implications can however be suggested now. For example, evidence of hurdle effects in the questions would suggest that they will also occur in classroom activities in science. Teachers perhaps need to pay attention to these effects, as they hinder pupils' progress in science. How to deal with the effects is another matter. Practice at a skill will only be effective as a strategy to aid learning if the pupils understand:

– the purpose of the skill;

– the way in which it functions;

– the manner of deploying it in a variety of contexts and contents.

Finally, some of the across-category work highlighted similar demands which were assessed using different modes of response. One could consider the results of this work as indicating that certain modes underestimate or undervalue what children can do or their potential for doing it. If this viewpoint is not accepted, then at a minimum allowing only one form of response to pupils provides a single and often narrow insight into their achievements. The use of several forms of response allows a much richer and therefore more useful picture to emerge. If pragmatics dictates that only *one* type of response can be used, then this report provides a lot of evidence to enable an informed selection to be made.

# 13

## Cross-age discussion

### 13.1 Introduction

Do pupils make sufficient progress in the development of the processses and concepts of science as a result of their school experience? Progression with age is a difficult matter to discuss. It involves both a measured change in performance between groups of pupils of different ages, and a decision about whether that change is appropriate. In order to judge whether the level of performance has risen or fallen, a common scale is needed which can be used for pupils of all ages. This compares with a scale on a rule used for measuring height; it can be used to measure a change, but will not indicate whether it is appropriate. For this, some judgement has to be made, some criteria applied, which might not be the same for different populations. An acceptable pattern of increase in height with age, for example, would differ for adolescent boys and girls. Even if the question of judging the appropriateness of the change is set aside, the need for the use of a common scale raises difficulties in the case of performance in science.

If that which is to be measured is as simple as height, not only a common scale, but also a common range of that scale, can be used for all ages. (A ruler 7 ft long covers the whole population, and there can hardly be an adverse backwash effect on the growth of individuals, of whatever height, as a consequence of its use.) The same cannot be said in the case of the measurement of performance of a complex activity like science, where performance level is measured as the outcome of a number of interacting factors. We can consider some *limited* aspects of the complex activity of measurement of performance by reference to a simple activity, such as high jumping. Here there is a common scale—the shifting heights of the bar—but the range offered to pupils of different ages is likely to differ. For 11 year olds, no one would think it necessary to go on raising the bar above five feet, even though an exceptional pupil might clear this height. Indeed to insist that *all* 11 year olds attempt such a jump might well decrease their enthusiasm for the activity. On the other hand, if the purpose is to compare performance of 11 year olds with that of 16 year olds, then the bar must not only start at the same height as before, but must be raised to a height which only a few 16 year olds would fail to clear. In the case of high jumping, the content of the test is not in doubt; whatever the age of the jumper, the question is much the same: can he or she clear the bar at a given height? Once a competitor has failed, there is

no need to attempt further 'questions', because they can be so neatly graded for difficulty. Thus adverse backwash effects on the younger group can be avoided.

However, when the field of activity is switched from high jumping to the complex reality of science activity in schools, the problems increase considerably. The range of difficulty in the questions must, like the range in the height of the bar in the high jump, be sufficient to accommodate both age groups. But problems arise because of the complex nature of the subject, and the lack of a simple and absolute hierarchy of questions. Whereas pupils do not grow *extra* legs—only stronger legs—between the ages of 11 and 16, they undoubtedly aquire additional knowledge and experience, both of which interact with the developing science 'process-skills' which have formed the focus of the APU assessment work. Perhaps the most obvious example of the problem occurs in those domains relating to the application of science concepts, where the list of concepts to which pupils are likely to have been exposed is different, and differently balanced, at different ages. The contexts with which pupils are familiar will also change, particularly from 11 to 13. While pupils of 13 will in general have become accustomed to school laboratories and the equipment to be found in them, many 11 year olds have yet to meet their first bunsen burner. Even the type of language available for successful communication will have changed. The analogy with high jumping becomes severely strained. To measure progression with age, the use of a common scale, and a common *range* of that scale, appear to be necessary; but the backwash effect of the use of the appropriate range may, for younger pupils, be adverse.

### 13.2 Early views: age-appropriate tests

The extent to which the goal of cross-age comparisons at the domain level (as opposed to the question level) should be pursued has been the subject of much discussion in the Steering Group, Monitoring teams, Validation groups and others. Teachers in liaison groups were generally of the opinion that the assessments should be age-appropriate; some were concerned lest their pupils should be confronted with tests which were outside their experience, while others were worried in case their older pupils were to reject questions as

158

puerile. They argued that wide ranging tests may produce invalid results as well as damage the image of science for their pupils. (This paralleled the concern about GCSE examination at 16+, though the argument was about ability-appropriate, rather than age-appropriate, tests.)

The first task of the Science Working Party (which pre-dated the Steering Group) was described in the Consultative Paper (DES, 1977) as follows:

'To identify criteria for evaluating the performance which pupils might be expected to achieve through their work in school'.

This could be taken to imply an expectation that assessment, in general, would be age-related, since pupils do different work in school at ages 11 and 16. This is the case even though the spread of performance on identical test questions at the two ages shows considerable overlap.

In a later publication from the Science Steering Group, the 'Science Progress Report' (DES, 1978), there was a discussion on the framework for test construction. A three-dimension grid was proposed or ages 11, 13 and 15, the axes being: process categories; concept areas; and context. But 'naturally, the grids relating to each age at which monitoring is to take place need not be identical'. The idea that tests at different ages might well have different characteristics was elaborated on subsequent pages. Two further quotations from the same report make this clear:

'...Whilst the same process categories will be the framework for assessment at 11, the range of sub-processes within each category will be restricted. Teacher groups are among those helping the science team in the selection of the sub-processes most appropriate to 11 year olds'.

'...There will therefore be no classification of questions according to context, and the grid at 11 is two-dimensional, involving process and concept only'.

The idea of using a very limited number of questions at more than one age was raised later in the report:

'...It has been noted that many (questions) are suitable for administration at two age levels. If such questions are used, there will be an opportunity to report results which show how performance changes with age...'

'...The questions employed in this way will therefore be carefully chosen as a result of pilot trials to be those which give particularly useful results and which stand on their own'.

From then on team members began to arrange to write such questions and include them in the category question pools at the two (and sometimes three) ages concerned. There was no reason to suppose that the

'overlap questions', as they were then called, would be drawn in the random selections which made up the tests at different ages, and so space was allowed in the test packages for their inclusion. Meanwhile preparations for pilot-testing and monitoring continued on the assumption that subcategory pools of questions in the bank would be different at different ages, and that domain tests would therefore also be different.

## 13.3 The move towards cross-age comparisons

It was not until the surveys were well under way that there was a move towards more substantial, if not complete, overlap for some subcategories of the framework. This move was coupled with a review of questions and mark schemes in the age-related pools. The purpose of this review was to strengthen correspondence between pools in terms of the intepretation of definitions. Question types in any subcategory had been defined by a set of question descriptors common to all three age groups (the current version is in Appendix 4). No similar descriptors had been thought appropriate for mark schemes. Indeed in some cases closely similar, if not identical, questions existed in pools at two ages with different mark schemes and sometimes different maximum marks. This was because a level of response thought acceptable from an 11 year old pupil may not be so regarded when offered by an older one. Although, in the circumstances of age-appropriate banks, this situation is perfectly legitimate it can cause misinterpretation of results, so the opportunity to rationalise questions and mark schemes was taken whenever it proved feasible.

At this stage, 1982–84, some subcategory pools of questions were modified so as to bring about complete overlap between two or more ages; in such cases identical test packages were used in the final survey in 1984. In other subcategories, for various reasons, this was not feasible, though the rationalisation procedures may have greatly increased the degree of overlap between pools at different ages. In these categories, the number of common questions selected for use in the survey could not be controlled, given the random selection procedures required for test construction. In some subcategories there remain differences in question presentation or administration procedures which preclude valid comparison.

The advantage of having common banks at two or more ages is obvious: direct comparisons of performance can be made between ages in relevant subcategories. But there are, of course, associated penalites; one is the danger that pupils and teachers may see the tests as less appropriate for a particular age range than before; another is the decrease in continuity, over the first five years, of those subcategories which underwent substantial modification. However, since for all categories questions were continually being added to the bank in order to bring it up to its optimum operating size, this loss of continuity is not restricted to the 'overlap' sub-categories, although it is more marked in these than in others.

The opportunity for direct comparison of performance across ages by inspection of mean scores for domains is limited. There is no *complete* domain overlap between ages 11 and 13, although there is a substantial overlap of banked questions in **Use of graphs tables and charts**, and in **Interpretation of presented information**; and some overlap in **Planning parts of investigations**. While there are some common questions in **Performance of investigations**, the administration procedures are so different that comparison of performance is of doubtful validity.

Between 13 and 15, there is complete overlap in three sub-categories. In **Use of apparatus and measuring instruments** there is a set of tasks comprising a Fixed Test which remains the same, for both ages, from year to year. In **Observation** and in **Planning parts of investigations** the question pools are identical and so are the survey test packages. Among the individual problems set to assess **Performance of investigations** there are several which are common. A discussion of the performance of 13 and 15 year old pupils in these subcategories can be found in the age 15 review report (DES, 1988b).

## 13.4 Alternative strategies for cross-age comparisons

Several ways of comparing performance between pupil populations of different ages (other than the use of identical subcategory tests) have been used during the course of the five surveys carried out so far:

(i) using individual questions;

(ii) using scores on subcategories having age-appropriate question pools;

(iii) using specially designed sets of questions or 'probes'.

### (i) *Comparison using individual questions*

Performance on individual questions has been inspected. Each year, several questions have been included in the test packages at two or more ages in addition to those needed for assessment of the sub-categories. An example from the first survey is the question 'Watering can' from **Applying science concepts** (see Report No. 1 at age 13, DES, 1982a). Sometimes such questions have been selected by chance from corresponding pools at different ages as part of the test for a particular subcategory, and the opportunity to present the results in the relevant report has been taken. The results are straightforward to interpret because the question and mark scheme are given, and the suitability of the questions at the relevant ages can be judged by the reader.

### (ii) *Comparison using scores on subcategories having age-appropriate question pools*

Performance in a given subcategory at one age has been compared with that at another age, even though the questions in the respective pools, and the tests drawn from them, differed. Table 13.1 (p.161), taken from the age 11 review report, shows an example of such comparisons. It is not sensible to compare the actual level of performance in any given subcategory across the two ages; but because of the commonality of the assessment framework, and therefore the meaning of the sub-category titles, it *is* of interest to note common patterns of performance. For example, the profiles of performance across subcategories are similar, and so is the variation (or lack of variation) in scores for boys and girls (see also Occasional Paper No. 4, Johnson and Murphy, 1986).

### (iii) *Comparison using specially designed sets of questions or 'probes'*

Comparison has been made of performance across age groups on sets of questions which have been constructed for a particular purpose, usually to illuminate some area of the assessment programme where problems of interpretation have arisen. One such area was the relationship between pupils' ability to read information from presented data, to describe a pattern in that data, and to make specific predictions from it (see Age 13/15 Report No. 3, DES, 1985a). Another was the relationship between pupils' ability to plan an investigation with varying degree of cueing in the form of diagrams of equipment or real equipment, described in the same report. A third was the relationship between performance in reading scales of real instruments, of photographs and of diagrams of the same instruments. (Chapter 6 of this report and the 13/15 Report, DES, 1985a, give results for ages 13 and 15 separately. The control of variables at ages 11 and 13 was investigated, and discussed in the Age 13 Report No. 4, DES, 1986a.)

'Probe' packages or sets of questions such as those described in (iii) above give results which appear easy to interpret; often all the questions and mark schemes involved have been presented in the relevant report; and in any case, apart from the larger size of the type-face which has invariably been used for age 11 pupils, the set of questions was identical at each age. There are, notwithstanding, certain difficulties of interpretation. There is no doubt about the size of differences which exist, in terms of mean scores, between performances of pupil populations of different ages. What *is* in doubt is the degree to which these differences might have been influenced by the need to select material accessible to the complete age range. For example, in the 'probe'

**Table 13.1**  *Subcategory performance levels at ages 11 and 13 (1984 survey)*

| Subcategory | | Age eleven All | Boys | Girls | | Age thirteen All | Boys | Girls | Degree of overlap in question pools |
|---|---|---|---|---|---|---|---|---|---|
| Reading information from graphs, tables and charts | mean | 62.2 | 62.5 | 61.8 | | | | | |
| | s.d. | 0.6 | 0.7 | 0.7 | | | | | |
| | | | | | using | 65.8 | 64.6 | 67.0 | sub-stantial |
| | | | | | | 0.6 | 0.8 | 0.7 | |
| Representing information as graphs, tables and charts | mean | 57.4 | 57.1 | 57.6 | | | | | |
| | s.d. | 0.7 | 0.8 | 0.8 | | | | | |
| Making and interpreting observations | mean | 44.3 | 44.1 | 44.5 | | 37.2 | 36.1 | 37.9 | minimal |
| | s.d. | 1.1 | 1.0 | 1.2 | | 0.7 | 0.8 | 0.6 | |
| Interpreting presented information | mean | 34.0 | 34.9 | 33.2 | | 42.4 | 43.1 | 41.9 | partial |
| | s.d. | 0.5 | 0.6 | 0.5 | | 0.5 | 0.7 | 0.6 | |
| | mean | | | | Biol. | 27.0 | 27.5 | 26.6 | |
| | s.d. | | | | | 0.4 | 0.6 | 0.5 | |
| Applying science concepts | mean | 30.4 | 31.5 | 29.3 | Phys. | 29.0 | 30.6 | 27.4 | minimal |
| | s.d. | 0.5 | 0.6 | 0.5 | | 0.4 | 0.5 | 0.5 | |
| | mean | | | | Chem. | 27.9 | 27.4 | 28.3 | |
| | s.d. | | | | | 0.5 | 0.6 | 0.5 | |
| Planning parts of investigations | mean | 32.4 | 31.6 | 33.3 | | 32.0 | 31.2 | 32.9 | partial |
| | s.d. | 0.5 | 0.6 | 0.6 | | 0.5 | 0.6 | 0.6 | |

relating to reading from and interpreting presented data, contexts, formality of language and mathematical aspects were controlled so that problems associated with these three factors should not, of themselves, prevent young pupils from demonstrating their ability in the particular 'process-skills' under examination. Had such modifications not been made–for example had decimal numbers or science laboratory contexts featured in the questions–it is possible that differences in performance between the three age groups shown in Figure 13.1 would have been wider.

**Figure 13.1**  *Variation with age in mean scores for three different demands\* in using and interpreting data*

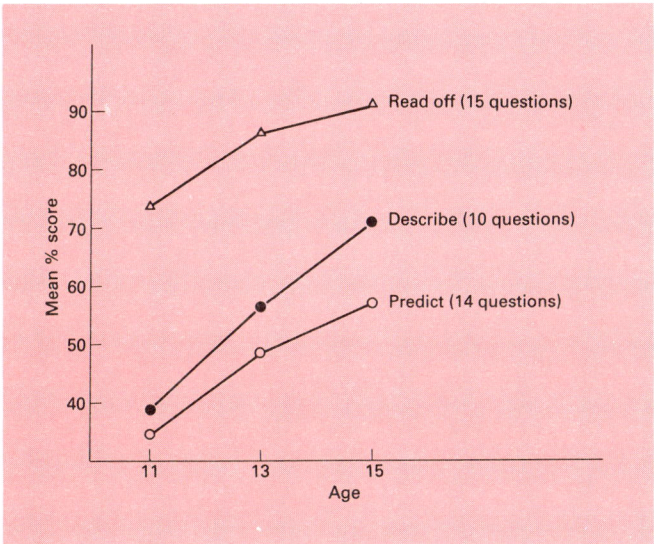

\* In this 'probe' the question stem (which contained the presented information) was the same for all three demands.

This difficulty is representative of one which recurs throughout the framework: to what extent should difficulty factors which are not those of particular concern in a given subcategory be suppressed in order to allow the assessment to be suitably focused? The problem reaches its peak in **Application**.

## 13.5  The difficulties of cross-age comparisons in 'Application'

In the APU Science assessment, questions have been grouped into categories according to the 'process-skill' intended to be the question-focus. Category 4, at one time described throughout as 'making sense of new information' now includes, in its second section, **Applying science concepts**. This is split at ages 13 and 15 into three subcategories concerned respectively with the concepts of the biology, physics and chemistry regions of the agreed list (see Appendix 5). At age 11 there is no such split and therefore one subcategory only. The 'process skill'–**Applying science concepts**–is in this case, by definition, bound by the range and nature of the concept statements listed; since these are different at each of the three survey ages, it is not possible to arrange for more than minimal overlap between any two ages. For example, there are 9 sections of the 'list of science concepts and knowledge' which comprise the chemistry region, labelled E1 to F4. Only in three of these sections are there any statements for age 11 assessment. This is hardly surprising; one would not expect primary school pupils to have any experience of the periodic table, for example. Overlap, in terms of concept statements, is much greater between ages 13 and 15. Indeed it is greater than one might at first expect. This is because when the list was first established, the third set of statements on each page was restricted, as stated in the preamble to the list itself, to 'science concepts and knowledge commonly taught by the end of the basic course, that is by the end of the third year, and will be used in testing all 15 year old students in the sample'. The reason for such restriction is obvious: many pupils cease to study one or more of the sciences after the end of the third year, so that questions involving matters not commonly covered until the fifth year would be likely to meet with little response, and so produce little information at great cost. This restriction need not restrict the *difficulty* of the questions in the bank; however, a question will be difficult for a different reason than would one involving the wave-particle duality, say, or the mechanism of inheritance.

Although there is, therefore, considerable overlap of concept statements between ages 13 and 15, there is very little overlap of questions in the two banks. It is often the case that the questions themselves are very similar; it is the mark schemes which differ. An answer which is considered acceptable from a 13 year old may not be so considered when offered by a 15 year old. Thus comparisons of performance across ages in the **Application**

category have been restricted to those made with respect to isolated questions designed for the purpose and initially included in test packages in addition to those randomly selected to represent the subcategories in the survey. Many such questions have been marked in such a way that types of response, in addition to simple numerical scores, have been identified. (See, for example, the question 'Kettle and bath' reported in the Age 15 Report No. 1, DES, 1982b.)

## 13.6  Summary

Repeated attempts have been made during the assessment to arrive at a satisfactory strategy for comparing performance across ages. Each method has certain drawbacks which have been discussed in the preceding sections. The results, expressed as mean scores for single questions, for identical groups of questions or for non-identical subcategory tests, need very careful interpretation. Some of the more useful findings concern the *patterns* of performance which are characteristic of pupils of all three ages.

## 14.1 Introduction

Many points about the significance of the monitoring results and their implications have been brought out in the summary and discussion sections of previous chapters. The aim of this chapter is to review these briefly and in general terms. This must be done in the light of the way in which the assessment framework was constructed to serve the aims of the monitoring. This issue is reviewed in section 14.2. After this follow discussions of the way in which the effectiveness of this framework is now understood (14.3), and of the implications for teaching and learning (14.4), for assessment (14.5), for policy (14.6) and for the monitoring itself (14.7).

## 14.2 The assessment framework: its structure and function

The categories and subcategories of the framework described in Table 1.1 were established in time to be used for the first survey in 1980; they were the outcome of discussion which was strongly influenced by the proposal for a cross-curriculum model of assessment first expressed by B. W. Kay in 1975 ('Trends in education', No. 2, 1975.) Science was here regarded as a particular way of thinking about and tackling problems, rather than as a compartmentalised package of knowledge, which could be encouraged and applied in many subject areas and not confined to the traditional science disciplines. The effect of the attempt to implement this model was to emphasise 'science processes' and to devalue the recall of facts *as an end in itself*. Other considerations were pushing the science framework in the same direction; the need for a single assessment to cover pupils of all abilities at a given age made the specification of required content a daunting task. Superficially, at least, 'science processes' appeared more universally testable than science content.

It was clear from the outset that within the arena of 'science processes' there existed significant sub-divisions, and that it was necessary to break down the global description of school science as '*ways of thinking about, and tackling, problems*' into a number of categories which were individually recognisable and meaningful and, as far as possible, mutually independent. Given the aim of relating performance to the circumstances in

which pupils might learn, it seemed necessary to try to relate performance within each of these limited aspects of science to certain background variables so that remedial action could be more effectively designed than on the basis of a single agglomerate score. In order to carry out this exercise tests giving reliable scores for each category were needed.

If trends in performance over time were to be detected, the choice lay between using the same fixed test for a category over and over again, or ensuring that different tests could be arranged, which were nevertheless equivalent both in difficulty and in nature. The first option, a fixed test, was rejected, except for the category concerned with **Use of apparatus and measuring instruments**; reasons for this exception are given in Chapter 6. For all other categories and sub-categories, apart from Category 6, **Performance of investigations**, equivalent tests were preferred, provided that they proved on trial to be concerned with a sufficiently generalisable 'process' or skill. The equivalent tests were to be generated by random selection of a prescribed number of questions from a pool devoted to the category or subcategory—ie, the domain—under consideration.

These influences and constraints resulted in questions which were unusual in two different respects. These were:

– questions were designed to test a 'science process' or skill and not recall of knowledge alone;

– each question had to match one or other category—to make much heavier demands in one direction than in others. Because of the need for random selection in the making up of tests of a particular category, a question structured to span the framework could have no place in the category pools.

A further consequence of the decision to generate equivalent tests in this way was the need for large pools of questions for each domain; this, and the need to refine the definitions of the domains, led to the introduction of generalised descriptors of questions which had been found, by trial and error, to be suitable for a given domain.

The discussion this far applies to the substantial components of Categories 1 to 5. Category 6 is quite different. It is synthetic rather than analytic in intent. This is the one activity in which the various aspects of performance are tested together; because this leads to exercises which require extended time and intensive assessment, it can only produce sets of case studies rather than statistically reliable average scores. The decision that this peculiar yet central aspect should be assessed in practical tests with open-ended problems is a very clear expression of the view of science that underlies the rationale for the monitoring.

It has not yet been possible to judge the suitability of the framework for all the purposes intended: the sub-structure of the assessment framework has been changing in two ways during the time since it was first proposed: the number of questions in the bank has been increased very considerably in the attempt to reach the optimum number required for the production of tests by the chosen method; and the fine structure of the subcategories has been modified to take account of information gained as a result of survey analysis. No trends over time have so far been noted which cannot be attributed to these changes, and although some consistent patterns of performance in relation to background variables have emerged, it is not immediately clear what action, if any, should be taken as a result. This is due in part to the *nature* of those background variables about which information could be gathered, and partly to the likelihood of their interactive effects. For example there is a consistent trend in levels of performance, in almost all categories, across catchment areas, as shown in Table 4.2. Few clear patterns have emerged connecting performance and school characteristics; even where positive association has been found, as between high performance and large class size, the variable concerned has been shown to be confounded with others—in this case, with ability range of the class. Nevertheless the categories clearly have potential use for these two purposes; meanwhile analysis of responses has directed attention to quite other areas of interest, which are discussed in section 14.3.

During the course of the surveys, more and more information has been gathered about the circumstances in which pupils learn while at school. Performance has not so far been related to all the school variables about which data have been collected, but the information about school resources has itself sometimes been disturbing. For example, the lack of balance with respect to subject of qualification among those teaching science in schools had already been discussed in Chapter 2. The shortage of teachers qualified in Physics, and to a lesser extent in Chemistry, is well known. However, any overall lack of balance is not simply *reflected* in the teaching pool for pupils in the early secondary stage: it is exaggerated, since specialist examination classes have first call on teachers qualified to match these specialisms. Indeed among general science classes at the 13 year old stage, only about one in ten is likely to be taught by a teacher with a qualification in Physics. Attention is also drawn, in the same chapter, to an impending rather than current problem; it concerns

laboratory provision. Although at present there is little indication that 13 year old pupils cannot be taught in a laboratory where this is appropriate, it does appear that many schools have too few laboratories to implement a programme of practical science courses for all their pupils up to the school leaving age. The shortage is likely to be most severe among secondary intermediate schools in Northern Ireland (particularly in girls' and mixed schools) but will also be likely to occur in many schools in England and Wales. It is suggested that about a quarter of the Comprehensives with sixth forms and a third or more of those without have too few laboratories to allow the proposals to strengthen practical work in GCSE assessment to be implemented. This almost certainly means that 13 year old classes will be moved out of laboratories to allow older pupils in*.

## 14.3 The framework in action

Although the subcategories were defined to be as independent of one another as possible, it has always been clear that, when real pupils responded to real questions, more that one 'process-skill' was going to be deployed. There was likely to be some interpretation, some observation, or some use of symbolic representation whatever other 'process-skills' were required. Such overlap between categories was unavoidable, and all that could be done was to ensure that the main burden of the required response lay clearly in the relevant category. However, what has become clear during the course of the first five surveys is the extent to which performance has been affected by factors other than those which formed the foci of the subcategories of the framework; many of these have proved to be common across categories. The sometimes unexpected effect of the context of a question, or of its specific content, has been reported and confirmed for particular categories; so has the effect of formality of language, or of the need for the application of certain concepts or for quantification. A series of probes both within and between categories has led to a growing body of understanding of the effect of these factors, and of other demands which operate across more than one category, such as the need to identify and relate variables. A discussion of some of the effects on performance of this sub-structure of the framework, which interacts with the defined categories, can be found in Chapter 12.

Questions representing a given subcategory, then, although focused on a particular 'process-skill' are nevertheless varied with respect to other demands. In any single question, or indeed in only small groups of questions, the effects of these demands may all but swamp those characteristics of the category under investigation. However, in the APU surveys, very many

---

* Although what is stated in this paragraph refers to the time of the assessment programme surveyed in this report, it is all still broadly true.

questions are used in each subcategory test and so these effects tend to cancel one another out.

In some subcategories, analysis indicates that the 'process-skill' is more trammelled by variable effects lying outside the subcategory definition than in others. **Observation** is a case in point, as indicated in Chapter 7. In such a case, it is more difficult to obtain a single reliable score. It is also more difficult to discern the educational significance of any score obtained. It may be that such complications contribute to the lack of consistent relationships between subcategory performance and school variables.

Attention has been drawn, at several points and particularly in Chapter 12, to the evidence that the mode of presentation and of response for a question can present demands which prevent pupils from showing their ability to the full. There do not seem to be cases where question results could over-estimate pupils' ability: answering a 'process' test by recall could occur, but the chances of this happening seem to be small given the diversity of question contents. It follows that average subcategory scores will in general be depressed by presentation and response hurdles. It is also possible that such hurdle factors may themselves be related to school and other background variables, thus further obscuring the effects of such variables on science performance scores.

A problem of a quite different kind has arisen since the initial establishment of the framework. This has to do with the desire to compare performance across ages. The original intention was to use a framework which was almost identical across ages as far as 'process-skills' were concerned but very different with respect to the contexts and content of questions, and to the science concepts to be expected. The aim was to have 'age-appropriate' banks of questions so that, among other things, variation in performance between sub-groups of pupils of a given age but with different backgrounds would be maximised. As work progressed, interest became concentrated on the development with age of science 'process-skills', so that where it seemed feasible, corresponding question pools in the banks at the three ages were merged. In some sub-categories, this enabled direct comparisons to be made of the performance of pupils of different ages. Some of the advantages and disadvantages of this move are discussed in Chapter 13.

Since assessment at age 13 is not conducted in all curriculum areas monitored by the APU, it is pertinent to consider the particular value of the age 13 results. This is harder to do than one might imagine, because all of the work at ages 11 and 15 has been conducted in relation to the age 13 work, and so the question of how the schemes at those two ages would have been composed in the absence of age 13 monitoring is almost impossible to answer. After this, there would be the question of how such results would have been interpreted. It is certainly true that much of the inter-pretation across the 11–15 gap would have been subject to quite disabling uncertainties, because of the effects of curriculum variability in the latter years of secondary schooling: in this respect the original motives for including age 13 have been justified. The analysis of pupils' responses to questions and tasks at the intermediate age has helped clarify the nature of some difficulties the younger children experience as well as the successes of the older ones. In addition, the identification of 'plateaux' in the performance of 13 and 15 year old pupils in the same tasks has been significant in developing our understanding of pupils' capabilities. The 11–13–15 year old sequence of results, therefore, provides a rich resource for generating and testing hypotheses about development of pupils' understanding and learning in science. For reasons explained above, strategies for exploiting this resource to the full are only just being developed.

## 14.4 Implications for teaching and learning

Although it was always hoped that results of the surveys would be of use to teachers and their pupils, the initial reaction of science teachers to the proposed framework was mixed. However now that it has become more familiar, it also appears to have become more popular. There are probably several reasons for this. Because of the current overload of content and concepts on examination syllabuses, and thus on the school science curriculum, an emphasis on 'process' rather than content is seen to be desirable. At a time when rapid changes in technology make it hard to predict exactly what a pupil will need to know after leaving school, the acquisition of scientific 'ways of thinking about, and tackling, problems' is thought to be potentially more useful than the memorising of a large body of knowledge. A small proportion of teachers see 'processes' as being more accessible to less able pupils than 'knowledge', and so regard the framework with favour. Whatever the reason, the idea of testing pupils against 'process criteria' has become more acceptable.

Another reason for teachers' evident interest in the monitoring has already been discussed in the particular case of the **Observation** category (Chapter 7). It is hard to cross the gap between commitment to a new set of aims and explicit, concrete realisation of these aims in pupil activities. It is one thing to applaud a move to encourage observation in pupils, but another matter entirely to think of practical tasks, involving a range of content, which are likely to develop observation skills. The teams encountered this difficulty and needed many person-years to compose the questions. Because they are valid and of good quality, the monitoring questions help teachers to solve this very difficult problem. However, because the questions survey overall outcomes without regard to how pupils attain them, they may seem more attractive for teaching than they really are.

There are certainly many results from the surveys which will be of value to teachers. Some will have alerted them to likely gaps in their pupils' understanding; questions or tasks used in the surveys may well be helpful in suggesting means of checking up on competence in specific directions. For example, can a particular pupil read information from tables? Does failure at this point account for lack of success elsewhere? Perhaps a decreasing lack of interest in matters electrical stems from the almost universal inability to read the scale of an ammeter. At the other end of the spectrum, reports of the performance of investigations may encourage teachers to offer opportunity for practical problem-solving with less direction than is common, and to discuss general procedural skills in a situation which is meaningful and motivating for individual pupils.

However, the difficulties and dangers that might arise from wholesale adoption of questions written for the science surveys are indicated in many sections of this report. For example, a teacher might be attracted to a particular group of practical questions designed to test observation skills. Such a group would by intention, and for survey purposes, cover a wide range of content. However, for an individual pupil, the tasks within the group might well seem unrelated and might therefore confuse because their common purpose is not perceived. Skilful judgement in the selection and use of the questions would be essential. In particular, it would be necessary to help pupils to discuss the conceptual assumptions they held about the entities they were observing so that they could reflect critically on how different observers 'see' different aspects: to serve this purpose, questions could well be related to the particular topics being taught at the time. It would also, in general, be necessary to grade questions by difficulty and to understand, and perhaps explore with pupils, the possibilities that modes of presentation and response could be barriers to the full expression of their ability. Here the detailed examinations of the sub-structures and complexities lying within each subcategory, which have been a prominent feature of several chapters of this report, will become essential parts of any attempt to relate monitoring questions to use in schools. The potential values for teaching have been established in the experience of the last few years, but it seems essential to make much more progress in understanding the individualities of questions and of pupils before ways to achieve this potential can be recommended with confidence.

Any increase in time spent in developing pupils' understanding of 'process skills' results in less time spent on a wide coverage of concepts. Any such shift in the curriculum will bring with it problems as well as benefits. The monitoring results have shown that an emphasis on the 'process-skills' is likely to raise communication problems between teacher and pupil. It has been noted for example that pupils often answer questions which they have not actually been asked, and that this might be because they expect questions to require them to

recall and repeat something that they have already been taught. This tendency occurs in most categories, in response to a variety of demands, whether to read off information, to make observations, to describe a pattern in information, or to conduct an investigation. If pupils are expected to respond in a different way, it may be necessary to develop methods and a language in which teachers and pupils can discuss this aim explicitly. Pupils will have to grasp the nature and the purpose of the various 'process-skills' if they are to be willing to explore and extend them across a variety of contexts.

## 14.5 Implications for assessment

The APU assessment has been *criterion-referenced* to the extent that questions representing a given sub-category were defined by a set of general question-descriptors (see Appendix 4). These descriptors took account of the particular 'process-skill' which formed the focus of the subcategory but allowed other factors to vary. The facility of a question written to match any given descriptor was found to vary over a wide range because of the effects of these other factors. However a test composed of a sufficient number of questions provided a stable overall criterion against which to measure population performance, as already explained. It is very much more difficult to arrange for criterion-referencing in the case of the assessment of the individual, because that individual would need to answer all the questions in the test. (In the survey the sixty or so questions used for each subcategory were split between several equivalent sub-samples of pupils, and no single sub-sample had to address all subcategories of the framework.) The only way to reduce the number of questions needed per criterion would be to make the criteria even more specific, so that each takes account not only of the 'process-skill' which is the focus of assessment but also of one or more of the factors which have been shown to have a marked affect on performance. This leads to an absurd and unmanageable number of *different* criteria, and the *total* number of questions needed for the assessment of an individual's performance remains high.

A single subcategory score would necessarily conflate several levels of performance even if the range of the subcategory could be described by a homogeneous set of criteria. Analysis of the possible sub-structure in relation to the relative facilities of different questions in a subcategory pool can indicate how a sequence of levels might be derived (see for example the discussion in Chapter 5). More work needs to done with the existing data, but it seems clear that one result will be that it will not be possible to establish attainment of levels within homogenous criteria without large numbers of assessment questions.

A second feature of the APU assessment has been the inclusion of a great deal of *practical testing*. Where attempts were made to write 'parallel' questions with a written response, it was found that performance was generally lower. For example, the artificial burden of planning without feedback depressed performance. Thus it seems that practical ability needs to be tested in a practical mode.

Categories 1 to 5 represent an *analysis* of scientific performance. The above discussion has considered some of the implications of using this type of assessment for individual pupils. The assessment debate has been extended in Chapters 11 and 12 to compare performances in Category 6 investigations with performances in other subcategories. In Category 6 pupils perform in the context of a *whole* task. The structure of the monitoring has placed this type of assessment in a central position and accorded the results equal significance with those of the domain-referenced categories. This is because the results serve as a 'key' to the interpretation of pupils' scientific performance across the framework. The monitoring results have shown that the 'whole task' context influences pupils' performance on many aspects of scientific activity, some of which are assessed in the other categories. In addition, the category provides information not available from an assessment of the components of scientific performance. An example of this includes pupils' ability to develop a measurement strategy to solve a problem. For these reasons any assessment of an individual pupil's scientific achievement which relies on the component activities alone will be limited. Such an assessment strategy is quite likely to underestimate pupils' achievements; it also misrepresents the activity of science.

Proposals for the conduct of examinations leading to the GCSE include references to criteria-related grades (see GCSE General Criteria, HMSO, 1985), which are described as 'definitions of the standards of performance in different aspects of this subject to be met by the candidate if he or she is to be awarded a particular grade'. These are to be distinguished from grade descriptions, such as those listed, for example, in the GCSE National Criteria for Science (HMSO, 1985). They are to be seen not simply as a general summary of the likely performance of a candidate reaching a given GCSE grade, but as means of determining that grade. It is clear from the arguments above that the task of establishing these grade criteria is a formidable one. The working parties of the Secondary Examinations Council charged with the task in Biology, Chemistry, Physics and Science certainly found it so, and their solutions to the problem range from references to very specific to very general criteria. Their suggestions for grade criteria are described in the reports of the separate working parties (SEC, 1986). It seems likely that the adoption of such criteria as an effective determinant of grades will depend on the use of a very much larger number of questions than can easily be set in a terminal examination.

Some of the grade criteria relate to practical assessment;

it is recommended that assessment should take place as far as possible during meaningful on-going investigations. This is in accord with the findings of the APU surveys (see Chapter 10 and 11 for a discussion of this), if pupils are to be given the opportunity to demonstrate their strengths rather than their weaknesses.

The probable consequences of the proposals are clear: if criterion-referencing and tests of practical ability (especially those involved in a whole rather than a fragmented investigation) are to feature in future public examinations as is proposed, it seems inevitable that a large proportion of the assessment must be conducted in school and over an extended period of time. The problem then would be to *integrate* teaching, learning and assessment in order to avoid continuous and unremitting testing*.

## 14.6 Implications for policy

Several of the issues discussed above, particularly in 14.4 and 14.5, carry implications for policy so that this section has to look briefly at these same issues from a different perspective. Three points are discussed, concerned respectively with background variables, aims of science education and continuity over time.

*Background variables*

For background variables, the data can be interpreted as showing that educational outcomes have such a complex dependence on circumstances and provision that it is not possible to produce dramatic improvement by any single isolated input. The fact that home background seems to have more effect than any aspects of resource that have been investigated does not prove that such resources do not matter: it only shows that their variations over the system have smaller effects than the variations in home background. Thus if resource variations over the country were to increase, the resource effects might become more evident. Furthermore, because no measure of teacher quality could be used, no direct evidence is provided on the potentially important effect of increasing the resources devoted to in-service training. The clear importance of catchment area raises broader questions of social policy. Within the confines of educational policy it may suggest that initiatives aimed at off-setting effects of home background or catchment area might deserve priority in any attempt to secure an overall improvement in performance. Further analysis of the monitoring data to determine whether clear and consistent characteristics of low achievement can be identified would provide valuable data to inform such policy initiatives.

---

* References to the GCSE in this report date from 1985. Courses started in schools in autumn 1986 and the first exams were taken in autumn 1988.

*Aims of science education*

For the aims of science education, the monitoring gives prominence in various ways to aspects of this field which are currently being emphasised as policy priorities. The assessment aspects have already been discussed. One general feature there, that complex and detailed work is needed to determine possible directions in practice for pursuing the overall aim, is clearly implied also by the work on process aims and on open-ended experimenting. Good output measures have been produced; clear links of these to various input effects do not exist. For policy purposes therefore, the internal mechanisms which determine how the workings of the teaching and learning system can produce better outputs have to be better understood. The APU surveys provide clues and useful instruments for such work, but cannot be a substitute for it. Above all, in science the survey reports have peculiar value in clarifying the targets and the criteria to which such inquiries should be addressed.

*Continuity over time*

If it is correct to emphasise the intricate nature of the problems involved in understanding how performance may be improved, it follows that it is only possible to produce improved understanding by work that has a consistent orientation over a prolonged period. It is also very likely that improvement itself will depend on a policy that works consistently over time on a broad front. However, new initiatives and priorities, and new perceptions of educational need, are always arising. Any monitoring system must be flexible in responding to such changes, but if a consistent strategy for the work were to be abandoned in the flux of such changes, then it is very probable that potentially useful outcomes would be lost altogether.

## 14.7  The future of the monitoring

The survey methods and question banks that have been developed, together with the results in the 1980–84 phase, provide an extensive base for future work on assessing trends over time. It seems hardly likely that detectable changes will be observable over a time span of less than five years and there will in future be inevitable tension between repeating for comparability and changing in the light of improved understanding and of changing needs.

However, the understanding and use of present results, and interpretation and development for the future, all require further detailed analysis of the existing work. Some of this must be explorations of the data already collected (eg as hinted in section 14.5). Some will be the testing out of hypotheses about why pupils respond in different ways to different questions in the same subcategory, so that small scale in-depth work with pupils will be needed. Finally, full realisation of the advantages of having test results at several ages might depend on following a particular cohort of pupils over several years to correlate in detail their changes in response with age and school experience.

If such studies can be carried out, the understanding already achieved will be expanded and the extensive resource of data already acquired will have been more thoroughly used. More particularly, it will be possible to appraise and to realise, at least in part, the aims of deploying the monitoring resource for teaching and learning and for new forms of assessment. If and when the result of such additional studies can be related to the monitoring outcomes, it seems likely that the view of the significance of monitoring may be profoundly altered, in much the same way as the experience of five years of monitoring has produced an outlook in this report quite different from, but not inconsistent with, the view expressed in documents written up to 1980.

# References

Comber L. C. and Keeves J. P. (1973). *Science education in nineteen countries* Stockholm: Almqvist & Wiksell.

DES (1977) *Assessment of Scientific Development (a Consultative Paper)* London: HMSO/DES

DES (1978) *Science Progress Report 1977–8* London: DES

DES (1979) *Aspects of Secondary Education in England* London: HMSO

DES (1981) *Science in Schools. Age 11: Report No. 1* London: HMSO

DES (1982a) *Science in Schools. Age 13: Report No. 1* London: HMSO

DES (1982b) *Science in Schools. Age 15: Report No. 1* London: HMSO

DES (1983) *Science in Schools. Age 11: Report No. 2* London: DES

DES (1984a) *Science in Schools. Age 13: Report No. 2* London: DES

DES (1984b) *Science in Schools. Age 15: Report No. 2* London: DES

DES (1984c) *Science in Schools. Age 11: Report No. 3* London: DES

DES (1985a) *Science in Schools. Age 13/15: Report No 3* London: DES

DES (1985b) *Science in Schools. Age 11: Report No. 4* London: DES

DES (1985c) *Science 5–16: A statement of policy* London: HMSO

DES (1986a) *Science in Schools. Age 13: Report No. 4* London: DES

DES (1986b) *Science in Schools. Age 15: Report No. 4* London: DES

DES (1988a) *Science in Schools. Age 11: Review Report* London: DES

DES (1988b) *Science in Schools. Age 15: Review Report* London: DES

DES (1989) *National Assessment: The APU Science Approach* London: DES

Ebbut, D. (1981) *'Girls' science: boys' science revisited'* in Kelly A., The Missing Half. Manchester University Press

Erikson, B. H. and Nosanchuk, T. A. (1979) *Understanding Data* Milton Keynes: Open University Press

Foxman et al (1985) *A Review of Monitoring in Mathematics* London: DES

Gamble, R., Davey, A., Gott, R. and Welford, G. (1985) *Science at Age 15* APU Science Report for Teachers: 5

GASAT (1983) *Contributions to the second GASAT Conference* Institute of Physics, University of Oslo

GCSE (1985) *General Criteria* London: HMSO

GCSE (1985) *National Criteria for Science* London: HMSO

Gott, R. (1984) *Electricity at Age 15* APU Science Report for Teachers: 7

Gott, R. and Murphy, P. (1987) *Assessing Investigations in Science at Ages 13 and 15* APU Science Report for Teachers: 9

Harlen, W. (1983) *Science at Age 11* APU Science Report for Teachers: 1

Harlen, W. (1987) *Planning Scientific Investigations at Age 11* APU Science Report for Teachers: 8

Harlen, W., Palacio, D. and Russell, T. (1984) *Science Assessment Framework, Age 11* APU Science Report for Teachers: 4

Hobbs, E. D. et al (1979) *British Columbia Science Assessment 1978,* General Report Volume 1. British Columbia; Ministry of Education

Johnson, S. and Bell, J. F., (1985) *Evaluating and predicting survey efficiency using generalizability theory* 'Journal of Educational Measurement'

Johnson, S. and Murphy, P. (1984) *The Underachievement of Girls in Physics: towards explanations* 'European Journal of Science Education', 16

Johnson, S. and Murphy, P. (1986) *Girls and physics: a discussion of APU survey findings* Occasional paper No. 4 London: APU

Kay, B. W. (1975) *Monitoring Pupils' Performance* 'Trends in Education' No. 2 London: HMSO

Mortimer, P. and Blackstone, T. (1982) *Disadvantage and Education* London: Heinemann

Murphy, P. and Gott, R. (1984) *Science Assessment Framework, Ages 13 and 15* APU Science Report for Teachers: 2

Murphy, P. and Schofield, B. (1984) *Science at Age 13* APU Science Report for Teachers: 3

NAEP (1978) *Science Achievement in Schools* a summary of results from the 1976–7 National Assessment of Science; Washington: Education Commission of the States

SEC (1986) *Science Draft Grade Criteria* London: Secondary Examinations Council

Smail, B. (1984) *Girl-friendly Science; Avoiding Sex Bias in the Curriculum* York: Longman

Tukey, John W. (1977) *Exploratory Data Analysis* Reading, Massachusetts: Addison-Wesley

Welford, G., Harlen, W. and Schofield, B. (1985) *Practical Testing at Ages 11, 13 and 15* APU Science Report for Teachers: 6

# Appendix

# 1

# Notes on sampling, test distribution, marking and survey analysis

The pupils who took part in the 1984 survey were selected, as usual, according to a two-stage stratified cluster sampling scheme. In the first stage a random sample of schools was selected, and this was followed in the second stage by the random selection of pupils of the appropriate age from within each of the participating schools. The sample survey scheme and other aspects of this Appendix are described in the technical review of the science survey programme (DES, 1989).

**Selection of schools**

Before selection began, the school population was stratified with respect to the variables *size, type* and *region*. The relevant regional classification within England is shown in Table A1.1.

Four *size of age group* classifications were imposed: *up to 80 pupils, 81–160 pupils, 161–240 pupils* and *more than 240 pupils*.

Four *type of school* categories applied in England and Wales: comprehensives with pupils up to age 16, comprehensives with pupils up to age 18, middle

schools, other maintained schools and independent schools. In Northern Ireland, technical colleges were distinguished from schools, and schools were identified as grammar or intermediate, and further subdivided according to their management system into controlled or maintained/voluntary schools.

Within England schools were selected from within each region-by-type-by-size classification in numbers which reflected their presence in the school population as a whole (ie schools were selected by proportional random sampling): in other words, if x per cent of the schools in England containing 13-year old pupils were 11–16 schools of size 81–160 pupils in the Midlands, then x per cent of the English school sample should be of this type. Within Wales and Northern Ireland schools were also selected by proportional random sampling from the type-by-size or management-by-size classifications, respectively, but these countries were deliberately over-represented relative to England in the final sample so that pupil performance estimates of reasonable accuracy could be produced.

**Table A1.1**  *The regions of England*

| North | Midlands | South |
|---|---|---|
| Merseyside* | West Midlands* | Greater London* |
| Greater Manchester* | Hereford and Worcester | Bedfordshire |
| South Yorkshire* | Shropshire | Berkshire |
| West Yorkshire* | Staffordshire | Buckinghamshire |
| Tyne and Wear* | Warwickshire | East Sussex |
| Cleveland | Derbyshire | Essex |
| Cumbria | Leicestershire | Hampshire |
| Durham | Lincolnshire | Hertfordshire |
| Humberside | Northamptonshire | Isle of Wight |
| Lancashire | Nottinghamshire | Kent |
| North Yorkshire | Cambridgeshire | Oxfordshire |
| Northumberland | Norfolk | Surrey |
| Cheshire | Suffolk | West Sussex |
| | | Isle of Scilly |
| | | Avon |
| | | Cornwall |
| | | Devon |
| | | Dorset |
| | | Gloucestershire |
| | | Somerset |
| | | Wiltshire |

* Metropolitan counties in 1984.

**Table A1.2**  *The sample of schools*

| | England | Wales | Northern Ireland |
|---|---|---|---|
| Invited to take part | 385 | 139 | 164 |
| Unable to take part | 45 | 37 | 38 |
| No reply | 4 | – | – |
| Initial acceptance, later decline | 4 | 1 | 3 |
| Tests not returned or returned unused | 9 | 8 | 6 |
| Schools participating | 323 | 93 | 117 |

Table A1.2 provides details of the numbers of schools invited to take part in the survey, and of those which finally participated. The participation rates for England, Wales and Northern Ireland were 85 per cent, 68 per cent and 73 per cent respectively.

**Selection of pupils**

The pupils chosen to take part in the survey were selected from all of those in the participating schools who were born between 1 September 1970 and 31

August 1971. Pupils were selected by reference to their dates of birth, and the range of birth dates specified varied according to the size of age-group in the school, so that roughly equal samples of pupils would be selected from each school.

The circus practical tests, for economic reasons, were administered to groups of nine pupils at a time (pupils working independently). Pupils were randomly selected for the practical tests from those taking the written tests.

The only pupils explicitly excluded from the survey were those in special schools or in units designated as 'special' within normal schools. However, the head-teacher of each selected school was told that discretion could be used in withdrawing particular pupils from the testing sessions if it was felt that participation would cause undue distress. Just over 14,000 pupils were chosen to take part in the survey, and just 30 pupils were withdrawn from testing by their headteachers. Clerical errors of one kind or another resulted in the overall loss of test results for fewer than one per cent of pupils at the final analysis stage.

### Test administration

The questions which were used in this survey to represent each subcategory were chosen at random from the pool of questions for that subcategory (ie a 'domain-sampling' approach to question selection was employed). Table A1.3 shows the number of questions selected from each subcategory pool. This complete set of questions was then sub-divided into three, four or six subtests to be administered to different, but similarly representative, random samples of pupils.

Table A1.3  *The sample of questions*

| Subcategory | Number of subtests | Number of questions selected |
|---|---|---|
| Using graphs, tables and charts | 6 | 90 |
| Making and interpreting observations | 3 | 45 |
| Interpreting presented information | 6 | 90 |
| Applying biology concepts | 4 | 60 |
| Applying physics concepts | 4 | 60 |
| Applying chemistry concepts | 4 | 60 |
| Planning parts of investigations | 4 | 60 |

Twenty-two different written test packages (each in two versions both containing the same questions but one version presenting these in the reverse order to the other) were administered to pupils in this survey. Most test packages consisted of questions from two different subtests. Each package was intended to last about an hour. There were four practical circuses; three circuses containing questions drawn from the subcategory pool **Making and interpreting observations** and one circus comprised of the fixed test of **Use of apparatus and**

**measuring instruments**. In addition, four individual practical investigations were administered to some of the sample pupils. There were also several packages which were not samples of questions from the subcategory pools but questions designed to investigate various aspects of science performance.

Each survey school was given a variety of the written test packages to be distributed at random among its sample pupils. Each pupil took just one of these. In addition, in each of a random subsample of the participating schools, subsamples of pupils taking written tests took part in a practical circus. Testing took place during November in the three countries.

Pupils who were in the sample but who were absent on the day on which the school undertook a written test session were given the relevant test if they attended school at any time within two weeks of the school's main test session. However 395 pupils did not complete their written tests because of absence from school during the two week period.

### Marking

The testers who were trained to administer the individual or group practical tests were also trained to mark the results of this testing. A detailed checklist has been devised for each individual category 6 practical task, and the administrators simply coded these checklists as the pupil attempted the tasks. In the group practical circuses, an occasional question would be marked at the time of testing but most would be marked as written responses at the end of the day.

For the written tests, pairs of markers were trained to mark one or other of the test packages, one of the pair marked all of the 'A' version scripts the other marked all of the 'B' version scripts (these represent equivalent random samples of between 250 and 300 scripts).

### Analysis

As the school sample was produced by a simple random sampling procedure within each stratum, it would be appropriate to apply the usual chi-square and other significant tests to the data if the statistical significance of any of the subgroup differences is of interest.

Throughout the report, any results presented for individual questions are raw sample statistics and have not been weighted in any way. Population mean performance estimates and their associated estimated variances were produced test package by test package for the subcategories contained in them. Where a subcategory was represented in two or more different test packages, the separate, independent performance estimates produced for these were combined. Full details are given in the associated technical report (DES, 1989).

The procedure requires that an appropriate subcategory percentage 'subtest score' be computed for each individual pupil, this being the simple sum of the pupil's scores on relevant questions as a percentage of the total possible score (after an initial adjustment of all question scores onto a common mark scale).

When producing the population estimates for each science subcategory in each test package it was necessary to weight the raw sample data to take account of the complex sampling scheme which was used to select the pupil sample. The method adopted here to produce a population mean estimate for any particular subgroup ('North', 'Comprehensive to 16', etc) was first to multiply each school mean by that school's size (ie by the number of pupils in that school of the appropriate age), to sum the resulting figure over all schools in that subgroup sample, and then to divide the whole by the total number of pupils of the appropriate age in those sample schools (technically termed a biased ratio estimate). Estimates were produced in this way for sample breakdowns by the stratifying variables, ie school location, school type and region. Weighted variance estimates were produced simultaneously–the relevant formula is to be found in any text on survey sampling. The overall population mean and variance estimates, and those for boys and girls separately, were produced by appropriately weighting the separate regional estimates before combining.

The subcategory mean estimates reported were produced by averaging the separate estimates produced for each test package which contained questions from that subcategory. The standard errors associated with these final mean scores were produced in the usual way for an average of independent variates by dividing the square root of the sum of the separate variance estimates by n (where n is the number of test packages involved). It should be noted that these standard errors, though following conventional practice applying recognised formulae, take account only of estimation errors arising from the sampling of pupils and schools. They do not allow for estimation errors arising from the sampling of questions, nor those arising from interactions between pupils or schools and questions. Computation of standard errors which should take this contribution into account is complex and time-consuming; the results of some preliminary analysis of the survey data do, though, suggest that the standard errors quoted in Chapter 1 could be multiplied by a factor of about three to approximate those which would apply if the question sampling influence were in fact taken into account (see Johnson and Bell, 1985; Johnson, DES, 1989).

SCHOOL NUMBER:

Assessment of Performance Unit, Department of Education and Science

# APU

ASSESSMENT OF PERFORMANCE IN SCIENCE

SCHOOL QUESTIONNAIRE

<u>AGE 13 SURVEY</u>

It is an essential part of the Science Monitoring exercise to relate the test results to information about the general provisions for science in schools. This questionnaire is designed to gather such information.

If a question has a number of coded alternative responses none of which exactly describes your particular circumstances please select the one which is closest to the actual situation. If a particular question cannot be answered in the form required then please leave the appropriate box(es) blank and attach an explanatory note to the questionnaire.

Many of the questions require numerical answers which are to be entered into boxes provided.

We realise that completing the questionnaire is an extra burden imposed on you, but we hope that you will understand that it is only with such information that full use can be made of the survey results.

Thank you for your help.

> *Before returning the questionnaire to the NFER, please ensure that information entered in Section II.4 is linked to pupils in the sample by completing column 9 of the Pupil Data form as given in the 'Instructions for completion of the Pupil Data form'.*

# APU SCIENCE: AGE 13 SURVEY 1984
## SCHOOL QUESTIONNAIRE

### I. GENERAL INFORMATION

#### 1. Age range and form entry

— What is the age range of your school?

— What is the number of forms on entry?
(eg if 5 form entry, enter 5)

#### 2. Timetable

— How many teaching periods are there in a calendar week?

— How long is an average teaching period (in minutes)?

#### 3. Laboratories and science technicians

For the purpose of this question, a laboratory is to be considered as a working space with services (gas, water, electricity), where pupils can do small group and individual practical work.

— How many laboratories does your school have?

— How many full-time equivalent science technicians do you employ?

#### 4. Finance for the current year

— Please indicate the size (in £) of your school's *general* capitation allowance for 1983/84 (in the case of independent schools, please indicate the amount of any regular income received by the school for teaching resources). £

— If your *science* department(s) received any external donations/grants (for example, from the PTA) during this same period, please indicate the total amount (in £) and the source(s). £

.................................................

— If possible, please indicate the total amount (in £) *spent* by your science department(s) in this period. (Include expenditure from special grants/donations, but *exclude* stationery expenses). £

— Approximately what percentage of this last amount is spent on books?

#### 5. Re-organisation

— if your school has recently been involved in any major restructuring (eg merger with another school) please describe below:

_____

_____

_____

#### 6. Science teachers

— How many teachers are currently involved in teaching science at any level in your school?

— Please give the science qualification of each teacher currently involved in teaching science. Use one column per teacher and indicate (i) the level of qualification and (ii) subject of qualification by entering the appropriate letter codes.

Please also (iii) tick to indicate whether the teacher currently teaches science to any 12/13 year old groups (ie any of the second year groups in an 11–18 secondary school)
and
(iv) use letter M or F to indicate the sex of the teacher.

(i) *Level of qualification*
D  Science degree
E  BEd degree or teaching certificates
H  HND
O  Other qualification, if none of above

(ii) *Subject of qualification*
B  Biology
C  Chemistry
P  Physics
G  General/Integrated science
A  Other physical science or applied physical science or engineering
S  Other biological science or applied life science
N  Not science

**Teachers**

| Qualification | 1 | 2 | 3 | 4 | 5 | 6 | 7 | 8 | 9 | 10 | 11 | 12 | 13 | 14 | 15 | 16 | 17 | 18 | 19 | 20 |
|---|---|---|---|---|---|---|---|---|---|---|---|---|---|---|---|---|---|---|---|---|
| (i) Level | | | | | | | | | | | | | | | | | | | | |
| (ii) Subject | | | | | | | | | | | | | | | | | | | | |
| (iii) Teaches 12/13s | | | | | | | | | | | | | | | | | | | | |
| (iv) Sex | | | | | | | | | | | | | | | | | | | | |

174

## 7. In-service courses

Please enter the number of teaching staff who have attended *in-service courses* or meetings on aspects of teaching science within the last three years, as follows:

(a) a course of advanced professional study leading to a certificate or award ☐

(b) a course amounting to more than three days in total but not included in the above ☐

## 8. For schools in Wales only

— Is the language medium (spoken and written) used by 12/13 year old pupils in science:

entirely Welsh ☐

entirely English ☐

both Welsh and English? ☐

## 9. Catchment area

Please give an indication of the catchment area of your school (catchment describes the environment from which the pupils come, rather than the location of the school). Please enter in the boxes A–E the approximate proportion of pupils drawn from each of the areas described below. These may be from one category of catchment area or from several. For example, if a school draws about 60 per cent of its pupils from a large city centre, about 30 per cent from less prosperous suburban areas and about 10 per cent from a prosperous suburban area, write in box:

| A | B 60 | C | D 10 | E 30 |
|---|------|---|------|------|

A.   Rural: few schools will have completely rural catchment areas, but some will draw their pupils from a mixture of farms, villages, small towns and/or small seaside resorts.

B.   Areas subject to the problems associated with city centres. This covers schools in the middle of large cities drawing pupils from crowded and run-down property or from new flats and houses built to rehouse families on the old sites. It also covers overspill developments and some sections of new towns to which the problems associated with city centres have been exported.

C.   Long established manufacturing areas. Socially, these areas would be relatively homogeneous: few pupils would come from very highly favoured groups, but very disadvantaged pupils would not present a notable problem.

D.   Prosperous suburban. Mainly owner-occupied, but including the more prosperous council estates.

E.   Less prosperous suburban. Mainly council estates. These areas would not suffer severely from social problems, but many pupils would have low motivation and aspirations.

Please enter proportions in boxes below:

| A | B 60 | C | D 10 | E 30 |
|---|------|---|------|------|

## II. INFORMATION RELATING SPECIFICALLY TO THE SCIENCE EDUCATION OF 12/13 YEAR OLD PUPILS

### 1. Science courses

— If all of your 12/13 year old pupils (ie the 2nd year in an 11–18 school) have a common curriculum in science please tick the appropriate box(es) to indicate the science course(s) which constitute this common curriculum:

General Science ☐    Biology ☐

Chemistry ☐    Physics ☐

Physics with Chemistry or Physical Science ☐    Other science ☐

— If your 12/13 year olds do *not* have a common curriculum, please indicate where the differences occur (eg more able groups separate sciences, less able groups General Science).

.................................................................

### 2. Organisation for science work

Please tick to indicate how 12/13 year old pupils are grouped for work in science.

☐ Mixed ability (teaching groups contain pupils across the complete range of ability in the school)

☐ Banding (teaching groups are roughly parallel in ability within each of a few broad bands)

☐ Setting (teaching groups are formed of pupils selected on the basis of their ability in science)

☐ Streaming (teaching groups are ranked by general ability)

☐ Other (please specify) ...............................

.................................................................

### 3. Resource materials

— If any groups of 12/13 year old pupils follow a General Science course, please indicate, by ticking the appropriate boxes, the main resource material used and any other resource materials which make a substantial contribution to the course:

| | Main resource | Substantial use |
|---|---|---|
| Nuffield Combined Science | ☐ | ☐ |
| Scottish Integrated Science | ☐ | ☐ |
| Insight to Science | ☐ | ☐ |
| Nuffield 'Themes for Middle Years' | ☐ | ☐ |
| Science 5–13 | ☐ | ☐ |
| School science department's independent material | ☐ | ☐ |
| Other published material: please specify: | ☐ | ☐ |

4.

Please complete the grid, giving information for *all science teaching groups* in which 12/13 year old pupils (ie the 2nd year in an 11–18 school) are taught, whether sample pupils are drawn from them or not. Two examples are given on the grid, one for a group of pupils taking 3 separate subjects and one for a group taking General Science.

*Col 1* These numbers are simply for linking the information on this page to the pupils taking the test. Please use these numbers when completing the Pupil Data form, to represent the science teaching group(s) to which each sample pupil belongs.

*Col 2* The school name (eg 2B) for each science teaching group.

*Col 3* The name of the course(s). Please use the following codes in suitable combinations:

G General, Integrated or Combined Science
B Biology
C Chemistry
P Physics
W Physics with Chemistry
O Other science

*Col 4* The number of pupils in the science teaching group.

*Col 5* The ability level of the pupils in the group. Please use the following codes (if necessary use combination of codes eg, HA, AL).

H High ability    R Remedial
A Average ability  M Mixed ability
L Low ability

*Col 6* The number of periods per calendar week allocated to the course(s).

*Col 7* The number of periods per calendar week that the course(s) is taught in a *classroom*, as opposed to a laboratory.

*Col 8* The science qualification of the teacher(s) on the course. If teaching group has more than one teacher, then give qualification of each teacher. If different teachers for different subjects then list in order of subjects as in column 3.

**Qualification**
D Science degree
E BEd degree or teaching certificate
H HND
O Other qualification

**Subject of qualification**
B Biology
C Chemistry
P Physics
G General/Integrated science
A Other physical science
S Other biological science
N Not science

| 1 Identifying number of group | 2 Name of group | 3 Course(s) followed | 4 Group size | 5 Group ability | 6 No of periods | 7 Periods in classroom | 8 Teacher qualific. |
|---|---|---|---|---|---|---|---|
| Example | 2A | PCB | 23 | M | 6 | 2 | DP, EC, EN |
| Example | 2B | G | 26 | AL | 5 | 0 | DC |
| 1 | | | | | | | |
| 2 | | | | | | | |
| 3 | | | | | | | |
| 4 | | | | | | | |
| 5 | | | | | | | |
| 6 | | | | | | | |
| 7 | | | | | | | |
| 8 | | | | | | | |
| 9 | | | | | | | |
| 10 | | | | | | | |
| 11 | | | | | | | |
| 12 | | | | | | | |
| 13 | | | | | | | |
| 14 | | | | | | | |
| 15 | | | | | | | |
| 16 | | | | | | | |
| 17 | | | | | | | |
| 18 | | | | | | | |

**Reminder**

*Before returning the questionnaire to the NFER, please ensure that information entered in Section II.4 is linked to pupils in the sample by completing column 9 of the Pupil Data form as given in the 'Instructions for completion of the Pupil Data form'.*

# Pupils' questionnaires

## Topics of interest

You have now finished your test—thank you for taking part in it.

Before you go we would like some more information. We have made a list of topics and would like to find out if you are interested in knowing more about them.

For each topic in the list put a tick in **one** of the boxes beside it to show how much it interests you.

**Would you like to know more about?...**

**Topics of interest**

| | Definitely yes | Quite a lot | Not sure | Not very | Definitely not |
|---|---|---|---|---|---|
| What gives fireworks different colours? | | | | | |
| How plants and animals respire. | | | | | |
| How to see round corners. | | | | | |
| How substances dissolve. | | | | | |
| Can vegetarians (people who don't eat meat) live without other animals? | | | | | |
| How does friction work? | | | | | |
| Why it's dangerous to throw aerosol cans on a bonfire. | | | | | |
| How animals respond to their environment. | | | | | |
| Is there such a thing as perpetual motion? | | | | | |
| How acids and bases react. | | | | | |
| How can we stop insects becoming resistant to insecticide? | | | | | |
| What is necessary for a steady current to flow between the terminals of a battery? | | | | | |
| Which materials are best for making saucepans? | | | | | |
| How animals reproduce. | | | | | |
| How to lift heavy weights with bags of air. | | | | | |
| How a change of state is caused. | | | | | |
| How does cutting down forests affect the air we breath? | | | | | |
| How mass differs from weight. | | | | | |
| Why jewellery is made from silver and not aluminium. | | | | | |
| How animals are adapted to the kind of food they eat. | | | | | |
| How bald tyres increase the chance of car accidents. | | | | | |
| Properties of metals. | | | | | |
| How to grow plants without soil. | | | | | |
| How to find the average speed of an object. | | | | | |
| Where does the water on the outside of cold drink cans come from? | | | | | |
| How plants and animals depend on each other. | | | | | |
| How balloons can be used to help teach deaf children. | | | | | |
| How elements vary in their relative activity. | | | | | |
| How do our lungs work? | | | | | |
| How pressure depends on force and area. | | | | | |
| Why is the sea salty? | | | | | |
| How animals are structurally adapted to their environment. | | | | | |
| How to mend a torch which doesn't work. | | | | | |
| How metals are distinguished from non-metals. | | | | | |
| Why are some twins identical? | | | | | |
| How light travels. | | | | | |
| How it's good that toothpaste is a base but bad that apples are acidic. | | | | | |
| Our ears and how we hear. | | | | | |
| Why it's hard to move in a space-craft. | | | | | |
| What the difference is between a solid, a liquid and a gas. | | | | | |
| Why the kiwi bird might become extinct. | | | | | |
| How energy is transferred from one thing to another. | | | | | |
| Why fibre glass and not metal is used for making cars that last. | | | | | |
| How plants make food. | | | | | |
| How do you prove you've broken a world speed record? | | | | | |
| How animals are trained. | | | | | |
| How sound travels. | | | | | |
| How to cross-breed goats and sheep. | | | | | |

## 'Out of school' activities

You have now finished your test—thank you for taking part in it.

Before you go we would like some more information. We have made a list of things that you may do out of school or that you may like to do.

Answer both questions beside each activity in the list by putting a tick in **one** of the five boxes only.

|  | How often do you do these things? | | | | | Would you be interested in doing more given the chance | | | | |
|---|---|---|---|---|---|---|---|---|---|---|
|  | Very often | Often | Sometimes | Once or twice | Never | Very interested | Quite interested | Not sure | Not very | Definitely not |

**'Out of school' activities**

| Activity |  |  |  |  |  |  |  |  |  |  |
|---|---|---|---|---|---|---|---|---|---|---|
| Go bird spotting. |  |  |  |  |  |  |  |  |  |  |
| Mend things or do jobs in the home using drills, screwdrivers or tools |  |  |  |  |  |  |  |  |  |  |
| Watch a science programme on TV–eg Tomorrow's World, The Living Planet |  |  |  |  |  |  |  |  |  |  |
| Watch science fiction programmes–eg Dr Who, Star Trek, Blake's 7. |  |  |  |  |  |  |  |  |  |  |
| Grow plants from seeds. |  |  |  |  |  |  |  |  |  |  |
| Play with Scalextric, or electric trains, etc. |  |  |  |  |  |  |  |  |  |  |
| Collect and study small animals such as caterpillars and insects. |  |  |  |  |  |  |  |  |  |  |
| Take equipment and things apart to see inside them–eg a radio, a hairdryer. |  |  |  |  |  |  |  |  |  |  |
| Draw plants or animals that have interested you. |  |  |  |  |  |  |  |  |  |  |
| Play games like snooker or billiards. |  |  |  |  |  |  |  |  |  |  |
| Read information in books about science–eg Science Now. |  |  |  |  |  |  |  |  |  |  |
| Read a science fiction book or magazine–eg Dan Dare, 2001: A Space Odyssey. |  |  |  |  |  |  |  |  |  |  |
| Design and then make something from construction kits such as Meccano, Lego, Bolt'n Build. |  |  |  |  |  |  |  |  |  |  |
| Collect fossils or interesting stones, shells or bones. |  |  |  |  |  |  |  |  |  |  |
| Repair or try to repair a broken electrical gadget–eg record player; rewire a plug. |  |  |  |  |  |  |  |  |  |  |
| Collect or study wild flowers and plants. |  |  |  |  |  |  |  |  |  |  |
| Use a computer to play games. |  |  |  |  |  |  |  |  |  |  |
| Use a computer to do things beside playing games. |  |  |  |  |  |  |  |  |  |  |
| Use a paper pattern to sew something to wear. |  |  |  |  |  |  |  |  |  |  |
| Use maps to help you when you go walking, cycling, etc. |  |  |  |  |  |  |  |  |  |  |
| Use special kits such as chemistry sets or electronic sets. |  |  |  |  |  |  |  |  |  |  |
| Use a magnifying glass or a microscope to see things more clearly. |  |  |  |  |  |  |  |  |  |  |
| Build models from kits such as Airfix. |  |  |  |  |  |  |  |  |  |  |
| Borrow books from the public library. |  |  |  |  |  |  |  |  |  |  |

|  | Yes | No |
|---|---|---|
| Have you got a sister? | ☐ | ☐ |
| Have you got a brother? | ☐ | ☐ |

Circus T ☐ ☐ ☐

Pupil Number ☐ ☐ ☐ ☐

Girl ☐

Boy ☐

You have now finished your test—thank you for taking part in it.

Before you go we would like your opinion about some of the questions in the test. Would you please read the following section carefully and answer the questions about the last TWO practical questions you did in the test.

Write down your letter and the station number you are sitting at:

letter ☐          station ☐

181

**Everything that follows on pages 1 and 2\* is asking about the question you have just completed.**

What was **this** question about?

_____

_____

_____

What did you think of the question? Put a tick in ONE box only:

☐       ☐       ☐       ☐       ☐

*Very*       *Quite*       *All right/*       *Not*       *Disliked*
*enjoyable*       *enjoyable*       *okay*       *much*       *it*

Explain **why** you thought that:

_____

_____

_____

_____

Do you think it was the sort of thing that should be in a science test? Put a tick in ONE box only:

☐       ☐       ☐       ☐       ☐

*Yes*       *Probably*       *Not sure*       *Not really*       *Definitely not*

Say **why** you think that:

_____

_____

_____

Please go on to the next page. . . .

\* i.e. pp.182–3 in this report.

Would you like to do more of this sort of thing in science?
Put a tick in ONE box only:

☐      ☐      ☐      ☐      ☐

*Very much*      *Quite a lot*      *Not sure*      *Probably not*      *Definitely not*

Why?

_____

_____

_____

Did you have enough time to do the question?

_____

_____

How well do you think you did on the question?
Put a tick in ONE box only:

☐      ☐      ☐      ☐      ☐      ☐

*Very well*      *Quite well*      *Average*      *Not so good*      *Pretty bad*      *Cannot tell*

Why do you think that?

_____

_____

_____

Please go on to the next page....

Now think about the previous question–**the one you did just before the one you are sitting at.**

Please answer the questions for that one now.

What was it about?

_____

_____

_____

What did you think of the question? Put a tick in ONE box only:

| ☐ | ☐ | ☐ | ☐ | ☐ |
|---|---|---|---|---|
| *Very enjoyable* | *Quite enjoyable* | *All right/ okay* | *Not much* | *Disliked it* |

Explain **why** you thought that:

_____

_____

_____

_____

Do you think it was the sort of thing that should be in a science test? Put a tick in ONE box only:

| ☐ | ☐ | ☐ | ☐ | ☐ |
|---|---|---|---|---|
| *Yes* | *Probably* | *Not sure* | *Not really* | *Definitely not* |

Say **why** you think that:

_____

_____

_____

Please go on to the next page. . . .

Would you like to do more of this sort of thing in science?
Put a tick in ONE box only:

☐       ☐       ☐       ☐       ☐

*Very much*       *Quite a lot*       *Not sure*       *Probably not*       *Definitely not*

Why?

_____

_____

_____

Did you have enough time to do the question?

_____

_____

How do you think you did on the question?
Put a tick in ONE box only:

☐     ☐     ☐     ☐     ☐     ☐

*Very well*     *Quite well*     *Average*     *Not so good*     *Pretty bad*     *Cannot tell*

Why do you think that?

_____

_____

_____

Please go on to the next page....

185

What was your favourite question in the whole test?

_____

Please explain why:

_____

_____

_____

How do you think you did on the whole test?

☐       ☐       ☐       ☐       ☐       ☐

*Very well*     *Quite well*     *Average*     *Not so good*     *Pretty bad*     *Cannot tell*

How do you normally do in science?

☐       ☐       ☐       ☐       ☐

*Very well*     *Quite well*     *Average*     *Not so good*     *Pretty bad*

What sort of things do you normally do in science?

_____

_____

_____

Do you want to continue doing a lot of science, or a little or no science, after the 3rd year?

_____

Please explain why:

_____

_____

_____

## Suitable jobs

You have now finished your test—thank you for taking part in it.

Before you go we would like to ask your opinion about the jobs in the list on the following page. We would like to know how suitable **you** think each job is—first for yourself, then for girls in general, and then for boys in general.

You can choose from a selection of five statements ranging from very suitable to totally unsuitable. Please tick only **one** box each time.

PUPIL NUMBER ☐☐☐☐

BOY ☐

GIRL ☐

How suitable do you think each of these jobs might be—

| Suitable jobs | For yourself? | | | | | For girls? | | | | | For boys? | | | | |
|---|---|---|---|---|---|---|---|---|---|---|---|---|---|---|---|
| | Very suitable | Quite suitable | Not sure | Not really suitable | Totally unsuitable | Very suitable | Quite suitable | Not sure | Not really suitable | Totally unsuitable | Very suitable | Quite suitable | Not sure | Not really suitable | Totally unsuitable |
| Teacher | | | | | | | | | | | | | | | |
| Bank manager | | | | | | | | | | | | | | | |
| Hairdresser | | | | | | | | | | | | | | | |
| Doctor | | | | | | | | | | | | | | | |
| Petrol pump attendant | | | | | | | | | | | | | | | |
| Clerical worker | | | | | | | | | | | | | | | |
| Plumber | | | | | | | | | | | | | | | |
| Machinist | | | | | | | | | | | | | | | |
| Computer programmer | | | | | | | | | | | | | | | |
| Member of Parliament | | | | | | | | | | | | | | | |
| Librarian | | | | | | | | | | | | | | | |
| Post office worker | | | | | | | | | | | | | | | |
| Office cleaner | | | | | | | | | | | | | | | |
| Farmer | | | | | | | | | | | | | | | |
| Scientist | | | | | | | | | | | | | | | |
| Caretaker | | | | | | | | | | | | | | | |
| Cashier | | | | | | | | | | | | | | | |
| Member of the Forces | | | | | | | | | | | | | | | |
| Factory worker | | | | | | | | | | | | | | | |
| Bank clerk | | | | | | | | | | | | | | | |
| Engineer | | | | | | | | | | | | | | | |
| Porter | | | | | | | | | | | | | | | |
| Shop assistant | | | | | | | | | | | | | | | |
| Solicitor | | | | | | | | | | | | | | | |
| Laboratory technician | | | | | | | | | | | | | | | |
| Architect | | | | | | | | | | | | | | | |
| Secretary | | | | | | | | | | | | | | | |
| Chef | | | | | | | | | | | | | | | |
| Bricklayer | | | | | | | | | | | | | | | |
| Journalist | | | | | | | | | | | | | | | |
| Nurse | | | | | | | | | | | | | | | |
| Police officer | | | | | | | | | | | | | | | |
| Social worker | | | | | | | | | | | | | | | |
| University lecturer | | | | | | | | | | | | | | | |
| Steelworker | | | | | | | | | | | | | | | |
| Garage mechanic | | | | | | | | | | | | | | | |
| Professor | | | | | | | | | | | | | | | |
| Café worker | | | | | | | | | | | | | | | |
| Electrician | | | | | | | | | | | | | | | |
| Typist | | | | | | | | | | | | | | | |
| Farm worker | | | | | | | | | | | | | | | |
| Factory manager | | | | | | | | | | | | | | | |
| Driver | | | | | | | | | | | | | | | |
| Shopkeeper | | | | | | | | | | | | | | | |

# Jobs and science

You have now finished your test—thank you for taking part in it.

Before you go we would like to ask your opinion about the jobs in the list on the following page. We would like to know how suitable **you** think each job is for yourself. Then we would like you to say how important you think science is for the particular job.

Answer both parts beside each job in the list by putting a tick in **one** of the five boxes only.

| Jobs and science | How suitable do you think each of these jobs would be for you? | | | | | How important do you think science is for this job? | | | | |
|---|---|---|---|---|---|---|---|---|---|---|
| | *Very suitable* | *Quite suitable* | *Not sure* | *Not really suitable* | *Totally unsuitable* | *Very important* | *Quite important* | *Not sure* | *Not really important* | *Totally unimportant* |
| Teacher | | | | | | | | | | |
| Bank manager | | | | | | | | | | |
| Hairdresser | | | | | | | | | | |
| Doctor | | | | | | | | | | |
| Petrol pump attendant | | | | | | | | | | |
| Clerical worker | | | | | | | | | | |
| Plumber | | | | | | | | | | |
| Machinist | | | | | | | | | | |
| Computer programmer | | | | | | | | | | |
| Member of Parliament | | | | | | | | | | |
| Librarian | | | | | | | | | | |
| Post office worker | | | | | | | | | | |
| Office cleaner | | | | | | | | | | |
| Farmer | | | | | | | | | | |
| Scientist | | | | | | | | | | |
| Caretaker | | | | | | | | | | |
| Cashier | | | | | | | | | | |
| Member of the Forces | | | | | | | | | | |
| Factory worker | | | | | | | | | | |
| Bank clerk | | | | | | | | | | |
| Engineer | | | | | | | | | | |
| Porter | | | | | | | | | | |
| Shop assistant | | | | | | | | | | |
| Solicitor | | | | | | | | | | |
| Laboratory technician | | | | | | | | | | |
| Architect | | | | | | | | | | |
| Secretary | | | | | | | | | | |
| Chef | | | | | | | | | | |
| Bricklayer | | | | | | | | | | |
| Journalist | | | | | | | | | | |
| Nurse | | | | | | | | | | |
| Police officer | | | | | | | | | | |
| Social worker | | | | | | | | | | |
| University lecturer | | | | | | | | | | |
| Steelworker | | | | | | | | | | |
| Garage mechanic | | | | | | | | | | |
| Professor | | | | | | | | | | |
| Café worker | | | | | | | | | | |
| Electrician | | | | | | | | | | |
| Typist | | | | | | | | | | |
| Farm worker | | | | | | | | | | |
| Factory manager | | | | | | | | | | |
| Driver | | | | | | | | | | |
| Shopkeeper | | | | | | | | | | |

# Levels of popularity of the activities listed in the pupil questionnaires

**Figure A3.1** *Percentage stating that they pursue each activity often or very often*

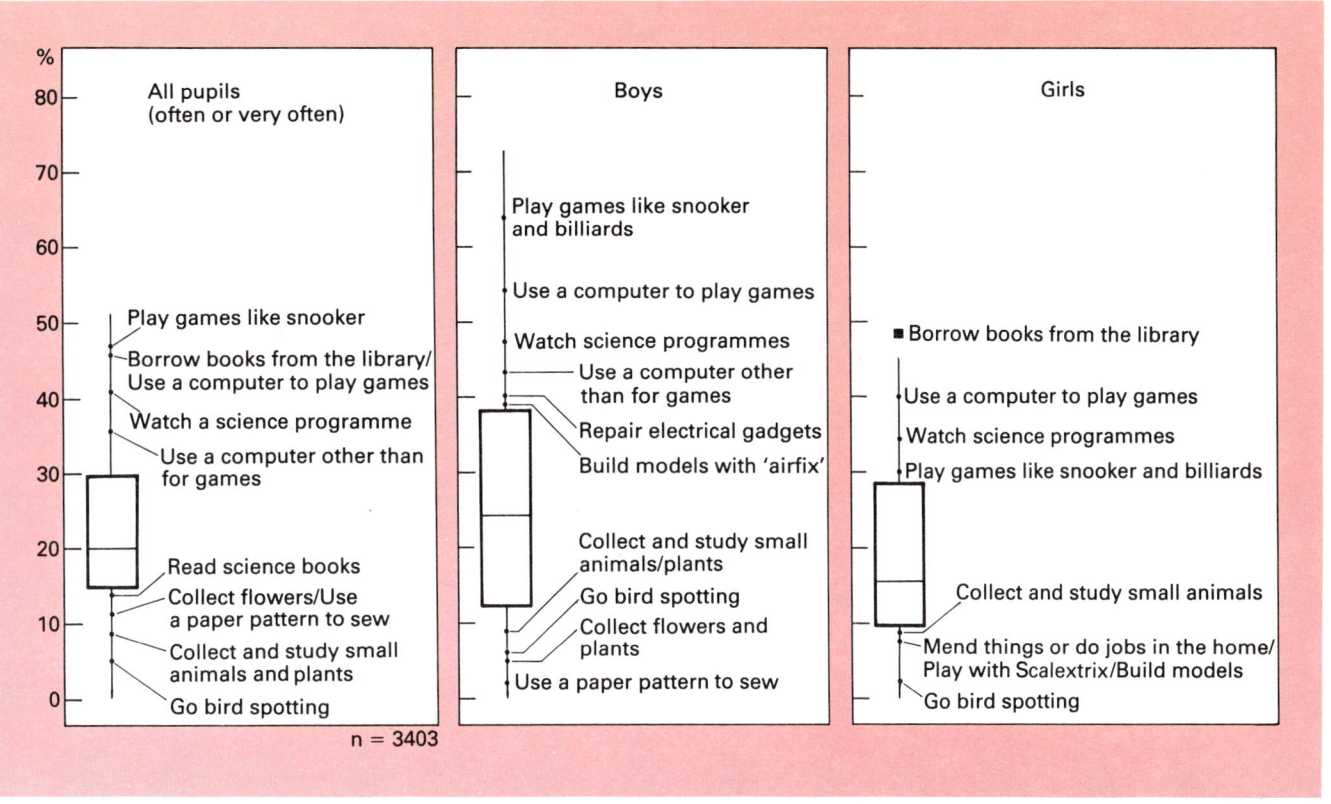

**Figure A3.2** *Distribution pattern by sibling gender for frequency with which activities are pursued*

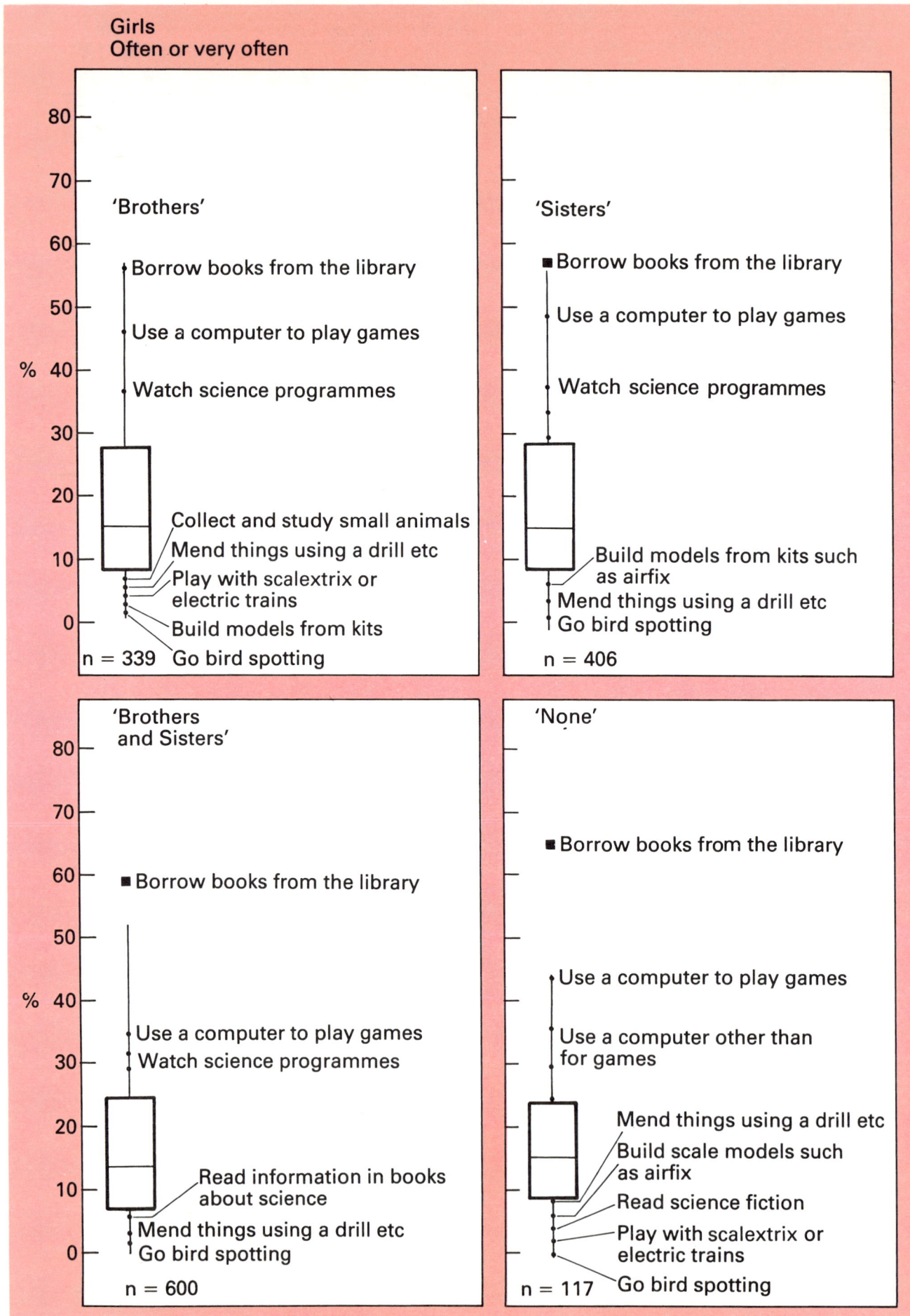

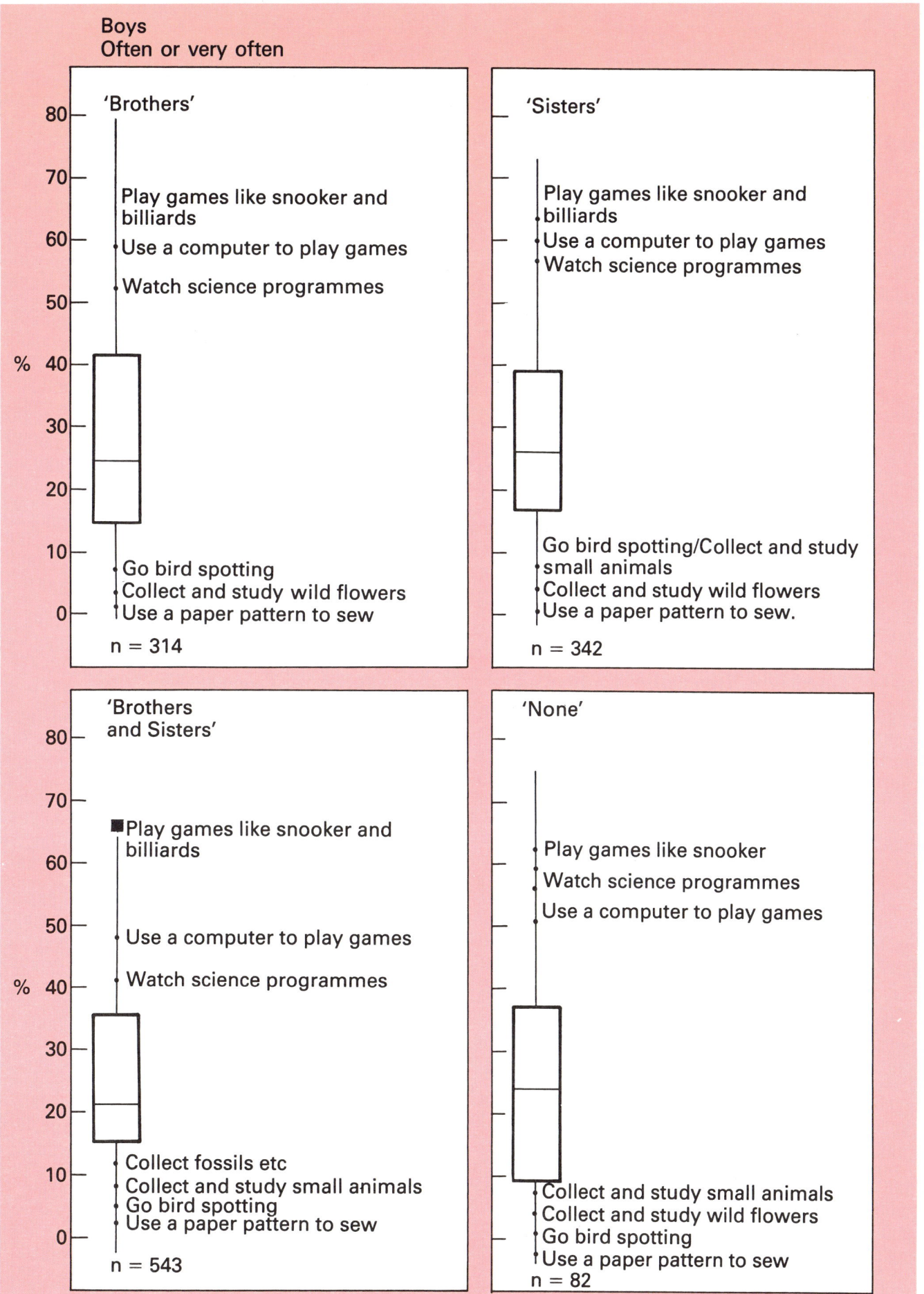

Boys
Often or very often

'Brothers'

Play games like snooker and billiards
Use a computer to play games
Watch science programmes

Go bird spotting
Collect and study wild flowers
Use a paper pattern to sew

n = 314

'Sisters'

Play games like snooker and billiards
Use a computer to play games
Watch science programmes

Go bird spotting/Collect and study small animals
Collect and study wild flowers
Use a paper pattern to sew.

n = 342

'Brothers and Sisters'

Play games like snooker and billiards
Use a computer to play games
Watch science programmes

Collect fossils etc
Collect and study small animals
Go bird spotting
Use a paper pattern to sew

n = 543

'None'

Play games like snooker
Watch science programmes
Use a computer to play games

Collect and study small animals
Collect and study wild flowers
Go bird spotting
Use a paper pattern to sew

n = 82

**Figure A3.3** *'Suitable jobs'. Percentages of boys and girls seeing jobs as suitable for themselves (contrasing sub-samples according to the suitability of 'teaching' for themselves)*

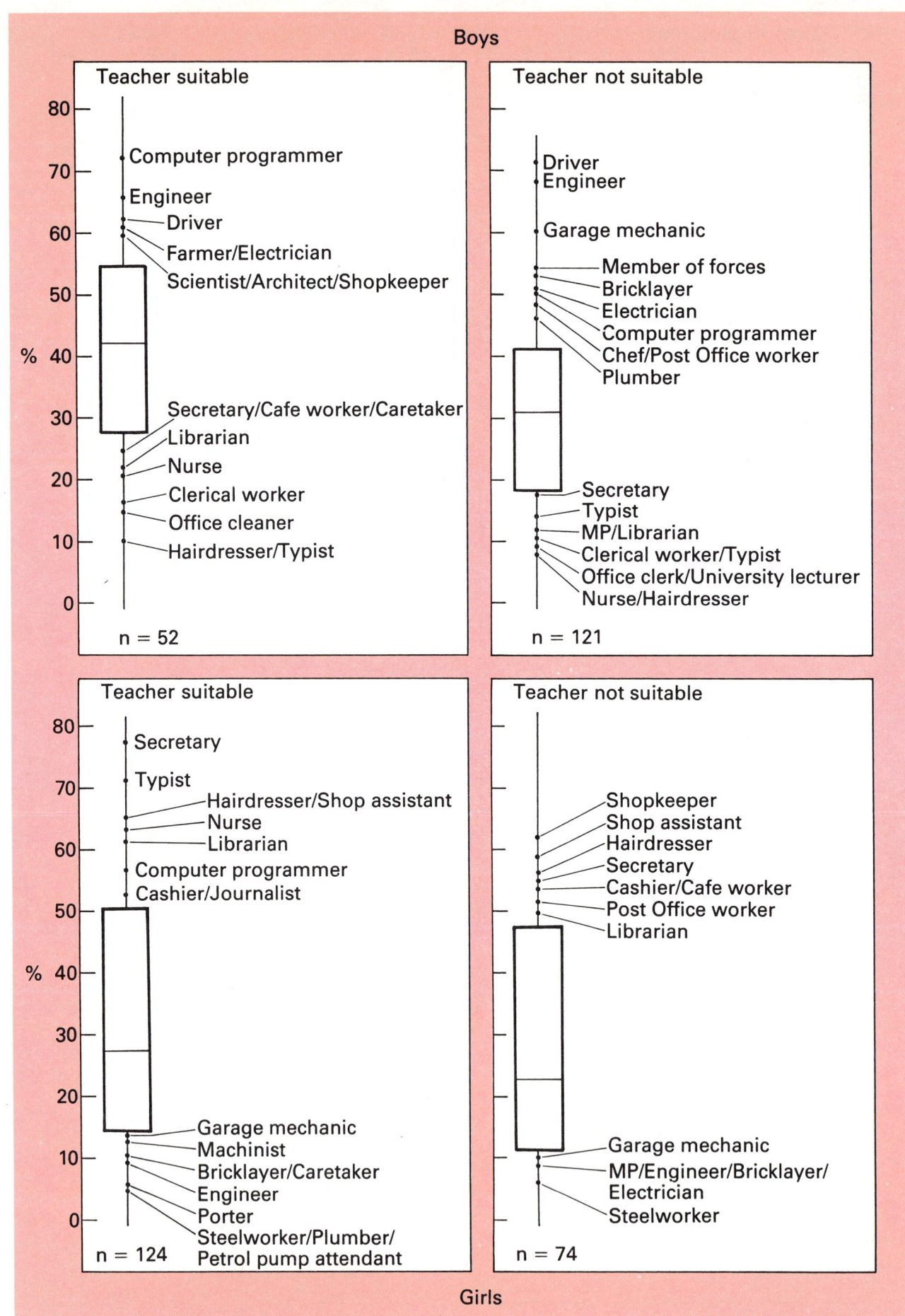

**Figure A3.4** *'Suitable jobs'. 'Percentages of boys and girls seeing jobs as suitable for themselves (contrasting sub-samples according to the suitability of 'architect' for themselves)*

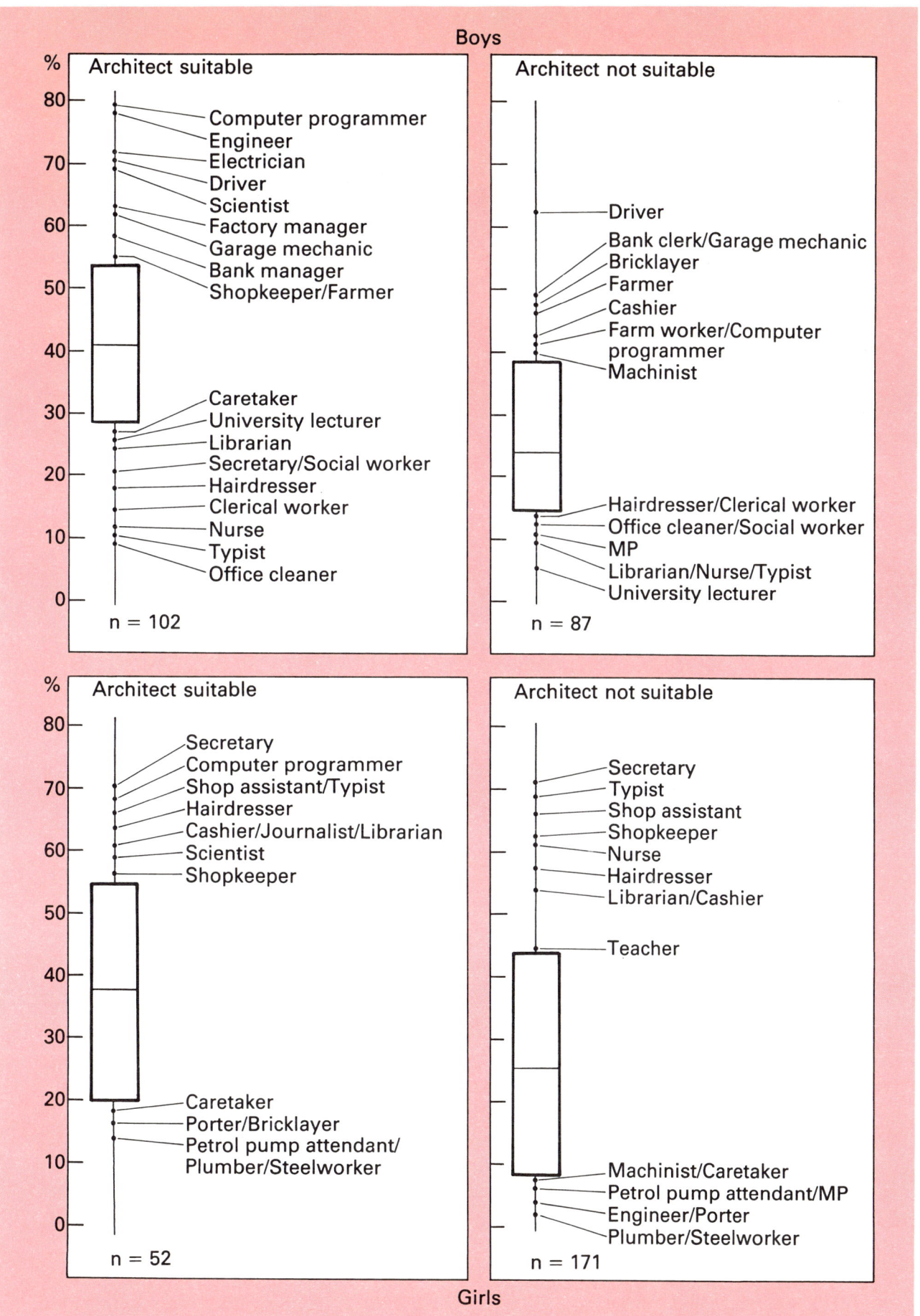

**Figure A3.5** *'Suitable jobs'. Percentages of boys and girls seeing jobs as suitable for themselves (contrasting sub-samples according to the suitability of 'social worker' for themselves)*

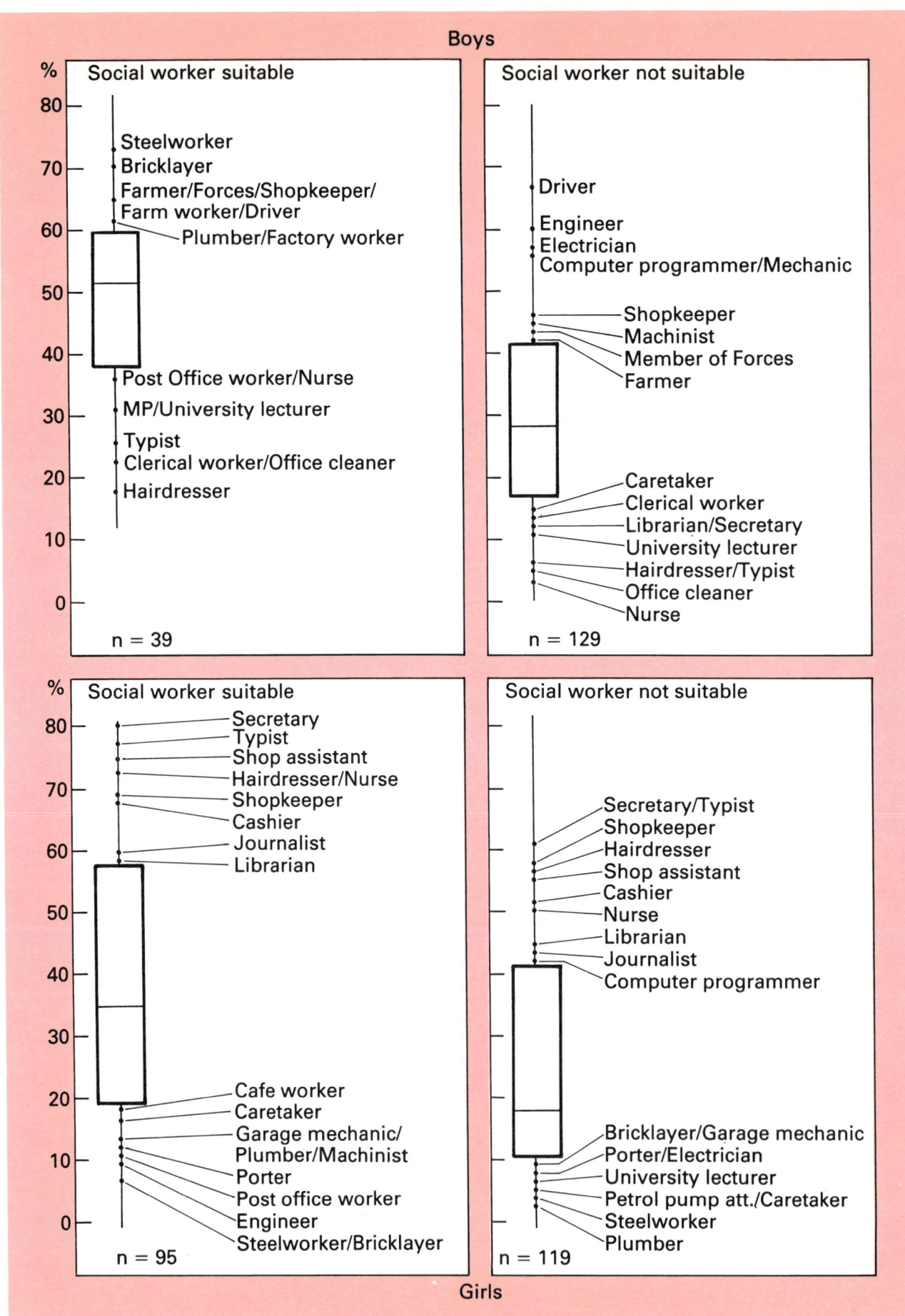

**Figure A3.6** *'Jobs and science'. Percentages of boys and girls seeing jobs as suitable for themselves (contrasting sub-sample according to the suitability of 'doctor' for themselves)*

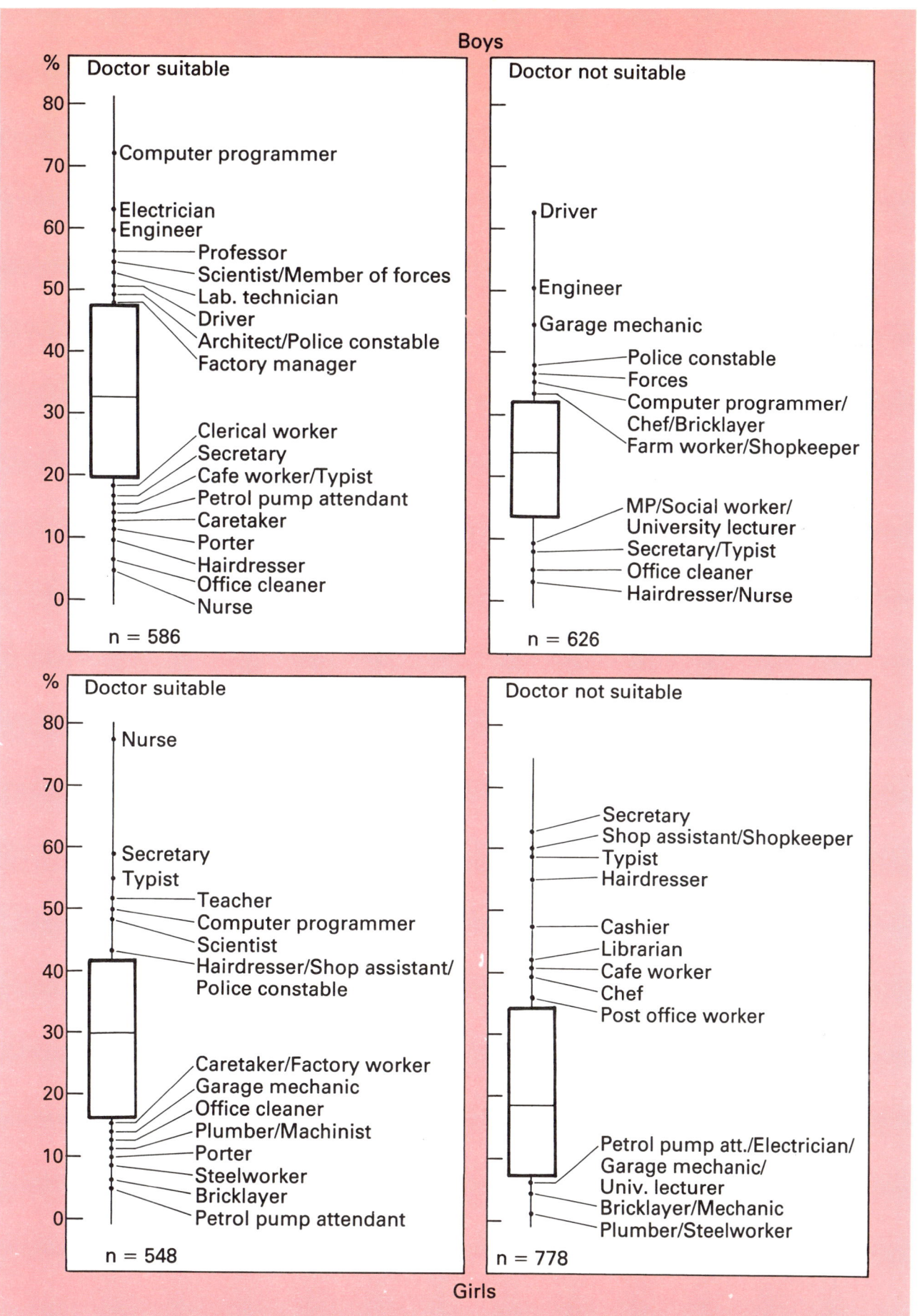

**Figure A3.7** *'Jobs and science'. Percentages of boys and girls seeing jobs as suitable for themselves (contrasting sub-samples according to suitability of 'architect' for themselves)*

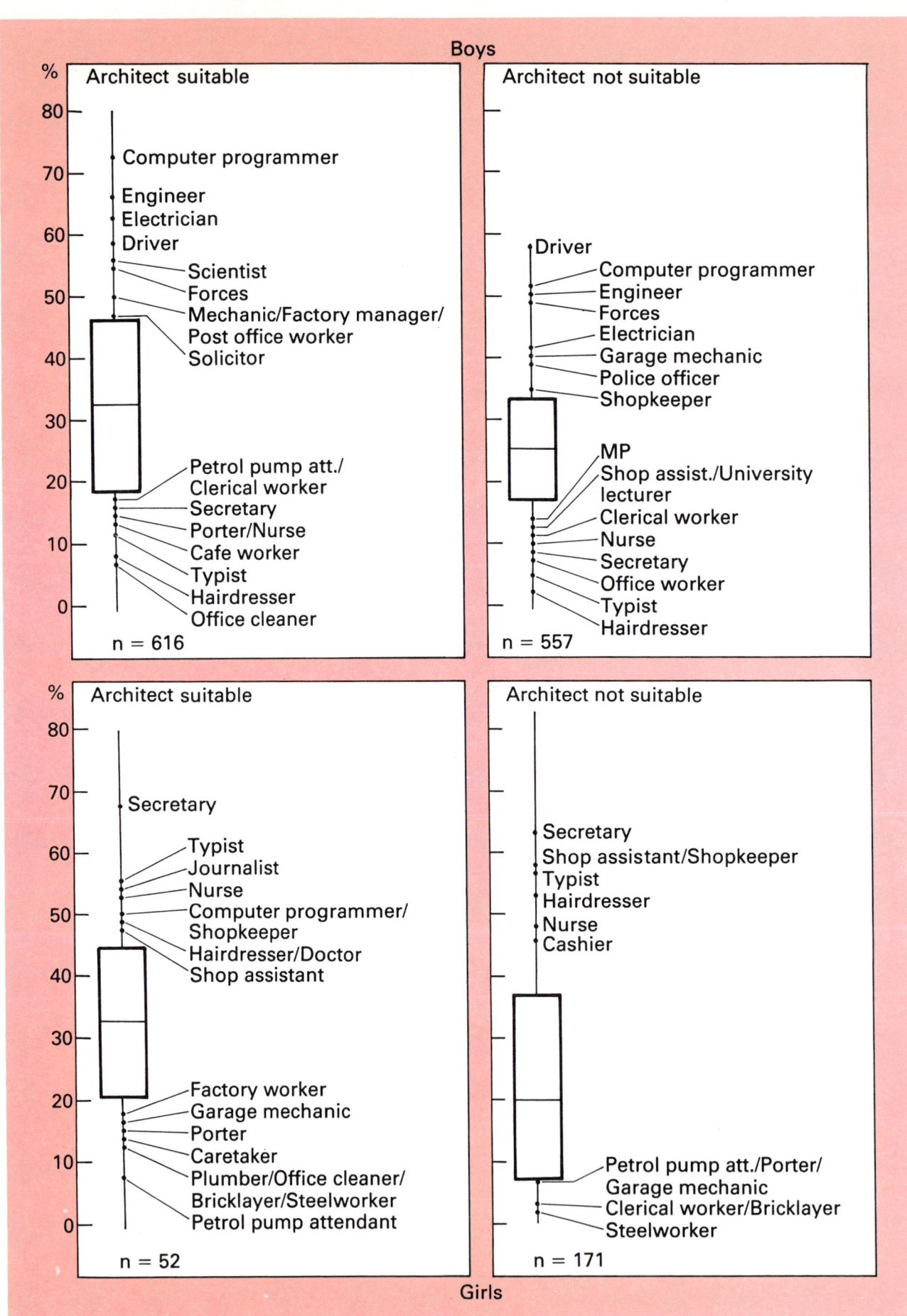

# Framework and Question types

The lists of question descriptors which follow have been used by members of the APU Science Monitoring Teams in writing questions to assess some of the processes and skills related to the assessment framework below. Subcategories shown in bold correspond to those listed in recent publications*.

*The assessment framework*

| Category | Subcategories | Mode of testing |
|---|---|---|
| 1 Use of graphical and symbolic representation | **Reading information from graphs, tables and charts**<br>**Representing information as graphs, tables and charts**<br>Using scientific symbols and conventions | Written |
| 2 Use of apparatus and measuring instruments | **Using measuring instruments**<br>**Estimating physical quantities**<br>**Following instructions for practical work** | Group practical |
| 3 Observation | **Making and interpreting observations** | Group practical |
| 4 Interpretation and application | i **Interpreting presented information**<br>Judging the applicability of statements to data<br>Distinguishing degrees of inference<br><br>ii **Applying: biology concepts**<br>**physics concepts**<br>**chemistry concepts**<br>Generating alternative hypotheses | Written |
| 5 Planning of investigations | **Planning parts of investigations**<br>**Planning entire investigations**<br>Identifying or proposing testable statements | Written |
| 6 Performance of investigations | **Performing entire investigations** | Individual practical |

*One or two question descriptors have been used only at age 11, and one or two only at ages 13 and 15.

# Category 1 : Use of graphical and symbolic representation

| Subcategory | Q.D. | Given | Outcome | Mode of Response |
|---|---|---|---|---|
| Reading information from graphs, tables and charts | 101 | A table of (a) figures (b) representative symbols (c) non-representative symbols | Read off information as directed | LR and CA |
| | 102 | A schematic representation of a process or series of linked events or relationships | Read off information as directed | LR and CA |
| | 103 | Vertical or horizontal bar chart | Read off information as directed | LR |
| | 104 | Pie chart | Read off information as directed | LR |
| | 105 | Graph | Read off information as directed | LR |
| | 106 | Graph and statement of what it represents | Name the variables on the axes | LR |
| | 107 | (a) line graph (b) points located by coordinates | Read coordinates of a designated point | LR |
| Representing information as graphs, tables and charts | 111 | Data and a partially completed table | Add further data to complete table | CA |
| | 112 | A partially complete schematic representation of a process, series of linked events or relationships and data to add | Add given data to complete schematic representation | Drawing |
| | 113 | Data and a partially completed bar chart | Add further data to complete chart | Drawing LR |
| | 114 | Data and a partially completed pie chart | Add further data to complete chart | Drawing LR |
| | 115 | Data and a partially completed line graph | Add further data to complete graph | Drawing LR |
| | 116 | Data in the form of pairs of related quantities | Draw axes, select scale and construct a bar chart | Drawing LR |
| | 117 | Data in the form of continuously varying quantities or pairs of related quantities | Draw axes, select scale and plot points and draw line graph | Drawing LR |
| | 118 | A pair of labelled axes, and (a) data (b) points to plot (c) data | Construct (a) bar chart representing data (b) points (c) line graph—as directed | Drawing LR |
| Using scientific symbols and conventions | 121 | Section diagram of assorted objects, and a list of names with some redundancy | Identify the objects by matching names to objects | LR |
| | 122 | A 3-D drawing of an experimental set-up using general lab. apparatus | Make a conventional section drawing | Drawing |
| | 123 | A conventional section drawing of a set-up using general lab. apparatus | Propose names for the components of the set-up | LR |
| | 124 | A 3-D drawing of a circuit | Draw a conventional circuit diagram | Drawing |
| | 125 | A conventional circuit diagram | Propose names for the components of the circuit | LR |

**Mode of response**
CA—Coded answer
LR—Limited written response

# Category 2 : Use of apparatus and measuring instruments

| Subcategory | Q.D. | Given | Outcome | Mode of Response | Mode of Marking |
|---|---|---|---|---|---|
| Using measuring instruments | 201 | Choice of units or description of physical quantities | Select from four or five alternatives | CA | 1 |
| | 202 | Physical quantity measured by a set up instrument | Give a value with units | LR | 1 |
| | 203 | Physical quantity, object or event, and instrument(s) for measuring or observing it | Employ appropriate instrument(s) to: give an answer or give a value with units or leave a measured quantity | LR LR A | 1 1 2 |
| Estimating physical quantities | 211 | Objects or events and units of physical quantities | Give a value | LR | 1 |
| | 212 | Supply of material and an amount specified | Leave or indicate the right amount of material | A | 2 |
| Following instructions for practical work | 221 | Instructions, in the form of a conventional diagram, for setting up apparatus for a stated purpose | Set up apparatus | A | 3 |
| | 222 | Detailed instructions for completing an unfamiliar task | Comply exactly with instructions to complete the task | A LR | 2 1 |
| | 223 | Detailed instructions for completing an unfamiliar task | Comply exactly with instructions to leave a product | A | 2 |
| | 224 | Instructions for task that explicitly refer to standard techniques used in laboratories | Following instructions, using the correct procedures, in order to complete the task | A | 4 |
| | 225 | Instructions for task that require standard techniques used in laboratories | Following instructions, recalling and using the correct procedures, in order to complete the task | A | 4 |

**Mode of response**
CA–Coded answer
LR–Limited written response
A–Action

**Mode of marking**
1 Assess written response
2 Inspect/check quantities at end of test period
3 Inspect each pupil's product during test period
4 Observe pupil and fill in prepared schedule

## Category 3 : Observation

Making and interpreting observations

| Q.D. | Given | Outcome | Mode of Response |
|------|-------|---------|------------------|
| 311 | Objects, photographs or diagrams | a) Group objects into self-defined classes<br>b) Identify rules used to classify the objects and add further objects to classes | Action<br><br>LR |
| 312 | At least two objects, events, photographs or diagrams | Give a specified number of similarities and differences or as many differences as possible | ER |
| 314 | Event | Make a record of change | ER |
| 315 | Objects and drawings, or photographs and drawings | Select the matching drawing | CA |
| 321 | Events | Make a record of observations and give an explanation | ER |
| 322 | Events and a list of explanations | Make a record of changes and select the appropriate explanation(s) | LR<br>+CA |
| 323 | Events | Make a record of changes and make a prediction consistent with the data | LR |
| 324 | a) At least two events, objects, photographs or diagrams<br>b) At least two events or photographs or diagrams and a list of predictions | a) Note the difference and make a prediction consistent with data<br>b) Note differences and select a prediction consistent with the data | LR<br><br>LR<br>+CA |
| 325 | Events | Make a record of changes and identify a pattern in the observed changes | ER |

**Mode of response**
LR —Limited written response
ER —Extended response
CA —Coded answer

# Category 4 : Interpretation and application

## 4i: Interpretation

| Subcategory | Q.D. | Given | Outcome | Mode of Response |
|---|---|---|---|---|
| Interpreting presented information | 401 | Data embodying a pattern, regularity or relationship | Generate a description of the regularity | ER |
| | 402 | Data as in 401 | Generate a description, and use to generate a prediction | ER +LR |
| | 403 | Data as in 401, and a minimum of four predictions | Generate a description and use to select a prediction | ER +CA |
| | 404 | Data as in 401 | Generate a prediction based on a regularity in data | LR |
| | 405 | Data as in 401 and a minimum of four predictions | Select a prediction using regularity in data | CA |
| | 406 | Data as in 401, and a minimum of four 'descriptions' | Select a description of the regularity in data | CA |
| | 407 | Data as in 401 | Generate a prediction and justify it | LR +ER |
| | 408 | Data as in 401, and a minimum of four predictions | Select a prediction and justify the choice | CA +ER |
| Judging the applicability of statements to data | 411 | Equivocal data and a statement (or pair of contradictory statements) | Assess and discuss validity of presented statement in relation to data | ER |
| | 412 | Data and a minimum of four statements | Assess the validity of the statements in relation to data and identify those consistent with it | CA |
| Distinguishing degrees of inference | 421 | A 'snapshot' of an event (in words or line drawing) and five possible accounts of it | Select the account which makes the fewest additional assumptions | CA |

**Mode of response**
ER −Extended response
LR −Limited written response
CA −Coded answer

## 4 ii : Application

| Subcategory | Q.D. | Given | Outcome | Mode of Response |
|---|---|---|---|---|
| Applying science concepts | 430 | Diagrams of stages in a sequence | Re-order according to accepted concepts | LR |
| | 431 | Data | a) Describe a relationship based on data and accepted concepts and use it to generate predictions *or* b) Generate predictions giving reasons based on data and accepted concepts | ER |
| | 432 | Data | Generate predictions based on data and accepted concepts | LR |
| | 433 | Data and a minimum of four predictions | Select a prediction giving reason based on data and accepted concepts | CA +ER |
| | 434 | Data and a minimum of four predictions | Select a prediction based on data and accepted concepts | CA |
| | 435 | Data, description of an event or situation | Give an explanation consistent with the data and accepted concepts | ER |
| | 436 | Data, description of event or situation, and one or more hypothesis/explanation | Assess validity of each hypothesis/explanation in relation to data and accepted concepts | ER |
| | 437 | Data, description of event or situation, and a minimum of four predictions or hypotheses/explanations | Select the best hypothesis/explanation in relation to data and accepted concepts. | CA |
| | 438 | Data, description of event or situation, and a minimum of four hypotheses/explanations | Select all the hypotheses/explanations which are consistent with the data and accepted concepts | CA |
| | 439 | Data and minimum of two predictions | Select one prediction and give reason based on data and accepted concepts | LR +ER |
| Generating alternative hypotheses | 441 | Data, description of event or situation where there is no single obvious explanation | Generate alternative hypotheses/ explanations consistent with data and accepted concepts | ER |

# Category 5: Planning of Investigations

| Subcategory | Q.D. | Given | Focus | Demand/Outcome |
|---|---|---|---|---|
| Identifying or proposing testable statements | 501 | Four or five statements, one of which: a) can be tested scientifically b) cannot be tested scientifically | — | Select the statement which can be tested scientifically Select the one which cannot be tested scientifically |
| | 503 | A general statement of opinion | — | Re-write as a (number of) statement(s), each of which can be tested |
| Planning entire investigations | 521 | A proposition in a testable form | — | *Plan* a procedure to test, resolve or determine the point at issue (taking into account control of variables and selection of equipment) |
| Planning parts of investigations | 515 | A statement of an investigation which may or may not include operational details of how the investigation is to be performed | Variables to be controlled | To select or generate variables in an investigation which should be kept constant, to explain why a certain variable should be kept constant, or to criticise the control of a particular variable |
| | 512 | A statement of an investigation | Variables to be changed (the independent variable) | To select or generate variables in an investigation which should be kept constant (controlled variables) and which should be systematically varied (independent variable) |
| | 516 | A statement of an investigation which contains operational details of how the investigation is to be performed | Variables to be changed (the independent variable) and controlled | To give or select or criticise operational details of the variables in an investigation which should be kept constant (controlled variables) and which should be systematically varied (independent variable) |
| | 514 | A description of a procedure specifying the variables changed (independent variable) and measured (dependent variable) | The problem being investigated | To select a statement of the relationship between dependent and independent variables |
| | 517 | A statement of an investigation with operational details of conditions which should be systematically varied (the independent variable) and, where appropriate, those which should be kept constant (controlled variables) | Operational details concerning the variable to be measured (the dependent variable) | To generate, select or criticise a procedure for measuring the dependent variable |
| | 518 | Describes an investigation, including details of operationalisation of dependent, independent and controlled variables | Procedures which ensure valid measurements of either the dependent or the independent variable | To explain how a given procedure ensures valid measurement procedure or say why it would not ensure validity of measurement |
| | 513 | Describes an investigation with experimental details, including the kind of measurement taken | The use of judgement/measurement in solving a problem | To describe how the measurement taken during the investigations could be used to solve the problem at issue. |

# The list of science concepts and knowledge for pupils aged 13

## Introduction

For the sake of brevity and clarity, in some statements use has been made of words with which the pupils would not necessarily be familiar. Such words are indicated by the use of quotation marks. In addition, certain qualifying statements, which it might not be appropriate to stress to pupils of the age in question, have been included in parentheses.

## Index to concept areas

Concept
areas

**A.  Interaction of living things with their environment**
1.  Interdependence of living things
2.  The physical and chemical environment
3.  Classification of living things
4.  Physical and chemical principles needed to interpret life phenomena

**B.  Living things and their life processes**
1.  The cell
2.  Nutrition
3.  Respiration
4.  Reproduction
5.  Sensitivity and movement

**C.  Force and field**
1.  Movement and deformation
2.  Properties of matter
3.  Forces at a distance
4.  The Earth in space

**D.  Transfer of energy**
1.  Work and energy
2.  Current electricity
3.  'Waves'

**E.  The classification and structure of matter**
1.  States of matter
2.  Pure substance
3.  Metals and non-metals
4.  Acids and bases
5.  Periodic table
6.  Atomic model

**F.  Chemical interactions**
1.  Solutions
2.  Reactivity
3.  Properties of a chemical reaction
4.  Some chemical reactions

## A    Interaction of living things with their environment

### A1    Interdependence of living things

Virtually all organisms are dependent on the presence and activities of other organisms for their survival.

Green plants use energy from the sun to make food by 'photosynthesis'. During this process the oxygen that is used by animals and plants is produced.

Some animals eat plants and some eat other animals, but all animals ultimately depend on green plants for food.

### A2    The physical and chemical environment

Air fills the space around or near the Earth's surface.

Water makes up a large proportion of all living things.

Soil is a mixture that includes rock particles, humus, water and air.

Substances taken from the soil must be replaced to maintain fertility.

Changes in the physical environment due to seasonal cycles are often matched by changes or events in the living world, such as fruiting or mating.

### A3    Classification of living things

There are many different plants and animals which between them show a variety of ways of carrying out life processes.

There are many different ways of grouping living things.

Plants may be distinguished from animals by the way they obtain food and by their cell structure.

Animals are classified into two major groups— invertebrates and vertebrates.

There are five main groups of vertebrates: fish, amphibia, reptiles, birds and mammals.

## A4 Physical and chemical principles needed to interpret life phenomena

The area of its surface affects the gain or loss of energy and matter from an organism or cell.

The ratio of surface area to the mass of an organism is critical for its survival and will reflect its relationship with its environment.

Animals that have a stable body temperature have a number of mechanisms for the control of loss of energy.

## B Living things and their life processes

### B1 The cell

The cell is the basic unit of most living things.

Cells have a nucleus and cell membrane.

Plant cells differ from animal cells in characteristic ways.

An organism may be formed from one or many cells.

Most cells reproduce themselves by division, which leads to growth or, in single-celled organisms, to new individuals.

### B2 Nutrition

All living things need food as a source of energy and of raw materials for growth and reproduction.

Green plants use simple substances from their environment to make their own food.

Animals require protein, fat, carbohydrates, minerals, vitamins and water.

Surplus food is stored as fat or carbohydrate.

All organisms are 'structurally adapted' to the kind of food they need.

All living things produce waste materials in carrying out life processes.

### B3 Respiration

Most living things take in oxygen from their surroundings to be used in the process of respiration.

All living things respire in order to make use of energy stored in food.

In respiration, energy is transferred from food with the release of carbon dioxide.

### B4 Reproduction

Living things produce offspring of the same 'species' as themselves.

Sexual reproduction involves two parents and the offspring will differ from their parents and generally from each other.

Sexual reproduction involves the fusion of two special sex cells, ova (eggs) and sperm or pollen; one cell from each parent.

The life cycle of all organisms repeats itself every generation.

### B5 Sensitivity and movement

All living organisms have means of receiving information from their environment.

In higher animals special organs are concerned with receiving different kinds of 'stimuli'. These are called sense organs.

In humans the senses include sight, touch, hearing, taste and smell.

The response to a 'stimulus' often results in movement.

Voluntary movement in many animals is brought about by contraction of muscles attached to a skeleton.

# C  Force and field

## C1  Movement and deformation

The average speed of an object is found by dividing the distance moved by the time taken.

Forces are necessary to change the motion of an object.

The turning effect of a force about a point is larger when the line of action of the force is further from the point.

Forces are needed to change the shape of an object. The force which an object can stand before breaking depends on its shape as well as the material from which it is made.

If materials recover their original shape after the applied force has been removed, the material is called elastic.

## C2  Properties of matter

Different substances have different masses for equal volume; the mass of a unit volume of a substance is its density.

If the volume of a given mass increases, its density decreases.

Pressure can be decreased by spreading the same force over a larger surface area.

Water tends to flow until its surface reaches a common level.

Particles of a substance are in constant motion. Diffusion of a substance is due to the random motion of individual particles.

Most substances expand as their temperature increases.

Objects completely immersed in a liquid displace a volume of liquid equal to their own volume.

Most liquids rise up into narrow tubes or crevices above the level of an open surface.

## C3  Forces at a distance

Magnets attract and repel other magnets and attract magnetic substances.

The region in which a magnetic effect can be detected is called a magnetic field.

There is a magnetic field surrounding the Earth.

Magnetism is induced in some materials when they are placed in a magnetic field.

An electric current in a coil of wire produces a magnetic field round it.

Some materials can be electrically charged by rubbing them with a different material.

Similarly charged objects repel each other, and oppositely charged objects attract each other. The force between such objects is stronger when the objects are close.

## C4  The Earth in space

The weight of an object on the Earth is the force with which it is attracted to the Earth.

The weight of an object may vary from place to place, but its mass does not change.

The apparent movements of the sun, moon and stars follow a regular pattern.

The Earth spins on its axis; this gives rise to night and day.

The Earth revolves in an orbit around the sun with its axis tilted with respect to this orbit; this accounts for seasonal changes.

The moon orbits the Earth as a natural satellite.

# D  Transfer of energy

## D1  Work and energy

There is a variety of sources of energy such as fuels (including food), other chemicals, deformed springs, capacitors and objects at a height.

Energy can be changed from one form to another but can never be created or destroyed.

Moving objects have energy which is transferred elsewhere when they are stopped.

The hotter a substance is, the more energy its particles have.

Different substances conduct heat at different rates.

## D2  Current electricity

A complete circuit of conducting material is needed for a steady current to flow between the terminals of a battery of a d.c. power supply.

Some materials conduct electricity better than others. Bad conductors are known as insulators.

## D3  'Waves'

Objects are seen because of the light they give out or reflect.

Light travels (in a uniform medium) in straight paths or rays.

Sound can be heard when objects vibrate in a 'medium'.

Sound requires a medium for its transmission.

# E  The classification and structure of matter

## E1  States of matter

In general a substance can be classified either as a solid or a liquid or a gas.

The behaviour of substances can be explained if it is assumed that matter is made of minute particles.

Solids have a definite shape and volume. They behave as if their particles are closely packed and held together.

Liquids have a definite volume and surface but no fixed shape. They behave as if their particles are closely packed but free to move.

Gases have no definite volume or shape. They behave as if their particles are free to move independently of each other.

A change in state does not involve a change in the chemical composition of the substance.

Changes of state caused by heating can be reversed by cooling and vice versa.

Changes of state always involve a transfer of energy.

## E2  Pure substance

A pure substance may be obtained from a mixture using one of several techniques, including evaporation, distillation, chromatography and filtration.

A pure substance is recognised by its characteristic chemical and physical properties (at STP) eg m.p., b.p., density and behaviour with other substances.

Pure substances may be classified into elements and compounds.

## E3  Metals and non-metals

Materials can be classified into groups in many different ways. One way is by sorting into metals and non-metals.

In general, metals can be distinguished from non-metals by their characteristic physical properties. These include high m.p. b.p., shiny appearance and conduction of heat and electricity.

Another way of distinguishing metals from non-metals is by their characteristic properties. These may include the nature of the oxide.

Some metals do not exhibit all these characteristic properties.

## E4  Acids and bases

Compounds can be classified into groups by their different properties. Acids and bases are two such groups.

Acids and bases have a characteristic effect on the colour of indicators.

Bases which are soluble in water are called alkalis.

In aqueous solution the degree of acidity depends on the substance.

The degree of acidity is expressed on a pH scale from 0 to 14.

A neutral solution has a pH value of 7; acidic solutions have pH values less than 7 and alkaline solutions pH values above 7.

## E5  Periodic table

Families of elements with similar chemical behaviour can be identified.

## E6  Atomic model

The atom is the smallest, characteristic uncharged particle of an element.


# F  Chemical interactions

## F1  Solutions

Some substances dissolve in water; others do not, but may dissolve in other liquids.

A liquid which will dissolve a substance to form a solution is called a solvent.

The substance which dissolves in the liquid is called a solute.

At a given temperature and pressure, the mass of solute which will dissolve in a given volume of solvent is limited and fixed.

For most solids solubility increases with increasing temperature.


## F2  Reactivity

A more reactive element can be used to extract a less reactive element from one of its ores or compounds.

The reactions of metals with water or dilute acid may be used to place them in a reactivity series.


## F3  Properties of a chemical reaction

A chemical reaction occurs when one or more different substances are formed from one or more original substances.

Most chemical reactions are initiated by an input of energy.

The total mass of reacting substances in any chemical reaction is the same as the total mass of products.


## F4  Some chemical reactions

On heating some compounds change colour due to loss of water. Often these changes are easily reversed.

When elements react with oxygen only they usually form oxides; this is an example of an oxidation reaction.

When a compound changes by losing oxygen, this is an example of a reduction reaction.

The oxidation of a metal by atmospheric oxygen is an example of corrosion.

Fuels such as coal and oil are formed by the gradual decay of plant remains under high pressure.

Large amounts of energy can be transferred from these fuels when they react with oxygen. This is an example of a combustion reaction.

# The fixed test ('Using measuring instruments')

<u>About this 'circus'</u>

This is a practical test.    Sometimes you will use science
apparatus, and sometimes other simple equipment.

The things you will need have been set out for you at nine
<u>stations</u> in a <u>circus</u>.  It is called a circus because,
wherever you start, you will move round so that you visit
all the stations in turn.
The supervisor will tell you when you are to move.
By the end of the test, you will have visited every
station.

In some questions, you may be told to use the letter on your
lapel badge.

Write your letter
in this space ➡ [          ]

> If you need help to read a question, put up
> your hand.
> Read every question carefully and be sure
> to follow the instructions given.

Station (1)

How long is this page? | 29.7 cm

a)  How much water is there in the measuring cylinder?

b)  How big is the force with which the rubber bands
     pull on the hook?

c)  What is the pressure of the gas at this gas-point?

d)  What is the temperature of the water in the flask?

e)  How long had the stop-clock been running before
     it was stopped? (It started at zero)

f)  Press the push-button to switch on the current.
     Read the current through the circuit on the ammeter.

g)  Press the push-button again.   Read the voltmeter.

h)  What is the mass of the object X?

i)  What is the length of the stick fixed to the rule?

Scale Readings

Station ②

a) Use the ruler to find out how much the spring stretches when you hang the load  X  on the end.

Stretch (extra length) . . . . . . . . . . . .

> *Take the load off the spring and leave it on the bench.*

b) Use the forcemeter to measure the force needed to lift the parcel marked 'P'.

Force needed . . . . . . . . . . .

> *When you have finished leave the forcemeter on the bench.*

c) Use the measuring cylinder to find out how much water the beaker will hold, up to the ring marked on its side.

Volume of water . . . . . . . . . . .

> *Leave the beaker and cylinder empty when you have finished.*

d) Use the stop clock to find out for how long the light stays on during one flash.

Time . . . . . . . . . . . . .

> *Set the stop clock back to zero when you have finished.*

Measuring

Station ③

> *This question is to find out how well you can use the kind of apparatus you measure things with.*

a)  Cut off a length of paper tape 47.3 cm long.
    Put it in the envelope which has your letter on it,
    and leave it on one side.

b)  Measure out 55 cm³ of water as accurately as you can and
    pour it into the small plastic beaker.  Put the beaker
    to one side.

c)  Put the plastic bag which has your letter on it on the
    balance to protect the pan.  Put on to it 68 g of plasticine.
    Be as accurate as you can.  Put the plasticine into the
    plastic bag and leave it on one side.

d)  Put the metal can with your letter on it on the balance,
    and put into it 82 g of sand.
    Leave the sand in the can  and put it on one side.

Deliver

Station ④

a) What is the temperature of the water in the beaker? . . . . . . . . . .

b) What is the volume of one of the marbles? . . . . . . . . . . . .

c) Pull the pendulum bob about 5 cm to one side and release it so that it swings freely to and fro.

   How long does the bob take to make one complete to and fro  movement?

   . . . . . . . . . . . .

Tech-check

215

a)  Use the magnifying glass to help you see what there is inside the circle on the card labelled A.
    Copy down what you see in the space below:

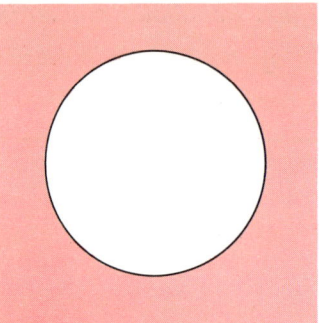

b)  The slide labelled B has been put on the stage of the microscope, which is almost ready to use.  All you have to do is to focus it. When you have done this, copy down in the space below exactly what you can see on the slide through the microscope.

Move the stage of the microscope down, away from the lens. Remove the slide and put it carefully back in its box.

c)  Put slide C on the microscope stage, and get it in focus. Move the slide around until the letters are in the middle of what you can see.    Copy them down in the space below.

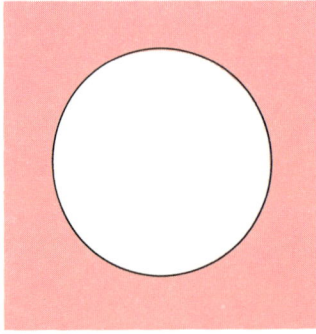

Lenses

Station (6)

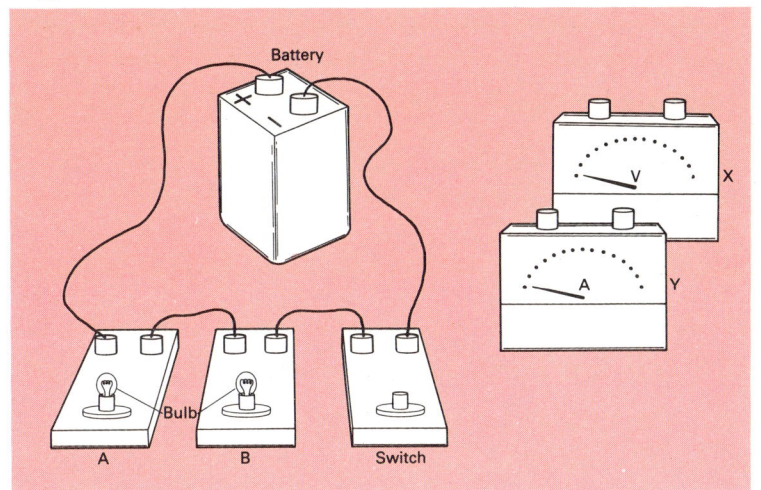

The circuit shown above is set up on the bench.
You are also given two meters labelled X and Y.

a)  Choose which meter will measure electric <u>current</u> and tick the box below:

Meter X [    ]          Meter Y [    ]

b)  Connect the meter in the circuit and measure the current.

Current is . . . . . . . . . . . . . . . . . . . . . . . . . . . . .

┌─────────────────────────────────────────────────────────────┐
│ *When you have done this, ask the supervisor to check your circuit.* │
└─────────────────────────────────────────────────────────────┘

Take out the meter you have just used.

c)  Choose  which meter will measure <u>voltage</u> (potential difference) and tick
the box below:

Meter X [    ]          Meter Y [    ]

d)  Connect the meter across bulb A and measure the voltage across bulb A.

Voltage is . . . . . . . . . . . . . . . . . . . . . . . . . . . . .

┌─────────────────────────────────────────────────────────────┐
│ *When you have done this, ask the supervisor to check your circuit.* │
└─────────────────────────────────────────────────────────────┘

┌─────────────────────────────────────────────────────────────┐
│ *When the supervisor has checked your circuits, disconnect the meter* │
│ *and put everything back as it was when you started.* │
└─────────────────────────────────────────────────────────────┘

Amvocirc

Station ⑦

> *You have been given five different liquids in bottles*
> *labelled P, Q, R, S and X.   Liquid X is the same as*
> *one of the others.*
> *Follow these instructions to find out which liquid*
> *is the same as X.*

a) First test liquids P, Q, R and S against each other:

Put liquid P into the first three test tubes to a depth of about 2 cm.

(You can use the special pencil to label them as you go).

Add an equal volume of liquid Q to the first tube, liquid R to the second and liquid S to the third.

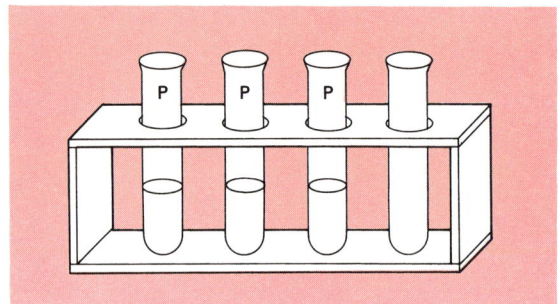

Record the results in the last column.

| Test tube | Liquid put in first | Liquid added | Results (if any) |
|---|---|---|---|
| 1 | P | Q | |
| 2 | P | R | |
| 3 | P | S | |

Carry on like this:

Put liquid Q into the next two test tubes:  add R to the first of these and S to the second.   Fill in the table as you go.

| Test tube | Liquid put in first | Liquid added | Results (if any) |
|---|---|---|---|
| 4 | Q | R | |
| 5 | Q | S | |

Put liquid R into the last test tube, add S to it, and complete the table.

| Test tube | Liquid put in first | Liquid added | Results (if any) |
|---|---|---|---|
| 6 | R | S | |

/continued on next page

b) <u>Now test the unknown liquid X.</u>

To do this, use four clean test tubes, and put in four new samples of P, Q, R and S, to a depth of about 2 cm.

Add an equal volume of X to each one.

Put the results in the table below:

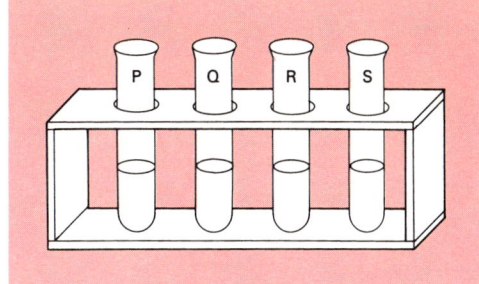

| Liquids | Results (if any) |
|---------|------------------|
| P and X | |
| Q and X | |
| R and X | |
| S and X | |

Which liquid do you think is the same as X? (tick one box)

P ☐          Q ☐          R ☐          S ☐

*Put all your used test tubes
in the container provided.*

Mystery Liquid (continued)

Station ⑧

In this question, you are not allowed to use
a measuring instrument. Instead, you are to
estimate (make your own best guess at) the
answer.

a)   How much coloured water is there in the plastic box C?

. . . . . . . . . . cm$^3$

b)   What is the area of the green paper leaf L?

. . . . . . . . . . cm$^2$

c)   How long is the wire that makes the circle?

. . . . . . . . . . cm

d)   What is the mass of the object G ?

. . . . . . . . . . g

e)   How much water is there in the tube T?

. . . . . . . . . . cm$^3$

f)   What is the temperature of the water in the flask?
     (It is safe to put your finger in it)

. . . . . . . . . . °C

g)   How long is the wooden rod?

. . . . . . . . . . cm

h)   Pull the elastic band to the line on the board
     marked E.   How much force is needed?

. . . . . . . . . . N

i)   What is the area of the top of the tube T?

. . . . . . . . . . cm$^2$

j)   What is the mass of the circle of wire?

. . . . . . . . . . g

k)   How many seconds do the wheels and axle take to roll
     down from the white line to the yellow one?

     (See the instructions with the apparatus)

Estimating

. . . . . . . . . . s

Station ⑨

a)  Cut off a length of tape 50 cm long.
    Put it in the envelope which has your letter on it,
    and set the envelope to one side.

b)  Take a plastic bag with your letter on it.
    Put 100 grams of dried beans in it. Seal the bag
    and 'post' it in the box provided.

c)  Take the other plastic bag with your letter on it.
    Put 100 grams of porridge oats in it. Seal it and
    post it in the same box.

d)  Take the beaker with your letter on it.
    Put 100 cm$^3$ of water into it from the tap.
    Put the beaker and water carefully into the
    box provided.

e)  Draw a line 11 cm long in the space below.
    You may use the 'straight edge' to help you.

Roundabout

# The 'scale readings' probe and unit codes

(a) How much water is there in the measuring cylinder?

    reading . . . . . . . . . .

    units    . . . . . . . . . .

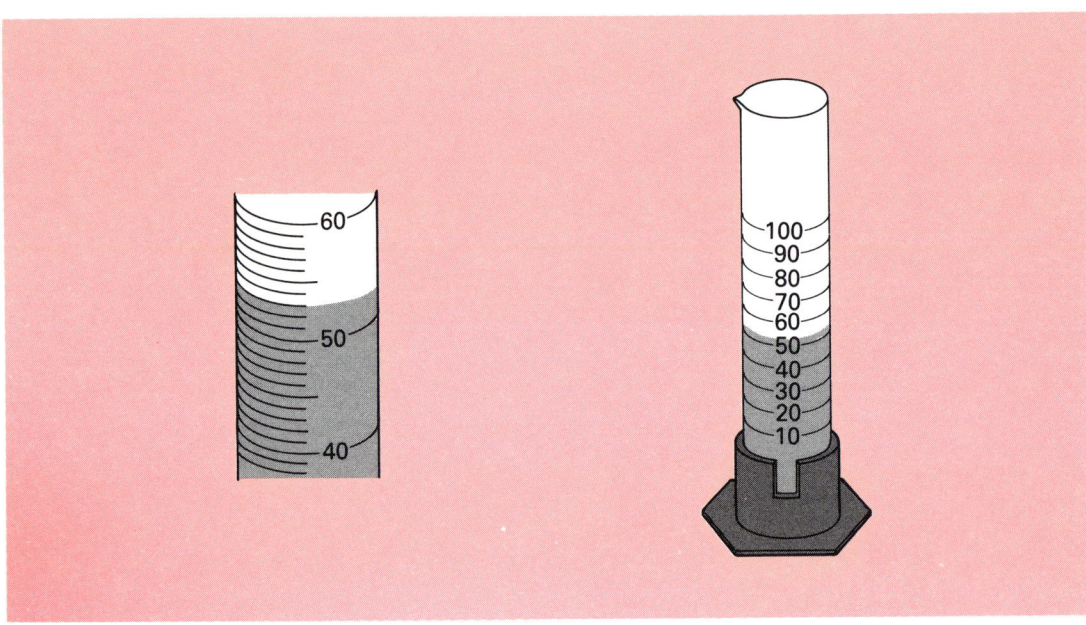

(b) What is the reading on the forcemeter?

    reading . . . . . . . . . .

    units    . . . . . . . . . .

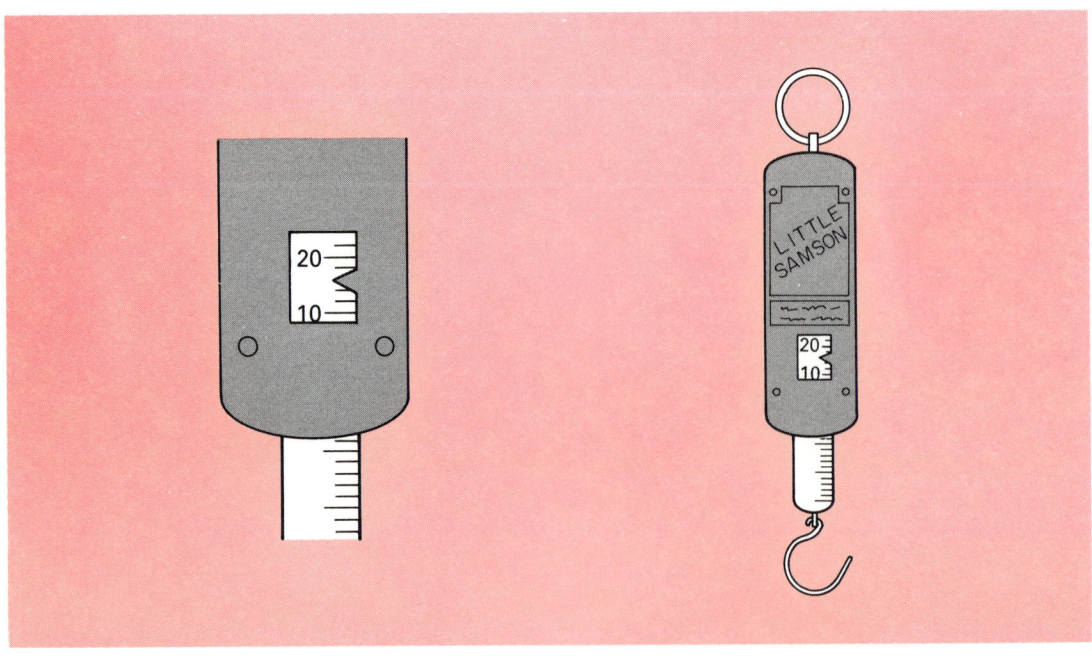

(c) What is the reading on the balance?

reading . . . . . . . . . .

units      . . . . . . . . . .

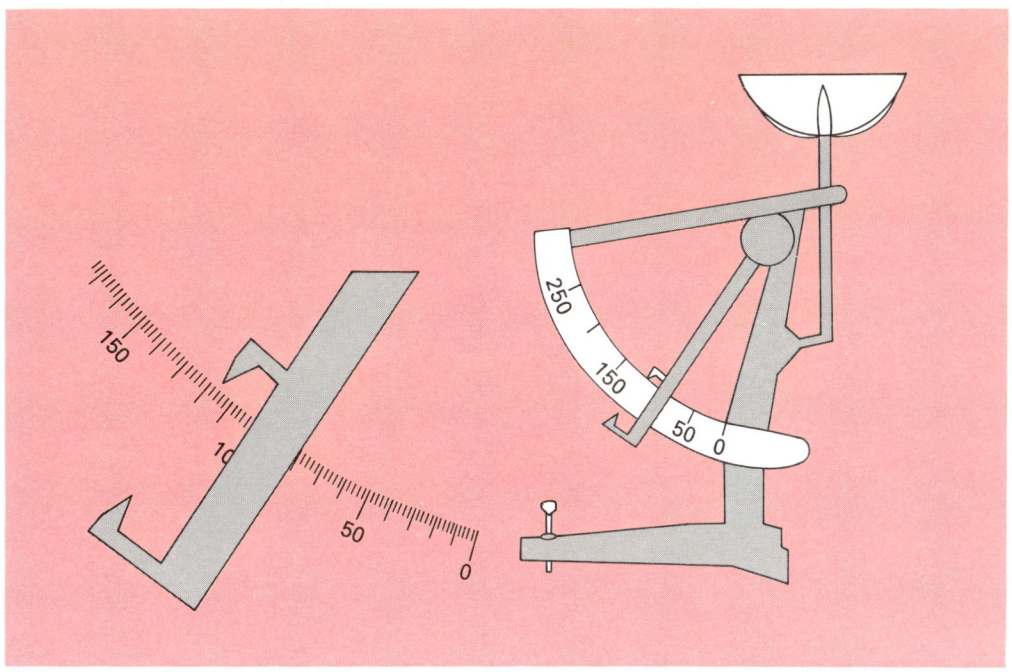

(d) What is the reading on the manometer?

reading . . . . . . . . . .

units      . . . . . . . . . .

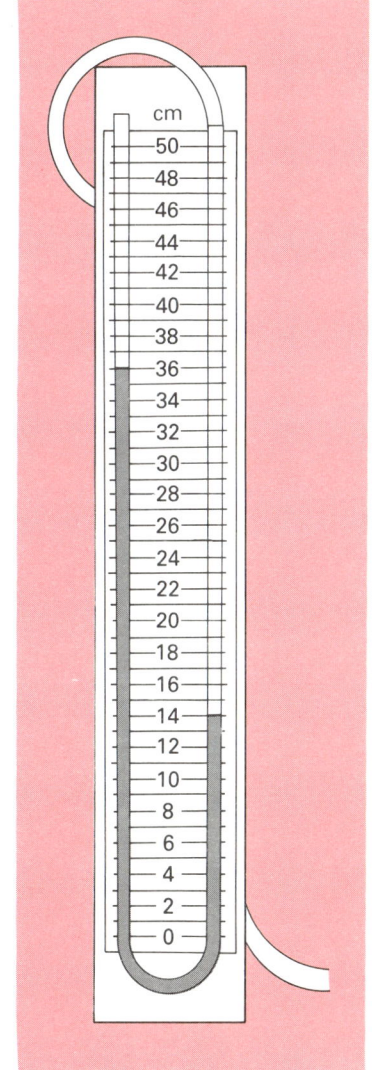

(e) What is the length of the rod?

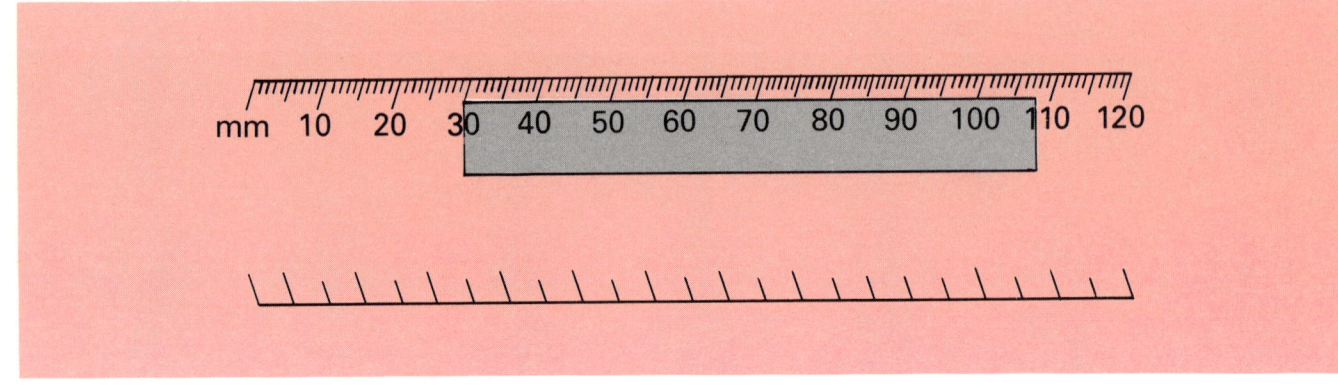

reading . . . . . . . . . .          units . . . . . . . . . .

(f) What is the temperature of the water in the flask?

reading . . . . . . . . . .

units     . . . . . . . . . .

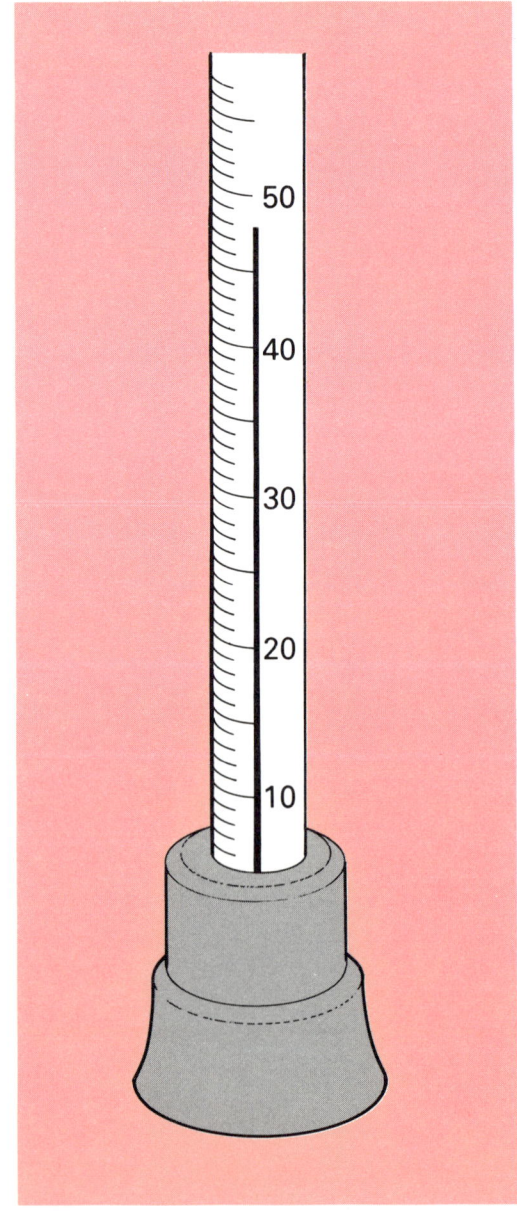

(g) How long had the stop-clock been running before it was stopped?
(It started at zero.)

reading . . . . . . . . . .

units . . . . . . . . . .

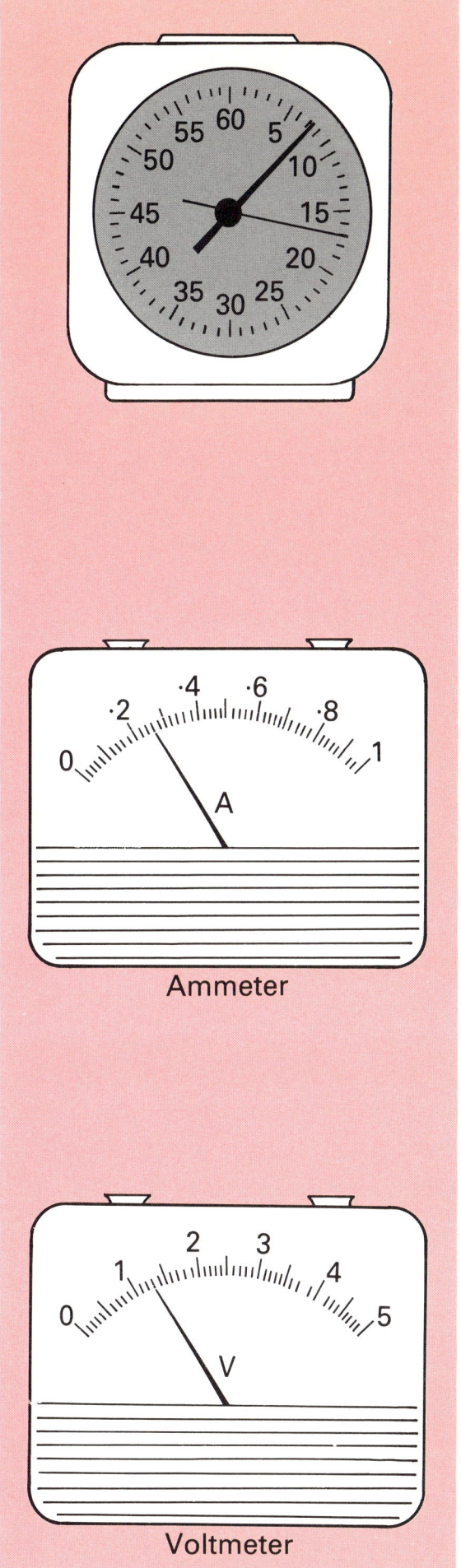

(h) What is the reading on the ammeter?

reading . . . . . . . . . .

units . . . . . . . . . .

Ammeter

(i) What is the reading on the voltmeter?

reading . . . . . . . . . .

units . . . . . . . . . .

Voltmeter

(j)  What is the reading on the syringe?

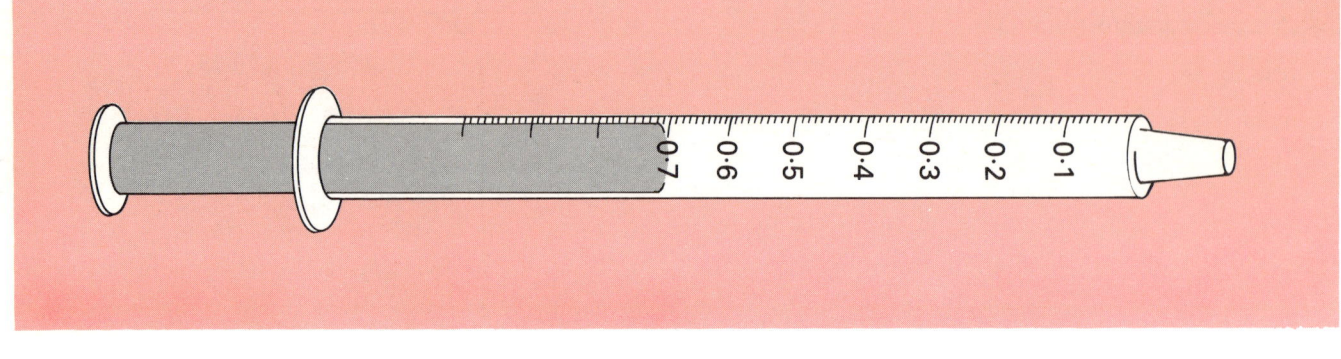

reading . . . . . . . . .                    units . . . . . . . . .

(k)  What is the reading on this syringe?

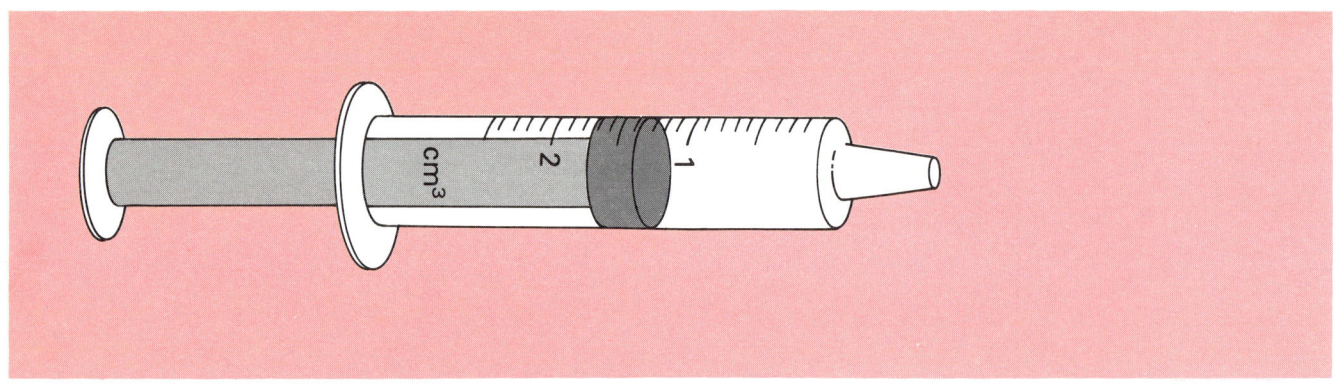

reading . . . . . . . . .                    units . . . . . . . . .

# Planning: further details

## Example A8.1 'Waterlevel' (1)
Mean score = 30 per cent

A group of pupils were investigating how quickly water flowed out from a container with a jet.

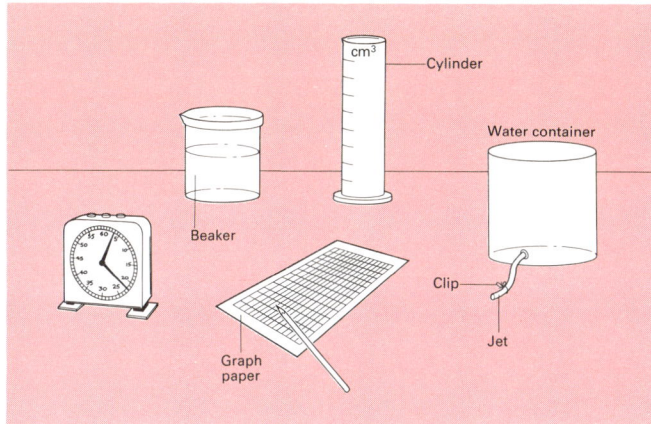

They wanted to find out <u>what difference the level of the water inside the container made to how quickly the water came out of the jet.</u>

This was what they did:

● They filled the container up to the point where the jet started.

● They measured how much water they had added.

What other measurements should they make to find out what difference the level of the water inside the container made to how quickly the water came out of the jet?

....................................................................

....................................................................

....................................................................

....................................................................

## Table A8.1 Results for 'Waterlevel' (1)

| Response | % pupils |
|---|---|
| Sufficient number of readings (3) and covering the full range | 14 |
| Sufficient number of readings stated plus the need for a reliable answer | 10 |
| Sufficient number of readings only | 40 |
| Less than three readings suggested | 8 |
| More than ten readings suggested | 2 |
| Number of readings unspecified | 10 |
| Controls stated | 2 |
| No response | 14 |

## Example A8.2 'Waterlevel' (2)
Mean score = 2 per cent

A group of pupils were investigating how quickly water flowed out from a container with a jet. The container was 35 cm high and had a volume of 1,500 cm$^3$.

*The illustration in Example A8.1 also applies to this example. It has been omitted from here to economise on space.*

They wanted to find out <u>what difference the level of the water inside the container made to how quickly the water came out of the jet.</u>

This was their experiment:

● They filled the container up to the point where water just started to drip out.

● They added a further 25 cm$^3$ of water.

● They timed how long it took to flow out.

● They repeated the experiment using 50 cm$^3$, 75 cm$^3$, 100 cm$^3$ and 125 cm$^3$ of water.

● They timed how long each volume took to flow out.

What do you think of the measurements they have decided to take? Do you think their results will tell them if the level of the water made a difference? Give the reason for your answer.

....................................................................

....................................................................

## Table A8.2 Results for 'Waterlevel' (2)

| Response | % pupils |
|---|---|
| Criticism: Volume intervals too small to judge | 1 |
| correct Range insufficient | 2 |
| Criticised the dependent variable | 1 |
| Criticised the experimental set up | 4 |
| Level makes no difference | 9 |
| Suggests an explanation | 26 |
| Criticised whole investigation | 1 |
| General statement (not fair test) | 1 |
| No explanation offered for criticism | 1 |
| Uncritical: measurement satisfactory | 2 |
| general statement | 12 |
| no explanation | 4 |
| States answer | 15 |
| Incomprehensible | 4 |
| No response | 18 |

**Example A8.3** *Cars*

A team of scientists were testing cars to find out if the distance a car took to stop in (the braking distance) was affected by the mass of the car.

They used three cars with different loads to find this out.

If it is to be a fair test they should be careful to keep some things the same for each car in case they make a different to the results. Suggest three things that should be the same:

(1) ...........................................................................................................

...........................................................................................................

(2) ...........................................................................................................

...........................................................................................................

(3) ...........................................................................................................

...........................................................................................................

Cars      B 5044      QD 515

                                              Score

Score 1 for each acceptable variable which needs to be controlled
eg, speed
      force on the brake pedal
      road surface, etc.

                                      Maximum ③

**Table A8.3** *Results for three questions—'Car range', 'Sweets range', 'Salty water range'*

**Cars range**

| Response | % pupils |
|---|---|
| Criticism: Measurement intervals too small | 1 |
| correct      Range insufficient | 2 |
| Criticises whole investigation | 12 |
| General statement (not a fair test) | 1 |
| No explanation offered for criticism | |
| Uncritical:  measurement satisfactory | 6 |
|            general statement | 11 |
|            no explanation | 1 |
| States answer or explains the outcome | 60 |
| Incomprehensible | 1 |
| No response | 5 |

**Sweets range**

| Response | % pupils |
|---|---|
| A greater number of readings needed | 35 |
| General statement (more readings needed) | 3 |
| Criticised the dependent variable | 2 |
| Criticised the experimental set-up | 2 |
| Criticised whole investigation | 5 |
| No explanation offered | 10 |
| Uncritical: | 18 |
|           no explanation | 8 |
|           states answer or explains outcome | 12 |
|           no response | 5 |

**Salty water range**

| Response | % pupils |
|---|---|
| Criticism:  time intervals too small | 1 |
|           cooling intervals too short | 1 |
|           need a longer cooling period and larger intervals | 2 |
| Criticised experimental set-up | 4 |
| Criticised whole investigation | 1 |
| General statement (critical) | 1 |
| Uncritical—measurement satisfactory | 4 |
| General statement (experiment satisfactory) | 28 |
| No explanation | 3 |
| States answer or explains outcome | 35 |
| Incomprehensible | 8 |
| No response | 12 |

## Example A8.4  'Ice shape'

A pupil plans an experiment to see if ice melts more quickly when it is put in water than when it is left in air.

This is what he did:

- Put one block of ice in a large beaker of water
- Put another block of ice out in the air
- Saw which block was the first to melt completely

He decided that to make it a fair test one of the things he would have to keep the same was the shape of the blocks.


Do you agree with him?

...........................................................

Explain your answer.

...........................................................

...........................................................

...........................................................

...........................................................

## Table A8.4  *Results for 'Ice shape'*

| Response | % pupils |
| --- | --- |
| **Explanation given for controlling the shape** | |
| The larger the block the slower it melts or the smaller the quicker | 34 |
| The larger the block the quicker it melts | 1 |
| Increased mass increases the time of melting | 1 |
| One shape is easier to melt than another | 1 |
| The greater the surface area the quicker it melts | 2 |
| The greater the surface area the slower it melts | 1 |
| Shape affects surface area | 1 |
| Size main theme: <br> eg   size affects the volume <br>        thin bits would melt quicker | 4 |
| Shape main theme: <br> eg   different shapes will give different volumes <br>        different shapes will give different weights | 10 |
| Other variables stated | 2 |
| General statement (will affect results) | 9 |
| No explanation | 3 |
| **Disagree that shape needs to be controlled** | |
| eg   size does not matter | 2 |
| mass not shape important | 10 |
| shape does not matter as long as the size and volume are the same | 10 |
| water and air temperature alone matter | 2 |
| size matters not shape | 1 |
| No explanation | 3 |
| States answer or explains outcome | 3 |
| Incomprehensible | 3 |
| No response | 3 |

# Additional information

## Introduction to practical testing

### *Chemical*

#### General points

— Pupil's name.

— Introduce who you are and why you are there.

— Explain how the pupil is involved and the school— (random selection) therefore by chance.

— Explain that it is a test of 13 year olds and not of individuals or their schools—so only a number goes on the form.

#### Aim of test

*We're interested in how people solve problems. There are lots of different ways of solving problems and it's how each individual decides to tackle a problem that we are interested in.*

*In particular we're interested to see if people solve problems scientifically.*

*By that we mean doing some practical work to collect accurate results on which to base the answer to the problem, so that the answer is a reliable one and not just (pupils' name)'s opinion. Is it clear what I mean?*

*You'll have two problems to look at in the test. You will have plenty of time to do each one and to think about what to do so don't think you have to rush. I will ask you some questions at the end and I will be taking notice of what you do as you go along.*

#### Introduction to the individual problem

*This is the problem I would like you to think about now.*

*Read it through to yourself carefully.*

Check that pupils can read (covertly!)
Read it with them if there are any problems.

Stress—*The main part of the problem is in the box.*

Read the contents of the box through with them.

*What do you have to find out?*

Check that the pupil mentions both the temperature and how broken up the chemical is.

Remind them of the two parts to the problem if they do not mention it.

#### Introduction to the apparatus

*What has been put out here has been chosen because it might be helpful. If anything is not helpful then you just ignore it. It is up to you to choose what you want to use. You do not have to use anything that's no help to you okay?*

— *This is the chemical I want you to investigate; you can use as much as you need to.*

— *You have got cold water in the container and hot water in the kettle. The hot water can be mixed with cold if you want to change how hot it is.*

— *You have two measuring cylinders if you want to measure volume.*

— *You have a clock if you want to time anything—it's green for go, red for stop and white for back to zero.*

— *You have a thermometer if you want to measure temperature.*

*You have:*

● *Five beakers if you want to use them.*

● *Stirring rods and spatula.*

● *A towel to mop up with if anything spills.*

*Is there anything you want to ask me about the apparatus?*

**Method of working**

*Now remember you choose what you want to do and what you want to use. It is up to you and it is what you decide to do that I am interested in.*

*You can change your mind if you want to and if something goes wrong so you have to start again it doesn't matter.*

*Remember to work carefully and scientifically so that your answer is a reliable one at the end.*

**Pupil record**

*Write your results or whatever you have taken particular notice of here (pointing)—not your method as I will be taking note of that.*

*Then here I would like you to explain what you have found out about what difference the temperature and how broken up the chemicals is makes to how long it fizzes for.*

**Table A9.1**   *Controls overall: the proportion of pupils exercising control of variables*

| % pupils | Paper Towel | Survival | Woodlice | Cars | Hot Wash | Swingboard |
|---|---|---|---|---|---|---|
| 100 | | | | | | |
| 90 | | | | | Detergent | |
| 80 | | | | | | Board release |
| | Water | Fastening fabric | | Initial treatment | | |
| 70 | | | No. of lice | End posn. Start posn. | Vol. water | |
| | Paper | | Damp | | | |
| 60 | | Can | { Area { Darkness | | Cloth size | |
| 50 | Soaking | | | | | |
| | | Cooling Vol. water | Posn. of lice | | | Amplitude |
| 40 | | | | | Timing Agitation | |
| | | Temperature | | | | |
| 30 | | | Timing | | Cloth dirt | |
| 20 | | | | | | |
| | Dripping | | | | Stirring | |
| 10 | | | | | | |
| 0 | | | | | | |

When you eat certain sweets they dissolve in your mouth and fizz.
They do the same thing in water.

This is what you have to find out:

> *What makes the difference to how long
> the sweets last for?*
>
> *Is it how hot or cold the water is
> or how much the sweet is broken up?*

You can use any of the things in front of you. Choose whatever
you need to answer the question.

(a) Make a clear record of your results here so that someone else can
understand what you have found out.

(b) Write your answer here.

..................................................................................................

..................................................................................................

..................................................................................................

..................................................................................................

# SWEETS

**Pupil Number** ☐☐☐☐☐  **Girl** ☐  **Boy** ☐

| | | 1 | 2 | 3 | 4 | 5 | 6 | 7 | 8 | 9 | 10 |
|---|---|---|---|---|---|---|---|---|---|---|---|
| **SURFACE AREA** | Surface area varied—whole | | | | | | | | | | |
| | —$\frac{1}{2}$ size | | | | | | | | | | |
| | —$\frac{1}{4}$ size | | | | | | | | | | |
| | —$<\frac{1}{4}$ size | | | | | | | | | | |
| | —crushed | | | | | | | | | | |
| | Temperature of water used—>80°C | | | | | | | | | | |
| | —60–80°C | | | | | | | | | | |
| | —40–59°C | | | | | | | | | | |
| | —20–39°C | | | | | | | | | | |
| **TEMPERATURE** | Temperature varied—>80°C | | | | | | | | | | |
| | —60–80°C | | | | | | | | | | |
| | —40–59°C | | | | | | | | | | |
| | —20–39°C | | | | | | | | | | |
| | Temperature measured | | | | | | | | | | |
| | Surface area tested—whole ● | | | | | | | | | | |
| | —$\frac{1}{2}$ size ◗ | | | | | | | | | | |
| | —$\frac{1}{4}$ size ◤ | | | | | | | | | | |
| | —$<\frac{1}{4}$ size | | | | | | | | | | |
| | —crushed | | | | | | | | | | |
| **SET UP** | Random/no variable varied | | | | | | | | | | |
| | Mass constant within ±10% for S.A. test | | | | | | | | | | |
| | Mass constant within ±10% for temperature test | | | | | | | | | | |
| | Volume of water measured—by eye | | | | | | | | | | |
| | —by jug/beaker | | | | | | | | | | |
| | Volume used—<10 cm³ | | | | | | | | | | |
| | —10–25 cm³ | | | | | | | | | | |
| | —>25–50 cm³ | | | | | | | | | | |
| | —>50 cm³ | | | | | | | | | | |
| | Volume constant within ±10% for—S.A. test | | | | | | | | | | |
| | —temperature test | | | | | | | | | | |
| | Stirred consistently | | | | | | | | | | |
| **MEASUREMENTS** | No apparent measurement | | | | | | | | | | |
| | Mixed measurement method | | | | | | | | | | |
| | Qualitative comparison | | | | | | | | | | |
| | Clock used | | | | | | | | | | |
| | Within ±3 s of starting point | | | | | | | | | | |
| | Within ±3 s of end point | | | | | | | | | | |
| | Timed—until end of fizzing | | | | | | | | | | |
| | —until all dissolved | | | | | | | | | | |
| | —until end of 'noise' | | | | | | | | | | |
| | (Note at the side) Other method | | | | | | | | | | |
| | Generalisation | | | | | | | | | | |
| | Reason for repeat | | | | | | | | | | |

**Controls**

Volume ☐

Mass ☐

Stirring ☐

233

When certain chemicals are placed in water they fizz and bubbles of gas are formed.

This is what you have to find out:

> *What makes the difference to how long the chemical lasts for?*
>
> *Is it how hot or cold the water is or how much the chemical is broken up?*

You can use any of the things in front of you. Choose whatever you need to answer the question.

(a)  Make a clear record of your results here so that someone else can understand what you have found out.

(b)  Write your answer here.

.............................................................................................

.............................................................................................

.............................................................................................

.............................................................................................

# CHEMICAL

**Pupil Number** ☐☐☐☐☐  **Girl** ☐  **Boy** ☐

| | 1 | 2 | 3 | 4 | 5 | 6 | 7 | 8 | 9 | 10 |
|---|---|---|---|---|---|---|---|---|---|---|
| **SURFACE AREA** Surface area varied—whole | | | | | | | | | | |
| —$\frac{1}{2}$ size | | | | | | | | | | |
| —$\frac{1}{4}$ size | | | | | | | | | | |
| —$<\frac{1}{4}$ size | | | | | | | | | | |
| —crushed | | | | | | | | | | |
| Temperature of water used—>80°C | | | | | | | | | | |
| —60–80°C | | | | | | | | | | |
| —40–59°C | | | | | | | | | | |
| —20–39°C | | | | | | | | | | |
| **TEMPERATURE** Temperature varied—>80°C | | | | | | | | | | |
| —60–80°C | | | | | | | | | | |
| —40–59°C | | | | | | | | | | |
| —20–39°C | | | | | | | | | | |
| Temperature measured | | | | | | | | | | |
| Surface area tested—whole ● | | | | | | | | | | |
| —$\frac{1}{2}$ size ◗ | | | | | | | | | | |
| —$\frac{1}{4}$ size ◣ | | | | | | | | | | |
| —$<\frac{1}{4}$ size | | | | | | | | | | |
| —crushed | | | | | | | | | | |
| **SET UP** Random/no variable varied | | | | | | | | | | |
| Mass constant within ±10% for S.A. test | | | | | | | | | | |
| Mass constant within ±10% for temperature test | | | | | | | | | | |
| Volume of water measured—by eye | | | | | | | | | | |
| —by jug/beaker | | | | | | | | | | |
| Volume used—<10 cm³ | | | | | | | | | | |
| —10–25 cm³ | | | | | | | | | | |
| —>25–50 cm³ | | | | | | | | | | |
| —>50 cm³ | | | | | | | | | | |
| Volume constant within ±10% for—S.A. test | | | | | | | | | | |
| —temperature test | | | | | | | | | | |
| Stirred consistently | | | | | | | | | | |
| **MEASUREMENTS** No apparent measurement | | | | | | | | | | |
| Mixed measurement method | | | | | | | | | | |
| Qualitative comparison | | | | | | | | | | |
| Clock used | | | | | | | | | | |
| Within ±3 s of starting point | | | | | | | | | | |
| Within ±3 s of end point | | | | | | | | | | |
| Timed—until end of fizzing | | | | | | | | | | |
| —until all dissolved | | | | | | | | | | |
| —until end of 'noise' | | | | | | | | | | |
| (Note at the side) Other method | | | | | | | | | | |
| Generalisation | | | | | | | | | | |
| Reason for repeat | | | | | | | | | | |

**Controls**

Volume ☐

Mass ☐

Stirring ☐

235

When you hang a load on a spring and let go it bobs up and down. The load bobs up and down faster on some springs than others.

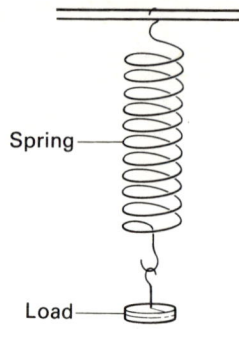

Spring

Load

You have been given a collection of different springs. This is what you have to find out:

> *What makes the difference to how quickly a load bobs up and down on a spring?*
>
> *Is it the <u>length</u> of the spring or the <u>diameter</u> of the spring?*

You can use any of the things in front of you. Choose whatever you need to answer the question.

(a)  Make a clear record of your results here so that someone else can understand what you have found out.

(b)  Write your answer here.

. . . . . . . . . . . . . . . . . . . . . . . . . . . . . . . . . . . . . . . . . . . . . . . . . . . . . . . . . . . . . . . . . . . . . . . . . . . . . . . . . . . . . . . . . .

. . . . . . . . . . . . . . . . . . . . . . . . . . . . . . . . . . . . . . . . . . . . . . . . . . . . . . . . . . . . . . . . . . . . . . . . . . . . . . . . . . . . . . . . . .

. . . . . . . . . . . . . . . . . . . . . . . . . . . . . . . . . . . . . . . . . . . . . . . . . . . . . . . . . . . . . . . . . . . . . . . . . . . . . . . . . . . . . . . . . .

. . . . . . . . . . . . . . . . . . . . . . . . . . . . . . . . . . . . . . . . . . . . . . . . . . . . . . . . . . . . . . . . . . . . . . . . . . . . . . . . . . . . . . . . . .

# SPRING LOAD

## LENGTH
Record the sequence of springs used (include springs that are re-used)

|  | Diameter |  |  |
|---|---|---|---|
|  | Fat | Medium | Thin |
| Long |  |  |  |
| Medium |  |  |  |
| Short |  |  |  |

## DIAMETER

## SET UP
Load used:
1.   2.   3.   4.
5.   6.   7.   8.
9.   10.

## MEASUREMENT

## TIMING

## COUNTING

| | 1 | 2 | 3 | 4 | 5 | 6 | 7 | 8 | 9 | 10 |
|---|---|---|---|---|---|---|---|---|---|---|
| Length varied | | | | | | | | | | |
| Number of springs used to vary length: —9 | | | | | | | | | | |
| —≥3 | | | | | | | | | | |
| —2 | | | | | | | | | | |
| Full range considered | | | | | | | | | | |
| Extremes only | | | | | | | | | | |
| Adjacent only | | | | | | | | | | |
| Diameter varied | | | | | | | | | | |
| Number of springs used to vary diameter: —9 | | | | | | | | | | |
| —≥3 | | | | | | | | | | |
| —2 | | | | | | | | | | |
| Full range considered | | | | | | | | | | |
| Extremes only | | | | | | | | | | |
| Adjacent only | | | | | | | | | | |
| Random/no variable varied | | | | | | | | | | |
| Load constant for length test | | | | | | | | | | |
| Load constant for diameter test | | | | | | | | | | |
| Same load used each time | | | | | | | | | | |
| Method of release—by dropping | | | | | | | | | | |
| —by pulling | | | | | | | | | | |
| Method of release consistent | | | | | | | | | | |
| Position of release consistent | | | | | | | | | | |
| No apparent measurement | | | | | | | | | | |
| Mixed measurement method | | | | | | | | | | |
| Qualitative comparison | | | | | | | | | | |
| Clock used | | | | | | | | | | |
| Within ±2 s of start | | | | | | | | | | |
| Within ±2 s of finish | | | | | | | | | | |
| Timed—fixed number of bounces | | | | | | | | | | |
| Number of bounces—0–5 | | | | | | | | | | |
| —6–10 | | | | | | | | | | |
| —11–20 | | | | | | | | | | |
| —>20 | | | | | | | | | | |
| Timed—to end of bouncing | | | | | | | | | | |
| Counted—number of bounces in set time | | | | | | | | | | |
| Set time—0–10 s | | | | | | | | | | |
| —11–20 s | | | | | | | | | | |
| —>20 s | | | | | | | | | | |
| Counted—to end of bouncing | | | | | | | | | | |
| (Letter code) Generalisation | | | | | | | | | | |
| Reason for repeat | | | | | | | | | | |

Hot drinks like tea or coffee are often served in large urns.
Someone waiting in a long queue for tea thought that the problem
was that the level of the tea was low and so the tea was taking
longer to come out.

You have been given a container with a jet which is like a model
tea urn. You can investigate if the level of the liquid does
make a difference to how quickly it comes out.

This is what you have to find out:

> *What difference does the level of the
> water inside the container make to how
> quickly the water comes out of the jet?*

You can use any of the things in front of you. Choose whatever
you need to answer the question.

(a)    Make a record of your results here so that someone else can
       understand what you have found out.

*Continued on facing page*

(b)  Explain how you worked out your results.




(c)  How would you explain to someone what you have found out?

.................................................................
.................................................................
.................................................................
.................................................................
.................................................................
.................................................................

# WATER LEVEL

Pupil Number ☐☐☐☐☐  Girl ☐  Boy ☐

| | 1 | 2 | 3 | 4 | 5 | 6 | 7 | 8 | 9 | 10 |
|---|---|---|---|---|---|---|---|---|---|---|
| **VOLUME IN** | | | | | | | | | | |
| Water added to the container | | | | | | | | | | |
| Water added up to the jet | | | | | | | | | | |
| Volume to jet measured | | | | | | | | | | |
| Initial volume measured—by eye | | | | | | | | | | |
| —by beaker | | | | | | | | | | |
| —by cylinder | | | | | | | | | | |
| Initial level marked | | | | | | | | | | |
| Initial level—distance measured | | | | | | | | | | |
| **VOLUME OUT** Container tipped/poured | | | | | | | | | | |
| Arbitrary volume out—flow judged qualitatively | | | | | | | | | | |
| —time of flow measured | | | | | | | | | | |
| Known volume out—flow judged qualitatively | | | | | | | | | | |
| —time for given volume measured | | | | | | | | | | |
| —volume in given time measured | | | | | | | | | | |
| Container emptied for each reading | | | | | | | | | | |
| Container partially emptied for each reading | | | | | | | | | | |
| Mixed set up used | | | | | | | | | | |
| Mixed measurement method used | | | | | | | | | | |
| **READINGS** Range of levels/volumes considered | | | | | | | | | | |
| Number of readings taken | | | | | | | | | | |
| Levels/volumes measured or noted with reasonable care | | | | | | | | | | |
| Clock started within ±2 s of start | | | | | | | | | | |
| Clock stopped within ±2 s of end | | | | | | | | | | |
| Difference between chosen volumes/levels out | | | | | | | | | | |
| Actual readings 1. 2. 3. 4. 5. 6. 7. 8. 9. 10. | | | | | | | | | | |
| Regular cover of range | | | | | | | | | | |
| Systematic cover of range | | | | | | | | | | |
| Adequate cover >4 readings spread over range | | | | | | | | | | |
| Inadequate cover—most readings nesting in part of the range | | | | | | | | | | |
| **TIME** Fixed time interval—0–5 s | | | | | | | | | | |
| —6–10 s | | | | | | | | | | |
| —11–15 s | | | | | | | | | | |
| —16–30 s | | | | | | | | | | |
| >30 s | | | | | | | | | | |
| Graph drawn | | | | | | | | | | |
| Generalisation* | | | | | | | | | | |
| Reason for repeat* | | | | | | | | | | |

RANGES
cm³

1,500 — A
1,250 — B
1,000 — C
750 — D
500 — E G
250 — F
0 —
Jet

(Letter code)
(A = 1; B = 2; C = 3; D = 4; E = 5; etc)

*Letter code

240

## 'Sweets' and 'Chemical' results

**Table A9.2**  *Number of readings of the independent variable—surface area*

| | % pupils | |
|---|---|---|
| Number of readings | Sweets | Chemical |
| 4 plus extremes (whole and crushed) | 1 | 1 |
| 3 plus extremes | 5 | 4 |
| 3 | 4 | 3 |
| 2 plus extremes | 61 | 43 |
| 2 | 14 | 28 |
| 0 | 13 | 21 |
| | n = 257 | n = 248 |

**Table A9.3**  *Number of readings of independent variable—temperature*

| | % pupils | |
|---|---|---|
| Number of readings | Sweets | Chemical |
| 4 | — | 2 |
| 3 plus extremes (hot and cold) | 19 | 18 |
| 3 | 10 | 14 |
| 2 plus extremes | 36 | 30 |
| 2 | 31 | 36 |
| 0 | 4 | 2 |
| | n = 257 | n = 248 |

**Table A9.4**  *Percentage of pupils testing each of the two independent variables*

Sweets

| | | | Temperature tested | | | |
|---|---|---|---|---|---|---|
| | | Group | (1) | | (2) | (3) |
| Surface Area tested | (1) | | 6 | (87) | 4 | 0 |
| | (2) | | 21 | | 56 | 0 |
| | (3) | | 3 | | 7 | 3 |
| | | | | | | n = 257 |

**Table A9.5**  *Percentage of pupils testing each of the two independent variables*

Chemical

| | | | Temperature tested | | | |
|---|---|---|---|---|---|---|
| | | Group | (1) | | (2) | (3) |
| Surface Area tested | (1) | | 3 | (78) | 4 | 0 |
| | (2) | | 20 | | 51 | 1 |
| | (3) | | 10 | | 10 | 1 |
| | | | | | | n = 248 |

**Table A9.6**  *Measurement of the dependent variable*

| | % pupils | |
|---|---|---|
| Method | Sweets | Chemical |
| Quantitative | 74 | 86 |
| Qualitative | 24 | 14 |
| Other | 2 | — |
| | n = 257 | n = 248 |

**Table A9.7**  *Style and content of pupils' record*

| | % pupils | |
|---|---|---|
| | Sweets | Chemical |
| Tabulated | 5 | 4 |
| Ordered (quantitative) | 40 | 59 |
| Ordered (prose) | 40 | 25 |
| Random | 10 | 8 |
| Specified—temperature | 91 | 94 |
| surface area | 81 | 71 |
| time | 68 | 80 |
| Units given—temperature (correct) | 25 | 23 |
| (incorrect) | 11 | 9 |
| —surface area | 55 | 62 |
| —time (correct) | 20 | 18 |
| (incorrect) | 45 | 60 |
| | n = 257 | n = 248 |

**Table A9.8**  *Pupil self-evaluation and 'prompts' given*

| | % pupils | |
|---|---|---|
| | Sweets | Chemical |
| **Pupil self-evaluation** | | |
| Increased the number of readings | 1 | 1 |
| Qualitative → Quantitative | 3 | 7 |
| Improved measurement technique | 2 | 2 |
| **Prompts** | | |
| Reasons for giving prompt: | | |
| No experiment considered | 1 | 0 |
| No understanding of the problem | 2 | 6 |
| Difficulty with the independent variable | 6 | 7 |
| Difficulty with the dependent variable | 5 | 5 |
| Effective prompts i.e. experiment commenced: | | |
| Problem perceived | 4 | 5 |
| Independent variables understood | 5 | 8 |
| Dependent variable understood | 1 | — |
| | n = 257 | n = 248 |

## 'Springload' results

**Table A9.9**  *Accurate experimental results for the different springs*

| Type of spring | | Number of bounces | | | | | Number of seconds | | | |
|---|---|---|---|---|---|---|---|---|---|---|
| Diameter | Length | 5 | 10 | 20 | 30 | | 10 | 20 | 30 | |
| Narrow | Short | 1.5 | 3 | 5 | 7 | seconds | 62 | 112 | 148 | bounces |
| | Medium | 2 | 4 | 7.5 | 10 | seconds | 29 | 56 | 82 | bounces |
| | Long | 2 | 5 | 9 | 14 | seconds | 22 | 46 | 68 | bounces |
| Medium | Short | 2 | 5 | 10 | 14 | seconds | 22 | 45 | 68 | bounces |
| | Medium | 3 | 6 | 12 | 20 | seconds | 15 | 31 | 47 | bounces |
| | Long | 4 | 8 | 16 | 24 | seconds | 13 | 25 | 37 | bounces |
| Wide | Short | 2 | 5 | 10 | 15 | seconds | 19 | 38 | 56 | bounces |
| | Medium | 4 | 8 | 15 | 24 | seconds | 13 | 26 | 38 | bounces |
| | Long | 5 | 10 | 20 | 30 | seconds | 10 | 20 | 30 | bounces |

**Table A9.10**  *Number of readings of the independent variable—length*

| Number of readings | % pupils | |
|---|---|---|
| | length | diameter |
| 9 | 42 | 42 |
| 8 | 1 | 2 |
| 7 | 3 | 2 |
| 6 | 12 | 13 |
| 5 | 4 | 4 |
| 4 | 6 | 6 |
| 3 | 12 | 13 |
| 2 | 11 | 12 |
| 1 | 1 | 1 |
| 0 | 9 | 5 |

n = 243

**Table A9.11**  *Measurement of the dependent variable*

| Method | % pupils |
|---|---|
| Quantitative | 80 |
| Qualitative | 18 |
| No apparent judgement | 2 |
| Quantative method: | |
| Timed fixed number of bounces | 35 |
| Counted number of bounces in a fixed time | 33 |
| Timed or counted to the end of bouncing | 12 |
| Qualitative judgement: | |
| Rate | 16 |
| Duration | 2 |

n = 243

**Table A9.12**  *Style and content of pupils' record*

| | % pupils | |
|---|---|---|
| | Springload | Swingboard |
| Tabulated | 7 | 7 |
| Ordered—quantitative | 53 | 75 |
| —prose | 29 | |
| Random | 5 | 13 |

n = 243    n = 523

**Table A9.13**  *Pupil self-evaluation*

| | % pupils Springload |
|---|---|
| Increased readings | 3 |
| Qualitative ➤ Quantitative | 20 |
| Improved measurement technique | 9 |

n = 243

**'Waterlevel' results**

**Table A9.14**  *Measurement of the dependent variable*
Percentage of pupils meeting defined criteria

| Method | % pupils |
|---|---|
| Quantified | 91 |
| Qualitative | 6 |
| Other | 3 |
| Qualitative method | |
| Varying the volume and measuring the time | 74 |
| Fixing the time and measuring the volume | 16 |

n = 249

**Table A9.15**  *Style and content of pupils' record*

| | % pupils |
|---|---|
| Tabulated | 4 |
| Ordered (quantitative) | 45 |
| Ordered (prose) | 37 |
| Random | 7 |
| Specified—level/volume | 88 |
| —time | 85 |
| Units—level/volume—correct | 67 |
| —incorrect | 8 |
| —time—correct | 37 |
| —incorrect | 45 |

n = 249

**Table A9.16**  *Pupil self-evaluation and 'prompts'*

| | % pupils |
|---|---|
| Evaluation | |
| Increases readings | 3 |
| Qualitative ➤ quantitative | 9 |
| Improved measurement technique | 1 |
| Prompt | |
| Independent variable understood | 3 |
| Dependent variable understood | 6 |

n = 249

**Figure A9.1** *Performance levels within stages—'Waterlevel'*

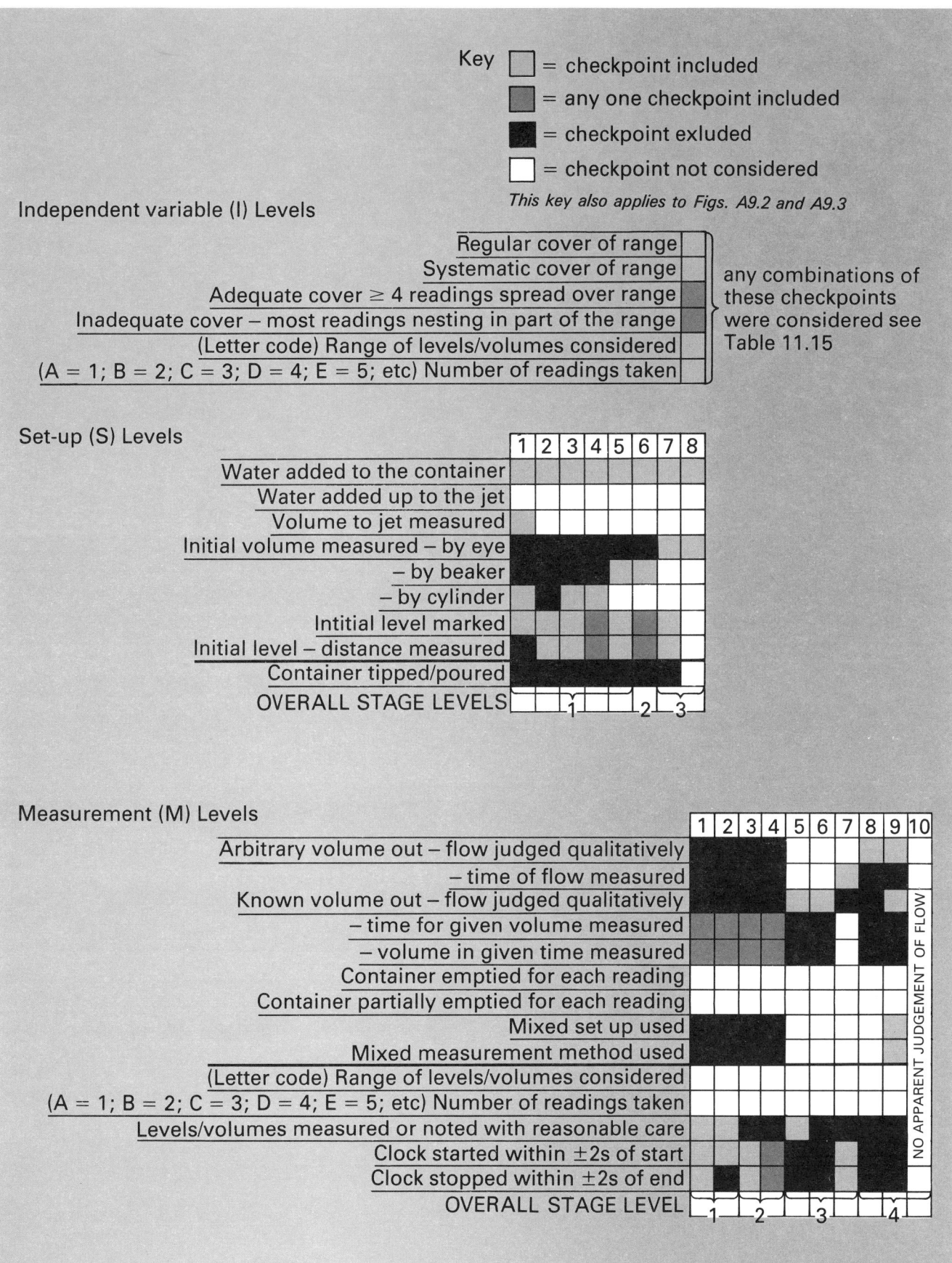

Key  ☐ = checkpoint included
 ▨ = any one checkpoint included
 ■ = checkpoint exluded
 ☐ = checkpoint not considered

*This key also applies to Figs. A9.2 and A9.3*

Independent variable (I) Levels

| | |
|---|---|
| Regular cover of range | |
| Systematic cover of range | |
| Adequate cover ≥ 4 readings spread over range | |
| Inadequate cover – most readings nesting in part of the range | |
| (Letter code) Range of levels/volumes considered | |
| (A = 1; B = 2; C = 3; D = 4; E = 5; etc) Number of readings taken | |

any combinations of these checkpoints were considered see Table 11.15

Set-up (S) Levels

| | 1 | 2 | 3 | 4 | 5 | 6 | 7 | 8 |
|---|---|---|---|---|---|---|---|---|
| Water added to the container | | | | | | | | |
| Water added up to the jet | | | | | | | | |
| Volume to jet measured | | | | | | | | |
| Initial volume measured – by eye | | | | | | | | |
| – by beaker | | | | | | | | |
| – by cylinder | | | | | | | | |
| Intitial level marked | | | | | | | | |
| Initial level – distance measured | | | | | | | | |
| Container tipped/poured | | | | | | | | |
| OVERALL STAGE LEVELS | | 1 | | | 2 | 3 | | |

Measurement (M) Levels

| | 1 | 2 | 3 | 4 | 5 | 6 | 7 | 8 | 9 | 10 |
|---|---|---|---|---|---|---|---|---|---|---|
| Arbitrary volume out – flow judged qualitatively | | | | | | | | | | |
| – time of flow measured | | | | | | | | | | |
| Known volume out – flow judged qualitatively | | | | | | | | | | |
| – time for given volume measured | | | | | | | | | | |
| – volume in given time measured | | | | | | | | | | |
| Container emptied for each reading | | | | | | | | | | |
| Container partially emptied for each reading | | | | | | | | | | |
| Mixed set up used | | | | | | | | | | |
| Mixed measurement method used | | | | | | | | | | |
| (Letter code) Range of levels/volumes considered | | | | | | | | | | |
| (A = 1; B = 2; C = 3; D = 4; E = 5; etc) Number of readings taken | | | | | | | | | | |
| Levels/volumes measured or noted with reasonable care | | | | | | | | | | |
| Clock started within ±2s of start | | | | | | | | | | |
| Clock stopped within ±2s of end | | | | | | | | | | |
| OVERALL STAGE LEVEL | | 1 | | 2 | | | 3 | | | 4 |

NO APPARENT JUDGEMENT OF FLOW

243

**Figure A9.2** *Performance levels within stages 'Springload'*

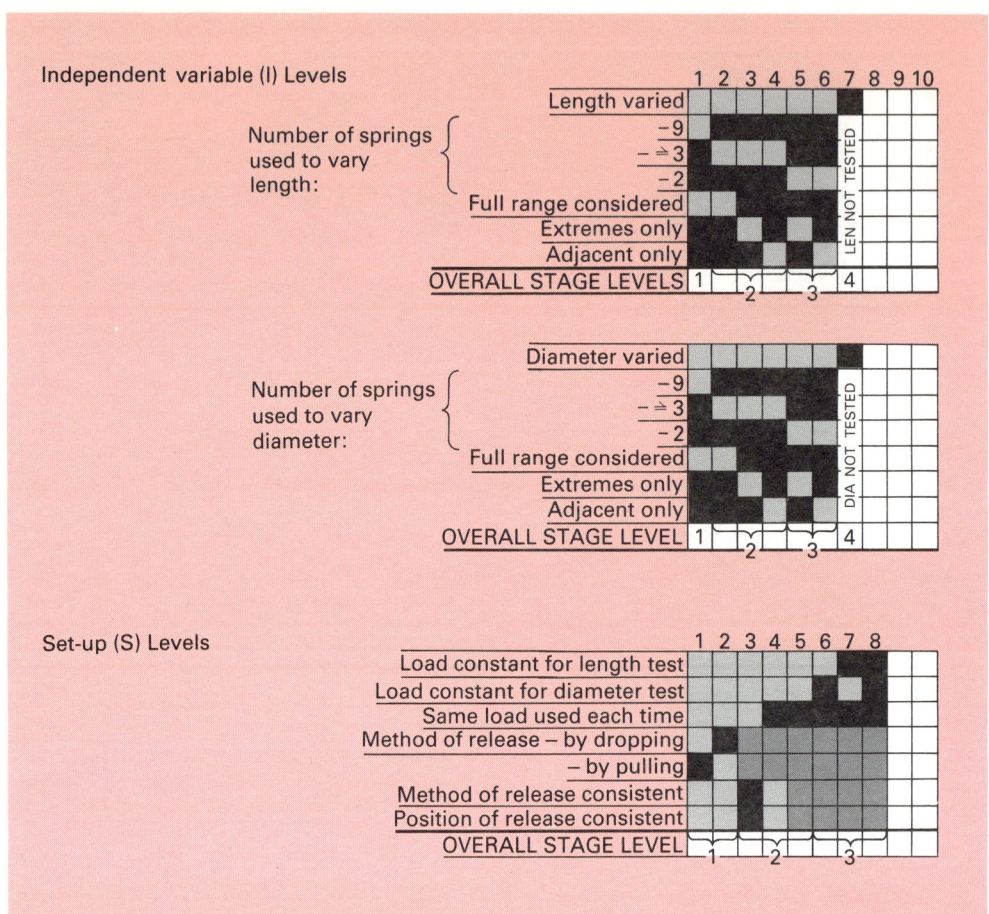

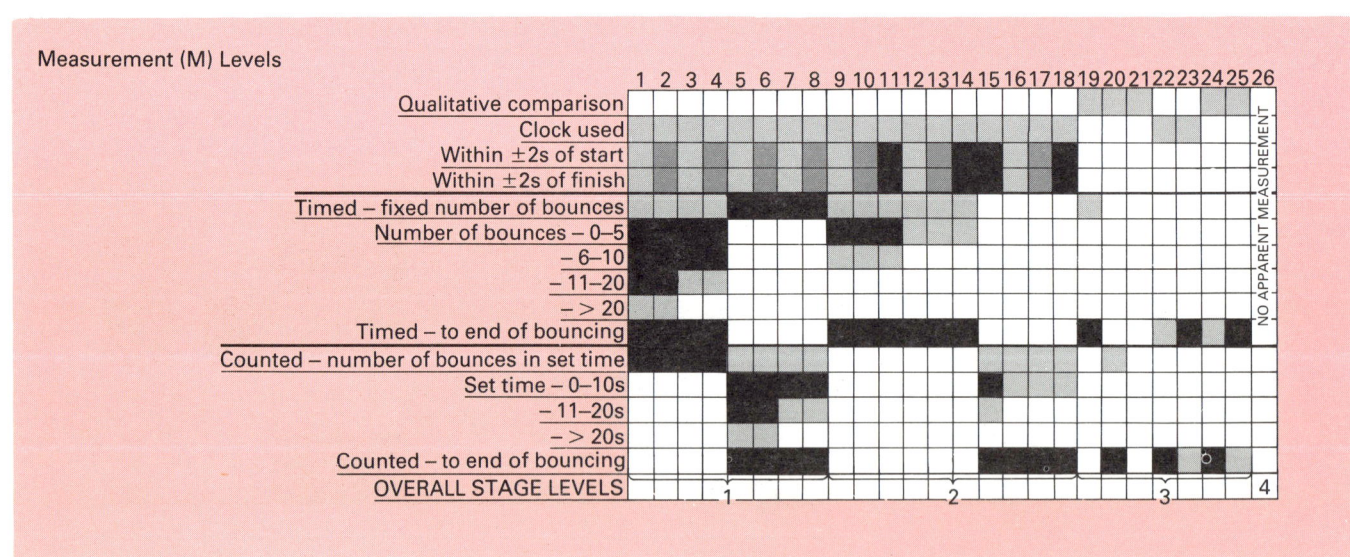

**Figure A9.3** *Performance levels within stages—'Sweets' and 'Chemical'*

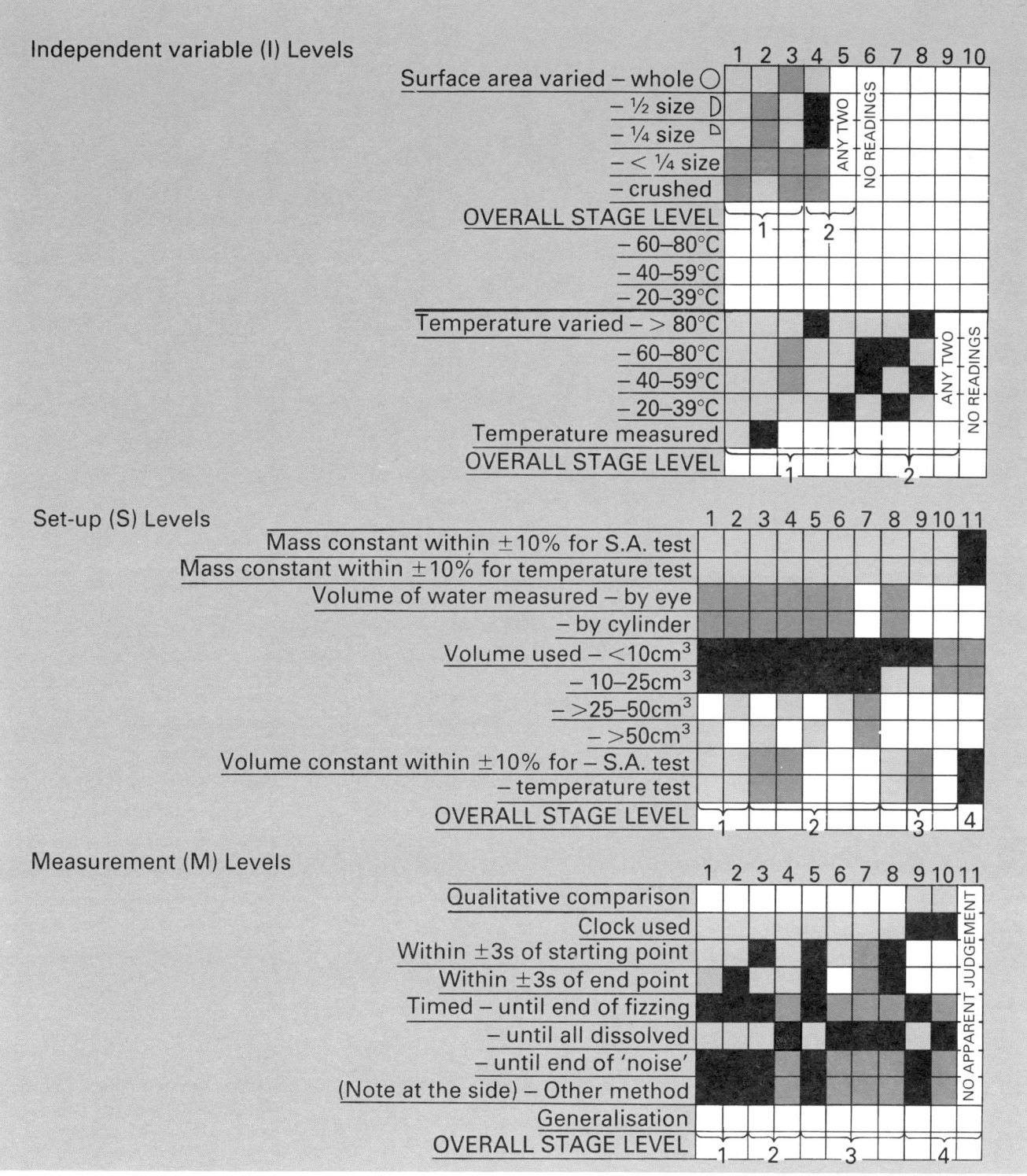

## Administrators of practical tests–1984 survey

### Group

*England*

| | |
|---|---|
| Mr B. Baker | (retired) Milford-on-Sea |
| Mrs D. Barton | St Thomas High School, Exeter |
| Mr R. Bibby | St Andrew's C. of E. School, Cobham, Surrey |
| Mr J. Calvesbert | Butley Middle School, Woodbridge |
| Mr D. Comber | Worcester College of Higher Education, Worcester |
| Mr J. Corrigan | Bedfords Park School, Southall, Middx. |
| Mr C. Curtis | Ashburton High School, Croydon |
| Mr P. Dalton | Beverley School, New Malden |
| Mr T. J. Denning | Madeley High School, Crewe |
| Mr C. G. Dew | Holy Cross Convent School, New Malden |
| Mr D. T. Fawbert | St Clere's School, Stanford-le-Hope, Essex |
| Mr P. Guest | Birmingham Education Authority |
| Mr J. Hopwood | Hummersknott Comprehensive School, Darlington |
| Ms L. Jefferies | The Radcliffe School, Milton Keynes |
| Mr A. Lawson | King Edward VII School, Sheffield |
| Mr M. J. McKay | Markland School, Worksop |
| Mrs J. Mitchell | Villiers High School, Southall, Middx. |
| Mr J. A. Reynolds | St Blaise RC School, Bradford |
| Mr G. Scurrah | Heysham High School, Morecambe |
| Mr M. Seddon | Swavesey Village College, Cambridge |
| Mr C. Turner | The Laurence Jackson School, Guisborough |
| Mrs S. Turner | New Parks School, Leicester |
| Mr T. Whiteley | Sydenham School, Bridgwater |

*Wales*

| | |
|---|---|
| Mr C. A. Garnett | Stanwell Comprehensive School, Penarth, S. Glam. |
| Mrs A. Garrod | Ysgol y Creuddyn, Llandudno, Gwynedd |
| Mrs S. Noake | Lewis Girls' Comp. School, Hengoed, Mid. Glam. |
| Mr T. N. Roberts | Ysgol Dyffryn Nantlle, Penygroes, Gwynedd |
| Mr R. J. Sharp | Whitchurch High School, Cardiff |
| Dr A. C. Thomas | Ysgol Gyfun y Strade, Llanelly, Dyfed |
| Mr P. Thomas | Pontarddulais Comprehensive School, Swansea |
| Mr P. D. Whitcombe | Coed-y-lan Comp. School, Pontypridd, Mid. Glam. |

*Northern Ireland*

| | |
|---|---|
| Mr J. Campbell | Coleraine Boys' Secondary School, Coleraine |
| Mr R. Conway | Armagh Secondary School, Armagh |
| Miss I. Dickson | Aughnacloy High School, Aughnacloy |
| Mr W. Ferguson | Crumlin High School, Crumlin |
| Miss A. Gavin | St Brecan's Boys' Sec. School, Londonderry |
| Mr J. McCloskey | St Patrick's Boys' Sec. School, Dungannon |
| Dr T. Mairs | Ballymena Girls' High School, Ballymena |
| Mr D. Muir | St Nicholas High School, Carrickfergus |

### Individual

*England*

| | |
|---|---|
| Mr J. Adams | Valentines High School, Ilford, Essex |
| Mr D. Boit | Priory School, Barnsley |
| Mr J. Breeds | MEd student, Kent |
| Mr J. Else | Lockleaze School, Bristol |
| Dr J. Evans | (on secondment) Oxford |
| Mr J. F. Faulkes | Fairfax Community School, Bradford |
| Dr R. Giles | Caterham High School, Clayhill, Ilford |
| Mr J. Goldsmith | Kemnal Manor School, Sidcup, Kent |
| Mr P. Hahn | Redewood School, Newcastle-upon-Tyne |
| Mrs M. Hodge | The Clarendon School, Trowbridge |
| Mr R. Jardine | Harlington Upper School, Hayes, Middx. |
| Mr J. T. O. Jones | Hatch End High School, Harrow, Middx. |
| Mr R. J. Lane | Oak Bank Grammar School, Keighley |
| Mr R. J. Lowries | North Leamington School, Leamington Spa |
| Ms S. Miller | South London Science Centre, London |
| Mr D. H. O'Neill | St Edmund Campion RC Comp. School, Gateshead |
| Mr W. Prickett | Stopsley High School, Luton |
| Mr R. Richards | Darrick Wood School, Orpington, Kent |
| Mrs J. Rothschild | Walworth School, London |
| Mrs P. Stevenson | King Edward VII High School, King's Lynn |
| Mr M. J. Tidball | St John Fisher RC School, Harrogate |
| Mr J. Westby | The Grove Comprehensive School, Newark |
| Mr P. E. Willcock | The Ordsall Hall School, Retford |

| | | | |
|---|---|---|---|
| Mrs F. Youlten | Archbishop Michael Ramsey School, London | Mr J. W. Turner | Monmouth Comprehensive School, Monmouth, Gwent |

*Wales*

| | |
|---|---|
| Mr C. H. Archer | Rumney High School, Cardiff |
| Ms C. Bowen-Jones | Ysgol Glan Clwyd, St Asaph, Clwyd |
| Mr D. Gwynne Morris | Brynh-ifryd School, Ruthin, Clwyd |
| Mr G. Harris | Brecon High School, Penlan, Powys |
| Mr D. Lloyd | (retired) Powys |
| Mr J. J. Palmer | Blackwood Comprehensive School, Blackwood, Gwent |
| Mr M. Tibbott | Pencoed Comprehensive School, Pencoed, Mid. Glam. |

*Northern Ireland*

| | |
|---|---|
| Mr S. Bradley | St Mary's High School, Limavady |
| Dr R. Floyd | Limavady Grammar School, Limavady |
| Dr J. Greenwood | Stranmillis College, Belfast |
| Mrs N. Haran | St Brigid's Secondary School, Omagh |
| Mr T. Lascelles | Quoile High School, Downpatrick |
| Mr L. Love | Castlederg Secondary School, Castlederg |
| Mrs P. Prenter | St Mary's High School, Downpatrick |
| Mr J. Watson | Grosvenor High School, Belfast |

# Membership of groups and committees

## 11.1 The Monitoring teams (January 1987)

**at King's**
Director — Paul Black

Research and Development (ages 11 and 13) — Patricia Murphy (Deputy Director)
Anne Qualter
Peter Swatton
Robert Taylor

**Secretarial Staff** — Julie Jones

**at Leeds**
Director — Fred Archenhold
Technical Director — Roger Hartley

Research and Development (age 15) — Geoff Welford (Project coordinator)
James Donnelly

Data Analysis — Sandra Johnson (Deputy Director)
John Bell

**Secretarial Staff** — Jan Akkermans

## 11.2 APU Steering Group on Science (January 1987)

| | |
|---|---|
| Mr A. G. Clegg, HMI, Chairman | Professional Head of the APU |
| Mr W. F. Archenhold | Director, Science Monitoring Team, University of Leeds |
| Professor P. J. Black | Director, Science Monitoring Team, King's College, London (KQC) |
| Mrs S. Dean | St Martin's College, Lancaster |
| Mr N. B. Evans, HMI | HM Inspectorate (Wales) |
| Mr A. Giles | British School Technology, Trent Polytechnic |
| Mr E. O. James | Deputy Head, Southlands School |
| Miss R. Jarman | Department of Education for Northern Ireland |
| Professor R. Kempa | Department of Education, University of Keele |
| Dr W. J. Kirkham | Director, Secondary Science Curriculum Review |
| Mr E. R. Little, HMI | HM Inspectorate |
| Mr H. Wilcox | Headteacher, Paganel Junior School, Birmingham |

## 11.3 Monitoring Services Unit (NFER)

Mrs B. Bloomfield—Head of Unit

Mrs A. Baker—Deputy

Mrs E. Elliott

Mrs M. Hall

Mrs B. Woodley

Mrs J. Cowan—Secretary

## 11.4 APU Consultative Committee

| | |
|---|---|
| Professor J. Dancy (Chair) | School of Education, University of Exeter |
| Miss J. E. L. Baird | Joint General Secretary AMMA |
| Dr P. Biggs | Senior Adviser, Wiltshire LEA |
| Mrs M. J. Bloom | Project Leader for Building and Civil Engineering, National Economic Development Office |
| Mr P. Boulter | Director of Education, Cumbria (ACC) |
| Dr C. Burstall | Director, National Foundation for Educational Research |
| Professor C. B. Cox | Department of English Language and Literature, University of Manchester |
| Mrs J. Davies | Howbury Grange School, Bexley |
| Mr G. Donaldson | Flint High Comprehensive School (NUT) |
| Mr I. Donaldson | NAS/UWT |
| Mr H. Dowson | Deputy Headmaster, Earl Marshall School, Sheffield (NUT) |
| Councillor G. Driver | Councillor, Leeds City Council (AMA) |
| Professor S. J. Eggleston | Department of Education, University of Keele |
| Mr A. Evans | Education Department, NUT |
| Mr D. Fox | Accountant, Chairman of National Education Association |
| Mr C. Gittins | Longsands School, St Neots (SHA) |
| Dr A. Grady | Middlesex Polytechnic |
| Mr P. L. Griffin | Windsor Clive Junior School, (NUT) |
| Mr K. S. Hopkins | Director of Education Mid-Glamorgan (WJEC) |
| Mr C. Humphrey | Director of Education, Solihull (AMA) |
| Mr S. A. Josephs | MacMillan Education Ltd. |
| Mr J. A. Lawton | Kent County Council (ACC) |
| Mr G. M. Lee | Doncaster Metropolitan Institute of Higher Education (NATFHE) |
| Mr J. M. Leonard | General Inspector, Walsall LEA (AMA) |
| Mr M. J. Pipes | Headmaster, City of Portsmouth School for Boys (NAHT) |
| Mr G. R. Potter | Director of Education, West Sussex LEA (ACC) |
| Miss C. L. Richards | (CBI) Understanding British Industry Project, Birmingham |
| Mr R. Richardson | Advisory Head, ILEA (NUT) |
| Professor M. D. Shipman | School of Education, Roehampton Institute |
| Mr P. Smith | Springfield Lower School, Bedford |
| Mr S. C. Woodley | The Kings School, Canterbury |

*Assessors*

| | |
|---|---|
| Mr A. Gibson | HM Inspectorate |
| Mr K. A. Smart | Department of Education for Northern Ireland |
| Mr N. Summers | DES |
| Mr D. Timlin | Welsh Office Education Department |

## 11.5  APU Advisory Group on Statistics (January 1987)

| | |
|---|---|
| Mr M. D. Phipps (Chair) | Administrative Head of the APU |
| Professor V. Barnett | Department of Statistics, University of Sheffield |
| Professor D. J. Bartholomew | Department of Statistics, London School of Economics and Political Science |
| Mrs B. Bloomfield | National Foundation for Educational Research |
| Mr T. Christie | Department of Education, University of Manchester |
| Mr J. Gardner | Chief Statistician, DES |
| Mr D. Hutchison | Chief Statistician, National Foundation for Educational Research |
| Mrs S. Johnson | Centre for Studies in Science Education, University of Leeds |
| Professor T. Lewis | Faculty of Mathematics, Open University |
| Professor R. Mead | Department of Applied Statistics, University of Reading |
| Mr A. Owen | Her Majesty's Inspectorate |
| Mrs V. Scott | WOED |
| Dr A. S. Willmott | University of Oxford Delegacy of Local Examinations |

## 11.6  APU Management Group (January 1987)

| | |
|---|---|
| Mr M. D. Phipps | Administrative Head of the APU |
| Mr A. G. Clegg | Professional Head of the APU |
| Mr P. J. Silvester | |
| Mr M. E. Malt | |
| Mr D. Sleep | |
| Miss H. Bennett | |
| Mrs M. L. Pooley | |
| Miss N. E. Mitchell | |
| Miss T. E. Pilborough | |

'Metal plates', 124
microscope, 69–70
'Milkman', 90
'minds eye view', 113
'mirror image' assessment, 77
mixed-ability classes, 7–8, 9–10
mixed sex schools, 11, 12
'model' of the problem, 133, 134, 138, 144, 147, 155
monitoring (future work), 168
monitoring teams, 1, 4
motivation (pupil), 55, 71, 121
Murphy, P., 2, 40, 42, 44, 109, 124, 125, 130, 153, 160
'Mushrooms', 89
'Mystery liquid', 70

NAEP, 14
National Criteria, 4, 167
networks, 52
'noise', 76, 77, 80, 120, 154, 156
  'background', 84, 85, 86–7
Northern Ireland
    pupils' science performance, 35–45
    sciences resources/provision, 5–8, 11–13
Nuffield Combined Science material, 7
number (independent variables), 134
numerical data, 47–8, 85, 86, 150–51
nurse (job suitability), 26, 28

observation, 2, 3, 160
  across-category issues, 154, 155–6
  history and present position, 72–4
  implications, 80–81
  tasks, 15, 20–21
  test results, 74–9
observations (making/interpreting), 2, 79, 161
  performance levels, 35–41 passim
  test results, 73, 75–7
observations (using), 73, 77–9
open-ended questions, 2, 90, 103, 164
organisational patterns (in science provision), 7–8
'other school subject', 2, 120
out-of-school activities, 3, 15, 18–20
  science-related, 33, 34
'outcome' questions, 20–21, 89, 120
overarching links (across categories), 157
'overlap' questions, 85, 195, 160, 161–2

'Painters', 90
paired statements, 15, 18, 89
'pairs' of jobs, 17, 24
'Paper towel', 125, 127, 128, 129–30, 132, 144, 153, 154
participation rates, 37–8
pattern types, 84–5, 88
patterns of performance, 37–9, 88, 162
patterns in space, 90–98
'Pendulum Swing', 69
perception (of problem), 126–7, 128–9
performance
  across-category issues, 3, 149–57
  cross-age comparisons, 158–62
  gender differences, 47, 52–3, 88–9, 104–6
  patterns, 37–9, 88, 162
  pupils' science, 35–45
  by question types, 83–4, 100–101, 118–20
  review (1983–84), 108–9
  summaries (graphical and symbolic representation), 1, 46–54
performance of investigations, 2, 3, 35, 55, 69, 119
  across-category issues, 149, 150, 152, 153, 155

further developments (1982–82), 130–31
historical background, 123–5
implications, 147–8
position (1981), 125–30
position prior to 1984 survey, 131–4
survey results (1984), 134–43
performance levels
  catchment area, 36–7, 164, 167
  concept areas, 101–3
  gender differences, 36, 40–45
  overall, 141–3, 146
  scale readings, 66–8
  subcategory, 1–4, 35–7, 44, 83, 160–61
periodic table, 103, 104, 105
photographs, 57–8, 60, 61, 62–4, 66, 67, 76
physical science, 17, 18, 33, 41
physics concepts, 2
  developmental history, 44
  performance levels, 35–7, 39, 44, 102, 104–5, 106
  question types (effects), 100–101
pictorial data, 47–8, 85, 86, 88, 117
pie charts, 40, 46, 51–2, 53
planning and carrying out (experiments), 127, 129
planning investigations, 2
  across-category issues, 149, 152, 153, 155, 156
  assessment of testable statements, 110
  entire investigations, 108, 117–20
  historical background, 107–8
  implications, 119–22
  parts of investigations, 35, 109, 110–20, 151, 154, 155, 160, 161
  performance by question type, 118–19
  performance review (1983–84), 108–9
'Plasticine', 69
plotting, 48, 49, 50–51
policy implications (assessment framwork), 167–8
'Pollen', 86, 98
'Polyglass', 78
Practical testing at ages 11, 13, and 15, 56, 57, 74, 124
practical tests, 2, 57, 66, 130–33, 166–7
practical work (instruction-following), 55, 56, 70
practically-based science courses, 11, 12
pre-set values, 57
prediction, 78–9, 82–3, 99–101
  spatial probe, 84–8, 91, 93–4, 97–8
prescriptive model, 125
presentation (independent variable), 134
presentation to pupils, 147
presented information, see interpretation (presented information)
'probe' questions, 3, 56, 57, 119
  across category, 153
  cross-age comparisons, 160–61
  patterns in space, 88, 90–97
problem-solving, 73, 109, 117
  performance of investigations, 124–9, 131–4, 143–5, 147
  planning investigations, 120, 121–2
problems, 110, 112, 152
  generation, 127
  model of, 133, 134, 138, 144, 147, 155
  perception, 126–7, 128–9
  reformulation, 73, 126–7, 128–9, 141
procedural skills, 166
procedural understanding, 125, 127, 143–4
'process' category, 72, 73, 74, 77, 101
process skills, 1, 2, 3, 41, 46, 83, 158, 161, 164–5, 166
professor (job suitability), 30, 31
prompts and prompting, 124, 134–5, 136
'prose' questions, 117, 119
pupils
  attitude to observation, 79
  attributes, 14, 16, 20, 34
  grouping strategies/size, 7–8

motivation, 55, 71, 121
questionnaire, 15–17
responses to questions, 20–21
understanding of science concepts, 103–4
see also boy(s); gender; girl(s)
pupils' interests and perceptions
  background, 14–15
  discussion of issues, 31, 33–4
  future research/implications, 34
  jobs (suitability), 22–8
  out-of-school activities, 18–20
  questionnaire development, 15–17
  task perception, 20–22
  topics of interest, 17–18
pupils' science performances
  biology concepts (applying), 42–3
  chemistry concepts (applying), 43–4
  observations, 40–41
  physics concepts (applying), 44
  presented information, 41–2
  reviewing performance patterns, 37–9
  subcategory performance levels, 35–7, 44
  use of graphs, tables, charts, 39–40

qualitative variables, 131, 136, 138–9, 140, 141, 145
quantitative variables, 135–6, 138–41, 143, 145, 150
question(s)
  attributes, 14, 16, 20
  banks, 1–3, 74–5, 107–9
  coded answer, 2, 83–4, 89–90, 94, 101, 103
  content, 1–2, 53, 72–3, 74, 75
  context, 1–2, 73, 120, 133, 156
  descriptors, 1, 72, 107, 159, 163, 166
  'explain', 101, 120
  groups, 46–7
  open-ended, 2, 90, 103, 164
  outcome, 89, 120
  overlap, 85, 159, 160, 161–2
  pools, 38–43, 83, 159–60, 165
  presentation, 119–20
  'probe', see 'probe' questions
  prose, 117, 119
  relationships, 84–5
  sampling effects, 37, 38
  selection, 56–7
  structure and function, 75, 78, 155–6
  type, 72–80, 83–97 passim, 118–20, 149
questionnaire data, 5, 12–13, 15–17
'Quick ticks', 87

random-sampling, 2–3, 37, 39
'Random coils', 91–2
'Random pipes', 91, 94, 97
rationalisation procedures, 2, 40, 41, 74, 75, 159
reading, 46, 48–9, 52, 151, 154, 161
readings (number), 141, 142, 143
rebound group, 91, 94–7
reclassification (grouping criteria), 75–6, 79
recording (data), 127, 129–30, 145
reformulation (problems), 73, 126–7, 128–9, 141
regularities (observation of), 74
relationship effect, 83, 84–5, 145
relationships and generalisation, 154–5
relevance (scientific), 16–17, 33, 73, 76, 78
rephrasing a general statement, 110
reporting levels (alternatives), 2–3
representation, see graphical and symbolic representation
research investigations, supplementary, 3
resources, 20–21, 76, 167
  data collection, 5
  laboratory provision and technician support, 10–12

Printed in the United Kingdom for Her Majesty's Stationery Office
Dd239899 4/89 C38 G443 10170